EXPLORING CULTURES
A PRENTICE HALL SERIES IN ANTHROPOLOGY

Contemporary Pacific Societies: Studies in Development and Change
Victoria S. Lockwood, Thomas G. Harding, and Ben J. Wallace

Crossing Currents: Continuity and Change in Latin America
Michael B. Whiteford and Scott Whiteford

Europe in the Anthropological Imagination
Susan Parman

The Legacy of Mesoamerica: History and Culture of a Native American Civilization
Robert M. Carmack, Janine Gasco, and Gary H. Gossen

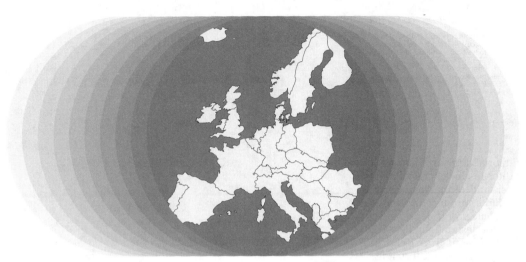

EUROPE IN THE
ANTHROPOLOGICAL IMAGINATION

EDITED BY
SUSAN PARMAN
CALIFORNIA STATE UNIVERSITY, FULLERTON

PRENTICE HALL, UPPER SADDLE RIVER, NEW JERSEY 07458

Library of Congress Cataloging-in-Publication Data

Europe in the anthropological imagination/edited by Susan Parman.
    p. cm.—(Exploring cultures)
    Includes bibliographical references and index.
    ISBN 0-13-337460-2
    1. Ethnology—Europe. 2. Ethnology—History. 3. Europe—Social
life and customs. I. Parman, Susan. II. Series.
GN575.E95 1997
306'.094—dc21   97-13591
                                                    CIP

Editorial director: Charlyce Jones Owen
Editor-in-chief: Nancy Roberts
Assistant editor: Anita Castro
Editorial/production supervision
   and electronic page makeup: Kari Callaghan Mazzola
Interior design: John P. Mazzola
Cover design: Bruce Kenselaar
Buyer: Mary Ann Gloriande

This book was set in 10/12 Palatino by Big Sky Composition
and was printed and bound by Hamilton Printing Company.
The cover was printed by Phoenix Color Corp.

© 1998 by Prentice-Hall, Inc.
Simon & Schuster/A Viacom Company
Upper Saddle River, New Jersey 07458

Printed in the United States of America
10 9 8 7 6 5 4 3 2 1

ISBN 0-13-337460-2

PRENTICE-HALL INTERNATIONAL (UK) LIMITED, *London*
PRENTICE-HALL OF AUSTRALIA PTY. LIMITED, *Sydney*
PRENTICE-HALL CANADA INC., *Toronto*
PRENTICE-HALL HISPANOAMERICANA, S.A., *Mexico*
PRENTICE-HALL OF INDIA PRIVATE LIMITED, *New Delhi*
PRENTICE-HALL OF JAPAN, INC., *Tokyo*
SIMON & SCHUSTER ASIA PTE. LTD., *Singapore*
EDITORA PRENTICE-HALL DO BRASIL, LTDA., *Rio de Janeiro*

CONTENTS

PREFACE

This book is intended to be used in classes on the Anthropology of Europe and the history of anthropology. It was written to encourage discussion of the history, paradigmatic shifts, cultural context, and future of the Anthropology of Europe in the development of anthropology, as well as provide insight into the protean entity that is "Europe."

On the one hand, this book is about the emergence of a specific focus of research in American anthropology—called the Anthropology of Europe—as described by some of the pioneer researchers in this field. On the other hand, it is about the history and identity of anthropology itself.

As an attempt to document some of the historical steps in the founding of the Anthropology of Europe in the United States, this book began as a session called "American Perspectives in the History of the Anthropology of Europe," held at the annual meetings of the American Anthropological Association in 1994. Most of the papers that were presented in this session are included as chapters in this book and represent an effort to address research in specific units of Europe. "Units" of Europe were variously defined at the session, from existing and former national units to transnational regions (France, Greece, Italy, Portugal, Ireland, former Yugoslavia, Eastern Europe, the European Union). All session participants had worked in Europe for at least twenty years and were actively involved in a subunit of the American Anthropological Association called the Society for the Anthropology of Europe; thus they were particularly well situated to address questions about how, when, where, and why they began to study Europe, and to consider what this implied for the development of anthropology in general.

I also invited several additional contributions, in part because they seemed particularly relevant to the intent of the book, which is to address issues in the history of anthropology, and also because they are good stories. Susanna M. Hoffman provides a narrative of the making of the film "Kypseli," a film widely used in anthropology classes; her thoughts on why she located the film where she did, and how she interprets this location, constitute an important part of the ethnography of anthropological studies of Greece, and should be read in conjunction with the papers by Jill Dubisch and Peter S. Allen.

Mark T. Shutes has done extensive research in Ireland; but his paper in this collection is not about this research experience but about the role that George Peter Murdock—"father" of the ambitious cross-cultural database, the Human Relations Area Files—played in his decision to make Europe his area of study. One of the last students of Murdock, Shutes gives quite a different picture of the man usually labeled a cultural determinist preoccupied with cross-cultural comparisons. Of particular relevance for this book are Shutes' observations about the role that Europe played in Murdock's own anthropological imaginings.

As a discipline traditionally identified with the study of the exotic Other (or the non-West), anthropology has played an important role in western society, helping western society define itself by marking boundaries and drawing distinctions between West and non-West, Us and Other. If Europe is the quintessential West, how can anthropologists study it and still be anthropologists (rather than sociologists or members of some other discipline traditionally associated with the analysis of western society)? How anthropologists have studied Europe—the place of Europe in the anthropological imagination—is the complex subject of this book and tells us something about the history, organization, and evolving definitions of American anthropology.

ACKNOWLEDGMENTS

I am indebted to the participants in this project, and to those who gave suggestions about "classics" in the Anthropology of Europe (in particular David J. Kertzer, Caroline B. Brettell, and Tony Galt). I am especially grateful for the critical wisdom, good humor, and creative thinking of my colleague William A. Douglass in organizing the symposium; and for the astute insights (and punning sensibility) of Michael Herzfeld, who served as a pensible, pundantic, and respunsible discussant for the punel (er, panel), and who facilitated my attendance at two important research conferences on Europe ("European Identity and Its Intellectual Roots," sponsored by the Joint Committee on Western Europe of the Social Science Research Council and the American Council of Learned Societies with support from the National Endowment for the Humanities, and at

Harvard by the Minda de Gunzburg Center for European Studies, the Department of Anthropology, and the Peabody Museum, held at Harvard under the direction of Michael Herzfeld on May 6–8, 1993; and "The Role of Anthropology in the Study of Europe, Prospects and Problems," sponsored by the Council for European Studies and held at Harvard October 14–16, 1994).

I am grateful to those at California State University, Fullerton, who honor and support the image of the "teacher–scholar," who recognize the significance of research for effective teaching, and who have given support for travel and research, and to the National Science Foundation and the National Endowment for the Humanities, who through their various support have validated the role of anthropology as a humanistic science (not to mention the study of Europe by anthropologists).

Working with Prentice Hall has been a pleasure. Thanks to Nancy Roberts (especially for her patience) and to Kari Callaghan Mazzola for her organizational skills in the process of bringing a compound document through production. I would also like to thank the following Prentice Hall reviewers: Janet E. Levy, *University of North Carolina at Charlotte*; Jill Dubisch, *Northern Arizona University*; and James Robert McLeod, *The Ohio State University*.

And finally, a very special thanks to my husband, Jacob Pandian, and our daughter, Gigi Pandian, who rode without complaint, and with much fortitude and encouragement, on the back of the bull.

Susan Parman

INTRODUCTION: EUROPE IN THE
ANTHROPOLOGICAL IMAGINATION

Susan Parman
California State University, Fullerton

The phrase "anthropology of Europe" is considered by many to be an oxymoron, or self-contradictory. Anthropologists are supposed to study the exotic Other—leopardskin chiefs, magical shamans, desert hunters, and Tibetan nomads who are thought to belong to a timeless present and to be preoccupied with dreams and kinship. This Other, the object of anthropological study, is conceived of, implicitly or explicitly, as the non-West. To study Europe is considered problematic as an anthropological project. To the usual humorous definitions of anthropology (ranging from "the study of the exotic by the eccentric" to "the study of the nude by the lewd") is added one that takes a backhanded swipe at those who choose to study Europe—"the study of people with particularly interesting local vintages" (Messenger 1991). To study Europe is often construed as an excuse for a holiday. Suffering and exotica are the stigmata of anthropological initiation.

If Europe is the quintessential West, how can anthropologists study it? And if they study Europe, are they still being anthropologists?

This book is as much about the history of anthropology (especially American anthropology) and the disciplinary boundaries of anthropology as it is about Europe. From the point of view of anthropology as a humanistic, scientific study of humankind from an evolutionary and cross-cultural perspective, there should be no difficulty including Europe in its subject matter. But because of the role that anthropology has played in Western culture for most of its history, as a cultural device to conceptualize Otherness, Europe has entered the anthropological stage, like a protean actor, in a predictable range of guises.

EUROPE IN THE ANTHROPOLOGICAL IMAGINATION

Anthropology, as Roy Wagner pointed out (1975, 10), is "the study of man 'as if' there were culture"; and the work of anthropologists is not only to invent, explore, and make useful the general concept of "culture" but also to invent particular cultures. Ethnography and particular peoples play key roles in the anthropological enterprise of helping anthropologists develop and define particular anthropological concepts. As Wagner (1975, 12) observed, "By forcing his imagination, through analogy, to follow the detailed conformations of some external and unpredictable subject, the scientist's or artist's invention gains a sureness it would not otherwise command. Invention is 'controlled' by the image of reality and the creator's lack of awareness that he is creating."

It has been suggested that Europe was not originally part of the anthropological imagination but was "discovered" and invented through a complex evolution of the discipline itself. According to this argument, anthropologists were prevented from pursuing their "traditional" subjects (rural, small-scale, self-sufficient, "isolated" tribal peoples represented by Trobriand Islanders, Australian aborigines, Andaman Islanders, and the memory cultures of American Indians) because of the breakdown of colonialism, and thus began to move hesitantly into Europe and the West and claim new anthropological subjects—initially groups that were similar to those they had studied (such as nomadic groups, marginal societies, and the "little community" of peasants), but eventually making tentative steps to fulfill its claims of universal holism.

There is some truth to these assertions. However, I would argue that Europe is much more than a geographical/cultural region composed of particular groups of people such as Irish Countrymen who have come to serve as external and objective reference points by which the anthropological imagination constructs interpretive models of categories such as "peasants" in "complex society." Europe has been present in the anthropological imagination for as long as there has been anthropology (indeed, Europe and anthropology have helped to create each other). Europe exists as a conceptual contrast, as a vehicle of occidentalism, to define and enforce the boundaries and hierarchical inequalities of Occident and Orient (West and non-West). It has also been used to define and serve as a testing ground for the distinguishing disciplinary features of anthropology itself.

Archimedes once stated that if only he could find a place to stand, he could use a lever to move the world. Cross-cultural comparison has always served as the platform for anthropological leverage to attack ethnocentric assumptions (e.g., "Not all children go through a stormy adolescence"; "Not all marriages are between one man and one woman, or even between men and women"). The history of anthropology has provided a platform for anthropologists to examine the implicit biases within their own discipline, or to use Margaret Mead's image, it has enabled anthropologists, as fish, to become more aware of the medium in which they are swimming. Examining the "anthropology of Europe" within the history of anthropology is an even more important step in this process because Europe, as the quintessential West, is the unexamined background of anthropological imaginings—the white page (racist connotations purposefully implied) on which the Rorschach of anthropological subject matter is printed.

The role of Europe in the anthropological imagination—as a conceptual contrast, as a region composed of particular groups of people used for a variety of purposes, as a goad to define the distinguishing features of anthropology itself—has been complex, sometimes paradoxical, often provocative. To sample some of the meanings associated with Europe that have been created in the anthropological imagination is the subject of this book.

THE BACKGROUND TO THE BOOK

In 1994, William Douglass and I co-organized and co-chaired a session sponsored by the Society for the Anthropology of Europe (a subunit of the American Anthropological Association) called "American Perspectives in the History of the Anthropology of Europe," with the explicit purpose of examining "the anthropology of Europe" as an historical event.

It is important to understand the larger context to which this session relates. The underlying questions that guided the formulation of this book—about theoretical paradigms and the historical context in which they emerged—stem not only from my involvement in anthropological research in Scotland since 1970 but from my interest in the history of anthropology generally, and particularly from a project with which I have been involved since 1990. In an inductive attempt to examine the dialectical relationship between traditional conceptions of anthropology (its focus on the exotic non-West) and the subject matter of Europe (the quintessential West), I began to read through the journal *American Anthropologist* from 1888 to the present, looking for how "Europe" was discussed. In other words, I treated the journal as a text in which, for the past hundred years, American anthropologists have been inventing Europe as a relevant part of anthropological discourse.

I presented my first review of the *American Anthropologist* material in a session at the American Anthropological Association in 1990 called "Cultural Disenchantments in the Anthropology of Europe: Making the Tensions Productive," organized by Sarah Uhl and Donna Muncey, and the second in a 1992 session called "Occidentalism," organized by James Carrier. In 1994, William Douglass and I co-organized and co-chaired the session on "American Perspectives in the History of the Anthropology of Europe."

Participants in the 1994 session were American anthropologists who had worked in Europe for at least twenty years, and who were asked to reflect on methodological and theoretical developments during their tenure. Their lives were not intended to be used as biographical accounts of inner emotional developments, of crises or psychoanalytic resolutions, but as stepping stones to the impersonal, as windows on the intellectual environment in which their own research in Europe developed. They were asked to reflect on how their interest in the anthropology of Europe developed, how they selected or discarded certain research concerns.

They were asked to consider whether there was such a thing as "the anthropology of Europe" when they started their fieldwork in Europe. Many agreed that it did not exist until the Society for the Anthropology of Europe was invented as a subunit of the American Anthropological Association; and most came to the study of Europe through "the back door"—a metaphor used by several participants in different ways, but which serves as a useful way of saying that Europe was not the primary target of their anthropological investigations. Many considered themselves "Mediterraneanists," a category that extended beyond the geographical boundaries of Europe and frequently beyond the disciplinary boundaries of anthropology as well.

They were asked to consider if studying Europe caused problems in graduate school—if the region was considered nonanthropological. Some said that they had some difficulty getting this topic accepted as an anthropological project. Susan Carol Rogers notes the challenge that awaits anthropologists wishing to do research in France, surrounded as they are by a mountain of scholarship very little of which has been produced by anthropologists. As a field that has relied heavily on an oral rather than a literate database, anthropology has a history of debates about historic versus contemporary foci, for both theoretical and pragmatic reasons. Once anthropologists take to the archives, do they become historians (or economists or political scientists) rather than anthropologists? Does studying Europe problematize the disciplinary boundaries of anthropology?

On the other hand, it may be argued that when anthropologists study Europe, they are not really violating what some consider to be their disciplinary cachet of studying the exotic non-West because they choose areas that represent the non-West within the West—the rural populations that speak dying or contested languages and practice exotic rituals, the small-scale communal society integrated by bonds of kinship, the culturally isolated nucleus that serves as a foreign land within which the anthropological imagination can roam freely. Indeed it may be said that they purposefully go about exoticizing the familiar (see Kertzer's chapter; Davis 1977 and Herzfeld 1987b) by extracting familiar behaviors and packaging them in unusual configurations (such as "honor and shame" or "limited good"). David Kertzer suggests that anthropologists studying Europe have tended to go to rural rather than urban areas in part because of the expectations of their profession—"in the field the air should smell of cow dung, not car exhaust"—to prove their suffering and link

themselves with prestigious field sites. And yet at a certain period of development in anthropological studies, it became legitimate to study urban in addition to rural areas, and to define anthropology as the universal study of
humankind rather than limiting its scope to the small-scale, the exotic, and the
non-West. What role did the study of Europe play in replacing the smell of
cow dung with car exhaust?

Participants were asked to consider what the main theoretical concerns
were in anthropology at the time they began their research, whether and how
these concerns changed over time, and what role studying Europe played in
these concerns (for example, did Europe provide a test case to examine generalizations developed in non-Western societies, or was the choice of Europe
irrelevant to the research?).

They were asked to consider the relationship between Americans studying Europe and their European colleagues. Although this topic is touched
upon by some of the contributors, it is a large and complex issue being dealt
with by many Europeanist anthropologists and is not taken up extensively in
this book.

And finally, they were asked to consider the relationship between
"Europe" and "anthropology." Does studying Europe help us think about
what "anthropology" is (and vice versa)?

THE ORDER OF THE CHAPTERS IN THE BOOK

The chapters in this volume can be read in any order, although there is a rationale for the current configuration. The project, from its very beginning, has
been rooted in epistemological concerns, addressing Europe not so much as a
geographical/cultural region but as a location on an intellectual map, a contested region in the anthropological imagination. Therefore I chose to begin the
volume not with Wilson's review of Irish studies (which was a logical possibility, given the recognition of Arensberg's *Irish Countryman* as a classic in the
anthropology of Europe) but with the chapter by Susan Carol Rogers,
"Strangers in a Crowded Field: American Anthropology in France." Rogers
places the anthropology of Europe in its organizational context and raises the
question of whether anthropologists can and should study economically and
politically dominant centers in Europe, or whether anthropology has primarily
located itself (and should remain) at the periphery.

Jill Dubisch's chapter, "Europe through the Back Door: Doing
Anthropology in Greece," deepens the discussion of center/periphery by
addressing Greece's paradoxical position as both central to a definition of
European/Western civilization and marginal to Europe, and highlights the
idea that identity (of a nation as well as of a discipline) is contested, negotiated, and relational. The chapters by Susanna M. Hoffman ("Bringing the
'Other' to the 'Self': Kypseli, the Place and the Film") and Peter Allen ("Europe
on Film") are both contrapuntal and supplementary to Dubisch's chapter, and

may also be considered a separate tangent (concerned with how Europe is represented in film). Hoffman made the film *Kypseli* not to extol the uniqueness of Europe as a culture area but to demonstrate the universality of the theoretical perspective of Levi-Straussian structuralism. Allen's chapter reviews films relevant to the anthropology of Europe and includes comments on Hoffman's film as well as discussion of the issue of marginality.

David I. Kertzer ("Representing Italy"), like Rogers, addresses anthropology's penchant for the rural and remote but affirms the importance of developing new paradigms, in particular urban anthropology. Caroline Brettell ("Returning with the Emigrants: A Journey in Portuguese Ethnography") and William A. Douglass ("Restless Continent: Migration and the Configuration of Europe") do the same with respect to internal and transnational migration.

With Thomas M. Wilson's chapter, "Themes in the Anthropology of Ireland," we turn to an historical perspective on the role that the study of Ireland has played in the anthropology of Europe. He documents the movement away from community studies to studies that deal with ethnicity, sectarianism, class, national and supranational identities, and thus he places Ireland squarely in the "mainstream concerns of the field" as well as in the political context of the European Union (a topic he addresses in another chapter).

Linda A. Bennett's chapter ("A Forty-Year Retrospective of the Anthropology of Former Yugoslavia") is, like Wilson's chapter, an intensive review of the anthropology of a particular area in Europe, and I have followed it with David A. Kideckel's chapter on East Europe ("Utter Otherness: Western Anthropology and East European Political Economy") for geographical reasons (although it could just as reasonably be placed with Rogers's chapter because of its disciplinary concerns, or with Dubisch's because of its discussion of marginality).

The two chapters on Eastern Europe remind us that Europe is a changing politico-cultural arena; thus it seems fitting to follow these with Wilson's second chapter, "An Anthropology of the European Union, from Above and Below." Europe is many things in the anthropological imagination (an Irish countryman, a linguistic-biological construction, an arena of "usness" with which to validate universal models, the apex of the colonial hierarchy, the West/Occident contrasted with the East/Orient, and so on), but most recently it is a political experiment in transnational unification that is being studied by anthropologists who have no qualms about embracing Europe's complexity both from above (at the level of the Eurocrats) and from below (the influence of the EU on local communities). The success of anthropologists in this enterprise has a great deal to do with how anthropology defines itself.

And finally, two chapters address the meaning and use of Europe in the history of American anthropology. Mark T. Shutes, as a former student of George Peter Murdock, describes the reasons that Murdock began to promote the study of Europe and to include more material on Europe in the Human Relations Area Files. Parman discusses three themes in the uses of Europe in the *American Anthropologist* up to the 1970s.

THEMES, QUESTIONS, AND ISSUES: THE RELATIONSHIP OF THE CHAPTERS TO EACH OTHER

The brief introduction to the chapters given previously does not do justice to the richness of ideas and interacting themes contained in them. For the remainder of this introduction I review, extract, relate, and in other ways interact with and suggest interactions among the arguments and points made in the chapters.

ORIGINS OF THE ANTHROPOLOGY OF EUROPE

Participants in the symposium were asked to address the question of whether they conceived of themselves as participating in an "anthropology of Europe," and whether Europe was considered an appropriate topic for anthropological investigation. Many chapters raised the question of when the subdiscipline of the "anthropology of Europe" emerged in the consciousness of American anthropologists. Many noted that they did not consider themselves Europeanists, in part because Europe was not considered the focus of "real" anthropology and in part because they backed into anthropology as an accidental setting for studying a topic such as gender, migration, or urban anthropology.

At the time Brettell did her doctoral research, there was no clearly defined "anthropology of Europe," and she did not consider herself a Europeanist (her dissertation advisor was an Africanist). She was familiar with ethnographies and categorizations of European culture areas but "backed" into Europe as an area that was relevant to general issues of migration and gender.

Rogers not only found that her choice of a European speciality was considered "odd by teachers and colleagues alike," but the fact that she chose to study France (a culturally and politically dominant nation in Europe that was the intense focus of other forms of scholarship) made her ask what anthropology had to offer that was different from other disciplines. She suggests that the crowded disciplinary field helps to explain why anthropologists stayed away from countries like France, but she also reaffirms the importance of anthropology's traditional alliance with difference so that it supplements other forms of scholarship in European Studies.

Kertzer began graduate school with the image of himself as an urban anthropologist hoping to work in an African city or in Latin America. Influenced by the chair of his department, who had worked in Sardinia, he went to Italy where urban-rural interpenetrations were similar to those described for Africa. The anthropological literature for Italy was full of remote peasant village studies (e.g., Robert Redfield's student, Charlotte Gower Chapman, studied the Sicilian community of Milocca in the late 1920s).

Dubisch found a dearth of anthropological materials on Greece when she was in graduate school, and only one faculty member who had worked in Europe (Spain). Greece, he told her, was "very oriental." She did not consider herself to be working in Europe, and Greece was her second choice, after the Middle East or North Africa, as areas where she could study gender roles. In Greece, she found other anthropologists (British and American) "united in our own marginal status in the discipline." They thought of themselves as Mediterraneanists rather than Europeanists, or as students of peasant societies. (Also see Ernestine Friedl's recent discussion of why she chose to study Greece, and in what intellectual climate she did so [Friedl 1995].)

Douglass credits Boissevain and Friedl (1975) with defining a new direction for Europeanist anthropology by issuing a challenge to anthropologists to deal with Europe not as a set of isolated villages (the predominant "island model" of small-scale peasant communities) but as a complex society. He argues that the Europeanist anthropologist's focus on little communities between 1950 and 1970 reflected the influence of British structure-functionalism and Redfield's work on peasant communities. Dubisch also notes the influence that British social anthropology had on her conception of "real" anthropology (also see Hoffman's comments about the final part of her film, *Kypseli*).

Fighting the stigma of being not quite legitimate participants in the geographical canon of anthropology, Dubisch and other anthropologists working in Greece sought legitimacy through organizational affiliation. The informal East European Study Group at the American Anthropological Association overlapped with their interests to some extent, but differed in sharing a common experience of socialist regimes. If anything, anthropologists who did research in Greece considered themselves Mediterraneanists without portfolio.

Dubisch points out that when the Society for the Anthropology of Europe held its first organizational meeting at the American Anthropological Association in 1986, Greece was in the process of being admitted to the European Community. Thus Dubisch's sense of disciplinary identity was doubly affirmed: she was studying an area now clearly defined as part of Europe under the aegis of an organization that billed itself as the "anthropology of Europe." No longer a vaguely defined Mediterraneanist or Old World Culture enthusiast, she had, like Greece, been stamped with a European identity. No longer limited to organizational affiliation with philosophers, poets, and political scientists, she could conduct her business as an accepted anthropologist.

Within European countries where American anthropologists went to do fieldwork, there were established organizations and disciplines for studying Europe, and anthropologists were suspect or considered inappropriately housed in their geographical location (see Rogers for an overview of which disciplines tend to concentrate on which European countries, and on changing patterns of anthropological research in Europe). As a graduate student, Brettell was directed to a political scientist who could only think to introduce her to his maid. Dubisch noted the importance of an anthropologist in Greece becoming familiar with, and situating him/herself in relationship to, Modern Greek Studies and other disciplines concerned with the study of Greece—to establish an interdisciplinary base. Wilson forged strong allegiances with political scientists in his work in Ireland and the European Union.

Organizationally, American anthropologists studying Europe linked themselves with other disciplines but felt marginalized in their own discipline. An occasional conference organized according to region and attended by representatives of many disciplines may have furthered networks of relationships but did not modify anthropologists' sense of marginal identity within their field. The "anthropology of Europe" as a recognized subdiscipline within American anthropology did not yet have an ideological or organizational home.

This was accomplished after the Society for the Anthropology of Europe held its first organizational meeting, as a subunit of the American Anthropological Association, in 1986. Susan Carol Rogers, whose observations about the territorial imperatives of different disciplines in European Studies provide an important perspective on the "anthropology of Europe" in this book, played a critical role in its founding and was its first president. Over the past decade the SAE has dramatically increased its membership and now provides over six hundred members with a variety of services, including an electronic discussion list (H-SAE, moderated by Anthony Galt), a newsletter (*SAE Bulletin*, edited by Patricia Gibson Heck), a *Directory* of members (the first edition edited by Susan Carol Rogers, David D. Gilmore, and Melissa Clegg, the second by Susan Parman, Donna Muncey, and Gary McDonogh), course design resource packets, bibliographies, annotated slide sets, and a guide to contacts with European anthropologists (*European Anthropologies: A Guide to the Profession*, edited by Susan Carol Rogers, Thomas M. Wilson, and Gary W. McDonogh). As expressed by the 1994–1996 president of SAE, David I. Kertzer, in a brochure describing the activities of the SAE, "the SAE is central to the professional identification of anthropologists specializing in the study of European societies."

ANTHROPOLOGICAL CONCEPTIONS OF "EUROPE"

The chapters in this volume vary in how they define the "Europe" of anthropological imaginings. Rogers points out that the Europe of interest to most scholars besides anthropologists (e.g., historians and political scientists) consists of those countries that are "dominant politically or culturally on the world scene," whereas the Europe of interest to anthropologists consists of countries "comparatively neglected" (until the 1980s, "Europeanist anthropology was dominated by rural village studies in the hinterlands of Mediterranean, Celtic or Alpine societies"). While others might agree with her that the anthropology of Europe is still preoccupied more with the exotic and peripheral than with the familiar, they give different reasons for why this might be so, and indeed many argue that this is no longer true.

Whereas Rogers suggests that anthropologists have been slow to study politically and culturally dominant countries such as France because they have been defined so thoroughly by other disciplines, and because they want to "retain a relative monopoly of scholarly knowledge about the peoples and places we study," others attribute such tendencies to anthropology's traditional concerns with marginality and smallness of scale, and, in fact, ask whether anthropology would continue to be anthropology if it did anything else. Although Kertzer admits that anthropologists of Europe have a tendency to exoticize the familiar (Davis 1977; Herzfeld 1987b), he characterizes his own concerns with urban studies in the Mediterranean as an attempt to come to terms with Europe as a complex, urban-industrial society, and says that the anthropology of Europe has changed to include the study of mainstream, universal processes. Bennett, although she chose an island town in which to do her fieldwork, was also concerned with "macro-level economic and educational changes in the wider society." Wilson argues that it is impossible to understand "local rural and urban communities [in Northern Ireland] without understanding ethnicity, sectarianism, national identities, class, and the overall importance of history in everyday life," and says that this has always been true.

Douglass, although admitting that anthropology has tended to focus on small peasant communities, also provides ample evidence of its long-term concern with internal and transnational migration. The diversity of the chapters in this collection—concerned with migration (Brettell, Douglass), urbanization (Kertzer), the European Union (Wilson), the effect of changes in political economy in East Europe on anthropological research (Kideckel)—indicates that the significance of Europe in the anthropological imagination is far too complex to reinforce a developmental or contrastive model of us/other, rural/urban, East/West, South/North, Orient/Occident, gemeinschaft/gesellschaft.

Hoffman's choice of location for the making of her film *Kypseli* indicates changes in the field of anthropology during the 1970s. Her purpose in making the film was to show that a common structural grammar existed in all cultures, in great as well as little traditions, in "us" as well as the "other." She sought to demonstrate this by using a structuralist approach in a European community, "the most 'us' of us." To represent a European community, she chose Greece, "a *radix* of the Western world," a place "resonant" with Europeanness, the "old man" of Western civilization. In addition, she followed in hallowed anthropological footsteps (Radcliffe-Brown; Malinowski; Mead) by choosing to study an island, and by accepting a definition of anthropology that focused on peasant communities in relatively isolated, rural locations.

Other contributors to this volume are less sanguine about the centrality of Greece in the Western tradition, and explore the marginality and ambiguity of Greece as European. Dubisch explicitly discusses her experiences of traveling to Greece as if she were traveling back in time; of the urban environment being more "barren" than other European cities; of the alien sounds of language and politics; of the ambiguity of Greece as being the originator of Western civilization but at the same time geographically and culturally marginal and thus necessitating the linguistic marking implicit in the phrase "modern" Greece. She discusses Campbell's use of the Sarakatsani as primordial Greeks, despite their marginality. The discussion of marginality was a common theme among the chapters, especially in discussing Greece (Allen; Dubisch), Portugal (Brettell), and Eastern Europe (Bennett, Kideckel).

The question, "What is Europe?" may be addressed in a different way (Dubisch asked it by saying, "Are we anthropologists *of* Europe ... or *in* Europe...?"). If the focus is on gender, migration, or urbanization, the answer may simply be, "Europe is a place where universal processes take place." If the focus is on typicality, essences, stereotypes, or identity (primordial or invented, exotic or familiar), the answer may be, "To be European is X" (implicitly or explicitly contrasted with Y), or "To be Greek is to be Z." In the latter focus, issues of occidentalism/orientalism, marginality and boundary-maintenance, and processes of identity-creation and negotiation are relevant.

When Dubisch asks what impact the concept of "Europe" has on anthropological research, she is asking a question that is at the heart of this book: how is "Europe" constructed in the anthropological imagination? This does not simply mean how do anthropologists define Europe. It also means how does "Europe," variously defined, engage anthropological attention. In the relationships that anthropologists have forged with places and processes defined, according to different criteria, as "European," what issues are defined, what questions asked? Perhaps Europe has no impact on anthropological productions (in Dubisch's terminology, we are simply anthropologists *in* Europe); or perhaps Europe has stimulated and provided a context for new areas of thought. For example, does the ambivalence that exists today about national and European Union identity influence current anthropological attention on identity construction? Were developments in urbanization, gender, and ethnicity stimulated by fieldwork in Europe? (See Parman's discussion of this issue in relation to the evidence provided in the *American Anthropologist*.)

MASTER TEXTS AND "CLASSICS": LURCHING TOWARD AN ANTHROPOLOGY OF EUROPE

Brettell quotes Jose Limon (1991), whose concept of "master ethnographic texts" refers to ethnographies considered so important that they influence future research and affect how an audience of present and future anthropologists perceive a people.

Why is a text defined as a master text? Why are some writings considered "classic"? (See also Wilson's discussion of the "sacred texts" of Arensberg and Kimball.)

Besides being a competent and clearly written statement, a "master text" probably also reflects the influence of personality, the prestige of schools, networks, and whatever else defines the politics of inclusion and exclusion. It may be controversial, lyrically written, topical (peasants, gender, urbanization, self), or promoted for personal and/or political reasons. Above all, it must meet Wagner's definition of ethnogrification of theory (see earlier discussion). In classic texts, the imagination of the writer (and the reader) engages the specifics of ethnographic detail and orchestrates this detail to produce insight. The master ethnographic text must be engageable—Hoffman's conjuring of structuralism from the use of public and private space in Kypseli, Arensberg's rendering of family and kinship in the West room—no matter how controversial. (See Parman's evolving list of "classics" in the anthropology of Europe, available in the archives of the electronic discussion list, H-SAE.)

Whatever the conditions that produce master texts and classics, the fact remains that we are seeing a pattern of geographical areas and research preferences. This is evident across disciplines (see Rogers for a discussion of disciplinary preferences in grant applications—e.g., historians prefer to study France, Germany, and Britain; art historians prefer France and Italy; political scientists like to study the European Union, etc.) as well as within the discipline of anthropology. One goes to Ireland to study peasants, Norway and England to study networks, the Mediterranean to study gender roles, honor/shame values, and patron-client relationships. Certain regions have become affiliated with certain research problems. We work out certain aspects of our anthropological agenda in Europe, and other aspects of the anthropological agenda elsewhere; or we include Europe specifically because we want to test the universality of anthropological models (Hoffman; Shutes). Appadurai (1986) used the term gatekeeping to refer to this tendency to link a particular place with a particular area of research.

The chapters in this book suggest that there has been a tendency in the history of the anthropology of Europe to exoticize the familiar, to create syndromes of difference (such as "honor and shame"), and to stress the study of the rural, the semiliterate folk, the small-scale, preferably on islands (in Kertzer's words, is the anthropology of Europe "merely a pith-helmeted form of rural sociology?"). The classic ethnography of Ireland is Arensberg's *Irish Countryman*, backed up in image by the film *Man of Aran*. The classic ethnography of Italy is Charlotte Gower Chapman's study of a small Sicilian community of Milocca. Two influential ethnographies of Greece, as Dubisch noted, are Friedl's village study of Greece, *Vasilika*, and Campbell's *Honour, Family, and Patronage* (1964), and Hoffman's film, *Kypseli*, was self-consciously located in an isolated peasant community on a Greek island.

For many years the island model of peasant/community studies dominated Europeanist anthropology (whether or not the peasant community was on an island, the community itself was treated as a self-contained unit), and to some extent continues to do so (see Kertzer's discussion of the anthropological yearning for "the simplicity of a manageable field setting...where...the scale is human, and the cow dung wafts through the air").

Douglass, on the other hand, challenges the idea that anglophone Europeanist anthropology has been "obsessed" with the study of isolated little communities, giving ample contrary evidence. He points out that migration has been a continuing feature of European and "Euro-settler" societies since the expansion of Europe outside of Europe in the fifteenth century. On the other hand, he admits that the model of community studies dominated the field from about 1950 to 1975, and he suggests that the preference for peasant communities is due in part to the influence of British social anthropology through the influence of Radcliffe-Brown and Robert Redfield at the University of Chicago. An important influence on American interest in European Spanish studies was an attempt to trace Latin American influences back to Spain. American anthropologists, studying peasants in Mesoamerica using a rural-urban continuum, went to Spain and studied peasant communities there. In the 1960s there was a plethora of review articles about peasants (e.g., Geertz 1962; Friedl 1963; Anderson 1965), and Susan Freeman went from the University of Chicago to do research in Spain, influenced not only by the British social anthropology presence in her institution but by British social anthropologists producing seminal studies of Spanish communities (Pitt-Rivers). The research that came out of this school of thought emphasized self-sufficiency and isolation rather than regional/national linkages, migration, tourism, and urbanization. Peasant studies and community studies by and large perpetuated the island model of anthropological units of study with its concomitant notions of tradition, conservatism, homogeneity (in ideology if not in fact, as Brettell points out), egalitarianism, organic solidarity, and cultural essences as opposed to the notion of culture as contested, negotiated, invented, and relational, in a society characterized by gesellschaft, stratification, class differences, and mechanical solidarity.

At the same time that he points out the long history of anthropological awareness of internal and transnational migration and the importance of looking at networks of relationship that extend beyond the little community, Douglass argues that small communities are an important part of the European experience and should not be dismissed as an intellectual interlude in theoretical trends within American anthropology. Other authors have justified the use of small communities in a variety of ways: they are condensed, manageable samples of a larger whole (Hoffman); they are primordial (Dubisch referring to Campbell); they are dynamic arenas within which national self-images are formed (Dubisch referring to Herzfeld); they provide the holistic and ethnographic vehicle for integrating micro and macro levels of analysis (Bennett; Wilson).

Gradually, however, changes within the field of anthropology itself led to changes in the way that Europe could be studied. Kertzer argues that leftist political currents supported a shift away from the view of peasants not as folkloristically interesting but as victims of exploitation. Such currents stimulated criticism of Oscar Lewis's "culture of poverty" thesis (see his comments on Belmonte's 1979 book, *The Broken Fountain*) and prompted an interest in the functioning of communism (Kertzer 1980). Researchers began to look more closely at the romantic myth of egalitarian communities, and to describe stratification systems. The island model of gemeinschaft/peasant community allowed for some role differentiation (primarily based on gender and kinship) but not the extreme differentiation that comes under the heading of stratification. Stratification is a symptom of large complex societies, not the gemein-schaft of small-scale societies. However, as Kertzer notes in his review of American anthropologists working in Italy, most work continues to be done on islands and in the rural south. In addition, anthropologists are drawn to border regions.

In East Europe, as described by Kideckel, a striking set of differences appear between how Western anthropologists (mostly American) study Eastern Europe, and how they study Western Europe. Western anthropologists studying Western Europe distinguish between the urban, stratified, literate, large-scale "us" and the "other" of rural, egalitarian, folk, small-scale communities, and are asking questions about who "we" are (what is the home toward which we are heading, what do we look like in the looking glass?). For Western anthropologists studying Eastern Europe, however, the whole of Eastern Europe becomes other, and anthropologists explore the otherness of unfamiliar customs, emphasizing the differences (the "utter other") rather than exploring the similarities.

Kideckel also provides an additional contrast: how Eastern European anthropologists studied Eastern Europe. Referring to Hofer's classic article (1968) that compared how Americans and Europeans studied European villages (the Americans characterized as slash-and-burn theoreticians with few ties to the community they studied, the Europeans as theoretically limited but ethnographically invested, long-term visitors), he notes that the conditions of doing fieldwork in Eastern Europe (the mutual demonization of East and West) forced Americans to develop closer ties with their communities of study in an effort to serve as cultural mediators between adverse politico-economic systems (for a detailed description of these ties concerning research in the former Yugoslavia, see Bennett's chapter). What resulted was a stronger ethnographic component (for example, in the work of the Halperns) that continued to be linked with theoretical inquiry into nationalism, social change, and political economy. Western anthropologists were giving a human face to socialism and deflating many cold war myths about socialist life. The breakdown of socialist East Europe in 1989 provides an interesting opportunity to examine changing theoretical perspectives and ethnographic practice. Kideckel notes a trend away from the ethnographic detail of everyday life toward explanations of how sociopolitical systems are transformed; and a focus on how to solve practical economic and political problems. East Europe has become not so much a place to be studied but a problem to be mastered. For Western anthropologists, it is also a cultural zone waiting to be theoretically defined.

ANTHROPOLOGY IN EUROPE, OR ANTHROPOLOGY OF EUROPE?

In the 1970s anthropologists became caught up in a surge of interest in world systems, processes that could be described independent of particular "culture areas." Urbanism, transnationalism, gender issues, and migration were universal processes, and anthropology was conceived of as a universal science of humankind, not just of the exotic, non-Western, savage Other.

As Brettell notes, urban anthropology began to appear as a distinct sub-discipline in the early 1970s, as indicated by the appearance of a new journal in 1972, and the publication of edited collections. Another topic of interest was migration. Douglass notes that his own work on migration among Basque communities was part of a larger wave of studies from the 1970s on. Dubisch comments that although she was interested primarily in "women's culture" in rural Greece, she was struck by the extensive migration and influence of "the City" (Istanbul), which changed her idea about the Mediterranean being full of self-contained moral communities. Her list of early studies of migration over-laps and complements that of Douglass.

Douglass argues that despite the appearance of the isolated peasant com-munity as the typical focus of early Europeanist anthropology, the theme of migration was a constant thread (e.g., he extracts comments from Arensberg's *Irish Countryman* and Pitt-Rivers's *People of the Sierra*, "the earliest example of anglophone Europeanist anthropology" and "anglophone Europeanist anthro-pology's quintessential and most influential little community study," respec-tively).

Brettell notes that the 1970s also saw the beginning not only of urban anthropology but of gender studies (e.g., Rosaldo and Lamphere 1974). Today issues of gender in Europe vary from honor and shame in the Mediterranean to general issues of the status of women, their power, their role in migration, and most recently, the construction of gender identity and the poetics of gen-der.

Thus from one point of view, one could argue that during the 1970s the anthropological study of Europe (or any culture area, for that matter) was irrel-evant in the anthropological imagination. Processes were universal; where they took place was of interest only in providing additional evidence about the nature of the processes themselves.

On the other hand, going to Europe was essential in the anthropological imagination because it validated the universality of anthropological models, separating it from its image as a discipline relevant only to the study of the exotic, the primitive, and the non-West.

In choosing to go to Europe, Hoffman was testing the question of univer-sality of anthropological models. The "point of anthropology," she said, was "to roll like a juggernaut across all landscapes toward the goal of describing the cross-cultural process of humankind." According to Shutes, this same moti-vation lay behind George Peter Murdock attempting to add more European material to the Human Relations Area Files, so as to expand the scope of ethnographic examples.

One can argue that studying Europe was a byproduct of the expanding interest of anthropologists in all cultures, including those of the West. As Kertzer noted, "Studying peoples in the 'west'…promises a way to recapture the generalizing aspirations of our discipline."

But it is also important to point out that the very fact of studying Europe made it easier to ask certain kinds of questions. Given assumptions about Westerners, it may be easier to pose research problems emphasizing decision-making individualists, which raises an important question about the points that Shutes makes in his chapter: was Murdock's epiphany historically contingent? It is also possible that new areas of interest can be more easily explored in Europe because Europe was not recognized as an acceptable, fully authentic, legitimate place for an anthropologist to do anthropological fieldwork; therefore, if an anthropologist works in Europe, it is more likely that he/she would borrow from other disciplines. Through their work on Europe, anthropologists have become more interdisciplinary, drawing on history (Brettell, Rogers; Kertzer's discussion of researchers in Italy incorporating history with ethnography), political economy (Brettell, Kertzer), political science (Wilson), and demography (Douglass).

MAKING THE FAMILIAR STRANGE

Orientalizing the Occident, or exoticizing the familiar (see Kertzer's discussion of Davis 1977 and Herzfeld 1987b), has been represented in a negative light in this collection, and many of the authors make a good case for anthropology to move out of the exotic margins and into the familiar centers of power, complexity, and hugeness (to use Rogers's example, to move from Vasilika to Versailles). I suggest, however, that wherever we pitch our tents (in small island peasant communities or in the back offices of high-powered Eurocrats), we should do our best to preserve the sense of the strange in the heart of the familiar—to disorient (not to Orient). This is not to argue with Kertzer, Davis, or Herzfeld (who were attacking the tendency, born of colonial power differentials, to create boundaries of essential otherness between Us and Them, Occident and Orient). And this is a slightly different point than the one Rogers makes about anthropologists preserving the strategic edge of marking out marginal territories in a crowded field. The ability of anthropologists to apply a cross-cultural perspective, to turn the familiar on edge, to develop a sense of distance from and cultural critique of that which we most take for granted, is what will make or break a successful anthropology of Europe. If we can do this, we will have truly come home—not to Europe/Us but to the central and critical task of our discipline. By studying Europe, anthropologists are in a position to dissolve the binary opposition of Us/Other with which anthropology has been engaged as part of its cultural heritage. In the process of making the familiar strange, by engaging Europe in the calculus of a universalizing cultural critique, they have the potential to turn the paradigmatic House of the Other into a common Global Home.

CHAPTER 1

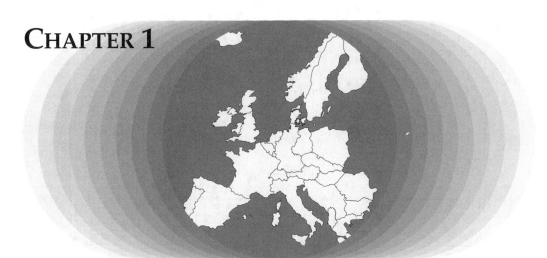

STRANGERS IN A CROWDED FIELD:
AMERICAN ANTHROPOLOGY IN FRANCE

Susan Carol Rogers
New York University

Two of the most striking characteristics of scholarship on France are that there is so very much of it, and that such a small amount has been produced by anthropologists. On the face of it, the same can be said of Europe in general: Knowledge about European societies has loomed large in the development of the cognate disciplines, while anthropology developed primarily as the study of nonwestern societies. This disciplinary division of labor appears to have substantially eroded over the past few decades. Among other signs is the dramatic development of Europeanist anthropology: Over the 1980s our discipline emerged as one of the principle components of European Studies as it is practiced in the United States, and the European area specialty became a highly visible one within our discipline.

Anthropology, it seems, can no longer be defined as the study of particular kinds of places or peoples, but has rather become one form of scholarly knowledge about societies that may also be known by other means. A variety of developments within Europe, the rest of the world, the academy, and the specific disciplines concerned have all contributed to this trend. One of the more familiar explanations for anthropology's turn westward is the salience of critiques—increasingly vocal over the 1980s—of our penchant for the "exotic other." Without a doubt, as the intellectual and moral foundations of anthropology's historic mission of producing knowledge about the non-European world were weakened, the legitimacy and attractiveness of focusing on European societies has been enhanced.

The curious case of France—its magnetic appeal to scholars in other disciplines and its relative lack of attraction to anthropologists—requires that this scenario be more nuanced, however. On one hand, the Europe of interest to most American scholars is actually a rather limited one, consisting primarily of France and Germany, secondarily Britain, with some marginal interest in Poland, Italy, and Spain, and not much attention to anywhere else. The countries for which American scholars have the strongest predilection are those that have been most dominant politically or culturally on the world scene, and correspondingly have the largest and most internationally prestigious indigenous scholarly establishments in the world.

The Europe that draws American anthropologists, on the other hand, is quite a different one: Europeanist anthropology in fact represents less of a departure from old habits than appears at first glance. Within the European domain, the old disciplinary division of labor has been largely reproduced because anthropologists have been relatively little attracted to those world powers most studied by indigenous and American scholars from other disciplines, instead clustering disproportionately in many of the corners of Europe that have remained comparatively neglected by others.[1] This pattern has two consequences, one convenient at the least, and the other positively salutary. First, anthropologists working in Europe, like those specializing in more conventionally "anthropological" settings, have frequently been able to skirt the daunting challenge of having to come to terms with and situate their own research with reference to massive bodies of extant scholarship, deeply entrenched paradigms, and substantial common knowledge about the places and peoples they study. Second, in tending toward the less familiar, anthropologists work in a considerably larger and more varied Europe than has conventionally been the subject of European Studies in the United States. Just as the anthropology of the "exotic," despite its putative sins, potentially broadens our sense of the range of human possibility and permits us to resituate our own experience, so the anthropology of Europe potentially broadens our understanding of the European or western world, inviting reconsideration of its more familiar bits.

This chapter is prompted by my curiosity, as an anthropologist of France, about why American anthropologists have been slower to undertake research in France than in some other areas of Europe, especially in view of the strong attraction of France for scholars from other disciplines. The puzzle, it seems to me, is its own solution. Ultimately, what distinguishes France from the places anthropologists have been more inclined to study is precisely that France, and ideas about what constitutes worthwhile knowledge about it, have been so thoroughly and prominently defined by others. Anthropologists specializing in western societies as elsewhere, accustomed to deriving their scholarly authority from knowledge of the unknown or little-known, are apt to be either disinclined to take on the task of redefining the well-known, or ill-equipped to do so credibly.[2] Anthropological knowledge about well-studied places like France does potentially offer valuable insights, precisely because it is apt to be derived from perspectives that are less Francocentric or entrenched in the established conventions of French studies than other forms of knowledge. On the other hand, the risk of displaying oneself as ill-informed, naive, and incompetent is, without a doubt, much greater in such a well-developed scholarly context. The alternative, acquiring sufficient conversance with at least some of those extant scholarly conventions to be able to address them convincingly, is a daunting challenge indeed.

To situate the anthropology of France, I will begin by sketching the geography of European Studies as currently practiced in the United States, before tracing the development of American anthropological interest in France over the past several decades. I will turn, finally, to a description of some of the better-established traditions of American and French research in France, helping to clarify, by comparison, the positioning of American anthropology.

THE GEOGRAPHY OF EUROPEAN STUDIES IN THE UNITED STATES

Tables 1-1 through 1-4 are drawn from data on applications for dissertation fellowships submitted to the Joint Committees on Western Europe (JCWE) and Eastern Europe (JCEE) of the Social Science Research Council (SSRC)/American Council of Learned Societies (ACLS) during a recent three-year period (1992–1994). Proposed doctoral research projects, analyzed in terms of disciplinary and country-focus distributions, provide a convenient basis for sketching the current and evolving geography of European Studies in the United States.[3] Data on proposals concerning Western and Eastern Europe have been tabulated separately for several reasons. First, they were handled by two separate committees, and neither the applicant pools nor the data available about them are exactly identical.[4] Second, while applications to the JCEE increased dramatically over the past decade—tripling between 1986 and 1995—the numbers remained much smaller than those submitted to the JCWE. Aggregation would, therefore, result in the data on Eastern Europeanist research being largely overwhelmed by patterns characteristic of Western Europeanists. As a region which has captured considerable public attention and is newly developing as a research focus, but which remains quite marginal to American Europeanist scholarship, Eastern Europe offers a revealing comparison to Western Europe.

Table 1-1 shows the disciplinary distribution of Europeanist research. For Western Europe, history clearly dominates, accounting for close to half of all submissions. Anthropology has become a second-tier discipline over the past decade, now accounting for about as many submissions as either political science or art history; these three together comprise about one-third of all proposals submitted. The remaining fifth of the pool is widely scattered among an array of disciplines.

TABLE 1-1 APPLICATIONS TO **JCWE** AND TO **JCEE** FOR DOCTORAL RESEARCH 1992–1994, BY DISCIPLINE

DISCIPLINE	WESTERN EUROPE		EASTERN EUROPE	
	N	%	N	%
History	325	45	67	29
Politics	97	13	70	30
Anthropology	84	12	11	5
Art History	80	11	6	3
Literature	34	5	16	7
Sociology	21	3	21	9
Economics	8	1	10	4
Other	77	11	29	13
TOTAL	726	101	230	100

No single discipline dominates the much smaller Eastern Europeanist pool, but political science and history together account for well over half of all proposals, in roughly equal numbers. The remaining two-fifths are composed of small numbers of proposals from each of a wide range of disciplines. Perhaps the most striking characteristic of this pool in comparison with that for Western Europe is the similarity between the two in the numbers of proposals from the "hard" social sciences (economics, sociology, political science): Students in those disciplines are about as likely to propose research in Eastern as in Western Europe, accounting for close to half of the smaller Eastern Europeanist pool, compared to less than one-fifth of the Western Europeanist proposals. In contrast, those in disciplines closer to the humanities (history, anthropology, art history) are many times more likely to choose a Western European focus. The difference may be attributable to the lesser emphasis generally placed on area expertise within the former set of disciplines, resulting in more rapid deployment of such newly accessible data sources. The current newsworthiness of Eastern Europe, and the considerable resources now being invested in its political and economic redefinition may also make the region relatively more attractive within those disciplines. In any case, the number of anthropology proposals is very small, both as a proportion of the Eastern Europeanist pool, and in comparison with the number of anthropologists proposing research in Western Europe. The lure of the unfamiliar does not appear to be drawing many anthropologists to Eastern Europe, perhaps in part because of popular perceptions of the region as being primarily of political and economic interest.

Tables 1-2 and 1-3 show the distribution of country specialties within the Western Europeanist applicant pool. Table 1-2 shows the striking importance of France (about 1/4 of all proposals), as well as a strong emphasis on a France-Germany-Britain core (almost 2/3 of all proposals). No less striking is anthropology's eccentricity with respect to this pattern. Compared to its 12 percent share of the total pool, our discipline accounts for a disproportionately small percent of projects in the core countries well-studied by others (especially France and Germany), and a very large proportion of those set outside of that core (especially Greece and Ireland, but also Spain and "other").

Table 1-3, showing the distribution of geographic focus within each discipline (including only those locations drawing at least 7 percent of all proposals within the discipline), reveals more detail in this pattern. Among Western Europeanists, proposals from each of the other major disciplines tend to be heavily concentrated on two or three countries and otherwise lightly scattered geographically. Each discipline has its own distinctive pattern, although there is substantial overlap. Historians are drawn primarily to France, show considerable interest in Germany and Britain, but are relatively little inclined to go elsewhere. Art historians are proportionately even more attracted to France; Italy is a distant second country of predilection. Political scientists are least

TABLE 1-2 APPLICATIONS TO JCWE/SSRC FOR DOCTORAL RESEARCH 1992–1994, BY COUNTRY FOCUS; % ANTHRO/NONANTHRO BY COUNTRY FOCUS

COUNTRY	N	% TOTAL	% ANTHRO	% NONANTHRO
France	173	24	6	94
Germany	129	18	5	95
Britain	94	13	10	90
Comparative[1]	49	7	0	100
Italy	49	7	14	86
Spain	42	6	24	76
European Union[2]	34	5	3	97
Greece	17	2	65	35
Ireland	13	2	46	54
Other	72	10	25	75
Indeterminate[3]	54	7	5	95
TOTAL	**726**	**101**	**12**	**88**

[1]Cross-national comparisons including at least one of the three countries above.
[2]Studies focusing on the European Union as an entity.
[3]Country focus either not relevant to project or not identifiable from project title.

TABLE 1-3   APPLICATIONS TO JCWE/SSRC FOR DOCTORAL RESEARCH 1992–1994, COUNTRY FOCUS WITHIN EACH DISCIPLINE (%; COUNTRIES DRAWING AT LEAST 7% OF DISCIPLINE'S PROPOSALS)

	HISTORY N = 325	POLITICS N = 97	ART HISTORY N = 80	ANTHROPOLOGY N = 84
France	31	7	40	13
Germany	22	20	8	8
Britain	18	—	9	11
Comparative[1]	—	20	—	—
Italy	—	—	14	8
Spain	—	—	—	12
EU[2]	—	27	—	—
Greece	—	—	—	13
Ireland	—	—	—	7
Other	—	—	9	21
TOTAL % SHOWN	**71**	**74**	**80**	**93**

[1]Cross-national comparisons including at least one of the three countries above
[2]Studies focusing on the European Union as an entity

likely to define their projects with reference to a single country. Studies of the European Union account for the highest proportion of their projects, and cross-national comparative studies (including at least one of the three core countries) are also frequent. When they do propose single-country studies, Germany is by far the country of choice. Anthropology projects, on the other hand, are much more widely and evenly spread out. No particular countries appear to dominate anthropologists' interests: Greece is as attractive as France; neither carries significantly more weight than Spain or Britain; and Ireland, Italy, and Germany are each almost as attractive as any of those. In contrast to any of the other major disciplines, the "other" category is the single largest one among anthropology proposals, comprising small numbers of projects located in an array of countries other than the seven listed here.

Table 1-4 shows the geography of Eastern Europeanist research. Poland is clearly the country of predilection, accounting for over one-quarter of all proposals, while Romania, Bulgaria, and Albania receive scant attention. Nonetheless, proposals for Eastern Europe are more evenly (albeit thinly) spread over a larger portion of the region than is the case for Western Europe. Further, a much higher proportion of Eastern Europeanist projects have a cross-national or supranational focus: About one-quarter are concerned with either East Central Europe or Eastern Europe as a whole. Political scientists

Table 1-4   Applications to JCEE/ACLS for Doctoral Research 1992–1994,
by Geographic Focus

	Total Pool		History N = 67	Politics N = 70	Anthro
	N	%	%	%	N
Poland	65	28	31	24	5
Czech/Slovakia	38	17	18	17	3
Germany	26	11	15	9	2
Hungary	24	10	7	9	0
Ex-Yugoslavia	15	7	15	3	1
Other Countries	10	4	2	7	0
Eastern[1]	29	13	3	14	0
East Central[2]	23	10	9	17	0
TOTAL	**230**	**100**	**100**	**100**	**11**

[1]Cross-national or supranational studies treating Eastern Europe in general

[2]Cross-national or supranational studies treating East Central Europe

working here, like those in Western Europe, are less inclined than historians to focus on a single country, but they also appear more inclined to take a country-specific focus than are their Western Europeanist colleagues. Indeed, in contrast to the Western Europeanist pool, there is little clear specificity by discipline in the geographic distribution of research projects. Although the number of anthropology proposals is too small to draw strong conclusions, they would seem to be more exclusively focused on specific countries than are those from other disciplines, but otherwise to share a similar geography with the major disciplines and the pool as a whole.

The old and venerable tradition of voluminous American scholarship on a Europe comprising primarily a few Western European countries would appear to be alive and well today. A recent arrival in this context, Europeanist anthropology has, to a considerable degree, taken the negative shape of this mold. Concerned with a broader area of Western Europe, anthropologists display no predilection for those countries most attractive to colleagues in longer-established disciplines, and do attend to those left largely unexplored by others. Eastern Europe, only recently readily accessible to American scholars again and the subject of considerable public attention, offers a special case of a relatively neglected European region. In the absence of any long-entrenched tradition of American scholarship there, the emerging geography of anthropological research appears quite similar to that in other disciplines. The unattractiveness of the region to anthropologists, compared to other less-studied areas of Europe, is more difficult to explain, but may be due in part to its visible status in the realm of current events, defined largely in terms of market and regime types.

This suggests that, for better or for worse, Europeanist anthropology has generally been conducted in a way that is consistent with a well-established convention in our discipline: By paying comparatively little attention to those countries that are most attractive to our compatriots and possess the strongest indigenous scholarly traditions, we have been able to retain a relative monopoly of scholarly knowledge about the peoples and places we study. Certainly Sicily, Andalusia, and Galloway are not as exclusively defined by specifically anthropological scholarship as were the Trobriands, Nuerland, or Tikopia. But neither have they been the subject of the same vast volumes of distinguished indigenous and American literatures as have France, Germany, or England. Furthermore, insofar as the specialist authority associated with the ethnographic enterprise derives from "having been there," it requires an audience that has not. Again, it is less remarkable to have lived in Crete or the Léon than in the Kalahari or the Amazon. But having spent time in Paris or Berlin is even less the province of specialists and indeed is too banal to carry much a priori authority at all. Finally, the international status hierarchy of scholars is such that the mere fact of being a well-educated, university-affiliated American undoubtedly confers less prestige or a priori legitimacy in Bucharest or Lisbon than in Bamako or Port Moresby, but very little at all in Edinburgh or Göttingen. Obviously there are few if any places in the world today about which American anthropologists can legitimately claim the same exclusive specialist expertise as did our ancestors. But it is equally unlikely that there are many locations in which our claims to expertise are as open to challenge as in the well-studied core nations of Europe.

AMERICAN ANTHROPOLOGISTS IN FRANCE

The geography of European Studies generally and of Europeanist anthropology more specifically are, of course, dynamic, reshaped by myriad factors across time. Over the past decade or two, the most dramatic shift in the field overall, as noted above, has been increased interest in Central and Eastern Europe since the fall of the iron curtain in 1989. Somewhat more difficult to document precisely is a growing interest in Germany, once about as attractive as Britain and a great deal less so than France. This shift has been most striking since 1990 and is undoubtedly explainable in large measure both by the new draw of the former East Bloc and by the substantial support offered by the German government for American research in Germany.[5] Research on the

European Union has also increased over the past decade, prompted by the evolution of the EU itself as well as by shifts within American political science tending to de-emphasize single-country research specialties (Hall 1995). The arrival of substantial numbers of anthropologists on the scene since the mid-1980s—the "success story of the past decade" in European Studies (Hall 1995, 9)—has broadened the geography of American scholarship in Europe considerably, but the geography of Europeanist anthropology has itself shifted somewhat during this period. Most notably, it would appear that this domain was initially heavily dominated by studies of the Mediterranean and Celtic fringes of the continent, but as it has become better established, anthropologists have increasingly ventured into those areas already colonized by colleagues in the sister disciplines. As shown in Table 1-3, anthropologists have still not adopted the pattern of disproportionate interest in France or Germany that is characteristic of other disciplines, but they are now as likely to conduct research in those two countries as in such earlier locales of predilection as Spain or Ireland.[6] This shift can be illustrated by the curious history of American anthropological research in France.

If we grant that at least until the 1980s, Europeanist ethnography was dominated by rural village studies in the hinterlands of Mediterranean, Celtic, or Alpine societies, it might be supposed that France would have been especially attractive to anthropologists: Well endowed with rural villages and a deep hinterland, it is the only European country that includes Mediterranean (Midi), Celtic (Brittany), *and* Alpine regions. Indeed, the best-known English language monograph on France probably remains Laurence Wylie's *Village in the Vaucluse*, first published in 1957. What is perhaps most remarkable about this engaging and widely read account of Mediterranean French village life, however, is that it apparently never inspired much subsequent American fieldwork in France. Wylie himself was originally trained in French literature and undertook his study to provide material for teaching French civilization in the context of a French department. He continued to work in France throughout his active career and was quite well-known among French social scientists; he was, for example, invited to deliver the keynote address at the inaugural meeting of the French Anthropological Association (1976). He was never directly involved in the graduate training of American anthropologists or other social scientists but, given the success of his book in the United States, it is nonetheless curious that it failed to launch any noticeable American ethnographic activity in France.

Almost a decade later, Barbara G. and Robert T. Anderson published their *Bus Stop to Paris* (1965), an historical account of a Parisian suburb. In some ways a mirror image of Wylie, the Andersons were professional anthropologists teaching in the United States for whom France was not the primary focus of interest. (Most of their other joint or individual publications treat Denmark, Europe in general, or the United States). Their book was well-read by American anthropologists interested in Europe, but made little or no impact in

France. In any case, it does not appear to have inspired any more American ethnographic interest in France than did Wylie's book.

Beginning in the early 1970s, however, a modest flurry of dissertation projects was undertaken in France by American students. While only three completed dissertations based on ethnographic research in France could be located in *Dissertation Abstracts* prior to 1973, about fifteen are listed over the subsequent ten-year period. As might be expected, most of these concern village studies in Mediterranean, Alpine, or Celtic France. Of these Ph.D.s, about half have remained within the anthropology profession (as roughly measured by current membership in the American Anthropological Association), but no more than two have retained France as a primary geographic focus of research. That is, almost without exception, everyone in that small cohort subsequently left the French scene, leaving behind few published traces or enduring French connections. (Publications resulting from dissertation research conducted during this period include Yoon 1975; Reiter 1975; Groger 1979; Brettell 1982; Anderson-Levitt 1987; Rosenberg 1988; Rogers 1991a). During the same period, Jennie Keith-Ross undertook a postdoctoral study of a retirement community in a Paris suburb, producing an excellent monograph (1977) that was as little remarked in France as in the United States. She, too, made her professional mark on the basis of research outside of France.

Prior to the 1980s then, France attracted no more than a handful of American anthropologists, and held virtually none of them. Since then, the picture has changed somewhat. Between 1983 and 1992, another fifteen or so dissertations based on ethnographic research in France were defended, still predominantly—though less exclusively—treating rural communities.[7] In a pattern similar to the earlier cohort, slightly more than half of these Ph.D.s have remained professionally active. But in contrast to the earlier group, almost all of these individuals have remained committed to research in France beyond the dissertation. Although no more numerous at the outset than those completing dissertations during the previous decade, they have already published a larger body of ethnographic literature on France than has the earlier cohort. (Publications include Mark 1987; Badone 1989; Boyarin 1991; Lem 1991; Jaffe 1993b; Beriss 1993; Reed-Danahay 1996). Furthermore, these individuals have generally been more successful or interested in establishing themselves within networks of French scholars than was the case of the previous decade's embarkment.

JCWE figures suggest that at least as many anthropology students will launch ethnographic dissertation projects in France during the 1990s as did in the 1970s and 1980s combined. Even allowing for uncompleted dissertations and postdoctoral career or specialty changes, it seems likely that by the turn of the century there will be a critical mass of American anthropologists of France and of English-language ethnographic literature treating French subjects. The emerging community of American anthropologists of France will probably be characterized for a time by a notably bottom-heavy age pyramid, and will certainly remain perennially strongly outnumbered by American colleagues from other disciplines (especially history), as well as by indigenous anthropologists of France. The future of this specialty area undoubtedly rests on the relationships forged over the coming years with scholarly traditions that, present earlier and more voluminously, have largely defined what is known and considered important to know about France.

OTHER ROADS TO FRANCE

As I have indicated, France's very modest attraction for American anthropologists stands in sharp contrast to its central importance to a number of other disciplines within the American academy. The magnetic appeal of France to the historians dominating European studies in North America provides one notable but not unique example, suggesting some of the forms and causes of this attraction. At least since the 1960s, France has been the single largest country specialty of those American historians working outside of the United States. There exist two sizable professional associations of American historians of France (French Historical Society, Western Society for French History), each with its annual meeting and scholarly journal. Most history departments in American colleges and universities include at least one historian of France, and it is virtually impossible for graduate students of history or undergraduate majors to escape without at least some exposure to the Hexagon.

The weight of France is attributable in large measure to the significance of French historiography to American historians. *Annales* history, dominant in France for the past fifty years, is concerned with the lives of ordinary people, and is focused almost exclusively on the history of France. A style of historical analysis that has been influential within the American academy, it has drawn large numbers of American historians to France, generating and sustaining a dense network of exchange between them and their French counterparts, together with a rough division of labor: Americans produce a disproportionate amount of nineteenth- and early-twentieth-century history (less prestigious in France), while the history of pre-Revolutionary France has remained more exclusively associated with indigenous historians. American historians of Europe further explain their proclivity for France by noting that they can dominate the English-language historical literature on France, a niche in which they are not compelled to compete with French colleagues, whereas they have no such competitive edge with respect to British historians of Britain. Germany, they say, is a less appealing place to work than France, and the rest of Europe is simply less important, historically and historiographically.

This assessment is reflected and reproduced in curricular and hiring practices, in turn shaping the choices made by those history students tabulated above. Much less likely to have been exposed to the history of Greece, for example, than that of France, Germany, or Britain, they are also less likely to encounter job openings for an historian of Greece than for one of France (although the competition for the latter may well be greater). This stands in contrast to standard practice in anthropology departments, where area special-ties are apt to be more broadly defined and little premium generally given to particular country specialties. Students who are exposed to Europeanist anthropology at all are not so likely to encounter it in a form privileging one or a few countries. Similarly, while becoming a Europeanist may well affect the number of positions for which an anthropologist is qualified, the fact of having worked in Portugal, for example, as opposed to Germany is unlikely to make very much difference. This means that an anthropologist is likely to face fewer professional obstacles to working in a place like Greece, but to be less well-pre-pared to work in a place like France, than his historian counterpart. The result is the relatively even spread of anthropological research in Europe as tabulated above, the larger Europe with which anthropologists are likely to be acquainted, the less intensive country-specific training they are likely to receive or dispense, and the greater difficulties they are likely to encounter in making credible contributions to the scholarship of the well-studied European countries.

If one key to American historians' attraction to France has been the draw of French styles of historical scholarship, the relationship between French and American anthropologies may provide further clues to the tepid appeal of France to American anthropologists. Certainly French anthropology enjoys considerable prestige within the American academy, but there has historically been very little sustained contact between our discipline and its French coun-terpart; Anglo-American and French anthropologies have evolved quite inde-pendently of each other, along strikingly different trajectories. Until quite recently, for example, French anthropologists were trained first in philosophy, moving to a specialty in anthropology only toward the end of their graduate careers; although this is no longer the case, basic conversance with philosophy remains a more crucial dimension of French anthropological thought than of Anglo-American. At the same time, extended fieldwork constitutes an essential cornerstone of the Anglo-American anthropological enterprise, but is treated rather more lightly by the French. In any case, while historical scholarship in France and the United States developed as the study of French and American national histories respectively, French anthropology, like Anglo-American, developed as the study of nonwestern societies largely devoid of indigenous research establishments. Even had there been sufficient cross-fertilization between the two anthropologies to inspire a shared geographic focus, that focus is unlikely to have been France. The study of France has been almost as marginal to French anthropology as it has been to American.

But not quite: There has been a move in France over the last several decades, as in England and the United States, toward extending the ethno-graphic enterprise to the western world. In the United States, this has implied a growing interest in the ethnography of North America and much of Europe; in England, increased attention to British and continental societies; in France, it has meant almost exclusively an interest in France. Although the anthropology of France remains somewhat marginal to the French discipline as a whole, it has been considerably more influential in reorienting the discipline and has drawn proportionately many more and better-established French anthropologists than has been the case within American anthropology. Furthermore, as this specialty emerged in the early 1970s, French anthropologists of France carefully situated their enterprise with respect to older traditions of scholarship on France. Initially retaining the idea that anthropological analysis was best suited to "cold" traditional societies, they were concerned primarily with reconstructing and analyzing pre-World War II life in rural communities (e.g., Zonabend 1980; Karnoouh 1980; Claverie and Lamaison 1982; Segalen 1985). They distanced themselves from folklore studies, instead assertively retaining styles of analysis associated with anthropology and cultivating ties with prestigious *Annales* history, as a more legitimating and intellectually lively way of approaching the study of traditional societies in France (Chiva 1987; Lenclud 1987; Segalen 1989). *Annales* historians, especially the substantial numbers then interested in rural France, meanwhile found in anthropology a new source of research problems, insights, and explanations, as well as legitimizing association with a bona fide social science (Burguière 1978; Goy 1986).[8] Over the past ten years, French anthropologists of France, now working within a well-established specialty area, have largely abandoned their flirtation with the history establishment, as well as the study of historical or rural societies. A substantial amount of French anthropological research now focuses on something called "modern" or "contemporary" society, usually located in institutions or groups associated with urban France (e.g., Le Wita 1988; Zonabend 1989; Abélès 1989; Segalen 1990; Althabe et al. 1992; Bellier 1993; Gaboriau 1993). Although French ethnography of France has only a slightly longer history than does American, it has become considerably better established and more visible, generating a substantially larger literature that includes both monographs and programmatic or theoretical statements.

American anthropologists' interest in France has occasionally been used to help legitimize the move toward France as an ethnographic fieldsite (e.g., Abélès 1995), but more often our French colleagues remain perplexed by the small numbers, junior status, unfamiliar research questions, apparent naiveté, and guarded enthusiasm for France that we have to offer them (e.g., Barbichon 1991). Although we too began with a preoccupation with rural communities, now increasingly displaced by a focus on other types of settings, the American and French ethnographic projects in France have remained quite distinct and unrelated. The analytical tools brought to bear, conceptions of the ethnographic enterprise, general knowledge of France, relationships to our fieldsites, and intended audiences, all distinguish French from American research (Reed-Danahay and Rogers 1987; Rogers 1991b).

French anthropologists, like American historians of France, generally bring to their research in France a conversance with long-established traditions of French scholarship rarely readily accessible to American anthropologists, professional identities carrying strong implications of expertise within the academic worlds we occupy, and well-established (albeit newly so in the case of French anthropologists) modes of producing new knowledge about France. French anthropologists further bring the familiarity of the native to their research settings, while American historians enjoy a long-occupied niche in the highly elaborated French research establishment. These advantages arguably come at the cost of a strongly Francocentric view of the world, appropriately alien to the sensibilities of most American anthropologists. They, nonetheless, also help to situate American anthropology as a kind of poor cousin with respect to scholarship on France. The massive volume of knowledge generated by American historians, French anthropologists, or scholars working in other intellectual traditions certainly cannot be disregarded by American anthropologists seeking to produce credible scholarship on France, and indeed it potentially provides an invaluably stimulating complement to our foreign ethnographer's eye. On the other hand, it can be overwhelming, disorienting, and disheartening. Anthropologists working in France, unlike those working in much of the rest of the world—including parts of Europe—are not engaged in defining the little-known, and are unlikely to survive professionally for long if they operate as if they were. Certainly the mere fact of having lived for a time in France lends no special authority to the anthropologist's knowledge; too many others have done the same. The anthropology of a place like France involves learning enough about other ways of knowing to be able to redefine the well-known, an exercise for which the conventions of our discipline do not especially prepare us. It promises new ways of knowing about such places insofar as our discipline does equip us to situate them in a broader, less well-known world. In the end, it is neither surprising nor alarming that anthropologists have not rushed in greater numbers to those small parts of the world so well-trodden by others.

CONCLUSIONS

My experience in France, no less than the experiences of other contributors to this volume, has been significantly shaped by the fieldwork I have conducted there—as unique in detail as, but generally similar to, fieldwork conducted anywhere in the world—and by the fact that my choice of a European specialty was considered odd by teachers and colleagues alike. In this chapter, however, I have focused on the scholarly world within which anthropologists of France operate, because it is the omnipresence of well-established and influential scholarly traditions that makes France substantially different, at least in degree, from the places studied by most anthropologists, including many Europeanists. Furthermore, much of my discussion has concerned European Studies generally, perhaps reflecting the attitude of many French people and scholars of France that France in many ways represents the epitome of Europe. Certainly, European Studies as practiced in the United States amounts, in considerable measure, to French Studies. This centrality, the broadly shared assumption that one might see all of Europe—or enough of Europe—from a French vantage point, also distinguishes France from the kind of places in Europe and elsewhere that have more usually attracted anthropologists.

The credibility of anthropological knowledge about a place like France rests in part on a reversal of the usual basis for establishing the value of our insights: In treating France as a place worth knowing about, we are not running counter to common wisdom, but are faced instead with the task of showing that we have something worthwhile to add to what is already known about it. The challenges of venturing onto territory that has been well-defined by others can hardly be overestimated, and accounts in significant measure, I would argue, for the relatively slow development of an anthropology of France.

Currently fashionable critiques of anthropology's penchant for the "exotic other" often imply that anthropologists should abandon the relatively unfamiliar locales and peoples that have historically been the subject matter of our discipline, focusing instead on phenomena closer to home. The case of France, however, suggests that such an endeavor may be easier to declare than to credibly execute. Furthermore, while there is certainly no reason why the ethnographic map of the world (or of Europe) should not extend into the powerful nations well-studied by others, as indeed is now happening, it would be unfortunate if our frame of reference were to become as restricted as that of our colleagues in other disciplines. The familiar world is, after all, a rather small one. If we have anything new to say about it, it is, in significant measure, because of the broad cross-cultural perspective our discipline has historically equipped us to bring to that small part of the world. We can and should act on the claim that anthropologists have as much of value to say about Strasbourg as about Sardinia. But it is at least as important for us to go on insisting that Europe includes Vasilika no less than Versailles.

ACKNOWLEDGMENTS

Thanks to Kent Worcester of SSRC and Jason Parker of ACLS for providing both the quantitative data used here and some ideas of what to make of them. Thanks also to the members of the 1995 Joint Committee on Western Europe (JCWE) for their comments on an earlier version of this chapter, to Peter Hall for making me think in new ways about European Studies, and to Nicholas Wahl for making room for me in his version of French Studies.

NOTES

1. The geographic distribution of chapters in this collection provides a good illustration of this point. Quite representative of Europeanist anthropology of the past twenty years, it is strikingly eccentric with respect to European Studies in general. Most notable are the absence of any chapters on Germany or England, and the presence of chapters on Greece and Portugal.

2. This line of argument is consistent with the geography of anthropological scholarship outside of Europe as well. For example, British social anthropologists were drawn earlier and in larger numbers to the study of African societies than to the equally exotic Indian colony. The existence of a well-established Sanscritist tradition—considerable indigenous and British scholarly expertise regarding India—but no comparable body of recognized knowledge regarding the African colonies undoubtedly helps explain the difference.

3. It would undoubtedly be revealing to further break down the country units used here. For example, although the numbers of anthropologists proposing research in Britain and Italy is roughly proportionate to their numbers in the Western Europeanist pool, it is quite possible that they tend to conduct their research in different regions of these countries than do colleagues in other disciplines. My general point, however, can be made with reference to the cruder nation-state units to which the data used here most easily lend themselves.

4. For example, only U.S. citizens are eligible for JCEE fellowships, while foreign nationals attending American universities may apply to the JCWE. On the other hand, the JCWE is more restrictive with regard to disciplinary orientation, requiring a substantial social science or history dimension, while the JCEE is more receptive to literary research.

5. For some years, German funding for research in Germany has been available to American students and scholars through various foundations and programs, but beginning in 1990, the German government made a more concerted effort to encourage German Studies in the United States by granting substantial sums to three American universities for the development of "Centers of Excellence" in German Studies. The French government also funds American students conducting research in France, although the total amount has always been less than that provided by the Germans.

6. This trend may further explain why anthropologists have not been more inclined to work in Eastern Europe, now that the region has become more accessible. Had the cold war ended by 1979, the Slavic fringe might well have become another area of predilection for Europeanist anthropolo-

gists. By 1989, however, the core nations of Western Europe had become plausible—and apparently more appealing—options.

7. As in the earlier period, there are no strongly dominant university affiliations. Of the thirty-three dissertations identified over the 1973–1992 period, five were defended at the University of California-Berkeley, four at the University of Michigan (all in the 1970s), and one or two each at nineteen other universities.

8. Note that some American historians—including some working in France—have also borrowed from anthropology but, unlike their French counterparts, they have been much more likely to turn to theoretical literature produced by anthropologists of nonwestern societies (especially Victor Turner, Mary Douglas, and Clifford Geertz) than to the ethnography of the places they study. At the same time, it should be noted that history occupies a considerably less prestigious niche in the American academy than in France; American anthropologists, therefore, have had less to gain by hitching their wagons to history than did their French counterparts.

CHAPTER 2

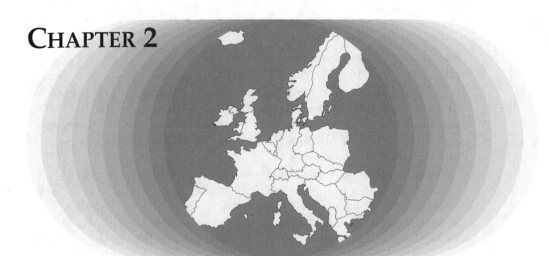

EUROPE THROUGH THE BACK DOOR: DOING ANTHROPOLOGY IN GREECE

Jill Dubisch
Northern Arizona University

Let me begin with coffee. When I first worked in Greece, in 1969–1970, two kinds of coffee were available in most of the areas in which I traveled: thick, usually highly sweetened coffee served in small cups (sometimes referred to as "Turkish" coffee) and instant coffee ("Nescafe") served mostly to tourists who found the local coffee unpalatable. When I asked for coffee, waiters would assume that, being a foreigner, I was asking for Nescafe. "No, *Greek* coffee," I replied the first time this happened, sensitive (so I thought) to the connotations of calling something Turkish in contemporary Greece. "Oh, you mean *Turkish* coffee," the waiter replied. Thus corrected, the next time I asked for coffee, I asked for Turkish coffee. "You mean *Greek* coffee," the waiter admonished me. And so it went.

In part, this little linguistic dance served to remind me that I was a foreigner, situating me "outside," despite my attempt to act like an "insider" by ordering Greek coffee. But I think there was something more than putting a stranger in her place involved here. This terminological game over coffee, I suggest, also represented Greece's ambiguous and ambivalent position between East and West, a position that I now find reproduced in myself as an anthropologist.

Greece is an anomaly in the study of Europe. It has been described as being "on the margins" of Europe (Herzfeld 1987b) and as Europe's "frontier" with the East (Diamandouros 1993). At the same time, the Byzantine past (to which contemporary Greece is, in some respects at least, the heir), the long period of Ottoman rule over areas that are now part of the present Greek state, and Greece's historic ties with cultures to the east have made Greece's status as a European nation ambiguous, both in its own eyes and in those of others.[1]

When I first chose Greece as my fieldwork site in graduate school, little anthropological work had been done there. In fact, I was hard put to find material to read when I was working on my dissertation proposal, and even resorted to novels about Greece for background on the country and culture, a far cry from the extensive array of anthropological (and nonanthropological) books and articles to which those embarking on fieldwork in Greece can now turn.[2] The only professor on my graduate school faculty who had worked extensively in Europe (Spain) had visited Greece only briefly. "It's very oriental," was all he could say to me about it.

Unhelpful though his comment was, it did accord with my own impressions when I had visited Greece during a tour of Europe several years earlier. To make the trip from Rome to Athens, as I did at that time, was to enter a different world. The urban landscape of Athens seemed rather barren to me, compared to other European cities. The language was strange and indecipherable. So were the politics—in my brief visit I was tear-gassed out of a restaurant near Constitution Square during a political demonstration.

And yet I experienced both familiarity and excitement when I stood on top of the Acropolis and watched the sun set through the columns of the Parthenon. I had the sense that all during my trip through Europe I had been traveling backwards in time and now had arrived at the beginning of things— or at least of things European.

This brings up another point about Greece. While it does not stand alone in being on the margins of Europe or as a frontier to the east (similar comments could be made about parts of Eastern Europe, including Russia), Greece does have a unique position in that it is also viewed as the originator of western civilization.[3] In fact, so prominent is the image of ancient Greece in the western view, that cultural anthropologists working in Greece find themselves in an odd position, as we are often assumed by those outside the field to be archaeologists working on ancient Greece. Indeed I know of no other language or culture in which the contemporary version is the marked category, and must be constantly designated by the word "modern" ("modern Greece," "modern Greek").[4]

What is the significance of this for the anthropology of Europe? To begin with, when I first did research in Greece, I did not consider myself to be working in Europe. In fact, Greece was my second choice of research sites. I had originally wanted to work in the Middle East or North Africa and, for reasons too complex to go into here, changed my fieldwork site to Greece, retaining, however, my original research project on gender roles and women's worlds. Thus, like the faculty member who described Greece as "very oriental," I suppose that I, too, saw it as part of a more eastern world, different enough to serve as a context in which to investigate "the other" even when I moved my fieldwork site westward from the locale I had originally proposed.

Though I was unaware of this when I left for Greece in 1969, there was a small cadre of anthropologists, mostly American but also some British, who were undertaking research in Greece at about the same time. We spanned a large area, from the islands to the Peloponnesus, to Athens, to northern Greece. But we became united in our own marginal status within the discipline, having worked in an area that was both exotic and, at the same time, not quite exotic enough to be considered "real" anthropology.[5] Hence, it was difficult for us to find an intellectual home in any regional study group or association. At the annual American Anthropological Association meetings, we would meet sometimes with the informally organized East European Study group. While they welcomed us, our problems were, for the most part, different from theirs, since they were all struggling with the difficulties of doing research under socialist regimes. Nor was there any organized Mediterranean Studies group in American anthropology with which to affiliate ourselves.

Nonetheless, it is within the context of "the Mediterranean" that much of the early study of Greece was placed and to which many of us turned, at least at first, for a comparative setting in which to place our own research. Insofar as "the Mediterranean" encompasses both the West (southern Europe) and the East (North Africa and parts of the Middle East), it provided a different framework for the study of Greece than does the anthropology of Europe. It is to a discussion of that difference and its significance for both anthropologists and Greeks that I now turn.

ANTHROPOLOGY IN GREECE

The anthropology of Greece, for Americans at least, was heavily impacted by two important ethnographies that appeared in the early 1960s. The first was Ernestine Friedl's *Vasilika*, which was published in 1962. The other, *Honour, Family, and Patronage*, published in 1964, was by British anthropologist John Campbell. Campbell's book focused on shepherds living in a mountainous area of northern Greece, Friedl's on an agricultural village in the fertile plains of central Greece. Campbell's work on the Sarakatsani shepherds reflected the "exoticizing" process found particularly in the earlier anthropology of Europe, a process which sought to legitimize anthropological work in a region that would otherwise seem too familiar, by accentuating the differences from contemporary Western societies and the parallels with "primitive society" in the communities being studied. Campbell placed his ethnography in the context of studies of "Mediterranean society," suggesting that the social forms observed among the mountain shepherds had their parallels in other parts of the Mediterranean region (Campbell 1964, v). Friedl, on the other hand, situated her study in the broad context of the "Old World cultures," cultures that owed a number of their basic features to their derivation from the civilizations of the

Near East (Friedl 1962, 2) and in the context of the study of "peasant society" (Friedl 1962, 4).[6]

These larger contexts, in which the anthropology of Greece has been placed, both determine, and are determined by, the particular problems chosen for study. Anthropological studies situated in the context of the Mediterranean have tended to focus on "honor and shame" as a moral system characteristic of the region,[7] leading to a variety of debates about the utility of honor and shame as a conceptual scheme, and its uniqueness as a Mediterranean feature.[8] Not only does the Mediterranean generate a specific set of anthropological questions, it also separates Greece, along with the rest of southern Europe, from Europe "proper," placing it in an "exotic" position, preceding "Europe" and in some sense "primordial," representing an earlier, archaic form of society and culture.[9]

In his study of the Sarakatsani, Campbell picked a remote mountain community whose way of life set them off from the neighboring populations. At the same time, he saw the Sarakatsani as having "always been" Greek and declared that, "They still hold to what the villagers describe as 'the old customs,' moral attitudes in family and community which a hundred years ago were general throughout Greek mountain communities, and still persist today though in conflict with other values of urban and alien origins" (1964, 6).

Campbell's compelling study was a basic work for those of us beginning our research in the late 1960s and early 1970s, and despite the fact that most of us chose for our own fieldwork communities distant both geographically and in their way of life from that studied by Campbell, his work on the Sarakatsani shepherds somehow created for at least some of us a sense that what he studied was the "real" Greece. This was true even for me, though I had chosen my original dissertation topic because of dissatisfaction with Campbell's discussion of Sarakatsani women.[10] Perhaps because of the community Campbell had chosen, or the way he described it, his book seemed like "real" anthropology, at least as I had been taught to that point.[11]

Perhaps part of what underlay this acceptance that at least some of Campbell's analysis should be applicable to our own studies, even if our communities were very different from his, was a tacit acceptance of the notion of "Greece" itself. That is, while we knew that there were regional and ecological differences among Greek communities, we uncritically assumed that they all existed within a real entity we could call Greece. We were not entirely wrong in such an assumption, of course; all of these communities were included within the contemporary Greek state, and were subject to similar national processes. But we were perhaps naive, accepting Greek nationalist ideology about Greekness, an ideology that presents the nation as more or less homogeneous and as historically continuous.

The interplay between nationalist ideology, western conceptions of Greece, and the anthropology of Greece is complex. Campbell saw the Sarakatsani as having "always been Greek," with the implication that they rep-

resent that Greekness in some primordial way. In some sense, then, this justifies his choice of such a community for anthropological study, marginal as it
may have been within the large context of Greece as a whole. Michael
Herzfeld, on the other hand, in his book *The Poetics of Manhood*, justifies the
anthropological choice of "obscure, peripheral communities" in places such as
Greece on somewhat different grounds, pointing out the vital role that such
communities play in the formation of national self-stereotypes and in collective
representations to the outside (Herzfeld 1985, xvi). Thus he suggests that certain features of the Cretan community he studied are important not because
they were typical of Greece and Greeks,[12] but because they play an important
role in certain formations of national self-image and values.

As American anthropologists found themselves working in a wide range
of Greek rural (and occasionally urban) communities, they came to formulate
different sorts of problems for study than those shaped by the issues of a
Mediterraneanist anthropology. Often these problems originated in the particular situations in which individual researchers found themselves, as well as
being shaped by certain emphases (such as cultural ecology) within American
anthropology itself. My own experience is a good example. Originally I began
fieldwork with a problem generated through my reading of Campbell.
Dissatisfied with Campbell's portrayal of Sarakatsani women, and wondering
if they viewed their culture in the way in which Campbell described it or if he
had presented only a male point of view, I set out to see if there was a
"women's culture" in rural Greek communities that differed from the culture
of men (see Dubisch 1986). However, when I had been in the island village
where I did my research for just a short while, I was struck by a different phenomenon—the high level of out-migration from the village to Athens and the
extensive web of relationships this set up between city and village, a topic I
had not seen discussed in any of the literature I had read to that point.
Moreover, I discovered, as I questioned villagers further, such migration had a
long history. In the preceding century, and up to the Greek defeat in Asia
Minor in 1922 (still referred to as the "catastrophe"), villagers had migrated
regularly to Constantinople, "the City" (as many villagers still called Istanbul),
and there had even been a village postman who went back and forth with mail
and packages. This certainly challenged my own prefieldwork view of the self-
contained moral community of the Mediterranean, as shaped by the writing of
Campbell and others.[13] As it turned out, I was not the only anthropologist
beginning fieldwork at this time who was struck by this phenomenon, and
since that time there have appeared a number of articles written on Greek
migration and migrants.[14] It was in part through such experiences that a number of anthropologists working in Greece during this period came to view the
communities we studied in the wider comparative context of peasant societies.[15] This was especially, though not exclusively, true of American anthropologists. Seeing Greece in this way, as a peasant society rather than only as
part of a Mediterranean region, locates it differently, both conceptually and
geographically, generating a different set of questions and placing Greece in a

comparative context that could include not only other European societies but also Asia and Latin America.[16]

If some of us working in Greece from the late 1960s onward did not feel comfortable viewing Greece in the context of the Mediterranean (and with the problems generated by such placement), this did not mean that we saw Greece as part of Europe. Perhaps Greece was too "oriental," poised between East and West, for us to see it as truly European. Indeed, it was this uncertainty about where we "belonged," intellectually and organizationally, that left many of us feeling "marginal."[17] Despite this feeling, however, many of the issues explored by anthropologists working in Greece mirrored larger interests and theoretical trends within the discipline and paralleled work done elsewhere in Europe as well. These issues included the cultural ecology of peasant farming[18] and rural-urban migration, as well as community relations, kinship, and family structure.[19] In addition, gender has been an important subject of interest to anthropologists working in Greece. While this last concern might seem to be driven by Mediterraneanist conceptions of honor and shame, much of the work on gender in Greece, especially by Americans (including myself), has paid little or no attention to issues of honor and shame, but has rather been driven by debates over "the position of women," as articulated in Friedl's 1967 article.[20] (More recent writings on gender in Greece have also examined the construction of gender identity and the "poetics" of gender.[21])

In addition, Greece has also generated special problems and topics of its own for research. Greek funerary practices, for example, with their often elaborate mourning rituals, the custom of secondary burial found in many areas, and the highly developed poetry of women's mourning laments, have attracted considerable attention from both anthropologists and folklorists.[22] Another topic that has been peculiar to Greece is the study of refugee communities formed by peoples who fled to Greece following the catastrophe of 1922, their problems of adaptation, and their continuing identity as refugees.[23] In most of these earlier studies, anthropologists in Greece, like anthropologists elsewhere in the region, focused their research on small, mainly rural communities.[24]

The number of anthropologists working in Greece has increased in recent years, and—not surprisingly—recent anthropological studies there have tended to reflect current interests and theoretical concerns within anthropology, including reflexivity, performance, the role of history, and issues of modernity and postmodernity.[25] In addition, anthropological work in Greece has recently come to be criticized by an emerging generation of Greek anthropologists.[26] These anthropologists, like other native anthropologists, have had to work with theoretical models and analytic categories which were not only developed by a western European and American social science, but which also drew their original inspiration from cultures far removed from Europe (see Gefou-Madianou 1993, 161). At the same time, though they come from a culture to which is attributed the roots of western civilization itself, and to whose ancient past is attributed the beginnings of anthropology, until recently at least, Greek students of anthropology had to seek out foreign institutions in order to study that to which their own cultural inheritance is claimed to have given birth (see Herzfeld 1987b).

Most Greek anthropologists have chosen Greece as their fieldwork site, sometimes studying the communities from which they themselves, or their families, have come.[27] A number of these anthropologists are active with the European Association of Social Anthropologists. This work by Greek anthropologists has added an important dimension to the anthropology of Greece, one with significant implications not only for the anthropology of Greece but more generally for our reflexive understanding of anthropology itself. For all of these reasons, then, Greece does not simply provide another context for research driven by contemporary issues and concerns, but is itself, as Herzfeld has argued, a particularly appropriate area—on the margins of Europe, at the divide between self and other—in which to generate anthropological self-examination (Herzfeld 1987b).

Recent work in Greece, however, has not only been shaped by current concerns within anthropology, but also by the growing—though to my mind still incomplete—inclusion of such research within the anthropology of Europe.

GREECE IN THE ANTHROPOLOGY OF EUROPE

As part of what has been termed the second wave of anthropologists, following Friedl and Campbell's work in Greece (Papataxiarchis 1991), I find that my work has mirrored the general trends in the anthropology of the region. My earlier work focused on rural-urban migration and on gender.[28] My more recent research, however, has moved away from the village and community studies that in the past characterized anthropological work in Greece. My study of a Greek pilgrimage site examines (among other things) issues of identity and its construction in both a local and national context, and seeks to relate these to current theoretical concerns within the discipline of anthropology (Dubisch 1995). At the same time, my work has felt the impact of the growing interest in, and formal organization of, the anthropology of Europe.

After I returned from fieldwork in the fall of 1986, I gave a paper at the AAA meetings, in a session organized by Ellen Badone titled "Orthodoxy and Folk Belief in European Society." It was, as I recall, the first time I was part of a "Europeanist" session at the AAA meetings (rather than a Mediterranean Europe or a Greek session, or a session organized topically). At that same meeting, the Society for the Anthropology of Europe held its first organizational meeting. This was also the period in which Greece was in the process of becoming a full-fledged member of the European Community. Thus I, the anthropology of Greece, and Greece itself were all moving toward inclusion in the political and intellectual category "Europe." And since then, most of my work has been presented and published in a new context: the anthropology of Europe.

The question "Is Greece part of Europe?" would thus seem to be answered. This chapter was originally presented as part of a panel organized by the Society for the Anthropology of Europe on the history of the anthropology of Europe and is now included in a reader on that topic. Greece is now part of the European Union. Most Greek anthropologists belong to the European Association of Social Anthropologists and publish in volumes generated by that association's conferences. Thus Europe has come to provide both an intellectual and an organizational context for anthropology in and of Greece.

At the same time there remains a sense of ambivalence and even marginality for Greeks and for anthropologists in and of Greece. We understand that "Europe" is a construction, just as is "the Mediterranean." At the same time, it is "real" in its power as an idea, in its political consequences, in its role as a context for anthropological research. And it may be regarded with ambivalence by those over whom Europe (and in a larger sense the West) extends its cultural and political hegemony (as illustrated in the following cartoon from a Greek newspaper).

Translation: Headline: How European Is the Greek?
First Panel: "I was born a Greek ..."
Second Panel: "... and a European I will die."

Cartoon by Ilia Makri. Published in *I Kathimerini*, June 7, 1990.

Earlier I suggested that placing Greece in the context of the Mediterranean or in the context of peasant society generates, and is the consequence of, attention to certain kinds of problems. What kinds of problems, then, result from placing Greece in "Europe"? There are several I could discuss here, but I will point out one that is of particular significance today. Placing Greece in Europe highlights issues of identity: the ways in which national and ethnic identity are formed and reformed, the impact of the concept of "European-ness" upon personal and group identity, the processes of contesting of and resistance to hegemonic political and cultural constructions of identity. Such issues have played a role in Greek political and social life since that country's inception as a nation (and before), as the concept of Greekness was forged from, and applied to, a range of populations differing in their history and way of life. But these issues have taken on a new critical import in the wake of the disintegration of Yugoslavia and the Soviet Union and in the context of the European Union, as many Greeks see Greece's cultural identity and political integrity threatened. I suggested earlier that anthropologists working in Greece in the late 1960s and early 1970s somewhat naively accepted the notion of "Greece" itself. More recently, however, and particularly as anthropologists have become more sophisticated in their use and understanding of history, there has been more anthropological examination of the process of creating a national Greek identity, and of the political and historical forces that have shaped this process.[29] (There is an important reflexive issue here as well, for our own identity as anthropologists is implicated insofar as we subdivide ourselves on a national basis: anthropologists of Italy, of Greece, of Spain, etcetera.[30])

All of this calls up a larger question: Are we anthropologists *of* Europe (or Greece) or *in* Europe (or Greece)? Do we study European cultures, or anthropological problems in the context of those cultures? To what extent does the concept of Europe itself also give us parameters and issues for study? Does the intellectual construction of Europe, like the political construction of Europe, exclude as well as include?[31] We need to ask ourselves not only what possibilities the creation of "the anthropology of Europe" brings, but what limitations it imposes as well. While for me, and for a number of other anthropologists, the institutionalizing of an anthropology of Europe has proved tremendously stimulating for both theory and research, it is important to remember that we have not so much *become* anthropologists of Europe as we have *created* ourselves as such.

On a final note, let me return to my original topic. Although Greek/Turkish coffee and Nescafe are still found in Greece, one now finds in cities and towns throughout Greece cafes and bars with espresso machines. I can now avoid my coffee dilemma, if I wish, by ordering an espresso or cappuccino, a clearly *European* choice. To paraphrase the Greek in the cartoon, then, I began my career as an anthropologist of Greece but it seems that I shall retire as an anthropologist of Europe. However, I cannot forget that I came to the study of Greece not because it was Greece but because it was the context for a problem. So, like certain Greeks, I sometimes feel ambivalent in "Europe" and occasionally wonder if those of us working in Greece should resist the "Europeanization" of our subject matter. Or should we accept that we have indeed entered Europe, albeit "through the back door"? Perhaps. But I hope that we will continue to leave that door open, if only just a crack.

Notes

1. For a discussion of this issue, see Herzfeld (1987b). The ambiguity is reflected in a variety of sources, including accounts by travelers who visited Greece during the nineteenth century following the establishment of an independent state of Greece. (See, for example, Bremer 1863.)

2. There were a number of publications by Greek and French sociologists and geographers on rural Greek communities put out by the Social Science Research Center in Athens in the 1960s, but I did not become aware of these until I got to Greece.

3. It was such a view that led thousands of western European "Philhellenes" to support the Greeks, directly and indirectly, in their struggle to achieve an independent state (St. Clair 1977). At the same time, Greece's politics and its status as an underdeveloped country have tended to keep it on the margins of democratic, industrialized western Europe.

4. We can see this also in the name of the Modern Greek Studies Association. Although, during the general business meeting at the organization's 1991 symposium, the suggestion was made that the designation "modern" be removed from the association's name (a suggestion that met with general approval), the name has not yet been changed.

5. One of my anthropology professors from college, though he never said so directly, was clearly disappointed that I had selected Greece for my fieldwork (rather than, for example, Native Americans, his own field of study).

6. Although Friedl and Campbell both published in volumes on the Mediterranean, Friedl's comparative context (whether implicit or explicit) has always seemed to me to be wider than this region. It may be that "the Mediterranean" has always been a more important concept for European anthropologists, and the British in particular, than for Americans, who perhaps felt less need to exoticize the area since it was, in some respects at least, more inherently distant, and hence less in need of exoticizing, than it was for Europeans. Two volumes on the Mediterranean in which both Campbell and Friedl had articles are Pitt-Rivers (1963) and Peristiany (1965).

7. Patron-client relations were another focus.

8. The literature on this includes Davis (1977); Gilmore (1987); Peristiany (1965); Pitt-Rivers (1977). Critiques of the category "Mediterranean" include Fernandez (1986); Herzfeld (1980, 1987b); Pina-Cabral (1989). For a recent discussion, see Sant Cassia (1991).

9. In this sense, some of the earlier anthropologists of the region could be seen as looking for earlier forms of their own society, just as the nineteenth-century evolutionists looked for early forms of human society generally among "primitive" peoples. This may also be one of the reasons for the anthropological emphasis on "honor and shame," as archaic values in eclipse in modern western European cultures. For a good statement of this, see Pitt-Rivers 1966; also Peristiany 1965. This approach is also exemplified in Susanna Hoffman's 1974 film *Kypseli*. For a discussion of these issues, see Dubisch 1995, 194–205.

10. See Dubisch 1986.

11. This may have been in part because both my graduate and undergraduate training had a strong emphasis on British social anthropology.

12. The issue of "typicality" was addressed, with somewhat heated debate, in the 1975 New York Academy of Sciences Conference on Greece. Ernestine Friedl's comments on this issue, from an anthropological point of view, were perhaps the most reasoned in the debate. (See Dimen and Friedl 1976.)

13. As it turned out, however, there had also been out-migration from the shepherd community Campbell had studied; he simply had not written about it in his ethnography. For an interesting discussion of this, see Dimen 1976.

14. Among both earlier and more recent works are Allen 1976; Costa 1988; Dubisch 1977; Kenna 1977, 1993; Stott 1993; Sutton 1988. In addition, some of the publications of the Social Science Research Centre in Athens mentioned earlier dealt with internal migration (e.g., Moustaka 1964).

15. These two approaches were not exclusive. There was a category of "Mediterranean peasantry," defined not on the basis of a system of moral values but according to ecological conditions and consequent farming practices and social organization (see, for example, Wolf 1966).

16. Another context was interdisciplinary. Within the Modern Greek Studies Association, for example, the problem for anthropologists became not the situating of Greece within anthropology but the situating of anthropology within scholarly studies of Greece.

17. An important event for those of us working in Greece was the 1975 New York Academy of Science conference on regional variation in Greece and Cyprus, organized by Ernestine Friedl and Muriel Dimen, which brought together many of the anthropologists (along with other social scientists) who had worked in Greece. While this may have relieved some of our

sense of isolation insofar as we found ourselves working in concert with others, it did not change our sense of marginality within the larger context of the discipline.

18.   See, for example, articles by Aschenbrenner, Gavrielides, Koster and Koster, and others in Dimen and Friedl 1976.

19.   See, for example, Bialor 1976; Currier 1976.

20.   My edited volume, *Gender and Power in Rural Greece* (1986), for example, as well as an earlier article (Dubisch 1974b), dealt with issues of women's status with little mention of honor and shame.

21.   For example, Herzfeld (1985); Loizos and Papataxiarchis (1991); Seremetakis (1990, 1991). There have also been several recent works on changes in gender roles; see, for example, Cowan 1991; Galani-Moutafi 1993, 1994. I am including here British and Greek anthropologists, as well as American. While there are still differences among the various approaches, they have strongly impacted each other, and Greek anthropologists have received training at both American and British schools.

22.   Such works include Caraveli (1980, 1986); Danforth and Tsiaras (1982); Dubisch (1989); Kenna (1976, 1991); Seremetakis (1991). The subject of death is not unconnected to gender since Greek mourning laments and many of the funerary practices and observances are the province of women.

23.   Works by Hirschon (1989) and Salamone (1987) are examples. Danforth's 1989 book also focuses on a refugee group.

24.   One exception is Hirschon 1983, 1989.

25.   I would include here such works as Cowan (1990); Dubisch (1995); Faubian (1993); Herzfeld (1991); Seremetakis (1991).

26.   For a discussion of this, and of the role of the native ethnographer, see Gefou-Madianou (1993). For a recent criticism of anthropological approaches to death in Greece, see Panourgia (1994).

27.   See, for example, Galani-Moutafi 1993, 1994; Papataxiarchis 1991.

28.   See Dubisch (1972, 1977, 1983, 1986).

29.   Among the first to do so was Herzfeld (1982, 1987b). More recent works include Karakasidou (1993); Sant Cassia (1992). Such analysis has not proceeded without controversy, however, because it challenges Greek nationalist ideology and can be seen as politically threatening, especially in the wake of the creation of a Macedonian state in the former Yugoslavia. Both Karakasidou and Herzfeld have been attacked in the Greek and Greek-American press.

30.   See Sant Cassia (1991) for a similar discussion.

31.   For example, it may create scholarly and conceptual barriers, in addition to the political ones, in comparative research on Greece and Turkey.

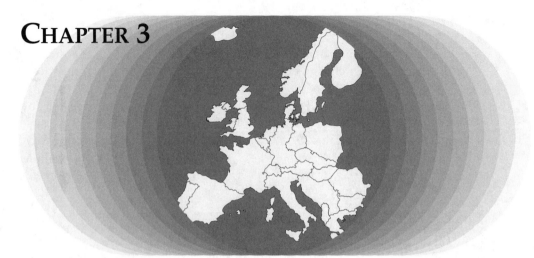

CHAPTER 3

BRINGING THE "OTHER" TO THE "SELF": KYPSELI—THE PLACE AND THE FILM

Susanna M. Hoffman

Certain courses in life are picked because of concerns that pulsate at partic-ular times. The path may seem focused, meaningful, even a sort of quest when elected. Then direction shifts, meaning drifts, and the chosen course leads the chooser to destinations unknown. It is as if you as a person, researcher, traveler step into a river, expecting to cross to a certain shore. Instead you are buoyed along through roiling eddies to far shoals you did not envision. Such is the nature of my story. It is the tale of how an anthropologist chose to conduct a precise academic study in Europe and ended up a feminist filmmaker and writer of popular nonfiction, including food books.

EUROPE

Europe. At the time I embarked for the place to conduct anthropological research, anthropologists—or more specifically structural anthropologists, of which I decid-edly was one—had come face to face with a paradox arising from within their own studies. When Levi-Strauss, Griaule, and others demonstrated that Amazon, African, Oceanic and Northwest Coastal cultures unraveled logical patterns of symbolism, that their order expressed lyric and poetic beauty and bespoke per-haps the nature of the human mind, the question insidiously arose: Could western people possibly be as sophisticated as their counterparts who flourished far out-side the erudite, long self-glorified framework of western thought?

   The question was the flip side of the one that had ostensibly driven anthropology for the decades of its history, though I wager the flip question was always the secret query. At issue was not whether isolated or parochial people were like us, but whether we were like them. Were we perhaps even as fascinatingly grammatical, elegantly organized, and symbolically revealing as they? Up to this point it had seemingly become an evident and enlightened truism of our discipline that every sort of people, regardless of the size of the population, obscurity, place of dwelling, or path far deviant from the mainstream of human development, could throw some light upon the social environment of every other people. But the nagging issue that now arose was, could we cast any illuminating beam upon ourselves?

In response, students of structuralism began to examine phenomena within the culture that produced them. Claude Levi-Strauss took his analysis from kinship systems to mythology, including western myth. In the overture to *The Raw and the Cooked* (1969) he expanded his ideas to include European music and poetry. His conversations with G. Charbonnier (1969) covered subject matters running from Picasso to steam engines. Other structuralists in France began to focus their investigations on a variety of topics within modern western life. Lacan, in deft turn-about, probed psychoanalysis (Ehrmann 1970). Dumezil brushed off European folklore for yet another go-around (Littleton 1966). Rifaterre turned his attention to Baudelaire's poetry, while Ripparere attempted to formulate a structural approach to all literature. Foucault dissected a Velazquez painting much as one would a drosophila, while Derrida strove to unravel popular fables concerning the Eiffel Tower (Caws 1970, 197–215).

Adherents of structural anthropology in Britain were not lying quietly beside the Avon. They, too, were expanding their interests to explore form and content within their own cultural tradition. Edmund Leach traced an analytical thread that led from the analysis of Native American mythology to ancient Greek legends and carried on to the Judeao-Christian Bible (1969). Mary Douglas was investigating the logic of Hebraic law (1966, 41–56). From the concepts of cultural taxonomy, marginality, disorder and dirt, both were prying out the sense within Genesis, Deuteronomy, virgin birth, food and blood taboos, and other matters that were part and parcel still to modern times and literate thought.

None of these hearties, however, had used a structural approach as the basis of fieldwork in a European community. Though a structural format had been applied to villages on Pacific islands, in South American rain forests and the African heartland, the "turf" of the western world lay abashedly unplowed. I, in my structuralist glow and graduate student greenness, decided to amend that. With all the accompanying hubris, I was convinced that if what was being said about these remote communities were true of the human mind, it would be true everywhere, even among the more lettered. Moreover, what was true of the "other" would be true of the "self." I resolved to expand structural studies on things close at hand as my idols were doing, but in an ethnographic way. I would experiment with a structural approach as an explanatory system and basis for understanding a more mainstream community—in fact, one among ourselves. I would conduct a structuralist village study in the seat of "our" tradition, among the most "us" of us. I would go to Europe.

Europe, therefore, was not a site I fell or backed into. Quite the opposite of many anthropologists who ended up Europeanists, I became a Europeanist on purpose and with a particular goal in mind. I was determined to show that among a community within our own tradition, the kinship system, the general ideology, and such items as our spatial and temporal arrangement were linked by a common structural grammar. The study was to compare to the structurally integrated sort that Levi-Strauss claimed for small populations along the Amazon, in Southeast Asia, or native America. Of course, since the study I had in mind was first and foremost about the nature of humanity and the human mind and not about a culture area, that the study take place in Europe was not an absolute requirement. I only needed to show that the same phenomena that occurred among remote people also appeared among people who dwelled within a literate milieu. The endeavor could have taken place within the context of any "great" tradition. I could have gone, say, to India or China. But if I were to pursue my second aim, to demonstrate that the phenomena true of the "other" were as true of the "self," Europe was my only possible proving ground, my own, so to speak, Bikini atoll.

Once I decided on Europe, my choice of where *in* Europe followed, I thought, a logical and linear process. As is par for the course for a first-time-site-picking tyro anthropologist, however, it turned out that thought process was about as plumb as the river Meander. If I were to conduct a study at a site within a great tradition, I wanted to go to a font of that tradition, a hub where that tradition flourished early and where a version yet endured. That made the pick of where to go relatively simple. There was no lady and no tiger. There was only one portal. It had to be Greece.

Just as Europe was not a site I fell into when I chose to do my fieldwork there, Greece was not at all in my mind the easternmost part of the west or a sort of orientalized enclave within Europe as some other anthropologists thought of it. To me, Greece represented a mainspring of European tradition, a *radix* of the western world, and also, despite the invasions it had seen, a site where that culture had long persisted. After all, every European seat had seen much conquest by fellow Europeans and extraneous others. Few had the resonance that Greece has. The reader must remember that I received my anthropological training at the University of California at Berkeley. To say that I well knew the complete and unabridged "culture" history of Europe, starting from before Zeus spied the maiden of the same name, is a mild understatement. Due to my professors, their nature, and the nature of Berkeley's holistic anthropological tradition, I was more than extremely well-versed in the exact steps of human arrival to that chilly subcontinent, at least as was best surmised at the time. I knew the immigrations of practically every individual Indo-European, his or her language family, brooch style, cart type, and horse stock. I knew when and from where each wave of Indo-European speakers came, where they wandered and finally settled, although as we all know they have not yet all settled. I knew all the locations of the lonely, lofty lairs of the remaining pre-Indo-European speakers, how and when those incursive Finno-Ugrics and Ural-Altaics came. I was further grounded in how the whole shebang developed over the next millennia and how they shipped themselves and their traditions to farther shores, including North America.

Greek-speaking people were, of course, among the first, if not the first, Indo-European speakers to enter what came to be called Europe.[1] Western civilization most certainly first flourished among the Hellenes, notwithstanding present controversy over where some of the ideas propagated derived (Bernal 1987). Despite the other Indo-Europeans and non-Indo-Europeans who overran them, Greece was to me the "old man" of western civilization and, sitting near the Acropolis, hints of "survivalism" notwithstanding, I cannot but still think so.

GREECE

Having selected Greece for my fieldwork, I was next faced with where to go in Greece and what kind of community to choose. I wanted some rein on cultural influence and certainly the size of the site, so a city, such as Athens, or a tourist mecca, such as Delphi, would not do. A more isolated or rural site with a long western tradition was the goal. I did not intend to conduct a "peasant" study; still I felt bound by the parameters of anthropology. I also believed a small, rural community might reveal more of the intertwined cultural grammar I sought. I was further influenced by other European village studies, although it was not exactly my purpose to turn one out. After a due amount of research, plowing through every volume I could find from archive to the Blue Guide, I chose the island of Thera.

On Thera's mysterious cliffs, a long and remarkable history had transpired. The island had been occupied first by Minoans, but a massive eruption of Thera's own volcano practically erased the Minoan civilization across the eastern Mediterranean. (Fouque 1869 and 1879; Marinatos 1939 and 1950; Galanopoulos 1958; Ninkovitch and Heezen 1965; Dumas 1983; Pellegrino 1993). In due time, after the cataclysm, Phoenicians arrived on the now crescent-shaped island, the remaining rim of the volcano. They were followed by very early Greeks. Some of the oldest Greek writing is found on Thera. The name Thera comes from prince Theras the Autesionos who, along with other Lacedaemonians from Sparta, conquered the island from Dorian Greeks around 1000 B.C. During the flowering of ancient Greek civilization, Thera was a center of trade and a seat of rulers. Battus of Thera, following a command of the Delphic oracle, established the famous colony of Cyrene on the coast of

North Africa (Naupliotou 1937). In the Roman era, the Greek kings of Egypt, the Ptolemies, were educated at the gymnasium on Thera. Christianization took place from the second to the fifth centuries A.D. and Greek Byzantium commanded the island until after A.D. 1000. All these layers unfolded in one long-lasting city, now called ancient Thera, situated atop the island's highest mountain. During the era of Italy's great seafaring might, Venetians took over the island. They deserted ancient Thera to build five other towns, which they crowned with castles. Although Turkish invaders eventually took over the island, they oversaw it without greatly populating it. The island was, in fact, never completely depopulated as were some Cycladic islands. Some descendants of the original Greek dwellers perhaps always remained.

Besides all of these reasonable reasons to choose Thera as my locus to unravel a western cultural structure, I had yet another. The tiny island was reputed in all the literature to hold some three thousand churches, and I thought, once again in a seemingly sensible, but ultimately sophomoric manner, that any people with that many churches must be seriously symbolic. They would be expressing themselves like three thousand Eratos. They would parade before me puzzles such as those delivered by that most enigmatic of all oracles, the impish Delphic one. I would find amid their behavior runes reflecting the island cultural organization as prevalent as I found wild oregano. Sadly, it turned out, the island's only "Enigma" was its most famous nightclub and Therans were not operating at all on the higher plane of symbol and sign with their bounteous churches. They were merely amassing coin and, as people almost everywhere do in one manner or another, counting coup. As soon as a Theran family had enough money, it turned out, its members built a private chapel in order to display to all their new-found worth and rank. Most of the churches were simply the island equivalent of a Mercedes Benz. However, I didn't know this at the time and I went there.

KYPSELI

Of the twelve villages on the island, two held the dubious distinction of being the most "backward." In these, said the island sages, I would find intact the most old traditions and see in action the most customary way of life. Of course, I would also find no running water, no electricity, and only a pumice dust trench of a road, but I was game (not so game, however, as to go to the one that was quite distant from the island's major town). The closer site made it more possible for me to follow the link between the village and town, I told myself. In truth, it also more easily granted the weary, over-ogled anthropologist an occasional escape and allowed me to indulge the grand American tradition of consumer therapy when times got rough. Shopping, however, disappointed. Practically the only items available for purchase in what was called "the market" were a *denakaki* of unfiltered kerosene and a two-week-old Herald Tribune. In the village there was but one sparsely supplied store. It featured Gala Nou Nou (condensed milk), Tide, *bikibaou* (baking powder), and under the oil cloth-draped counter great flat plates of dried cod. I call the village Kypseli. I stayed more than two years. I have been back continuously for the past twenty-five.

To my gratification, my experimental ground yielded all the fruit I had hoped for. The social and cognitive organization I was looking for, so clear and lyrical among isolated people, was equally present and equally elegiac among these denizens of a great literate tradition. I found that the Greek villagers expressed a sophisticated logic to their cultural order. Here in a European village, as with Amazon tribes and other remote peoples, factions of persons defined by incest laws stood distinct from one another. Following the dictates of incest prohibitions, marital exchange united these separate factions. Moreover, even among these Europeans, the symbolic categories and the structural pattern utilized to separate and differentiate human groupings were recapitulated in other arenas. The codification that appeared in the kinship reemerged in the wedding ceremony, wove through the engagement proceedings, unfolded again in the spatial disposition of homes and village as a whole, showed up in the time schedule of the villagers' day, replayed in the village dances, beliefs, jokes, and taboos, and emerged in the behavioral roles of paterfamilias and matriarch. These multitudinous elements within the maze of village custom intersected and made sense within a holistic context. I entered Kypseli as Theseus wandering in the labyrinth only to discover the labyrinth was not a tangled maze but was laid out in a grid.

ORGANIZATION BY GENDER

In the heady haze of structuralist true belief, I expected to find in unmined Kypseli a social organization revealed in all sorts of abstractions. I thought I would discover Hegelian dialectics springing forth from the village's tightly circled grape vines, poetically oppositional categories hidden among the laundry lines, thesis, antithesis, and synthesis popping up like red eggs from Easter bread. Instead the dualism, including the ever-hidden triad, fleshed out quite, well—quite corporeally. The rules, beliefs, and roles in Kypselian society operated according to a very basic division, that of gender, and employed a very bodily surface sign, that of male and female. The people eschewed bears. They utilized no eagles or wolves, or other environmentally borrowed symbols to arrange their human groupings or segment their world. They paid little heed to barbers. Though there were carpenters and shoemakers, no occupational or other literary categories extended to social factions nor to divisions of other matter, material or immaterial. Though last names defined families to some degree, the scant eight or so patronyms in the village defined no major social unit. Rather, the organizational distinction operated according to sex.

As with the use of totemic animals to categorize persons and things, the employment of gender categories arises from sensory perception. A phenomenon existing in nature—heard, touched, smelled, usually seen—is lifted from its physicality and used in an abstract or cultural way to sort all manner of not-connected matter, matter that has nothing to do with the actual, natural phenomenon. Of all the natural occurrences, more so than distinctions based on animals, or stars, or other physical objects, the sensory perception of gender distinction is immediately, readily, and constantly available. One has but to look at almost any living creature, almost any time, to confirm that sexual distinction exists. Thus gender category when used as the sorting device, even on goods that bear no gender, that are in fact without sex, seems directly justifiable, and as a consequence the use of gender to classify things and sunder them constitutes a deeply ingrained method of arrangement. Gender distinction is so available, so close at hand, that the cultural use of it throughout the human community is widespread. Any cultural system based on it results in a tenacious pattern.

In the village of Kypseli, gender was attached to paraphernalia and phenomena that were not gendered in reality at all. It was wielded to separate and distinguish time and space in days, at dances, in the home, in church, and across the entire village span from plaza to periphery. Lines of descent, property, the sides united at weddings, the choreography of ritual were indexed by male and female stamp. Personal names crisscrossed by gender, gender line, and alternate generation so that not only were there but eight last names in the village, there existed only about eight first names as well. Even the villagers' nicknames bore gender and passed down descent lines in gendered fashion.

Yet, despite the utter dualism of gender distinction, true to what I hoped to find, beneath the duality of male and female persons and goods lay a triadic design in which, in contradiction to their equality in apparent category, female items were actually bound between male elements. They were like a book between bookends. Male and female emblems constituted only the surface sign. Although a woman and her possessions seemingly commanded one side in marital exchange, in truth her father and brothers held control over both her and her belongings. Women and female goods crossed from father to husband in marriage, never quite leaving the father, never quite belonging to the husband, suspended between both. Cohesion in the village derived from women and female goods transferred between male factions—two of them to be exact. On close examination, in lyrical reiteration of the marital and kinship pattern, one could see that female segments of time, space and so on were likewise circumscribed by male articles on either side. The residential section of the village, a female area, since in Kypseli all the houses belong to women, was bound between the male-dominated central square and the encircling fields of the village periphery which belong to and are the province of men. The women's section of the church stood sandwiched between the central section in front of the altar, occupied only by men, and the area where most of the men spend Sunday service and which the women eschewed, the church courtyard. In the daily cycle of time men rose and embraced the day first, then left the village to work. Women buzzed about the village by day. Men returned from the land by evening and took charge of village life again by night.

Women and female items consequently occupied a problematic position in the village social structure. Despite the overt independence of women and female goods in symbol, female items always dangled betwixt males. Which one was the owner was the question. Due to the nature of marital alliance, kinship line, and property rights, it was impossible to ascertain exactly to which discrete male, or male social segment, females belonged. I retract my earlier statement that the only "enigma" was the island's most famous nightclub. Women, their time, their space, their things, were the island's true riddle.

To deal with the ambiguous nature of women and female goods, village ideology rose to the occasion. Kypselian belief, rather than unraveling exactly to which male or social segment any one woman, her pots, pans, and goats belonged, lumped all women into one overriding category, that of woman. All were declared to share the same characteristic, a characteristic which, if it did not clarify a woman's position, at least announced her problematic nature. All women were believed dangerous, all defiling. Men and male things were orderly items that things female threatened. Though I had not intended to delve into the then blossoming Mediterranean studies of honor and shame (Peristiany 1965, 1967; Campbell 1964; Pitt-Rivers 1971, 1977), nevertheless, I ended up with a study colored by gender and very much dealing, if not with male honor and female shame, at least with male purity and female danger. I have certainly not been alone in dealing with gender issues in Greece (Peristiany 1965, 1967; Campbell 1964; Clark 1983; Dubisch 1974a, 1983, 1986; Loizos and Papataxiarchis 1991; Herzfeld 1985; Hirschon 1984; and others). But my attempt was to unearth the grammar by which reality was segmented and categorized in Greece, and to explore the poetry of the belief system that reiterated the structural arrangement.

The most significant thing about Kypseli was that all of it showed. The pattern—not just the duality of male and female, but how the female element was bound between two male elements—was amazingly and graphically visible to the eye. Even the male purity and the female precariousness was discernible within the village confines. It appeared clearly in the use of courtyard, honorific celebrations, idleness and work. It showed up in how prayer was given and how a party progressed, in who took on public office and who delved in behind-the-scene mystic matters. I realized I had a rare opportunity. With the village grammar, the surface duality, the underlying triad, and the consequences prominently demonstrable, I decided that rather than write the requisite book, the study could be—should be—presented in film.

KYPSELI—THE FILM

To publish the study in film, of course, meant a number of considerations. It would mean eliminating much of the kinship and linguistic data. It would require much explication. Yet, such a publication would show, indeed demonstrate, as no written treatise could, the cultural divisions and how the symbolic categories interplayed on many planes. In pursuit of this goal, I sought out a fellow anthropologist who had made prior ethnographic films, engaged a camera operator, and applied to the National Endowment for the Humanities for funding. The film was to be a first: an ethnological film, not an ethnographic one. It was intended to demonstrate the theory and show interpretation in a situation perfect to reveal both. I believed so strongly in the importance of this film that when no funding had yet come through (and films are very expensive) I went ahead with the work anyway. With my two comrades I would at least get the essence of the study "in the can," i.e., photographed, even if we didn't have the coin to develop it, cut it, narrate it, and complete it. But on Columbus Day, October 12, 1972, America found us. While in the village and with most of the study already photographed, we received notice that the National Endowment for the Humanities had funded the endeavor and we had the finances to finish the movie.

The film was photographed in 1972, completed and released in 1974. It has proved enormously successful. *Kypseli: Women and Men Apart—A Divided Reality* is the third best-selling anthropology film ever made. Even twenty years later it remains the biggest selling and renting ethnographic film of its academic distributor. Reminiscent of the admonition "beware of what you ask for" (because it always comes out with an unexpected twist), however, the study's nature influenced its interpretation and ended up both categorizing the film and categorizing me. Like a Moebius strip, my intent as filmmaker and anthropologist and the audiences' perception fused together, back to back yet contiguous, with one sometimes inside, sometimes outside, the other taking over. *Kypseli: Men and Women Apart—A Divided Reality* has also been subject to the changing tides of what is popular in anthropology, and seen through the lens of each of these trends, has received different diagnoses over time.

Because films, like eagles and bears and genders, are directly sensorially perceived, a filmmaker sometimes overlooks the fact that they are received with more plasticity by the audience than are written works. The filmmaker endeavors to mold the viewer's reading, but can never fully control it. I intended *Kypseli* to present a structural study, to elucidate theory, and to illuminate an "ideal" analysis, though I believed my ideal analysis as an anthropologist was quite close to the "real" view shared by the Kypselian villagers. The film received that reading, but also a number of other interpretations. First and foremost, because of the nature of the subject matter, the symbolic categories, and the division of reality shown, it was taken as a feminist study. Many viewers received it as a work that displayed the place and role of women in Kypseli with bearings on the position of women in many societies.

I do not object to the perception. I am and was a feminist and a feminist anthropologist. It is just that in conceiving the film and constructing it, I had not taken into consideration that I was dealing to a certain extent with the same model I was showing, thus redoubling the world view. The film demonstrated not only the Greek perception and grammar, but one that we, in another strand of much the same cultural tradition, to a certain extent share. Many in the audience perceived the work through somewhat the same perceptual lens the villagers employ with somewhat the same ideology—or a reverse of it—to remedy it. The corporeal nature of the categories shown in the film looked downright fleshy, not abstract, and led to my work being interpreted in a fleshy way as study of gender rather than of social organization. The film in odd consequence was lauded as a vanguard, an early feminist study, and certainly one of the first feminist films. To this day, it finds a large audience in woman's studies departments and classes.

Within the feminist reading, some of *Kypseli's* viewers have interpreted the film as showing how women are mistreated, how caught in webs of exchange and viewed in their social realm as less valued persons than males, their lives are sorrowful. I did not intend this translation. I strove to demonstrate in picture and narration, particularly as the film unfolds, that the women of Kypseli participate in their own cultural pattern, and they do, albeit I call the irony of it "bittersweet." The women, like the men, are products and perpetrators of their own culture. The presentation is a structural one, not psychological. Structure does not imply emotion or malevolence or value. The reaction, I believe, again arises from the sensory perception film entails.

In the film I treat Kypseli—or at least the narration states twice—that the village is not only an example of a people who are part and parcel of a long literate tradition but, as had been the purpose of my original study, that Kypseli represents an instance of "our own" cultural tradition rather than a distant and different "other" society. Of the issues the film stirred, this one received, if not the most hue and cry, still a considerable amount. In fact, *Kypseli* has been critiqued not merely for stating that what was presented in the film extended to the rest of European society, but for utilizing a Eurocentric model in the first place (Herzfeld 1987).

Of course, that was the very point. I intended the looking glass through the looking glass, or a mirror within a mirror, and intended to ask if we, with our own model, from our own Eurocentric perceptions, could say anything about us? The question arises, does the film's statement apply to the rest of those who share the European tradition? Does it apply to us quasi and other Europeans? Does the bride's family at an American wedding sit on the sinister side of the church? How long is it since we have had women "of the night?" My own mother found the woman who accused William Smith of rape (in the recent controversial trial) at fault for crossing into improper territory and at an improper hour for a person of the female category, and she was not alone in her view. What was the woman doing there with him and at that time of night? Women in our social realm transfer between families along with money, changing name from one male family to another, and we see few females behind the altar. Do we not still hear arguments that women should remain at home and that only men should venture into the workplace? Do we employ a division of cultural items according to gender, then justify that division on sensory perception? It is true that if an anthropologist tries to generalize from one village to the next, much less one tribe to the next, or even more so from one country to the next—even within a cultural area—roiling ensues. Greece, as I mentioned earlier, continues to be considered by many to be less than eastern European, almost non-European, and villages are more and more considered marginal. Yet to me, European or non-European, city or village notwithstanding, the point of anthropology is to roll like a juggernaut across all landscapes toward the goal of describing the cross-cultural process of humankind. However, to do that in the cultural area of self as opposed to other, would, as I should have realized, stir reactions.

What has always unsettled me about the film is quite other; it is how the film slips at the end from structuralism to structural-functionalism. I felt I had little choice but to make that slippery slide, since the thing had to end. There is always the problem of *denouement* in the cinema. Yet, I always rued it and felt that someday someone from the higher flights of anthropological purism would "catch me" with my theories down. Instead, ten years later, the film was once again hailed as a vanguard. It seemed it had become vogue to marry later, purer structuralism with earlier, slightly more rag-tag structural-functionalism and to pronounce the marriage quite an adept and apt one. I had accidentally (well, semi-accidentally) come upon that union, though I was not so insightful as to see its looming value. I was not so much avant garde as seeking a conclusion, and cultural grammars, no matter how lyrical, leave a viewer a bit high and dry. The acclaim over that union once more shows that social scientists, like artists, cannot be sure how a work will be seen as paradigms shift over time. As I stated earlier, you enter a stream quite purposefully, only to be carried to unexpected shores. Our work as anthropologists also shifts under the slide rule of current thought. As much as I still prefer to do ethnology, the whole endeavor has made me highly value good ethnography.

The film has also been critiqued, as many anthropological studies of the time, especially of villages, are now, as not really reflecting the larger society, as isolated, marginal, disappearing. Europeans and Americans also claim, though they took to structuralism like layer cake as long as it was only applied to art, myth, and Eiffel towers and not their own social organization, that should the pattern shown, gender categories and all, be true, it is old and no longer functions. That may be so, but I was trying to bite the apple for the core, and I believe from the grit of both the study and the response that I got there.

I myself do not see exactly why *Kypseli* is in any way controversial. As a film, true, even today it stands almost alone as an ethnological film, one that enters with the anthropologist's preconceived explanation rather than, like journalism, just following and reporting how a people act and what they say.

No denying, *Kypseli* does not have any "natives" telling their version. (Hoffman 1988c). Yet I continue to find the pattern that *Kypseli* portrays viable. Twenty-five years have passed. I go to the village almost yearly. With electricity, television, tourists, and modernization, matters in the village have now much changed. And they have not changed. Women go to the tavern but only with their husbands, and they will sit only outside on the patio; they never go inside. Young girls do work even after marriage, at least until the first child is born, but then they go "home" and remain there. Women do get to choose—or at least have more choice over—their own husbands, though they feel they only have one or two turn-downs available and had then best comply. Although dowry is delegitimized in Greece, every village girl receives a complete house along with all its furnishings as she approaches a marriageable age, and it becomes the marriage home. Indeed, daughters' houses in the village have grown ever more expensive and elaborate. More marriages occur outside the village population, but most continue to take place within it or with persons from nearby villages. And, while women move about more freely, when traipsing about with a group of four last summer, one had to return home to serve her husband his meal. The food was all cooked and sitting on the stove, but he would not put the food on a plate for himself, not unlike many American men who still come home and expect their dinner ready and served. Women even today abide in both native village and neighborhood, while the men shift residence. Family unity remains strong in Kypseli, though village unity has crumbled somewhat with Greece's overall modernization.

CONCLUSION

The study I did and the film I published led to more work on European, or western, society—in fact on popular American culture. Following the male and female theme, I co-conducted a small study on American women and the stages, or timing, of their lives. The insights from the Kypselian work combined with the themes voiced by contemporary American women seemed worthy of bringing to a larger audience, and when I presented them to a commercial publisher, they were lapped up. So, from the Europeanist work, indirectly I was led to write a popular book on patterns of male and female relationships in America. (Hoffman 1980, 1988a) that came out in four languages. I am following it with another popular book on the changes in women's lives provoked by sexual freedom, the torn fabric of our lives, our changed partners, new twists in independence and dependency, new manifestations of depression. I began to write newspaper columns and articles with the anthropological and Europeanist eye I developed from my work in Greece and America. I became so inundated with writing projects, I left my university position—a tenured one—and now do something I never expected to do when I embarked on that first research trip. I write full time and in the popular genre. I write about and for a western folk, namely Americans, although my books have been published in a number of European and other countries worldwide. I enjoy writing for the popular audience and working with commercial publishers. The audience is avid for the lore. The publishers are avid for the material. In writing for and about America, I use the age-old anthropological technique, participant observation, and conduct research as if my fellows were strange. Not many anthropologists actively study Americans in an academic or laic vein. If my popular books seem again to follow the feminist track of the gender question, it is because I am a woman. Not only that, but 75 percent of the American book buyers are women, an interesting comment on gender, gendered objects, and gendered activity in our world, and it behooves a commercial author to heed the audience. My popular writing has led to one more unexpected eddy. Writers of pop psychology usually have their practices to provide them money between books or to supplement their book sales. Without a regular job to rely on, pop anthropology writers are rather up a creek. An old hobby has led me to write food books as well as other nonfiction, one even a best seller (1988b, 1990, 1996, 1997). I call it the sideline that ate my life. I feel even these do not stray far from my original calling, my anthropology. They do not stray far even from structuralism, for the classifications and categories of food and cooking are most amazing. Food is a major theme of all and certainly of our culture at this time. Present-day urban Americans talk about food down to the detail of which herb and what baby vegetable. I must say I enjoy the process of writing a tidbit, as it were, of food archeology or anthropology in a tidy two hundred words or less, not to mention devouring the fruits of my labor.

To temper my popular work, I continue to study and write about Greece (Hoffman 1993a, 1993b, 1995) and other academic matters (Hoffman 1994, 1995b). Of course, not having an academic position, to be Mary Douglas-ian about it, has made me an anthropologist "out of place," but I prefer to think of myself as popularizing rather than polluting, and sharing wisdom rather than witchery. Still and all, if button-holed by some irascible person to name my profession and my "area," I always call myself an anthropologist and Europeanist, not a Mediterraneanist, author, or even a cook. I still think of myself as a Europeanist. I feel that, in some sense, to attempt to unravel European or western culture anthropologically, especially what may be core structure or traditional pattern, is now almost salvage anthropology, not unlike what has been conducted on numerous disappearing isolated peoples. Europe has rapidly urbanized and become a melting pot, as has America. In its own Moebius maneuver, Europe has also become Americanized, entwining what was and is into a complex knot.

Europe, the image, the place, was thus for me from the start a testing field of a particular type of analysis. Greece was the deepest soil in which to dig, Santorini a fertile acre, and Kypseli the furrow. I ponder yet if studying Europe was, is, somehow more than just studying ourselves as a culture, but studying ourselves personally. Are those of us who work there curious not just about particular European features or universal cultural patterns, but about the very traditions that still effect our very lives?

I think, for many anthropologists who studied and continue to study Europe, the answer is yes. Overtly or covertly, there is some sort of return. I am reminded of my great aunt Annie who said, when she heard I was about to leave on my first trip there, "Europe, Europe, I was never so happy to leave a place." I am always happy in every sense to go back to where I did my field-work, though none of my four grandparents came from anywhere near it. I am always happy to plunge, as if into a deep sea, into the cultural patterns that to some degree molded my own existence. I freely admit, however, some of them are the ones I hope, by the enlightenment of my research there, by what Kypseli, the film, and my continuing research in Europe and America show, by seeing the "self" through the "self," to change.

Note

1. Most scholars agree that Greek-speaking people were among the first Indo-Europeans to enter Europe, although recent evidence points to an earlier arrival of Indo-Europeans to central and north central Europe than was previously thought. Many scholars also now concur that the Ural-Altaic language family, many of whose speakers arrived later in the European subcontinent, probably derives from the same "proto-proto" linguistic root as Indo-European. The areas of origin of both language groups were likely adjacent to one another and numerous linguistic correspondence exist between the two language families (Mallory 1989).

CHAPTER 4

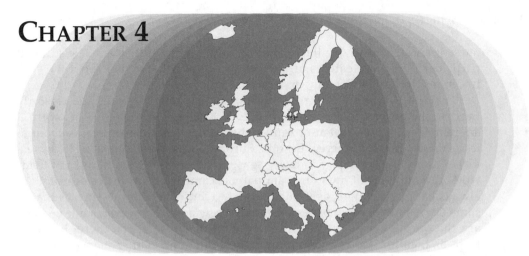

EUROPE ON FILM

Peter S. Allen
Rhode Island College

A version of this chapter was originally prepared for presentation at a breakfast round table sponsored by the Society for the Anthropology of Europe at the annual meeting of the American Anthropological Association (AAA) in Washington, D.C., November, 1991. The present version is substantially revised and enlarged and further incorporates information on films produced since 1991. The Society for the Anthropology of Europe has shown an increased interest in ethnographic film over the past few years. They are in the process of compiling a directory of ethnographic films on Europe that should be completed sometime in 1998, and they have been promoting the use and appreciation of film for the study of Europe in their sponsorship of round-table discussions at the annual meetings of the American Anthropological Association. In addition to the round table cited above, Gary McDonogh and Cindy Wong did one on European feature films at the 1995 AAA annual meeting and I was scheduled to do one on archaeological film and video on Europe at the 1996 meeting.

Anthropologists have used films and other visual materials in the classroom from an early date. Far more than for almost all other disciplines, the teaching of anthropology is enhanced by use of the visual image. Films and videos can be used both inside and outside the classroom in a number of ways and the potential for pedagogical utility is enormous.

Nevertheless, for the majority of anthropologists, films and videos are used to illustrate aspects of the peoples and cultures being taught and, perhaps less often, to stimulate discussion. Films, by their very nature, tend to be descriptive rather than theoretical and thus cannot be used in the same way that books and articles can.[1] However, they can be very useful for familiarizing students with other cultures and as points of departure for discussion and analysis. The validity of the old saw that "a picture is worth a thousand words" is much appreciated by any anthropologist who has struggled to describe the "other" to his or her students and tried to bring to life exotic behaviors of far-away peoples. And although television has helped shorten the distance between cultures and helped familiarize current generations of students with other cultures, films and videos continue to be a valuable classroom resource. One of the challenges faced by anthropologists working in European areas is to find compelling films and videos to illustrate the peoples and cultures with which they deal. This chapter addresses some of the issues represented by this challenge.

THE MARGINALIZATION OF EUROPE

Like the ethnography of Europe (see Herzfeld 1987), the filmography of Europe has been marginalized. This is evidenced by several factors. First of all, few films on Europe are counted among the recognized classics of the genre: *Nanook of the North*, *The Hunters*, *Dead Birds*, etcetera. Nor do we have a substantial and coherent body of films or videos on any European society as we do for more "exotic" places like Africa and Latin America, where filmmakers like John Marshall (!Kung/San films) and Timothy Asch and Napoleon Chagnon (Yanamamo films) have produced prodigious corpi of films on specific groups. Moreover, like much of the ethnography of Europe, the filmography of Europe often focuses on the more "exotic" (and, ironically, already marginalized within Europe) peoples of the area. Consider, for example, the two classics, *Man of Aran* and *Land without Bread*. Both deal with very marginal peoples in atypical or even anomalous circumstances, and, in the case of *Land without Bread*, it could be argued that the situation is actually pathological, at least in the eyes of the filmmaker. It could further be argued that the creators of these films, Flaherty and Buñuel respectively, exaggerated the circumstances of the subject societies by selective editing that distorted the true situations of these two peoples. There are some scholars who argue that *Land without Bread* is actually a kind of hoax or parody (Sitney 1985; Winston 1995), although this is disputed (Aranda 1976; Barnouw 1983; and Mellen 1978).

Moreover, these films, like many of the films on Europe that anthropologists find useful, were not made by anthropologists nor were any anthropologists consulted. Thus, they have certain limitations that must be accounted for when being used in the classroom. Ethnographic "truth" has been compromised in many ways. For example, in *Man of Aran*, Flaherty exaggerated the harshness of life in the Aran Islands and disguised evidences of modernization, much as he did in *Nanook of the North*, to strengthen his theme of man against nature. For the modern anthropologist this can be both an asset and a handicap. On the one hand, films like *Man of Aran* can be used to show what life was like in a premodern world. On the other hand, if students take the information presented at face value, then they are getting a false impression of life in the Aran Islands at the time the film was shot.[2] Similar problems exist with *Nanook of the North*.

The setting of another European classic, *Farrebique*, is hardly marginal, nor are the people depicted as marginal, but evidently the director, George Rouquier, did not consider French farm life in the 1940s interesting (exotic?) enough for a documentary, so he doctored his subject, creating a scripted and acted film, a procedure he repeated in his 1987 sequel, *Biquefarre*. Real peasants, rather than actors, are used in these two films and both are excellent works—rich in ethnographic data and artistically sensitive—but the introduction of a plot with intrigue and conflict is jarring to some and certainly detracts somewhat from the ethnographic value of these productions.

This tendency to concentrate attention on marginal peoples continues. For example, most ethnographic films on Greece, the region with which I am most familiar, focus on marginal peoples and/or exotic themes. *Kalogeros* is a good case in point: It documents a bawdy local ritual that involves cross-dressing and other behaviors alien to the majority of Greeks. The subjects live in small isolated villages in northern Greece quite apart from the mainstream of Greek culture. Another film, *Anastenaria*, deals with a cult of firewalkers who are well known in Greece, but who nevertheless represent a tiny fringe group there. They are universally regarded in Greece as "exotic" and marginalized, their actions viewed as bizarre and anomalous by most Greeks. The actual participants in this ritual amount to only a few dozen individuals in the larger Greek nation. *Kypseli: Women and Men Apart—A Divided Reality* is another film on Greece with a very wide distribution, but its subject matter is a remote village chosen for its isolation and resistance to change and modernization. It is hardly representative of mainstream Greece. *Aegean Sponge Divers*, another well-known film on Greece, likewise features marginal people engaged in anachronistic activities. The films of Colette Piault and Barry Machin also depict marginal Greeks, although they deal with themes that have a broader significance for Greek culture and society in general.

This fascination with the exotic and atypical has continued to the present in Europe, as exemplified by the listings in Grenada Television's *Disappearing World* series. Of the approximately fifty titles in the series, only five are from Europe, all of which feature marginal peoples—gypsies in *Across the Tracks: Vlach Gypsies in Hungary*; Basque shepherds in *The Basques of Santazi*; transhumant Spanish shepherds in *The Villagers of the Sierra de Gredos*; Sami (Lapps) in

An Invisible Enemy; and Albanians in *The Albanians of Rrogam*. Gypsies, by definition, are marginalized peoples and thus no further comment is necessary for
this film. Ironically, if there is anything exotic about the lives of the Basques in
The Basques of Santazi, it is not shown in this film. However, the people are
marginal and, consistent with the theme of the series, in the throes of cultural
change as their traditional way of life succumbs to the forces of modernization.
The Villagers of the Sierra de Gredos concentrates on a "dying" lifestyle in an
attempt to capture something of a more traditional (i.e., exotic) past in a
remote Spanish mountain village, very much in keeping with the series title.
The subject of *An Invisible Enemy* is the impact of the nuclear disaster at
Chernobyl on a population of Sami in Finland. Although many Europeans
were adversely affected by the Chernobyl tragedy, and some more than the
Sami, it is these traditional nomadic peoples who are featured in this production. Predictably enough, the most recent title in the *Disappearing World* series
for Europe is *The Albanians of Rrogam*, a film about the least-known and thus
most marginal and exotic of all Europeans. Thus, all five of the films in the
Disappearing World series dealing with Europeans focus on traditional or marginalized people living in remote or inaccessible parts of the continent.
Moreover, the series editors have turned down at least one proposal to do a
film on Greece with a more prosaic subject (Charles Stewart, personal communication), although one cannot be sure this particular project was rejected
because Greece is not exotic enough, or for some other reason; nor am I sure
that such factors play any conscious role at all in the editors' decisions regarding films. Nevertheless, the proposal was rejected.[3]

The marginalization of Europe is reflected in its representation at ethnographic film festivals and in the listings of catalogues and guides. At the
Margaret Mead Film Festival, arguably the premier showcase for ethnographic
films in the United States, only seven (13 percent) of the fifty-three films
screened in 1995 dealt with Europe, and at the American Anthropological
Association Film Festival the same year, Europe accounted for only three
(about 7 percent) of the forty-one films shown. These figures are consistent
with those from past years (e.g., in 1992 only four [13 percent] of the thirty-two
films shown at the Margaret Mead Festival had European themes, and the figures for the American Anthropological Association Festival were three [about
7 percent] of forty-five films shown). On the other hand, films on European
subjects have consistently won prizes at the AAA festival as evidenced by their
prominence on the list of prize winners for the past decade in the 1995 program for the annual meeting of the American Anthropological Association (at
least one film on Europe was a winner in all but one year). In the catalogue of
anthropological films from the collection of the Extension Center for Media
and Independent Learning at the University of California at Berkeley, there are
three pages of listings for films on Latin America (twenty titles), three for films
on Asia (thirty-three titles), two for Africa (seven titles), while Europe falls into
the "Miscellaneous Ethnography" category with less than half a page and only

four titles. The Institute für Wissenschaftlichen Film in Göttingen, Germany, has recently published four volumes of guides to its collections, one each for Africa, Asia, Australia/Oceania, and Europe. The one on Europe is actually the second longest (Africa is the longest), but fully half the titles are for Germany and thus reflect the bias of the collection toward the country in which it is housed. Minus the German titles, this would be by far the slimmest volume in the series. In the latest edition of Karl Heider and Carol Hermer's *Films for Anthropological Teaching* (1995), films on Europe comprise only five percent of all listings. Europe fares considerably better in archaeology. In the second edition of *Archaeology on Film* (1994), Europe accounts for more than 25 percent of all entries. Percentages in both guides are consistent with those of earlier editions. Part of the discrepancy between the percentages of productions with European themes in *Films for Anthropological Teaching* and *Archaeology on Film* can probably be attributed to individual orientations and expertise—all four of the compilers of *Archaeology on Film* are Europeanists whereas Heider and Hermer are not—as well as to the different nature of ethnography and archaeology. There are a good number of films on the archaeology of Greece and Rome, for example, which helps swell the numbers of films on the archaeology of Europe.

How can we account for this marginalization? Certainly some of it is a direct reflection of Europe's position in anthropology generally—marginalized in print, marginalized in film. But there are other reasons as well. One lies in the history of the genre. Ethnographic film has its roots in the depiction of the exotic "other". Because the basic outlines of most European cultures are fairly well known to most western audiences, ethnographic films on Europe have not always played the same role for anthropologists that ethnographic films from other parts of the world have played. The earliest ethnographic films transported audiences to faraway places and brought them into contact with cultures radically different from their own. Most European peoples are familiar to western audiences of ethnographic film and are not the "other." Consequently, in the past relatively few films of an ethnographic nature were produced on European subjects, and those that were, like *Man of Aran* and *Land without Bread*, tend to focus on marginal, less familiar subjects. Moreover, for Europe we do not have a John Marshall, a Robert Gardner, a Timothy Asch, a David and Judith MacDougall team, or even a Jean Rouch (although he did make one European film, *Chronicle of a Summer*). All of these individuals have made large numbers of high quality ethnographic films on various cultures around the world, and in a very real sense, their work has been instrumental in defining the genre. Their names and their films are inevitably associated with the category ethnographic film, whereas films on Europe, even those by important documentarists, do not have quite the resonance of those on non-European subjects. And yet, the pedigree of Europe is not bad—Flaherty (*Man of Aran*); Buñuel (*Land without Bread*); Rouquier (*Farrebique* and *Biquefarre*); and even Rouch, as just noted. However, none of these individuals has a significant body of work in the area comparable to Marshall's for the !Kung/San; the MacDougalls' for Africa; Asch's for the Yanamamo; or Gardner and associates' for India. There are only single films for all but Rouquier, and his two are a primary film and a sequel on the same subject.

Another possible explanation for the marginalization of ethnographic films on Europe and the general dearth of such films is the problem of shooting films in one's own society and in western society in general. Those making films on less technologically advanced people have had an advantage for two reasons. First of all, as colonialists or neocolonialists, they have been able, consciously or unconsciously, to intimidate their subjects. Just as early anthropologists found the colonial environment much to their liking and were able to collect the kinds of data that would never have been made available to them by members of their own societies had they sought them, filmmakers working in preliterate societies have been able to make films that could not have been made in their own societies. Secondly, many of the subjects of films in preliterate societies had very little comprehension of the medium and its uses. Despite the fact that filmmakers from Flaherty onward have often arranged for their subjects to view their finished products, it is unlikely that many of the subjects fully understood the complexities of films and the uses to which they would be put. This helps explain why the vast majority of films on European subjects deal with marginal and isolated peoples. Filmmakers have approached and dealt with them as anthropologists and filmmakers working in less developed countries have approached and dealt with their subjects.

THE FUTURE OF EUROPEAN FILMOGRAPHY

Things are beginning to change, however, and they can be expected to change even more now that video is so inexpensive and, at one level, so easy to use. Signs of change, however, appeared even before the video revolution. For Spain, there is the work of Jerome Mintz and for Greece, that of Colette Piault. Both Mintz and Piault have created impressive corpi of films focusing on particular localities and personalities—Andalusia for Mintz and Epirus for Piault. We also have the excellent book/film combination of Donald Pitkin, both entitled, *The House that Giacomo Built*. And there are some fine individual films on Europe that are relatively unknown. *Village of Spain* is one of my favorites and, even though it is not profound in any way, it does convey a good sense of life in a preindustrial peasant village. An absolutely first-rate piece entitled *The Shepherds of Berneray* received excellent notices when it was released in 1981, and distribution rights were quickly acquired by the Museum of Modern Art. The film is still available, but little known. I recently polled three prominent ethnographers of Scotland and none had even heard of the film, much less seen it. *Kypseli: Women and Men Apart—A Divided Reality*, a film on sex roles in

Greece, is an innovative and provocative film and is still vastly popular despite what some consider serious flaws in its basic argument (Allen et al. 1978).[4] Peter Loizos' two fine films on Cyprus, *Life Chances* and *Sophia's People*, also deserve mention for, although they are set geographically some distance from Europe, the subjects—Greek Cypriots—are thoroughly European in their culture and orientation.

Nor should we overlook the rich and extensive body of mostly folkloric films on virtually all European countries that exist in their own countries, but which, for the most part, are not available with English language sound tracks and are not distributed in the United States or Great Britain. Most are more folkloric than ethnographic or they are so ethnographic and specialized as to be of little interest to anyone but a specialist. Examples of the latter would be films like *Western Norway: Manufacture of a Barrel* and *Holstein: Making a Rope*. Nevertheless, some are good—for example, the work of Nestor Matsos in Greece. Some countries are much better represented than others, but almost all countries have produced something along these lines. A number of titles (including the two mentioned above) are available from the collection of the *Encyclopaedia Cinematographica* through the Pennsylvania State University Audio-Visual services, where listings for Europe equal those for Asia, but are only half the number for Africa.

Some older works with tremendous ethnographic value are also being rediscovered. At two recent festivals of archaeological film in Europe (Cinarchea in Kiel, Germany, and AGON in Athens, Greece), several films of Francesco Alliata were shown. Alliata made documentaries on Sicilian fishermen in the late 1940s before turning his talents to feature films (among others, he produced *Vulcano* and *Carrozza d'Oro*, both starring Anna Magnani and the latter the last film directed by Jean Renoir.) His documentaries—*Tuna Fishing*, *Between Scylla and Charybdis*, and *Underwater Hunters*—are minor masterpieces and will no doubt be more widely screened now that they have resurfaced. The same is probably true of Vasilis Maros' *Kalymnos*, an absolutely fabulous film also shown at AGON.

Moreover, there is evidence that some filmmakers have been able to penetrate into the heart of modern industrial western society. *Steaming*, a recent film done for the BBC by Ashtok Prasad and Steven Standen, examines male intimacy in the steam baths of London's East End. Naked men parade unselfconsciously through this film and it could easily be compared to John Marshall's *Men Bathing*, which depicts San Bushmen engaged in bathing and horseplay in a shallow lake in the Kalahari Desert.

Overall, there are great lacunae. There are virtually no ethnographic films available in the United States on the low countries, Germany and Portugal, and very few on Great Britain. For Finland and Scandinavia there are plenty of films on the Lapps, exotic and marginal people, but virtually none on other peoples of these countries. And, with the exception of the former Yugoslavia, there are very few titles in distribution here from central and Eastern Europe despite the presence of a very active and vibrant film industry in Hungary, Czechoslovakia, Romania, and Poland. The ethnography of Europe has been reasonably well-served by commercial film production, although this could probably be said for virtually any part of the world. Nevertheless, worth noting are such films as *Bandits of Orgosolo*; *Salvatore Guiliano*; *Padre Padrone*; *Bread and Chocolate*; *The Feather Merchant*; *The Round-up*; *Jean de Florette*; *Manon of the Spring*; and dozens upon dozens of others of this type.

In the long and even the short run, prospects for ethnographic film in Europe are bright. More and more ethnographic films and videos are being made on European subjects. The advent of inexpensive high quality video technology has been responsible for a boomlet in ethnographic productions. Moreover, like the written ethnography of Europe (Allen 1992 and 1994), the filmography is getting some serious attention and gaining wider acceptance in the discipline, although it still lags somewhat behind the progress of the written word. The unpretentious works of Mintz and Piault are good examples of this trend and good indications of what we are likely to see more of in the future.

Among the better films on Europe produced in recent years are the following, all of which won prizes of some kind at the annual film festival of the American Anthropological Association: *Romeria: Day of the Virgin*; *Voyage from Antiquity*; *Ave Maria*; *Perico the Bowlmaker*; *The Charcoal Makers*; *Man in the Ring*; and *Jakub*.

Archaeological films on European subjects, like ethnographic films, have also been marginalized and exoticized, especially in recent years. Some of the best straightforward older productions, like *The Tree that Turned the Clock Back*, are almost completely out of distribution and unavailable,[5] and relatively few new productions of this caliber have been released. A team of German adventurers has produced a large number of films on archaeological sites over the past six or eight years and more than a dozen deal with European sites. These have been shown nationally on the Discovery cable channel in the United States under the series title *Terra X*, and some are now being distributed by Films for the Humanities and Sciences of Princeton, New Jersey, but none are very good.

Some European sites are not accessible for filming, so other arrangements have to be made. A good example is the case of Lascaux Cave, now off-limits to all but a few privileged specialists. Until recently the only film of any quality on the famous cave was *Lascaux: Cradle of Man's Art*, a production from the 1950s. The poor organization of this film and the lack of opportunity to shoot new footage prompted archaeologist Leslie Freeman to acquire rights to this production's footage, which he reorganized, adding some commentary of his own, and ending up with *The Lascaux Cave: A Look at Our Prehistoric Past*. This piece is an improvement over the original classic, but it is not the same thing as shooting one's own film, something that is unfortunately not possible at Lascaux today.

A large number of films on European archaeology are produced every year and shown at a variety of festivals (see Lazio 1995), but there is little demand for them in the United States so they are rarely given English subtitles or soundtracks and distributed here. Those that do manage to find an audience here are the glamorous ones—those focusing on underwater sites, archaeological "mysteries" (usually the concoction of the producer rather than the archaeologist), or sites with high recognition quotients like Stonehenge or the Parthenon. One recent success was the BBC's production of *Iceman*, a captivating film on a fascinating subject that was shown as part of the NOVA series. It chronicles the recovery of the body of an individual more than five thousand years old from an alpine glacier.

Unfortunately, the market for documentary films in the United States is driven largely by the television syndrome and if a production is not "broadcast quality," then it has little chance of being shown. Even when respectable scientific films on the archaeology of Europe are done, the distributors often find it necessary to hype their promotion with titles that include such buzz words as "mystery," "secret," or "The search for...." This makes it difficult for the potential viewer to distinguish between productions of substance and those from the *Terra X* and other such series.

In general, there is cause for optimism with respect to the situation of ethnographic and archaeological film in Europe. Good films and videos are being made and there seems to be increasing interest in the medium. At the recent (May 1996) Göttingen International Ethnographic Film Festival, twelve of the thirty-one films shown had European subjects, a far greater percentage than either of the previous Göttingen festivals. The Society for the Anthropology of Europe, a subgroup of the American Anthropological Association, is in the process of preparing a comprehensive guide to films and videos on Europe. Once it is finished, it should help stimulate interest and disseminate information about productions.

Notes

1. Perhaps the only exception is the film *Kypseli: Women and Men Apart—A Divided Reality*, which purports (with some degree of validity) to be the only ethnographic film that aims to be theoretical as well as descriptive. And although it achieves this purpose in large part, unfortunately the particular theory advanced has not found a very receptive audience.

2. *Looking for the Man of Aran*, a new film produced at the Granada Center for Visual Anthropology by student Sebastian Eschenbach, examines the impact of Flaherty's film on the islands and their inhabitants.

3. David MacDougall has recently made a film for the BBC, *Tempus de Baristas*, about three goatherds on the island of Sardinia, marginal people in a marginal place.

4. Despite some less than favorable reviews, *Kypseli* was for many years the most frequently rented film in the collection of the University of California at Berkeley, one of the largest academic distributors in the country.

5. The audio-visual department of my college owns a print of this film, but it is damaged. New prints or footage to replace the damaged part have not been available from the producer for more than a decade despite the fact that the film was only made in 1972.

CHAPTER 5

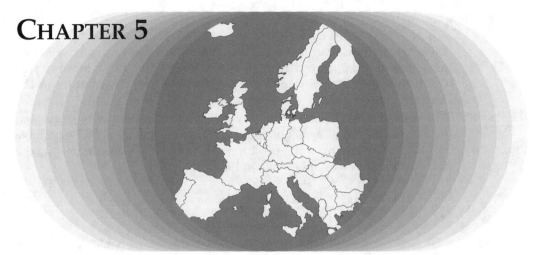

REPRESENTING ITALY

David I. Kertzer
Brown University

Doubting objectivity, disdaining objectivism, and not quite knowing what to make of the Other, American anthropologists have recently suffered from a self-absorption bred of epistemological malaise.[1] The crisis of ethnographic authority threatens to turn ethnography into a denial of anthropology's claim to be anything more than either conduits for more authentic (native) voices or simply an exotic locus for psychoanalysis. The malaise, though, goes beyond epistemology into politics, for the *cris de coeur* that punctuate any gathering of anthropologists these days stem less from questions of epistemology than from issues of power and morality.[2]

Anthropologists working in Western Europe might be thought mercifully immune from such political and ideological problems. Indeed, we might even try to cast ourselves as potential saviors of the discipline, despite the stigma that still clings vaguely to us for choosing field sites free of malaria or dysentery. In short, a case can be made that we are part of the solution rather than the problem. Studying peoples in the "west," we might argue, promises a way to recapture the generalizing aspirations of our discipline. Targeting Europeans, we may feel less morally encumbered by the stricture that our primary task should be a political/moral one of serving the people, and less defensive about the charge that we routinely impose our own categories and values on the people we study.

I have not been overly sympathetic to the handwringing taking place in anthropology about the evils of a discipline that seeks a generalizing language and set of concepts, and have found much of the moralizing (among my own undergraduates, and not just among our professional colleagues) over the "Other" to be misplaced. Yet, surveying the work of American anthropologists in Italy (as, more generally, in Europe) does give me pause. The danger is that, rather than help lead anthropology out of its paralytic state, work by American (I could add Italian here, too, but that topic is beyond the scope of this chapter) anthropologists in Italy remains vulnerable to some of the same criticisms that poor Malinowski now faces.[3] In short, it seems that we have gone to remarkable lengths to look at our fellow westerners and see the "Other."

The problems to which I am referring have been taken up in the context of the anthropology of Mediterranean Europe by various observers over the years, perhaps most notably by John Davis (1977) in his *People of the Mediterranean*, and Michael Herzfeld in *Anthropology through the Looking Glass*. Herzfeld (1987b, 11), for example, has charged that "the extension of ethnography to the circum-Mediterranean has created a need for exoticizing devices to justify research in what is otherwise a familiar cultural backyard." He notes that anthropologists' concentration on such topics as honor and shame, presented as hallmarks of these cultures, along with the unremitting village-level focus of so much of the anthropology done there, furthers this distancing, rendering the otherwise dangerously familiar into the satisfyingly exotic.

It was out of concern for just this trap into which we feared Mediterranean anthropology had fallen that Michael Kenny and I organized a panel at the 1977 annual meeting of the American Anthropological Association on "urban life in Mediterranean Europe." The panel led several years later to the publication of an edited book by the same title (Kenny and Kertzer 1983). In the introduction, Kenny and I lamented the lack of anthropological research in the urban areas of the region, which we linked in part to the insecure professional status of Europeanist anthropology. In short, anthropologists working in Europe were doing the best they could to imitate anthropologists working in the more prestigious field settings. The intrepid anthropologist must rough it; in the field the air should smell of cow dung, not car exhaust.

I opened my chapter on Italy for that volume with the observation that "Judging from the anthropological literature, one might well conclude that Italy is a nation of peasants living in remote and desolate villages" (Kertzer 1983, 52). Anthropologists, I wrote, "have converged on the small agricultural communities of the underdeveloped south, with some venturing to relatively isolated and small communities of the center and north" (1983, 59). In conclusion, somewhat portentously, not to say pompously (after all, I wrote the paper before I had hit thirty!), I opined: "The time is ripe for a shift in the rural preoccupation of anthropological study in Italy to a more balanced approach … if anthropologists do not shift their focus from peasants to urban-dwellers, we will be in danger of becoming as marginal to the academic community as our traditional research subjects are becoming to Italian national society" (1983, 70).

URBAN-RURAL LINKS IN ITALY

In this chapter, I would like to reflect on the extent to which the concerns I had back in the 1970s remain in the 1990s. I begin with a bit about the history of my own involvement in Italian anthropology.

When I first set off to graduate school right out of college in 1969, I fancied myself as a pioneer in a new movement, "urban anthropology," and identified myself as a (novitiate) urban anthropologist. The young Turk self-image that came with feeling part of this urban movement in anthropology was nourished by the absence of faculty at prominent graduate programs who had done urban fieldwork. A good part of the reason for my choice of Brandeis for graduate school was that it had just recently hired a young anthropologist (David Jacobson) who had worked in an African city. At the time, I had no idea I would end up working in Europe—in fact, I had been leaning toward Latin America.

Given my proselytizing zeal for urban anthropology, though, once the idea of Italy was planted (in good part due to the persuasiveness of the then chair of the Brandeis department, Alex Weingrod, who had worked in Sardinia), a sense of mission took hold. At the time, Italy was arguably the continental European country that had received the most attention (or close to it, running neck and neck with Spain) from anglophone anthropologists. Yet, despite the fact that by then almost half the population of the country lived in the thirty largest urban centers, there apparently had not been a single anthropological study conducted in an Italian city.

Unlike some of those drawn to the new field of urban anthropology (Tony Leeds, for example), I was never especially interested in studying cities as such, nor in investigating how cities differed from smaller communities. On the contrary, for me the value of urban anthropology stemmed from the belief that social life followed basically similar principles everywhere and that the division between the principles governing urban and rural life was largely artificial.[4] My subsequent experience has only reinforced this view, both in doing fieldwork and in undertaking historical research. Indeed, over the centuries there has been a constant flux of population between cities and their rural hinterland in Italy, belying scholars' apparent categorical imperative to contrast "city-dwellers" with "peasants."

This flux, and the penetration of rural in urban and urban in rural, have an intriguing parallel in the African sites where urban anthropology first took hold. There, what most struck anthropologists about the city was, on the one hand, the reproduction of rural life within urban borders, and on the other, the continuing importance of the social (and principally kin) ties linking urban dwellers to their rural communities of origin. In trying to trace these nongeographically bound relationships, anthropologists turned to network analysis. This enabled them to conceptualize webs of social relations outside of the traditional anthropological focus on specific localities.

MILOCCA

If we return, though, to the work done by American anthropologists in Italy, the quest for the remote and the rural can be seen from the very beginning. The professional anglophone anthropology of Italy dates back to the work of Charlotte Gower Chapman who was a graduate student at the University of Chicago in the 1920s, where she too saw herself as a pioneer. While American anthropology was solidifying its commitment to exotic island and Indian reservation locales, she sought to apply the newly developed methods of the discipline to peasant society. Indeed, hers was to be the second such application, following that of her Chicago mentor, Robert Redfield, who had just completed his study of Tepoztlan, Mexico. Significantly, Chapman's eighteen months of fieldwork in the Sicilian community of Milocca in the late 1920s was not her first major research project. Rather, her Italian work came immediately after her dissertation research, which focused on the Sicilian-American community of Chicago. It is worth reflecting on the fact that, even in the 1920s, anthropological research in an American city could be met with approval, as long as the focus was on an ethnic enclave. Yet, by contrast, in planning to undertake anthropological research in Europe, all efforts were made to locate the most remote rural community possible. It should also be noted that her manuscript was not published back in the early 1930s when it was completed, but only after being rediscovered and deemed a classic of community studies in 1971.

Chapman herself describes Milocca as "by no means typical" of Sicilian communities, being "much smaller" and "more isolated" than the average. It may not have been New Guinea, but it was "an hour's walk from the end of the nearest highway, and more than two hours from the nearest railroad station" (1971, ix). Despite the fact that even Sicily's agricultural population lived primarily in large communities (sometimes referred to as agro-towns), Chapman sought out a small village. Thus, the preferred anthropological peasant community was not even typical of peasant settlements, since the most typical were presumably too large for satisfactory anthropological treatment.

Milocca must be considered a milestone in the history of American anthropology, and there is little point here in rehearsing its many limits as seen by contemporary anthropological standards, limits largely identified with the community study approach. Chapman's work reflects two features that would mark the development of anglophone anthropology of Italy: the equation of anthropology with the study of the rural (indeed, the less-literate-the-better) folk, and the preference for anthropological work on Italy's two big islands—Sicily and Sardinia.

INTRODUCING HISTORY AND POLITICAL ECONOMY IN ANTHROPOLOGY

The pattern of these ahistorical community studies set in Italy's most remote areas—almost entirely in the mainland south and the two islands—continued as a number of foreign anthropologists began to venture into Italy in the 1950s and early 1960s. Topics such as honor and shame on the cultural level, and local-level patterns of family, kinship, and patron-client relations on the social level, dominated the work done in these years.

Major changes, though, began to take place in the late 1960s, changes traceable to developments in anthropology that can only be understood against the broader context of what was going on in American society at the time. The influence of the various forms of leftist political currents in the United States and Europe led to both a heightened interest in political econ-omy and a new view of the poor that saw them not folkloristically but, in adaptive terms, as victims of exploitation. Hence, while both the studies of Anton Blok (1974) and Jane and Peter Schneider (1976) continued in the tradi-tion of rooting their studies in rural Sicilian communities, they introduced both history and political economy into the anglophone anthropology of Italy.

My own initial project for my year of dissertation fieldwork in 1971–1972 similarly reflected the currents sweeping the United States at the time more than any distinctively Italian developments. Back then many of us were exer-cised about the "culture of poverty" thesis propounded by Oscar Lewis and taken up by Daniel Moynihan and others in the American public policy arena. My own master's research had been conducted in a working-class area of Boston, where I studied attempts to found a local branch of a national welfare rights organization, calling into question the culture of poverty interpretation. My first destination in Italy was Naples, where I considered continuing this line of research: Here I would try to overcome anthropology's romantic attach-ment to rural folk, yet hang on to some form of anthropological justification of the type Chapman herself had employed in her dissertation on Chicago's Sicilian Americans. While I did not go on to do this study, it is notable that the first urban anthropological monograph published in English—Thomas Belmonte's *The Broken Fountain* (1979)—had exactly this focus on a neighbor-hood of poor Neapolitans and the applicability of a culture of poverty explana-tion for their behavior.[5]

Yet my own choice of a dissertation project—leading ultimately to my first book, *Comrades and Christians* (1980)—was no less the product of contem-porary American political and social forces. Having spent as much of my time in the late 1960s organizing in the anti-Vietnam war movement as I did study-ing anthropology, I was intrigued by the success of Italy's Communist Party (PCI) and, in particular, the attachment to it of much of the Italian working class.

Moreover, inquiry into people's allegiance to the PCI also seemed to offer an ideal arena in which to demonstrate the value of an anthropological approach to urban research. Previous social scientific studies of the attractions of the Communist Party—based almost entirely on surveys and electoral analyses—seemed to me hopelessly inadequate and thin. On the other hand, my particular focus, on the struggle between the PCI and the Catholic Church for the allegiance of the working class, came from other sources, partly anthropological (given the theoretical development in anthropology's study of religion) and partly personal [a long story for another occasion, but see M. Kertzer 1947]).[6]

Although my study was based on fieldwork conducted in one of Italy's major cities, traces of the community study tradition were certainly present. The romantic side of this tradition was evident both in my selection of a (relatively) impoverished *quartiere* for study, and in its location outside the old walled part of the city, an area sprinkled with open fields and even a few farms. People lived not in high-rise apartment houses but primarily in three-story buildings not unlike those found in most nonurban areas of the country. It was an area where social networks were dense, people knew one another, and a good deal of social activity was organized at the local level. While I could not get to know everyone in the *quartiere* (which had 9,000 inhabitants), I did have some contact with a substantial proportion of the population.

AMERICAN ANTHROPOLOGY IN ITALY, 1975–1994

Although I thought I was able to demonstrate both the feasibility of conducting anthropological research in urban areas of Italy, and the fact that there were significant contributions to be made by anthropologists to the study of social life in Italian cities, my hopes that significant numbers of other anglophone anthropologists would begin to work in urban Italy proved to be in vain. It is worth reviewing very briefly the choices of research sites made by American anthropologists working in Italy over the past twenty years (limiting myself to those who have published in the period 1975–1994) to make this point and consider its implications. Although I have, no doubt, overlooked some published work, I believe that the scholars whose work I allude to here accurately represent the work done by American anthropologists in Italy in these years.[7]

The continued attachment of North American anthropologists to working on Italy's two main islands remains impressive. For Sicily alone, this includes at least seven anthropologists (I cite just one representative work from authors cited here and below): Cucchiari (1988); Giovannini (1981); Hilowitz (1976); J. Schneider and P. Schneider (1976); Triolo (1993); and Galt (1980) on Pantelleria, the island just off the Sicilian coast. For Sardinia, there are at least three—Brown (1981); Counihan (1984); and Magliocco (1993)—not to mention the McGill University project under Philip Salzman's direction, which has brought several Canadian-based anthropologists to the Sardinian mountains.

For the mainland south, I count at least ten, including Belmonte (1979); Berkowitz (1984); Breuner (1992); Douglass (1984); Galt (1991); R. Miller and M. Miller (1978); Moss and Cappannari (1976); and Pitkin (1985). By contrast, there are five American anthropologists who have published work in this period on central Italy: Blim (1990); Counihan (1988); Romanucci-Ross (1991); Saunders (1995); and Silverman (1975). For northern Italy, I count just Holmes (1989); Kertzer (1980); Saunders (1979); Ward (1994); Whitaker (1992); and Yanagisako (1991).

If we look instead at the scholarly monographs on Italy published over the past two decades as an indication of the kind of American anthropological work that has had the most impact, we may have an even more revealing picture. According to my rough calculation (again I apologize for works I have overlooked here), of the thirteen American scholars who have published monographs in the last twenty years based on Italian fieldwork, only three (Doug Holmes, Martha Ward, and I) did their work in the northern half of the country (that is, north of Umbria).

But the regional distribution by itself is only part of the story. If we were to plot on a map the places in Italy where American anthropologists have done fieldwork over the past twenty years, we would find not only a heavy concentration in the southern third of the country, but a strong tendency for the relatively few anthropologists working in the northern two-thirds of the country to work in small, generally peripheral communities. Although the northern third of the country is primarily urban, and filled with important cities like Milan, Turin, Genoa, and Venice, not to mention such important provincial centers as Brescia, Verona, Parma, and Modena, American anthropologists have studiously avoided such centers.[8] It seems that we are somehow drawn to the liminal reaches of border regions, as in the case of Saunders near the French border, or Holmes near the Yugoslav border, and Ward on the Austrian border, the latter two perhaps influenced by Cole and Wolf's (1974) earlier research spanning the Austrian-Italian border.[9]

By no means do I want to argue that work done in the south is less interesting or less important than work done in the north, nor that anthropologists do not have important contributions to make to our understanding of rural society or to societies at the crossroads of different cultures. Much of our most innovative work has been done in just such settings, and work done in rural areas can be the basis of works of more general theoretical significance. There have also been very important recent developments in the American anthropology of Italy—reflected by innovative studies such as those by Holmes (1989), combining history and ethnography to provide a new take on the development of worker-peasants in Friuli; by Blim, in his anthropologically pioneering look at small industry in central Italy; or Jane and Peter Schneider (1996), in their combined use of ethnography, oral history, and archival research in Sicily to provide valuable insights into the historical decline of fertility in Italy, to take just three of several possible examples.

If we look at the problem areas providing the focus of recent research by American anthropologists in Italy rather than the research site, the picture of stagnation that comes from a focus on field sites gives way to a more hopeful picture of innovation. Most notable here are the diverse works that focus more on history than on contemporary ethnography. Indeed, Italy has been one of the most productive sites in the move of American anthropology toward history. These include not only the studies by Holmes and Jane and Peter Schneider mentioned above, but various others. Some focus on medical topics, such as Peter Brown's (1981) work on malaria in Sardinia, and Elizabeth Whitaker's (1992) work on pellagra in northern Italy.[10] Others, like the Schneiders, focus on demographic topics, including William Douglass's (1984, 1991) studies of the impact of out-migration and household organization in an Abruzzese town, and David Horn's (1994) study of the role of the state and science in regulating reproduction in the Fascist era. Here I would also mention my own historical work on the transformation of sharecropping family life around Bologna (Kertzer 1984; Kertzer and Hogan 1989), and on the institutionalization of infant abandonment in the Italian past (Kertzer 1993). These studies combine a focus on culture and social life with the recognition of the role of the state in producing historical change. Other historical studies, like Galt's (1991) work on the impact of economic change on family organization in an Apulian community, following on John Davis's (1973) pioneering work on economy and kinship in Pisticci, illustrate why and how the historical dimension is so crucial to current anthropological work. These studies examine culture and social organization as ever-changing processes, and recognize the importance of using archival sources alongside the more traditional ethnographic methods.

Yet, all these positive developments notwithstanding, all is not right with the anthropological study of Italy (and I suspect these observations pertain to varying extents to the American anthropological study of other portions of Europe). We seem to be awfully slow in overcoming our primitivist past. Is anthropology merely a pith-helmeted form of rural sociology? What is it about anthropology that makes us eschew the urban life that totally dominates Italy? And why do we find the south in general, and Sicily in particular, so much more attractive to us?

CONCLUSION

Let me return in closing to the charges hurled at anthropologists (generally by other anthropologists—few others seem to care about this) as part of the self-critical mood identified variously with postmodernism, reflexivity, and anti-imperialism. Are we engaged in manufacturing a bogus Other, in exoticizing the familiar? And to the extent that we seem to be guilty of such impulses, what accounts for them?

Reluctantly, I think we have to plead guilty to these charges. There are a number of reasons for the development of the anglophone (and not just the anglophone) anthropology of Italy along these lines, as I have already discussed. But let me conclude by pointing to just one other, related, reason: our still deeply rooted commitment to a model of field research that—vilify it all we like—continues to rest on the community study model. In short, in the sixty-five years since Charlotte Chapman got the Prefect of Sicily to order the mayor to order the midwife to put her up and be sure she got to know what she wanted to know about Milocca (and one can only imagine what the Prefect thought this American woman was doing in such a village), we still pine for the simplicity of a manageable field setting, one we can get a handle on, one where people will know who we are, where the social boundary is clear, the scale is human, and the cow dung wafts through the air.

NOTES

1. For helpful comments on an earlier version of this chapter, I would like to thank Stanley Brandes and Susan Parman.

2. On the crisis of ethnographic authority, see Clifford (1988).

3. For a recent compendium of views by Italian anthropologists of the anthropological study of Italy, see Apolito (1993).

4. Of course there are also native views of the difference between city-dwellers and rural folk that are themselves worth examining. In Italy, Silverman's (1975) study of a small central Italian hill town shows the high value Italians place on "civiltà," identifying the urban with the civilized, and the rural with the uncouth.

5. Though, interestingly, Belmonte's interpretation swam rather against the anthropological stream at the time in leaning toward a culture of poverty explanation. It is also noteworthy that the first British-trained (though Italian) anthropologist to publish on urban Italy, Italo Pardo (1989), also focused on the poor of Naples.

6. It is curious that one of the only other fieldwork-based urban studies by an anglophone anthropologist in Italy, British anthropologist Chris Shore's (1990) work in Perugia, also takes as its subject the Italian Communist Party. Remarkably, this study was begun in 1981 (a year after my own *Comrades and Christians* was published), as a dissertation on "communism and Catholicism in an inner-city neighbourhood of Perugia" (1990, v). For my views of Shore's book, see Kertzer (1991).

7. Adding British anthropologists would not alter this picture. The best British anthropology conducted in Italy—works such as John Davis's (1973) study of Pisticci, and Caroline White's (1980) study of the Fucino area—have been done in the rural south.

8. Those doing historical research, rather than fieldwork, partially escape this pattern. Note especially the work of Horn (1991, 1994), based on Milan. Yanagisako's (1991) research in family history and industrialization in the Como area is another exception.

9. Italian, but British-trained, anthropologist Pier Paolo Viazzo (1989) should also be mentioned here for his excellent historical study of the Alpine border area of northwestern Italy.

10. See also Brown and Whitaker (1994).

CHAPTER 6

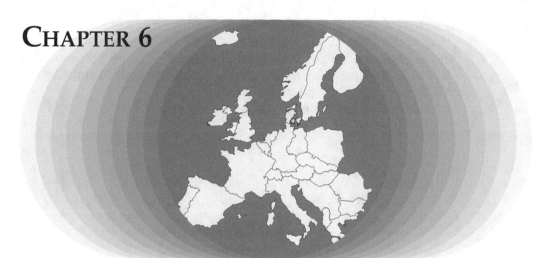

RETURNING WITH THE EMIGRANTS: A JOURNEY IN PORTUGUESE ETHNOGRAPHY

Caroline B. Brettell
Southern Methodist University

Although I am an ethnographer of Portuguese culture and society, I came to Portugal through the back door. For several years I had conducted fieldwork among Portuguese immigrants in New England, Canada (Brettell 1977, 1981), and France (Brettell 1982, 1984), and when I first set foot in Portugal it was because I journeyed there with emigrants who were returning from France for their summer vacations. My interest in immigrants was rooted in my training in urban anthropology, a subfield that was emerging in the early 1970s when I was in graduate school.[1]

For my dissertation, I chose to study Portuguese immigrant women in Paris, looking specifically at changes in social and economic roles that might be associated with the move from countryside to city. Subsequent to the year in Paris, I spent six months in Portugal. My goal for this part of the research was to look at the impact of emigration to France not only on the lives of women who had chosen to remain behind but also on the village community in general.

The decision to work on immigrant women was directly linked to the beginnings of the anthropology of gender, and more specifically to the publication of *Woman, Culture and Society* (Rosaldo and Lamphere 1974), a book that was coedited by one of my professors, Louise Lamphere. Although the study of migrant and immigrant women, as well as of the impact of male emigration on women's lives has blossomed into a rich field of investigation, when Susan Rogers and I, from our respective perspectives of France and Portugal, participated in a session about women and migration at the American Anthropological Association in 1976, the topic and the session drew little attention.[2]

My decision to work on the Portuguese in Paris grew out of my interest in exploring a situation of international migration where immigrants could move back and forth more easily between their homeland and the country of destination. What I was studying then is now called "transnationalism" and has become a major focus of research in the anthropology of migration (Schiller, Basch, and Blanc-Szanton 1992). Although I never used the concept of transnationalism, it was impossible to study Portuguese emigrants abroad without considering Portugal, just as it was impossible to consider Portugal without considering emigration.

Portuguese emigration is imbued with an ideology of return (Brettell 1979, 1990b) encapsulated in the concept of *saudade*, a word that loosely translates as nostalgia or yearning for the homeland. But when Robert Rhoades, who had worked in Spain, proposed a session at the 1977 annual meeting of the American Anthropological Association that would focus on return migration, it was turned down. I suspect that this too was because return migration had not yet been recognized as something central to anthropological interest. And yet two of us, again from the perspective of European-based research, knew that it was fundamental to understanding the populations with which we worked and the continent within which those populations resided. We were later vindicated; in 1986 a review essay on return migration by George Gmelch (1986a) appeared in the *Annual Review of Anthropology*.

Since 1976 I have spent a good deal more time in Portugal, continuing my exploration of the phenomenon of Portuguese emigration (Brettell 1986, 1993a, 1994), and adding to it an interest in folk catholicism (Brettell 1983, 1990a), property and inheritance (Brettell 1991), family history (Brettell 1989), and the intersection of anthropology and history (Brettell 1993b). Indeed, if my thinking about Portugal has changed from what it was in the mid-1970s it is in the direction of adding historical depth and historical analysis to almost anything that I undertake, and in some of this work I have collaborated with Portuguese historians (Brettell and Feijó 1991). It is probably safe to argue that by employing the wealth of historical records at their disposal, ethnographers of Europe have contributed important insights about social process and social change to general anthropological theory.[3]

When I began my work in Portugal under the guidance of a dissertation advisor who was an Africanist, there was no clearly defined "anthropology of Europe" although Arensberg (1963) had already attempted to delineate a series of culture areas within continental Europe and several important ethnographies of European communities had become part of the anthropological canon.[4] That Europe, and especially Paris, was not considered to be a place for anthropologists became most evident to me when I went to New York City for an interview at the Social Science Research Council as part of the application process for an SSRC grant. I was the first anthropologist whom several members of the committee had met. "The immigrants in northern Europe"—to their minds that was a topic for sociologists and political scientists.[5] Nevertheless, they awarded me the grant and later the head of the Western European program provided me with the name of a French political scientist to contact if I needed help with my research. When I met with him in Paris, he was at a loss to provide me the names of other scholars to approach, but he did offer me the name and telephone number of his Portuguese maid. He was apologetic; I was most grateful!

In 1974, as I set out to France to start research for my dissertation, I did not label myself a "Europeanist." I was an anthropologist and my choices of both research problem and fieldwork locale were shaped by questions that pertained to the discipline in general. My contribution was going to be to the anthropology of gender, and to the study of migration from an anthropological perspective.[6] And yet, prior to my journey to Portugal I had journeyed into Portuguese ethnography. I had read and been influenced by the "master texts," to borrow a phrase from José Limón (1991),[7] that were available at that time. Although perhaps less well-known than "classic" ethnographies such as *People of the Sierra*, *Vasilika*, or *Family and Community in Ireland*, or key articles such as Jane Schneider's "Of Vigilance and Virgins" (1971), these Portuguese master texts were wrestling with issues of widespread concern in anthropology, particularly among those working in peasant societies. Furthermore, a number of the themes addressed in these master texts are still relevant today, albeit viewed through a different theoretical lens.

In this chapter I take the reader on a brief journey through Portuguese ethnography. What this journey will reveal, at least from the perspective of Portugal, a country as much on the "margins of Europe" as Greece (Herzfeld 1987b), is that Europe is a vital place to address questions of general anthropological interest and has been all along. I also want to suggest, as I already have, for example, in my comments about migrant women and return migration, that some of the anthropological research in Europe, then as now, was on the cutting edge, although often not recognized as such because the theoretical frameworks or concepts by which such research was organized were not yet part of common anthropological discourse. Perhaps we suffered then, less so than we do now, from the fact that work done in Europe was not generally recognized as legitimate anthropology.

JORGE DIAS, CLOSED CORPORATE COMMUNITIES, AND THE ROOTS OF PORTUGUESE ETHNOGRAPHY

The earliest ethnography of Portugal was produced by native ethnographers and those of us who studied that country were and remain mindful of their contributions. Among the master texts were two produced by the Portuguese anthropologist Jorge Dias. Dias studied two communitarian villages, Vilarinho da Furna in the Alto Minho in northwestern Portugal (Dias 1981 [1948]) and Rio de Onor in Trás-os-Montes in the northeast (Dias 1953). Although Dias never mentioned Eric Wolf (1955, 1957a), it is evident that Rio de Onor and Vilarinho da Furna were examples of the "closed corporate community" that Wolf outlined in two important articles published in the 1950s. Portuguese ethnography, like that conducted by American anthropologists who first went to Spain (Freeman 1968a, 1970a), was shaped by the growing interest in peasant societies, an interest that had its foundations in the work of Robert Redfield, Sol Tax, and others who conducted fieldwork in Mesoamerica. Peasant studies blossomed after World War II and reached their apogee during the 1960s when three separate articles on peasant culture and society were published in the *Biennial Review of Anthropology* (Geertz 1961; Friedl 1963; Anderson 1965). In later reflections on these two field sites, Dias, who had by this time traveled to the United States and had perhaps become more familiar with the contributions of American anthropologists to peasant studies, wrote that these two remote mountain villages of Portugal offered him "the characteristics of the small community as defined by Redfield. They constituted autonomous homogenous groups, economically self-sufficient, clearly limited, isolated by grazing lands and sowing fields which traditionally belonged to the group" (Dias 1961, 83).

Vilarinho da Furna is a monograph rich in ethnographic data documenting housing and material goods, pastorage and agriculture, food and clothing, popular beliefs, dances and music, proverbs and riddles. Emigration is given a few pages, but, according to Dias, is perceived by villagers "as a place where money is earned, that is all" (1981, 282). To a great extent, emigration is played down to suit the model of an "autonomous and economically self-sufficient village," much as George Foster (1965) played down the impact of outmigration in his formulation of the concept of "limited good" as a defining feature of peasant society.[8] Where Dias accepted emigration as a mechanism of change, he did so with an attitude of nostalgia and concern for the world that would be lost (to paraphrase Peter Laslett [1965]):

> Emigration is one of the sources for the rapid loss of the values of popular culture as well as for the corruption of language through the appropriation of foreign expressions. These men who arrive from big countries, where they live in contact with more advanced civilization, lose their primitive naiveté and view the simple and traditional customs with disdain. (1981, 284)

In a more broadly theoretical essay, Dias (1961, 63) reiterated his concern for the passing of traditional society in Portugal. "Portugal," he wrote "has not escaped the implacable march of modern industrial civilization which threatens to reduce the enormous diversity of the forms of human life to a sad and monotonous uniformity." While it is hard to accept today the linear evolutionary model of social change that undergirds Dias's work, undoubtedly influenced, as Redfield also was, by Tönnies's opposition between *Gemeinschaft* and *Gesellschaft*,[9] it is important to note that Dias recognized that the nostalgia for the past among "civilized peoples" had "given rise to a new industry, the tourist industry, which creates an interest in folklore, regional restaurants, popular regional dancers, thus seeking to give illusions to things that no longer exist." In short, Dias, more than forty years ago, was making reference to a research problem that has become central to more recent ethnographic and historical investigation—the reinvigoration and reinvention of tradition (Hobsbawn 1983; Hanson 1989).

If communitarianism was one powerful theme in Dias's two ethnographies, the roles of men and women was another. In Vilarinho, he wrote "the woman continues to have an important role in social life, even to the point of participating in meetings of the Junta and she is the representative of the house by widowhood or the absence of her husband. She also takes an active role in agricultural work and her voice in the house is always listened to with respect, something that shows the matriarchal tendency of Minho that reaches the mountainous regions of the Minhotan north" (1981, 291).

By contrast, while women were described as essential to the economy and society of the villages of the Alto Minho, they were less so in Rio de Onor where Dias stressed the patriarchal basis of communal traditions. In Rio de Onor, Dias asserts "the woman has little economic value, her life practically reduced to the domestic tasks and a bit of help in the garden or in agricultural work when there are insufficient men in the house. Perhaps for this reason she has no political rights and ... assumes no public roles" (Dias 1953, 318–319). Elsewhere he alludes to the sexual restraint of women. "Except in rare cases, the relations between boys and girls are cordial, free, but without surpassing the limits established by public opinion" (p. 319).

Despite the discomfort that we might feel today with the theoretical framework used by Dias, in this work were seeds of important problems that were to shape later Portuguese ethnography as well as European ethnography more generally—issues of gender roles and gender ideology, of the relationship between women's status and productive activity, of regional variation, and of the relationship between an egalitarian ideology and social stratification. What Dias also did was to focus attention in Portuguese ethnography on the north, the region of Portugal where peasant culture dominated.[10]

In the Shadow of Redfield and Lewis: World View and Social Stratification in the Peasant Community

Although Dias's influence was probably more indirect than direct, both João de Pina-Cabral (1986) and Brian O'Neill (1987) addressed the question of egalitarianism and homogeneity in the peasant societies of northern Portugal in their ethnographic research of the early- to mid-1980s. The degree to which people in peasant communities were "all one" or socially stratified had been explored elsewhere in Europe as well as in rural village communities around the world. Indeed it is a theoretical debate that has existed since Oscar Lewis (1951) presented the anthropological community with an alternative vision of the Mexican village of Tepotzlán from that offered by Robert Redfield (1930) twenty years earlier.

Pina-Cabral, in a study of two rural Minhotan parishes on the southern side of the Lima River in the concelho of Ponte da Barca, does not deny the presence of social stratification—indeed he is one of the few ethnographers of rural European life to incorporate the bourgeoisie into his study—but his emphasis is on the ideology of equality, an ideology to which peer groups of children are socialized, and an ideology that is "a central corollary of the subsistence prototype" (1986, 130). "The open expression of status differences," he argues, "… is felt as antisocial and … undesirable" (p. 151). If communalism is not mentioned by Pina-Cabral, the experience of community is. This community is characterized by "folkways" (a Redfieldian model) that are in contrast to the impersonal stateways beyond its boundaries. Mutual cooperation is manifested in the value placed on friendship between households of unequal and equal wealth. Pina-Cabral explores how this equality is symbolically expressed—unequal relations of economic dependence between *compadres* as well as the spiritual dependence on saints is reshaped into a reciprocal relationship between equals (pp. 119, 163). It is only on ritual occasions—at weddings and funerals, for example—that the ideology that "all peasants are equal" is set aside.

Pina-Cabral's peasants, his subsistence prototype, are "other" to his bourgeois prototype. It is the bourgeois way of life that is characterized by hierarchy and mechanical solidarity. "For the bourgeois, social relationships are typically thought of as associative and a strong emphasis is placed on the external demonstration of economic differentiation" (p. 35). If subsistence typifies the peasant worldview, salary typifies the worldview of the bourgeois. Although Pina-Cabral does not focus extensively on emigration, the implication is that the salary earned from it is adapted to the needs of the subsistence prototype.

By contrast to Pina-Cabral, Brian O'Neill, working in a hamlet in northeastern Trás-os-Montes, aims in his ethnography to "dispute the contention that small, isolated mountain communities in northern Portugal are necessarily egalitarian in social structure" (1987, 1). O'Neill argues that hamlet life in northern Portugal is "ridden with inequality, internal conflict, and struggles to maintain positions of high economic and social rank." This inequality, or absence of homogeneity, is apparent in property ownership, forms of cooperative labor, marriage, and inheritance patterns.

Just as Redfield and Lewis's different versions of peasant society can be reconciled once we accept that they approached their subject matter with a different set of theoretical assumptions and methodological emphases, so too can

O'Neill, Dias, and Pina-Cabral. O'Neill claims that he was not interested in or left unfathomed "values, religion, or ideology" (1987, 16, 343). Pina-Cabral, while recognizing status differences as measured by wealth, expressly addresses ideology and symbols.

However, what is perhaps most interesting for our purposes here is that the dichotomous thinking that has characterized a good deal of anthropological work on peasant culture and society persists.[11] Of course such thinking has deep roots in representations of and writings about the peasantry. The blissful, bucolic peasant whom the French author George Sand defined as a representative of a good and noble reality by contrast with the artifice of modern life, can be compared to the vicious, backbiting, petty, and vindictive peasant who is the central character in the literature of Honoré Balzac or Émile Zola.

A MOVE AWAY FROM DICHOTOMOUS THINKING: THE PEASANT AND THE STATE

It was Joyce Riegelhaupt who, perhaps better than anyone else, attempted to abandon the dichotomous model that opposed city and country. Her collective *oeuvre* was an attempt to explore the myriad ways—economic, political, religious—in which the Portuguese peasant interacts with Portuguese society and the Portuguese state. Riegelhaupt was, of course, influenced by the work of Redfield and Wolf (1966), certainly more so than was Jorge Dias for whom these theoreticians were an afterthought. She went to Portugal in the early 1960s, choosing as her fieldwork site the small Estremaduran village of São João das Lampas, forty kilometers from Lisbon. What she found was that the people of São João lived "in the shadow of the city" (Riegelhaupt 1964). They participated fully in the national economy, providing much of the agricultural produce for the capital. However, increasing integration (São João was losing its "part-society" character) was not, in Riegelhaupt's view, the result of contact with the city, as Redfield had proposed, but of the penetration of national institutions into the village. Nonagricultural occupations, for example, brought the peasants of São João into contact with the syndicates and guilds of the corporate Portuguese state.

If these peasants were integrated economically, they were also integrated politically. Salazar's centralized *Estado Novo*, in Riegelhaupt's view (Riegelhaupt 1979), effectively eliminated all possibilities for local politics. Riegelhaupt went on to note that the largely administrative rather than political contacts between the Portuguese peasant and the Portuguese state made it impossible for the patronage systems that ethnographers had observed and recorded elsewhere in the Iberian and Latin American world to emerge with any force in the Portuguese context. This was an important observation about social as well as political organization that added a new dimension to the growing literature on patron-client relations within peasant societies.

Riegelhaupt's interest in the impact of the state on peasant society also emerged in her studies of religion. In "Festas and Padres," an article published in 1973 in the *American Anthropologist*, she showed how the priest, as an agent of the state, attempted to control the Portuguese peasant, and, alternatively, how the peasant resisted orthodoxy in favor of his or her more personal religion. Popular anticlericalism, in Riegelhaupt's view (1984), was not antireligious, but stemmed from distrust of the privileged position of the Catholic Church as an institution of the Portuguese state. If priests were the objects of suspicion, it was to some extent because of their secular roles as state agents who helped parishioners to secure building permits, obtain permission for emigration, or apply for social insurance. It is hard to underestimate the impact of Riegelhaupt's work on later work in the European context on the relationship between orthodoxy and popular religion (Badone 1990).

In her final work, Riegelhaupt turned to history, but here too she sustained her interest in the relationship of the peasantry to the state. Focusing on the Maria da Fonte uprising of the 1840s (Riegelhaupt 1981), she explored the process by which the state increasingly infiltrated the countryside through new laws, new roads, new taxes and, in the process, attempted to alter some of the most fundamental facets of local social and cultural life. If the new health laws requiring burial in new state-owned cemeteries rather than in the church or churchyard became the focus of the Maria da Fonte uprising, this was because the state was appropriating a fundamental aspect of the communal ritual life of village neighbors.

Although Riegelhaupt never categorized her work within the arena of political-economy, her overriding concern about the impact of the state moves thinking in that direction. It certainly influenced my own work on emigration by forcing me to consider the ways in which individual or family decisions about migration are shaped by state policy (Brettell 1993). Portugal, if not Europe in general, is a good place to test some of the models of political economy.

WADING IN THE WATERS OF THE ANTHROPOLOGY OF GENDER

Riegelhaupt also worked on issues of gender. In a 1967 article she drew attention to the informal networks of the women of São João das Lampas. These women had more contact with the city than did men; they were at the hub of information networks and men depended on them for knowledge about village events, issues, and personalities. They had informal power, a fact that undermined the appearance of the formal power of men.

Riegelhaupt's work, together with that of the French anthropologist Colette Callier-Boisvert (1966) on the "feminine rural community" of Soajo in the Alto Minho, were difficult to come to terms with in the context of the domestic-public model that emerged a few years later in feminist anthropology as an explanation for presumably universal male dominance. It was equally problematic to make sense of this work on Portugal in relationship to Michaelson and Goldschmidt's (1972) argument, based on an analysis of forty-six community studies, that peasant society was male-dominated. They pointed to strict social segregation and a division of labor by sex whereby men were engaged in higher prestige productive work.

Callier-Boisvert's (1966) study of Soajo suggested that this model of peasant society could not be applied to northern Portugal where men were frequently absent and where women had to assume important productive roles. Callier-Boisvert went on to note, this time in an article dealing with Portuguese kinship (1968), that while postmarital residence was generally neolocal, there was a powerful tendency to matrilocality. "Neolocal residence," she suggested, "is situated by preference in the same village or city, even in the same hamlet as that of the parents of the wife. There is therefore always a certain element of matrilocality in residence patterns" (1968, 91). The relationship between the absence of men and the matricentric characteristics of rural life in Portugal is one that I have explored in depth, as have other ethnographers of Portugal (Cole 1991). But it is also a theme of wider importance in the ethnography of southern Europe. Some time ago, Jeremy Boissevain, in an article on the anthropology of the Mediterranean (Boissevain 1979, 83–84) observed:

> that matrifocal uxorilocal families are reported among landless labourers on Portuguese latifundia and among industrial workers in Malta. The facts that in both cases attachment to landed property for economic purposes is minimal and that in both there is village-outward economic orientation allowing freer play of the strong mother-daughter tie do not suggest coincidence.

Of course, in the Portuguese case this matricentrism (a term I prefer to matrifocality) also exists in areas where there is a powerful attachment to the land, but where dense population has made male emigration imperative. The important point, of course, is that these observations were contrary to some of the dominant thinking about gender roles in peasant communities in general and in Mediterranean Europe more specifically.

Boissevain's article was both a review of and a response to John Davis's book *People of the Mediterranean: An Essay in Comparative Social Anthropology* (1977), a book that attempted to build on earlier formulations of the Mediterranean as a culture area. While there is no room here to enter into the debate about whether or not there is a unified region that we can call "the Mediterranean,"[12] the comparative problem that Boissevain raised is as intriguing to me now as it was when I first read the article. It is a problem that I would view as central to the anthropology of gender rather than one that merely typifies an ethnographic culture area.

HONOR, SHAME, AND ILLEGITIMACY IN PORTUGAL

If the domestic-public model was hard to reconcile in relationship to ethnographic data from northern Portugal, so too was the honor-shame model that John Peristiany (1965) had put forth as a unifying feature of the Mediterranean culture area. Indeed if there is anything akin to what Appadurai (1986) has labeled a "gatekeeping concept" for the anthropology of the Mediterranean region, it is the "honor-shame" complex.[13] As O'Neill has so aptly expressed it, "one need only think of social occasions in which anthropologists working in Europe are queried: 'Did your village have honour and shame?'" (1987, 16).

This model became immediately troublesome for Pina-Cabral, O'Neill, Sally Cole, and me when we were confronted with the extensive data on illegitimacy in our respective communities in northern Portugal.[14] O'Neill, almost as if in reaction to what he "knew" about European ethnography, went so far as to describe the community of Fontelas and its "astronomical" illegitimacy rates as "almost another planet" (1987, 16).

I, too, wrote in *Men Who Migrate, Women Who Wait* (Brettell 1986) of the world I had expected to find based on my theoretical reading and what I did find in the form of ratios of illegitimate births, which reached 13 percent in the later-nineteenth and early-twentieth centuries. Could I talk about "vigilance of virgins" and chastity codes? My explanation for the high incidence of illegitimacy was rooted in the connection with emigration—a slightly different approach from that of O'Neill, who situates illegitimacy within the system of property and social stratification. We do, however, concur that more women of the day-laboring social group (the *jornaleiras*) are or were unwed mothers than women of the *lavrador* or *proprietário* social groups. Although neither one of us used the word "class," it is a class-based model that we present in our interpretation of findings.

Our assessments are corroborated by the work of Cole (1991) in the northern coastal fishing village of Vila Chã and by the work of Pina-Cabral in the interior Minhotan parishes of Paço and Couto (1986). Landlessness and illegitimacy are correlated and the social makeup of rural communities was clearly much more complex than the anthropological literature often suggested. More recently, Colette Callier-Boisvert has returned to the village of Soajo to study celibacy and illegitimacy (1990). Describing illegitimacy as a "distinctive trait of Portuguese demography" (1990, 189), she attempts to situate it within the logic of a particular social system and, like me, points to its relationship with emigration. But while I document a rapid decline in illegitimacy in the 1930s and 1940s—a period when emigration was stagnant—in Soajo it rose. Callier-Boisvert links this to poverty and the precariousness of resources during this period, a period when "sexuality remained as a privileged domain where men could rival one another in a competition that involved their vanity" (1990, 199).

Callier-Boisvert's argument is similar to those that have been used to explain Iberian and Latin American *machismo* and, moreover, reproduces the Mediterranean masculinity cult that Gilmore and other Anglo-American ethnographers have written about (Gilmore 1987, Brandes 1980). Pina-Cabral not only stresses that this heightened masculinity is less characteristic of a region than of a social class, but also captures the tendency to essentialize that has been present in some ethnography of southern Europe. "One is therefore tempted to think that one of the reasons middle class and upper middle class young Anglo-American scholars are so deeply impressed with the agonistic display of malehood among southern European peasants is that they are so ignorant of working-class behavior in their own country of origin" (Pina-Cabral 1989, 402).

TOWARD THE TWENTY-FIRST CENTURY IN THE ANTHROPOLOGY OF PORTUGAL

In her book *Gone Primitive*, Torgovnick (1990) argues that when anthropologists go into the field, they demonstrate a tendency to ignore the modern. It is precisely this tendency that Gewertz and Errington (1991) reveal in Margaret Mead's work on the Chambri people of Papua, New Guinea. At the time of Mead's fieldwork in the 1930s, fifty-two percent of the men between the ages of fifteen and forty-five who were from the village where Mead lived were away working as migrant laborers. The majority had been exposed to missionization and some had become at least nominal Catholics. Yet we read nothing of this in Mead's ethnography. "That she did not take these articulations with a larger system into consideration," write Gewertz and Errington, "reflects her essentializing perspective" (1991, 81).

Despite Jorge Dias's nostalgia for the Portuguese past and his comfort with a theoretical framework that opposed city and country, I am not sure that he can be put in the same category as Mead—ignoring "the modern." He skirted over it perhaps, but nevertheless acknowledged that it was there. Other early anthropological work in Portugal, although focusing on rural communities and peasant society, did emphasize the relationship between the local community and the rest of the world, often through the mechanism of migration and emigration. The heirs to this work have continued in this tradition. And yet, what we have is still very much the study of rural ways of life and of peasant communities. If the ethnography of Portugal has been successful in articulating the relationship between small communities and the rest of the world in terms of emigration, we now need to explore it in terms of politics or culture. We also need more ethnography of urban populations in Portugal and more ethnography that explores the impact of new economic opportunities, including that derived from Portugal's entry into the European Economic Community. The impact of tourism or of modern institutions of health care are other arenas for promising investigation. Indeed, if medical anthropology is a viable, exciting, and growing subfield within anthropology, it has yet to influence seriously ethnographic research in Europe. In Portugal, women are no longer giving birth in the villages; the use of pharmaceuticals has become widespread; and the people perceive that new diseases and illnesses have entered their life and experience. As anthropologists we have paid some attention to traditional methods of healing but little to the way that traditional and modern medicine have accommodated one another. In short, Portugal, like Europe in general, has been and will continue to be an arena within which to address questions that are germane to the larger discipline of anthropology.

NOTES

1. The first issue of the journal *Urban Anthropology* appeared in 1972. Foster and Kemper published an edited volume titled *Anthropologists in Cities* in 1974. The year before, a collection on *Urban Anthropology* edited by Aidan Southall had appeared (Southall 1973).

2. Curiously, a special issue of *Anthropological Quarterly* edited by Judith Buechler, who had worked on Spanish immigrant women in Switzerland, had just appeared as Volume 49, number 1 (1976). See Brettell and deBerjeois (1992) for a recent review of the anthropological literature dealing with immigrant women in the United States, and Simon and Brettell (1986) for a broader overview.

3. One of the earliest works to recognize the value of history was Jane and Peter Schneider's study of Sicily (1976). More recent examples can be found in Maddox's (1993) work on Spain and Rogers's (1991a) on France.

4. Among them, of course, are Arensberg and Kimball's *Family and Community in Ireland* (1940); Julian Pitt-Rivers's *People of the Sierra* (1954); Ernestine Friedl's *Vasilika* (1962); Laurence Wylie's *Village in the Vaucluse* (1964); John Campbell's *Honour, Family and Patronage* (1964); William Douglass's *Death in Murelaga* (1969); and Susan Freeman's *Neighbors* (1970a).

5. Rural-urban migration was already a subject of anthropological investigation in Africa, Latin America, and Asia, but it was not yet recognized as something of importance in the European context, despite the fact that Latin Americanists like Judith and Hans Buechler were working on the topic. There were, of course, some community studies of Europe where outmigration was the focus of attention. The work of Stanley Brandes and William Douglass in Spain and of Peter Allen in Greece come to mind immediately.

6. In 1970, the American Ethnological Society focused on migration as a theme for its annual meeting and proceedings (Spencer 1970). This could

perhaps be taken as a signpost for the integration of this topic into the canon of topics of importance to anthropology. Another signpost publication, also in 1970, was William Mangin's edited volume *Peasants in Cities*.

7. Limón defines "master ethnographic texts" as texts that have or will "deeply influence the structure of later ethnographies" and that often affect the way the world views the people they represent (Limón 1991, 116).

8. An English anthropologist who worked with Dias, Patricia Goldey, focused more extensively on emigration in a village neighboring Vilarinho (Goldey 1981). Goldey has argued that historical emigration from this region was integrated with and supported the communal way of life and an egalitarian ideology. More contemporary emigration, conversely, has been the source of significant change, leaving the village "materially better off, but morally more isolated" (1981, 127).

9. Today we would label this kind of approach "orientalization" and yet the model to which Dias ascribed persists in a recent ethnography of the fishing community of Nazare published by Jan Brøgger. However, Brøgger, rather than recognize change, writes about "atavistic culture traits" and premodern survivals that "follow the medieval pattern ... of pre-Bureaucratic innocence" (Brøgger 1990, 11 passim). For further discussion of Brøgger's ethnography, see Brettell (1992) and Pina-Cabral (1991).

10. Even today, this emphasis remains. The major published ethnographies, with the exception of Cutileiro (1971), are all based on fieldwork in Minho or Trás-os-Montes. Exceptions are the work of Denise Lawrence (1988) and Cristina Bastos (1988) and some new work coming out of Portugal itself.

11. See Roseberry (1989) for a broader comment on the pervasiveness of oppositional thinking in anthropology.

12. For further discussion of this issue, see the comments following Boissevain's article: Gilmore (1982); Herzfeld (1980, 1987b); Galt (1985); and Pina-Cabral (1989). It is probably worth noting that the most vehement critique of the concept of "the Mediterranean" has come from Pina-Cabral, a Portuguese anthropologist trained at Oxford. It represents the discomfort, if not sometimes distrust, that some European-born anthropologists feel when faced with the ethnography of Europe produced by American and British anthropologists. See also Moreno-Navarro (1986) and Llobera (1986).

13. By "gatekeeping concept" Appadurai (1986, 357) is referring to concepts "that limit anthropological theorizing about the place in question and ... define the quintessential and dominant questions of interest in the region." Thus, lineages or segments are a focus of research in Africa, dual organizations and structured mythologies in South America, the manipulation of bodily substances in Melanesia, and reciprocity in Polynesia.

14.   It is interesting to note that Pina-Cabral, O'Neill, and I (in my second stint of fieldwork) were working at roughly the same time and we were all making extensive use of historical data, and yet we were working in ignorance of one another. We had all been influenced by the research in historical demography and family history emerging out of the Cambridge School under the guidance of historians such as Peter Laslett and Richard Wall.

CHAPTER 7

RESTLESS CONTINENT: MIGRATION AND THE CONFIGURATION OF EUROPE

William A. Douglass
University of Nevada, Reno

In 1975 Jeremy Boissevain and John Friedl published their edited work entitled *Beyond the Community: Social Process in Europe*. It is a watershed text that helped configure the direction of the Europeanist anthropology of the past two decades while setting it apart from earlier investigations—at least as conducted by anglophone researchers. The main criticism of the volume is that anthropologists—given their experience with primitive and tribal societies—were ill-equipped to deal with the complexity of Europe. "Consequently," according to Boissevain, "many have sought refuge in villages, which they proceed to treat as isolated entities. They have tribalized Europe" (1975, 11).

Like all generalizations, the foregoing one incorporates elements of both truth and hyperbole. To what extent, then, has Europeanist anthropology, particularly during its formative phase, regarded little communities to be social isolates? The question is of particular interest since Europe is, arguably, the continent most characterized by transnational emigration and internal migration. *Grosso modo* three European macrohistorical patterns make the point.

PATTERNS OF MIGRATION AND EMIGRATION

First, there is European imperialism and colonialism that began in the fifteenth century and are now seemingly in their final (if not finest) hour. Over the last half-millennium, the overseas expansion of European political hegemony essentially reconfigured the social, political, economic, and cultural realities of the entire planet. Indeed, there is a sense in which the spread of occidental influence at least partially defines the setting within which the anthropological investigation of *any* society, no matter how "isolated," transpires. In large measure, the common tropical ploy of dealing in the "ethnographic present" within anthropological discourse is the attempt to factor out European influence when studying a nonwestern people.

For present purposes, what is of interest are the opportunity structures created by the colonial empires of several European nation-states. Each became a kind of perdurable, transnational universe that affected the lives of all of its inhabitants. While enormous linguistic and cultural heterogeneity persisted within each, it is equally true that the defining nation-state provided its empire with a European lingua franca and hegemonic cultural tradition. Thus, even in the present essentially postcolonial period, much of the world is carved up into anglophone, francophone, slavophone, etcetera, spheres of influence—universes within which former colonizers *and* their colonized continue to share some sense of common destiny.

By definition, the establishment of the several European transnational colonial ventures supposed emigration. As administrators of, and religious ministers to, nonwestern populations, and as colonists on an expanding (at least from a European perspective) frontier, Europeans obviously constituted much of the social and cultural elite in their colonies. Thus began a two-directional exchange of persons, resources, capital, diseases, cultigens, and ideas between the several metropoles and their spheres of influence.

The second pattern of interest was the nineteenth- and early-twentieth-century transfers of Europe's "huddled masses," to what Denoon (1983) has called "Euro-settler societies." These would include places like Canada and the United States, Australia and New Zealand, parts of southern Africa, and the southern reaches of South America. No longer were Europeans emigrating within their own particular sphere of colonial influence as its social and political elite. Rather, the ranks of the new emigrants were swollen with lower-class persons, often from southern and central European areas lacking a colonial empire. In many instances the migrants were economic or political refugees—as often fleeing oppression as pursuing opportunity. As manual laborers they swelled the ranks of both agricultural and industrial work forces in maturing Euro-settler society economies.

Thirdly, since the industrial revolution began in Europe the continent witnessed an early, if uneven, massive rural exodus from the countryside to burgeoning urban-industrial complexes (Moch 1992). Migration of persons within Europe in response to urban attractions or employment opportunities has characterized Europe for several centuries. It assumes the many forms of domestic population transfers within particular nation-states, transnational migrations among them and, most recently, immigration from either the postcolonial spheres of influence (e.g., from the Commonwealth to Great Britain) or from adjacent impoverished areas (e.g., from North Africa to Spain, France, and Italy).

In sum, given all of the foregoing, it is inconceivable that twentieth-century anthropologists would have encountered *any* European little community unaffected by the consequences of the continent's migratory legacy in its many guises. Nor, indeed, were anthropologists insensitive to this reality. We need only consider that when Ernestine Friedl (1962) penned *Vasilika*, based upon her field research in a Greek village during 1955 and 1956, the villagers' migration strategies were given considerable attention. We are told that the system of dowering and inheritance turned, at least in part, upon providing some sons with the formal education to allow them to relocate successfully in urban areas (1962, 49–53) and daughters with the wherewithal to marry a townsman (pp. 65–68). Success or failure in meeting these goals determined a household's social status within Vasilika itself.

Village Migration Data

In 1960 Sydel Silverman conducted field research in the town of Montecastello in Umbria. In her book *Three Bells of Civilization: The Life of an Italian Hill Town*, she notes in passing that Montecastello had a floating population of day laborers who sometimes migrated seasonally for work elsewhere (1975, 54). At the same time, the *mezzadria* system, her central concern, was clearly in crisis since the younger farmers were leaving in order to escape its strictures (pp. 70–71). In analyzing the land tenure system, Silverman demonstrated the considerable extent to which, over the past three centuries, external persons and purposes had shaped Montecastello's social and economic destiny (pp. 75–98).[1]

I conducted field research in the Basque area of Spain in the early- and mid-1960s. The issues of transoceanic emigration and a palpable rural exodus were of paramount concern to the inhabitants of both Echalar and Murélaga, the Navarrese and Bizkaian villages in which I was a fieldworker for more than two years.

Table 7-1 details the migration experiences (and lack thereof) of 465 villagers from Echalar and 1,043 from Murélaga. The data derived from genealogical analysis of the active adult population in both villages during the early 1960s, as well as from the former generation of villagers.[2] In 1960 the population of Echalar was 1,186 persons and that of Murélaga 1,133 inhabitants.

Table 7-1 Migratory Experience of Villagers from Echalar and Murélaga, 1910–1965*

Reason and/or Destination When Migrating	Males		Females		Reason and/or Destination When Migrating
	Echalar *n* = 210	*Murélaga* *n* = 534	*Echalar* *n* = 255	*Murélaga* *n* = 509	
Resettlement as factory worker, shopkeeper, or in the service economy in another town in the Basque Country	27	65	69	141	Housewife or working in a factory or service industry elsewhere in the Basque Country
Resettlement as a farmer in a nearby village	6	9	5	50	Married to a farmer in a nearby village
Pursuing a religious career (priest or seminarian)	5	12	9	15	Pursuing a religious career (nuns)
Killed in the Spanish Civil War	3 (+2)**	10	—	9	Married to man sojourning in the American West
Serving in the Army at the time of interview	1	6	—	2	Married to man sojourning in Australia
In the (western) United States	18	113+	—	6	In the (western) United States
In Australia	—	44	—	8	In Australia
In Argentina	19	23	13	6	In Argentina
In Venezuela	1	20	2	11	In Venezuela
In other Latin American Country	1 (Chile)	7++	2 (Uruguay)	—	In other Latin American Country
In France	16	1	42	2	In France
In England	—	1	—	4	In England
In Spain other than the Basque Country	2	5	11	9	In Spain other than the Basque Country
Other	—	1 (Philippines)	—	1 (Morocco)	

*It should be noted that the totals for the migration strategies do not equate to an absolute total of migrants. For example, a nun living in Buenos Aires appears in both the religious and Argentina boxes. Such double-counting is not, however, common. At the same time there are other migration strategies (e.g., mariner, ballplayer), which are detailed in the subsequent text rather than in Table 7-1.

**Two men were killed fighting in Spain's African War.

+Includes two residing in New Jersey, one in New York, and one in Florida.

++Includes four in Cuba, one in Mexico, one in Chile, and one in Peru.

Several observations are in order. Of the 465 villagers sampled from Echalar, 254, or 56 percent, had some sort of migration experience. Of the 1,043 persons in the Murélaga sample, 581, or an additional 56 percent, had migrated or commuted. Thus, *more than half* of the villagers in both communities had employed some form of migration in formulating a life strategy.

It is evident that in both villages men were more likely than women to emigrate to New World Euro-settler societies. Thus, both villages provided men to the ranks of the Basque sheepherders of the western United States. Both had migrants in Argentina, Venezuela, and, to a lesser degree, other Latin American countries. There is no particular socioeconomic pattern discernible among them since their occupations ranged from manual laborer and taxi driver to the well-to-do storekeeper and retired rancher. In Murélaga there is a pattern of emigration to North Queensland, Australia, of men recruited to cut sugarcane.

There are occupationally and circumstantially driven explanations of migration in both villages as well. These include males killed elsewhere during warfare and the religious vocations of both sexes (with some predominance of nuns). A religious career could mean a minimal move to nearby Eibar or Bilbao to residence in Madrid, Barcelona, or Peru (one friar from Murélaga). Not listed in the table are the seven men from Murélaga and one from Echalar pursuing professional sports careers as pelotaris (handball or jai alai players), which might transpire within the Basque Country (a man from Echalar) or in Florida (a man from Murélaga). Then, too, there are the mariners who reside in the village when home from the sea but regularly travel throughout the world (nine from Murélaga and two from Echalar).

For women in both villages migration strategies include relocation to a nearby village as the spouse of a farmer (Murélaga 50, Echalar 5) or to a town within the Basque Country as a housewife, factory worker, shopkeeper, or servant (Murélaga 141, Echalar 69). The latter decision was roughly two and a half times as common for women as for men. Again, women were more likely than men to settle outside of the Basque Country, yet within Spain.

If emigration to Australia was unique to Murélaga, emigration to France was nearly so for Echalar. Situated on the French-Spanish border, the village provided men to the ranks of the timber-cutters in the Landes and Alps regions (seven of the sixteen males in France) and maids to hotels and private homes from Biarritz to Paris (thirty-eight of the forty-two females).

Indeed, "serving" accounts for a significant portion of female migration from both villages. In Echalar no fewer than seventy-one, or 28 percent of the sample, were reported as having worked as a domestic at some point; after France their most popular destination was the nearby Gipuzkoan coast from San Sebastián to the French frontier (sixteen). In Murélaga the ratio was more modest, yet forty-eight, or 9 percent, of the females counted, had served. Nearly half (twenty-one) had done so in the provincial capital and nearby major city of Bilbao.

Then there is the issue of commuting. In Echalar at the time of the survey seven men held jobs in the factories of nearby towns to which they commuted daily. In Murélaga fifty-seven men worked at jobs available either in nearby marble quarries or the more distant factories of the Eibar-Elgoibar industrial zone in Gipuzkoa.

Nor is an earlier colonial influence lacking in either community, as reflected in some of the more impressive stone dwellings. Then there is the son of Murélaga who, in 1711, became the archbishop of Lima, Peru (Douglass and Bilbao 1975, 6).

In sum, echoes of all three migratory legacies discussed earlier—empire, recent transatlantic mass emigration, and internal migration to urban-indus-trial opportunities—reverberate loudly in the streets, households, and minds of both Echalar and Murélaga.

In light of the foregoing, it would have been absurd for me to treat either village as a closed universe. Given the additional reality that at the time of my fieldwork whole families were abandoning their farms to resettle elsewhere, it is scarcely surprising that my main monograph dealing with the Basque Country is entitled *Echalar and Murélaga, Opportunity and Rural Depopulation in Two Spanish Basque Villages* (1975).[3]

I was scarcely unique in making migration the main focus of my research. By the 1960s and early 1970s other Europeanist anthropologists were smitten by the subject. Without any pretense of being exhaustive, and with apologies to the omitted, examples include Constance Cronin, whose *Sting of Change* (1970) looks at Sicilians in Sicily and then as immigrants in Sydney, Australia. Caroline Brettell's research in northern Portugal resulted in her impressive monograph *Men Who Migrate, Women Who Wait* (1986). Stanley Brandes focused upon rural exodus from a Castilian village to Madrid in his book *Migration, Kinship and Community* (1975). David Gregory (1978) and Hans and Maria Buechler (1981) documented the migration of Spanish laborers to Common Market countries.

Then there were the several unpublished theses such as Peter Allen's "Social and Economic Change in a Depopulated Community in Southern Greece" (1973), Susan Buck Sutton's "Migrant Regional Associations: An Athenian Example and Its Implications" (1978), Janet Schreiber Mogg's "To Eat the Bread of Others: The Decision to Migrate in a Province of Southern Italy" (1973), and Mark Gregory Wojno's "Countrymen Return: Colonial Migration and Rural Economy in Northern Portugal" (1982).

By the 1980s the Europeanist anthropological bibliography also contained the migration section of Michael Kenny and David Kertzer's *Urban Life in Mediterranean Europe: Anthropological Perspectives* (1983, 133–249). The Buechlers had edited a volume entitled *Migrants in Europe: The Role of Family Labor and Politics* (1987), and there were several Europeanist articles in the vol-ume *International Migration: The Female Experience*, edited by Rita James Simon and Caroline Brettell (1986). Most of the articles in these collections were either based upon the author's earlier research or were summaries of the previously published research efforts of others.

Three Classical Treatments of Migration

Despite all of the foregoing, and the examples could easily be multiplied, John Davis, in his critical book-length essay *People of the Mediterranean*, states that "Migration is another relatively neglected mediterranean topic" (1977, 29). While my disagreement with the statement may be a question of perceiving the glass as half-filled as opposed to half-emptied, at the very least I would argue that by the 1970s a considerable portion of the Europeanist anthropological literature failed to qualify for the little-community/social-isolate-syndrome criticism. The question then becomes whether it is more valid when applied to the formative phase of Europeanist anthropology. My answer would be a qualified yes, but what is of interest for present purposes are the qualifications themselves. We might consider the treatment of migration in three classical anglophone Europeanist anthropological texts.

MIGRATION IN IRELAND

Conrad Arensberg, in *The Irish Countryman*, regarded by many as the earliest example of anglophone Europeanist anthropology, since research for it was conducted in the early 1930s, tells us that

> Ireland is in many ways an old person's country. Where emigration carries youth away, old age is disproportionately numerous. (1937, 110)

Nor is emigration a net loss to rural Ireland, since

> [t]he new equilibrium has a place even where emigration removes the dispersed children altogether. The behaviours and sentiments of kinship "travel" with them. They send back remittances and passage money for nephews and nieces, brothers and sisters. There is a marked tendency for emigration from a local region to perpetuate itself. Sons and daughters of each generation go out to join the last. (p. 84)

We are told about one community in County Clare that staffed much of the Singapore Police Force after one of its native sons became the International Settlement's Chief of Police. Then there is the case of Seumas as related by his father. When an emigrant from a nearby town offered to help Seumas emigrate to Australia, where he was to work in his benefactor's hotel as a barman, there was nearly a family rift. It seems that

[a]fter this fellow went back to Australia, he sent over £50 for passage for Seumas. But didn't Seumas' sisters write from Boston and they swearing that if I let their brother go off from them to Australia I'd never hear from them again. So Seumas went out to America to his sisters.

Nor was Arensberg oblivious to the symbiosis between the Irish town and countryside, particularly as expressed through rural-urban migration. He tells us that

[t]he sons and daughters who must travel are forced out of the closely knit group in which they once had their being. Yet, unless they emigrate beyond hope of call, they do not drop out of sight. The sentiments of years of close association do not die out. It has been a matter of pride and duty with the farm father to provide well for his children. Wherever he can, he has found them an opening. He has sent them into the towns, into the shops, the professions, the trades, and into the Church. As in nearly all modern countries today, there is in Ireland a great and constant flow of population from country to city. Much of this is made up of farm sons and daughters. (pp. 80–81)

Finally, it is worth mentioning that this founding text for anglophone Europeanist anthropology is *not* a community study at all. Rather, it draws its examples quite broadly from several of the communities within the region of North Clare.

MIGRATION IN THE SIERRA

In his study *The People of the Sierra*, Julian Pitt-Rivers details the in-migration to and out-migration from Alcalá. Thus, we are told that 11.7 percent of the resident population of the town was born elsewhere, as was 17.1 percent of the rural sector of the populace. Both statistics are then disaggregated into outsiders who came to Alcalá from less than fifty kilometers distance and those from more than fifty kilometers away (1961, 24–25). Rather than a social isolate, Alcalá is depicted as receiving and contributing both to the region's highly mobile pool of landless laborers as well as to the ranks of an independent entrepreneurial class of tradesmen, millers, and charcoal-burners. Even the local agriculturalists are often in motion within the region as they either lease or purchase new holdings (pp. 25–27).

Then, too, we are told,

> It may appear surprising that in a place which has a high birth-rate and a declining population there should be so many outsiders. The number of sons of the pueblo living elsewhere is certainly far greater, though it is not possible to know exact numbers. Prior to the Civil War, some went to America. Many went to Jerez during the last century. Today they go in all directions—wherever it is possible to make a living. Most of all have gone to the Campo de Gibraltar in recent years, where the end of international hostilities has brought a boom in its traditional activity, contraband. (p. 26)

While in *The People of the Sierra* Pitt-Rivers provided what is, arguably, anglophone Europeanist anthropology's quintessential and most influential little community study, it should be noted that its author subsequently became a cultural thematicist *par excellence*, and hence a precursor if not a practitioner of Europeanist symbolic anthropology. After elaborating topics such as honor and shame (1962), honor and grace (1992), and the bullfight (1993) in Mediterranean society, Pitt-Rivers can scarcely be regarded as wedded to the little-community perspective.

MIGRATION IN SPAIN

The third work we might consider is Michael Kenny's *A Spanish Tapestry: Town and Country in Castile* (1962a). Based upon field research conducted in the 1950s, the work divides its attention between the Sorian village of Ramosierra and the urban parish of San Martín in Madrid. There is a sense in which the comparison is more artificial than natural since Kenny makes no attempt to demonstrate specific links between village and the city. That is, despite the fact that many Ramosierrans have resettled in Madrid, we do not meet them in San Martín. Rather, Ramosierra is the prototypical Castilian village with Madrid serving as its urban metropolis.

Conversely, the research paradigm is scarcely designed to treat Ramosierra as a social isolate (after all, it shares the pages of the text with San Martín). Nor are the Ramosierrans described in self-sufficient terms. Rather, we are told that many reside in Madrid. They return regularly to the village, often for its annual patronal saint's festival. Ramosierra has also sent her sons and daughters abroad. Kenny states,

> Close contact is maintained between kin and friends separated physically by emigration. It was an emigrant's boast that anything which happened in Ramosierra, however insignificant, was known within three days in Vera Cruz.... (1962a, 43)

Kenny explores the feedback effects upon Ramosierra of money, ideas, and persons from both Madrid and the village's Latin American diaspora. It is the returned emigrant who advocates the introduction of more modern industrial and agricultural techniques. It is the returned emigrant who sometimes prevailed upon the local authorities to ameliorate the harsh political restrictions that characterized Franco's Spain. Nevertheless, we are also told that the emigrant's role and lot in Ramosierra were fraught with ambiguity. Thus,

> [t]here is a certain romantic allusion here to the clean-limbed, poor but honest emigrant who 'hits the town with five cents,' starts with some lowly task like selling newspapers, and builds himself up by sheer hard industry into a leading business tycoon. No doubt this picture contains an element of truth; the early emigrant's lot was almost certainly a hard struggle; but it is equally true that, once he was established abroad, ties of kinship and friendship prompted him and his kind to help those who followed in their footsteps. This 'self-made man' technique is highly applauded in the village, but it does not automatically carry with it any notable prestige. All returned emigrants are rather scornfully referred to as *Indianos*, and it is evident that they are by no means welcomed back to the village fold with open arms. Though their money and their donations may be accepted as a matter of course, the emigrant has to work hard to win his own acceptance; hence his enthusiastic plunging into village affairs and fiesta ritual, and his ingratiating ways and generosity in the bars. Mistrust of 'foreign ways' and the 'city slicker' mentality acquired in the towns and abroad account in part for this feeling, but one of the less publicized, though by no means weaker, characteristics of the Castilian—envy—is its real basis. (p. 44)

CONCLUSION

In this chapter I have questioned the absolute, as opposed to the relative, validity of depicting anglophone Europeanist anthropology as obsessed with the little-community-as-social-isolate study. We might have considered other ways in which any European community is open to external influences, for example, the community as historical precipitate (its temporal aperture) or the community within its region and nation (its spatial aperture). It is the rare monograph that eschews such concerns altogether, while others make them their central focus.

However, rather than belaboring my earlier points, I conclude by turning the issue on its head. That is, if we accept that the critics of the little-community-study methodology had some basis for their criticism (which I do), then it is interesting to question why the approach came to characterize Europeanist anthropology, at least during its middle phase (or from about 1950 to 1975).

I believe that the answer lies with conjunctural realities within the intellectual history of our discipline. However, I do not subscribe solely to the overly simplistic view (which I have espoused in print on occasion) that as anthropologists moved into Europe, and given the discipline's legacy of studying culturally exotic and small scale units (tribes, islands), we gravitated "naturally" to backwater little communities where our singular method of participant observation would be most efficacious. The view is not entirely erroneous, and possesses some explanatory value in a general sense that becomes considerable in particular cases. However, to my mind, the attraction of the little community emerged as much for theoretical reasons as for methodological or heuristic ones.

I refer to the particular conjunctural moment (in the early 1950s) when the structural-functional approach of British social anthropology commingled with the emerging interest in peasant studies, particularly as championed by Robert Redfield.[4] The former was obviously both a product and producer of the study of small-scale social units treated largely as social isolates in both time and space.

Redfield was articulating the concerns of a discipline faced with the evident disappearance of its traditional subject matter—primitive society. In urging the study of peasant society in its stead, he was issuing a call for considering twentieth-century human reality in its own terms. Redfield envisioned a folk-urban continuum, as well as great and little traditions—and both their articulation and interpretation. If his paradigms are sometimes overly mechanistic and subject to criticisms—for example, that the overconcern with cultural survivals in order to establish the folk end of the continuum can easily lead to neglect of contemporary influences within peasant communities—in Redfield's view peasantries were part-societies whose very existence *required* articulation with wider social and cultural realities (1960).

For the Europeanist anthropology of the day this commingling of intellectual trends was not without its tensions. The functionalist paradigm when employed in large-scale social contexts becomes unwieldy from a methodological standpoint and less convincing from an analytical one. The emergence of urban anthropology lay somewhere in the future and was contemplated with ambivalence by many of the anthropologists of the day. Redfield's treatment of Chan Kom seemed more satisfying than his analysis of Mérida (the same is true of Kenny's description of Ramosierra compared with his weaker treatment of San Martín). In short, Redfield's contemporaries placed much greater faith in, and applied more enthusiastic attention to, the folk end of Redfield's continuum.

It was about this time that anglophone Europeanist anthropology began to expand dramatically—driven largely by the selection of the little community settings as venues for field investigation, however else the remaining concerns of a particular study might be defined (and, as we have noted, those concerns could vary considerably).

Having stated all of the foregoing, I nevertheless would argue that while there were clear, if complex, conjunctural disciplinary reasons for *selecting* the little community, Europeanist anthropology did not *invent* it. In this period of deconstruction and concern with the invention of tradition, I believe that the point is important. In the current revisionist climate the legitimacy of employing a little-community perspective at all has been called into question. I believe that this is unfortunate, since the little community is the expression of its own reality and relevance within the European experience. It occupies discrete space within Europe's social and physical landscapes. It confers upon its residents a part, indeed in most cases a significant part, of their social identity. In short, it is important to the actors themselves and while it does not equate to their entire social universe it constitutes one of its major constellations.

Consequently, if it would be erroneous to continue to conduct vacuum-cleaner ethnographic research in the little community setting, confident, as we were when functionalism was ascendant, that once all of the pieces are assembled the organic whole will become apparent, it is equally absurd to abandon the little community altogether. Indeed, despite its subordination and even denigration, de facto, Europeanist anthropology has never entirely lost its fascination with the little community. I suspect that this will continue to be the case. I further believe that in the future any particular little community study will be criticized and evaluated less as the anachronistic choice in some kind of either/or process of elimination with other possible subjects for anthropological investigation and more in terms of the wisdom of its premises and goals and the extent to which they were realized.

NOTES

1. In 1971 Silverman returned to the community for a restudy. In a section called "Ten Years Later" she notes, "It soon became evident that the main sources of Montecastello's affluence were external" (1975, 214). During the 1960s many Montecastellani had worked in Common Market countries and tourism had penetrated the town. There was also a discernible commuter culture to new nearby factories and construction projects. In short, the accelerated movement of persons in and out of town had profoundly reconfigured its social reality.

2. The data on sibling sets were collected in the early 1960s. Surveying and genealogical reconstruction encompassed two generations of villagers. Hence the outcomes reflect both the contemporary residence and migration histories (or lack thereof) of respondents and their siblings, as well as those of the previous generation. For contemporaries only persons fifteen years of age and older were included, for the ascending generation persons deceased before their fifteenth birthday were excluded. The historical

baseline for the genealogical reconstruction of the latter would be about 1910. Thus, the sample details roughly one-half century of emigration from the two communities. The discrepancy in the size of the two samples reflects a methodological distinction. The fieldwork in Echalar was completed before research was initiated in Murélaga. In the household survey for Echalar, sibling set information was elicited only for the present and previous heir or heiress of household, whereas in Murélaga it was collected for the affines as well. I do not believe that inclusion of the affinal data from Echalar would change its overall migratory profile materially.

3. Neither, once having become involved in migration studies, have I ever escaped their clutches. Thus, I subsequently chose to work in South Italy in a community characterized by extensive transoceanic emigration, as well as migration to destinations within Italy and other Common Market countries, which led to publication of *Emigration in a South Italian Town: An Anthropological History* (1984). Nor was my purview limited to the donor or sending community perspective, since I coauthored a study entitled *Amerikanuak: Basques in the New World* (1975). I subsequently conducted field research among Basque and South Italian sugarcane cutters in North Queensland (1996).

4. Curiously, the critique of little-community studies rarely cites their configuring text. Based on lectures given in Uppsala, Sweden, in 1953, or when the anglophone monographs in Europeanist anthropology could still be counted on one hand, Redfield's *The Little Community*, like so many classical texts, is more often ignored or dismissed than read. I would defy anyone to contemplate it and then contend that the founding fathers of anglophone peasant studies viewed the little community as a social isolate to be understood solely in its own contemporary terms. Chapter headings alone capture the richness and breadth of Redfield's approach (1960, V). The reader is invited to consider the little community as:

I. A Whole
II. An Ecological System
III. Social Structure
IV. A Typical Biography
V. A Kind of Person
VI. An Outlook on Life
VII. A History
VIII. A Community within Communities
IX. A Combination of Opposites
X. Whole and Parts

CHAPTER 8

THEMES IN THE ANTHROPOLOGY OF IRELAND

Thomas M. Wilson
The Queen's University of Belfast

Anthropological research in Ireland can be dated from the ethnographic research of C. R. Browne and A. C. Haddon in the 1890s (see Haddon and Browne 1891–1893), but its modern period was initiated with the field research conducted from 1932 to 1934 by Conrad Arensberg and Solon Kimball in a rural and peripheral area of County Clare, on the western seacoast of Ireland. The publications that resulted from this anthropological research (Arensberg 1937; Arensberg and Kimball 1968), which focused on social and cultural stability and change in the lives of poor farmers and their neighbouring townspeople, became so influential in the general anthropology and sociology of Ireland that they set the standard by which much of the anthropology of Ireland was judged up to the 1980s. The template for rural ethnographic research became, in fact, the community-based model espoused by Arensberg and Kimball, in which kinship and social structure were examined as a means of testing the theoretical model of structural-functionalism (Wilson 1984). This theoretical paradigm had been developed by British anthropologists who conducted fieldwork in the far-flung and exotic areas of the early twentieth-century empires, but at the time of Arensberg and Kimball's research it had only been applied in a few community studies in North America. Arensberg and Kimball's field work in rural Ireland was motivated by their desire to bring an anthropological perspective to a modern nation which, if not quite industrialized or modernized in terms of 1930s Europe, was clearly one of the civilized societies at the fringe of Europe's metropolises.

Thus, ironically, the attempt by Arensberg and Kimball to modernize the field of social and cultural anthropology (which, in shorthand, amounts to British and American anthropology respectively) resulted in a long period of theoretical and methodological dormancy, in which the majority of anthropologists researching in Ireland "felt the need to explain their research as an extension, validation, contradiction or variation of the work of Arensberg and Kimball" (Kane et al. 1988, 97). In this period up to the early 1980s, with a few exceptions mentioned below, anthropologists tested the theory, methods, and empirical findings of the path-breaking research in Clare, but in so doing seemed to confuse the issues at hand. As a number of Irish scholars concluded in 1988: "Far from being coherent, the follow-up to Arensberg and Kimball has simply been repetitive, or fitfully genuflective. Rather than examining their theoretical approach and ethnography, researchers interested in Ireland have experienced the classic work initially as a centripetal force; their own findings are then presented as centrifugal extensions of the touchstone" (Kane et al. 1988, 98). This chapter is a review of the major themes in the anthropology of Ireland that emerged as extensions of this touchstone, or that seemed to craft alternative bases to the research of the last twenty years. It concludes by identifying some of the areas of current interest and concern in anthropological research in Ireland, in particular those that may be of comparative European interest.

For over a generation after the seminal Clare study, anthropological research in Ireland was dominated by the analysis of family roles, generational relations, inheritance, marriage patterns, and a range of aspects of formal and informal kinship and social structure. These studies were almost exclusively done in rural settings. From the early 1970s, however, a series of critiques of the methods and theory of the Arensberg and Kimball type of community study began to appear. Their common theme was the notion that anthropologists should not generalize to any great extent from the Clare study, which in their shared view was rooted in the time and place of Clare in the 1930s (for a discussion of the debates regarding the theoretical intentions of Arensberg and Kimball, see Wilson 1984). As the post-Second World War research in Ireland began to be published, anthropologists, while analyzing their locales in terms of the findings of their two anthropological ancestors, began to make tentative criticisms of Arensberg and Kimball's data and methods. The simple departure point for this mild but growing criticism was that the Clare study did not seem to account for behavioral variations and disparate social structural formations throughout the island. Thus, Gibbon (1973) criticized Arensberg and Kimball's historical methods, Messenger (1964b, 1968, 1969, 1983) identified a host of cultural values and political factors that were to be found on the Aran Islands off the west coast of Ireland, but that were not mentioned or were not emphasized in the Clare research, and Brody (1973) reviewed the many ways that traditional farm life and rural community values were breaking down in the face of modernization and economic marginalization in the west of Ireland. These critiques notwithstanding, the majority of the anthropological studies conducted in the twenty years after the war took the Arensberg and Kimball study as their baseline. Even as some questioned the community model set out by Arensberg and Kimball, other anthropologists and sociologists simply tested the conclusions of the Clare study by either chronicling social change in Clare itself (in essence updating Arensberg and Kimball's findings; see Cresswell 1969) or by following Arensberg and Kimball's "Irish countrymen" to Dublin (see Humphreys 1966).

The contradictions developing in the anthropology of Ireland in this period can perhaps be best illustrated by the slightly different tradition in ethnographic research that began to emerge in Northern Ireland's anthropology in the years after "the Troubles"[1] returned in 1969. This divergent trend was also based on community studies in the mold of that of Arensberg and Kimball, but although the initial community studies of Northern Irish villages and cityscapes focused on networks of kinship and social organizational relations, much like their counterparts in the Republic of Ireland, different results were being obtained precisely because the cultural values and social structure of Northern Ireland were, at least on the surface, markedly different. No matter how hard they may have tried, no ethnographer of Northern Ireland's localities could ignore the facts of social class, nationalism, and sectarianism. As a result, the community studies of Harris (1961, 1972); Leyton (1966, 1970, 1974, 1975); McFarlane (1979); and Bufwack (1982), among others, attempted to describe the social structure of local village life in Northern Ireland, but at the same time account for the divisiveness and friction that cross-cut all levels of Northern Irish society. In the anthropology of Northern Ireland it was, and it remains, impossible to understand local rural and urban communities without understanding ethnicity, sectarianism, national identities, class, and the overall importance of history in everyday life. This was apparent in the first ethnographies published on Northern Ireland. In fact, it was in the earlier anthropology of Northern Ireland that the origins of much of the applied anthropological focus of today's ethnographic research can be found (Donnan and McFarlane 1989).

DEPARTURES FROM THE "SACRED TEXTS"

Although the 1980s was a time that ushered in a number of new developments in the anthropology of Ireland, the strong traditions in methods, research interests, and theories begun by Arensberg and Kimball continued apace, if perhaps for no better reason than to provide straw men to be destroyed. Much of the ethnographic research of the 1970s began to appear in print near the end of that decade and into the first years of the next (although some scholars continued to express concern that the majority of anthropological research projects conducted in Ireland have not resulted in publication, see Kane et al. 1988). The themes of these publications represented major departures from the themes of the "sacred texts" of Arensberg and Kimball, but perhaps because of the traditional nature of the anthropology of Ireland, many writings continued to focus on the same type of questions and analysis as had been outlined in Clare. Although many anthropologists began to identify and examine the ways in which the small peasant communities of the west of Ireland were unlike those of Arensberg and Kimball's day, and in so doing tended to characterize rural Ireland as declining, or even dying (see, for example, Brody 1973; Scheper-Hughes 1979; Messenger 1983), just as many continued to look at the structures and functions of kinship, social organization, marriage, the family, and the conditions of work and production that kept villages stable, peaceful, and relatively traditional in their concerns (see, for example, Kane 1979; Taylor 1981; Buckley 1982; Bufwack 1982; Shanklin 1982). The only lively scholarly exchanges to appear in print in the anthropology of Ireland revolved around issues of family form and function (see, for example, Gibbon and Curtin 1976, 1983a, b) and rural social and political patrons and clients (see, for example, Gibbon and Higgins 1974, 1977; see also Shanklin 1980), which were clearly related to the intellectual groundwork set by Arensberg and Kimball.

Much of this debate on the history and structure of Irish families is significant beyond Ireland, and it provides one of many areas in the anthropology of Ireland that demonstrates the usefulness of anthropological research for discovering and comparing the wide range of social formations to be found elsewhere in Europe. In particular, the debates in Irish social history and ethnography over the changing form of the family since the early eighteenth century can inform wider European discussion of the historical depth and cultural constructions that compose "family" units everywhere in Europe. In fact, the mechanization of Irish agriculture, the patterns of emigration, and the suburbanization and urbanization of Ireland have been contributing factors in the changing definition of families throughout Ireland. This transformation in the structure and function of Irish families does not mean, however, that larger extended families are no longer an important force in Irish social life, but rather that the local and regional patterns of family and residence are factors of which all scholars and policymakers of contemporary Europe must be aware. Since the 1930s, anthropology has been at the forefront of efforts to describe and explain family variations in Ireland, efforts that highlight the shifting and contested nature of all notions of "normal" European family structures.

Such continuities in research aside, however, the late 1970s and early 1980s also witnessed the beginnings of new research agendas, which paralleled those of scholars in North America, Britain, and the rest of Europe. A series of critiques, overviews, and scholarly calls to arms began to appear; all in essence were attempting to reset the research agenda for Ireland, north and south (see, for example, Wilson 1984; Donnan and McFarlane 1986; Jenkins 1986; Kane et al. 1988; Curtin and Wilson 1989b; Peace 1989). The changes in anthropological interest and research designs were partly a reaction to the transformations that both Northern Ireland and the Irish Republic had experienced. Much of Ireland had become urbanized and suburbanized. The war raged in Northern

Ireland. Both Irelands had joined the European Community. Economic reces-
sion had led to the return of emigration as a panacea for Ireland's social ills.
National radio and television services expanded and grew in influence. Each
night the images and events of Europe and beyond were brought into the
kitchens and sitting rooms of Irish households, encouraging processes of secularization, modernization, and internationalization. Leaders of other European
countries and the European Union itself became as familiar to the Irish as their
own politicians. National educational reforms, access to new markets in continental Europe, and advances in information and communication technologies
weakened the traditional ties of church and politics, increasingly forcing Irish
people onto the European and world stages, and opening up Irish society to
the twin forces of secularization and modernization. As a result, it became
unthinkable for ethnographers to characterize rural villages as sociocultural
isolates. Thus, the revisionist trends in the anthropology of Ireland focused on
many of the ways in which rural communities were tied to social formations
and economic and political structures external to the locality. In short, anthropologists began to investigate the ways in which the people of Ireland's farms,
villages, towns, and cities were linked to local and national institutions, and
they began to examine the regional and national processes of social change. As
a result, a boom in anthropological writing occurred, which included studies
of government and politics (Bax 1973, 1975; Komito 1984; Wilson 1989a), religion and churches (Eipper 1986; Taylor 1989), colonialism (Taylor 1980a, b),
urbanization (Gmelch 1977), migration (Gmelch 1986b; Gmelch and Gmelch
1985), rural industrialization and development (Kane 1977; Ruane 1989), social
and economic history (Messenger 1975; Vincent 1983), ethnic boundaries
(Larsen 1982a, b), and minorities (Gmelch 1986b).

SOCIAL CHANGE IN IRELAND AND NEW MODELS FOR ANTHROPOLOGY

The wide range of anthropological research interests in Ireland today, which
mark a break with many of the models that so dominated the field for fifty
years, is evidenced in two recent collections of ethnographic case studies. These
books, which deal with social change at local community levels in the countryside (Curtin and Wilson 1989b) and in the towns and cities (Curtin et al. 1993a)
of all Ireland, include essays from anthropologists from Ireland, the United
Kingdom, Canada, and the United States, are intended as textbooks, and have
been adopted in Irish universities as what might be seen as new models for
anthropological research and writing. Their chapters are a persuasive if only a
partial answer to the questions regarding relevance and applicability that were
posed by other scholars in the past (for example, Wilson 1984; Kane et al. 1988).
They and many other European and North American anthropologists have created many new research agendas in Ireland, squarely placing the anthropology
of Ireland within a variety of mainstream concerns of the field.

Anthropologists researching in Ireland today are concerned with issues of urban unemployment (Howe 1989a, 1989b, 1990; Blacking et al. 1989; McLaughlin 1989); rituals and religion (Crozier 1989; Szuchewycz 1989; Taylor 1989a; McFarlane 1989, 1994); international frontiers and sovereignty (Vincent 1991; Wilson 1993b); women's roles and rights in society (Gaetz 1993; LeMaster 1993; McLaughlin 1989; McCann 1994); the symbolic definitions to nation and state (Shanks 1994; Wilson 1994b); political violence and the state (Vincent 1989; Sluka 1989, 1992a, b; Feldman 1991); political rituals and symbolism (Cecil 1993; Wilson 1994b); suburban life and globalized culture (Varenne 1993a); tourism and rural development (Curtin and Varley 1989); ethnicity and minority rights and movements (Vincent 1993; Donnan 1994); intellectuals and the constructions of national culture (Sheehan 1993); consumer culture (Curtin and Ryan 1989; Wilson 1993c); and local and national history and historiography (Silverman 1989; Wilson 1990b; Silverman and Gulliver 1992; Vincent 1992). As impressive a review as this compendium of interests and achievements is, it is not complete. It serves in this chapter as an introduction to the depth and breadth of anthropological scholarship in and on Ireland. Anthropological research in Ireland has had its ups and downs, but it is alive and well, and willing and able to be involved in the scholarly effort to understand behavior and values in every walk and level of Irish life (for a longer review of the stereotypes and revisionist positions in Irish anthropology than this chapter allows, see Curtin et al. 1993b). There is no better example of the relevance and contemporary value of anthropological research for Ireland, and by extension in Europe as a whole, than in the anthropological analysis of social and political problems and policy.

Contemporary anthropology in Ireland has begun to address many of the concerns that involve anthropologists worldwide. This has been especially true in Ireland's towns and cities (Curtin et al. 1993b), where a variety of forces has brought the problems of poverty, homelessness, disease, racism, sexism, the environment, urban sprawl, and increased levels of violence to the forefront of everyday cultural consciousness. Anthropologists in Ireland were slow to react to the ways people have adapted to these problems, in part for the reasons outlined above but also due to the general nature of the field everywhere, but they are now investigating the impact and development of these problems in a variety of local contexts throughout the island. Although it may be fair to say that anthropologists in Northern Ireland have been focused longer on issues of social disintegration and their relationships to public policy formation (for a review of this, see Donnan and McFarlane 1989), the anthropological concern with matters of policy is now an all-island one. One of the longest-studied issues in urban life, and still one of the most serious in Irish towns and cities, has been the pressures young people face because of their rapidly changing economies and polities. Jenkins (1983) and Bell (1990) have chronicled youth culture in urban Northern Ireland, where young adults not only have to face the day-to-day dilemmas of unemployment, peer pressures, sectarianism, and deteriorating cities, but are also victims and agents of war.

YOUTH IN NORTHERN IRELAND

It is in the study of youth and their problems that anthropology yet again can provide valuable insights into policy construction, implementation, and administration. Although Northern Irish young people, especially in the ghettos of Belfast and Derry, may appear on the surface to be different from other youth cultures elsewhere in Europe, largely because of extreme religious sectarianism and the war violence that has been part of their daily lives, these differences may be illusory. Ethnic and racial prejudice and the violence of drugs and organized crime that are commonplace in many of the capitals of Europe may be little different in form from the patterns of urban street culture in Northern Ireland. Ethnographers in Northern Ireland can provide the information to social policymakers regarding both the national and the international dimensions to youth cultures, and the ways in which Irish young people have specific local needs, pressures, and desires. For example, unemployment is a common cause of youth unrest throughout Europe, but Irish and British nationalism are variants of identity among Northern Irish youth that are peculiar to Ireland. Nevertheless, they are aspects of youth identity that can be addressed in modified and integrated educational environments. The ways in which national and European social welfare policies have an impact in neighborhoods in Belfast, and are understood and accepted or rejected by locals, is one of the principal avenues by which anthropologists can aid in the building of a general and applied social science of the European Union (see, for example, Cecil 1989; Ogle 1989).

The violence that is an everyday aspect of youth culture in Northern Ireland does not seem to be as prevalent in the Republic of Ireland (although this remains a matter of more empirical inquiry), but the debilitating pressures of being educated, then unemployed, in a transforming national society that is itself becoming more marginalized in an expanding Europe are experiences shared by all Irish young people. The class dimension to the travails of Irish youth is but one factor that exacerbates the problems for some, as does the inherent sexism of a patriarchal Irish society (Gaetz 1992, 1993). Although emigration continues to serve a depressurizing function in Ireland, in particular for many young people, the traditional receiving countries such as Great Britain, the United States, and Australia are instituting measures to block continued Irish immigration. The movement of Irish youth in future may well be to the continent, where they will swell the ranks of unemployed and put pressure on the labor markets of other European nations.

"DOING THE DOUBLE"—SOCIAL POLICY AND ITS EVERYDAY EFFECTS

Anthropological research in Ireland serves as an example of the ways in which the realities of local social and cultural life often do not match the ideal constructions of national societies as seen from the spectrum of European centers, be they national capitals, core regions in states, or the key institutions and bodies of the European Union in Brussels and Strasbourg. The "democratic deficit" that seemingly marks the powerful apparatus of the European Union, where the only elected body, the European Parliament, has relatively little power in comparison to other Union bodies, affects the overall social science of the European Union. The anthropology of the European Union is small in scale and influence when compared with the vast literature in political science and economics on the European Union and integration, most of which is based on top-down and center-out perspectives on national trends. Policies determined in metropolises distant from the localities of Ireland often have a variety of effects on Irish everyday life that are both unintended and unnoticed by policymakers. To many Irish people, for example, national and European Union economic policies provide a variety of changing contexts for local initiatives. This is especially apparent in the informal and black economies, wherein any amount of statistical analysis cannot fail to omit a wide range of productive economic activities that define many local communities' notions of work, wealth, and class. For example, Howe (1989a, 1989b, 1990) has documented the many ways in which the Belfast unemployed make a living through a variety of legal and illegal actions. Their "doing the double" is an apt term for claiming social welfare benefits, sometimes in more than one location, while at the same time working in such occupations as laborers, taxi drivers, thieves, baby sitters, and bouncers. People in the borderlands between Ireland and the United Kingdom have made veritable fortunes through smuggling, especially in agricultural goods, tobacco, alcohol, and consumer durables. The many large bungalows and holiday homes that have been constructed along the Irish border not only reflect the wealth that has been made by large-scale smugglers, but they also indicate the thriving construction trade in the borderlands, where locals collect the dole (unemployment benefits) in both the Republic of Ireland and Northern Ireland, while at the same time working a full week off the books at construction. Smuggling and welfare fraud are often difficult for social scientists to document, but they are so essential to local community life that they are elemental to any ethnographic study of a community (for a review of aspects of the commodification of life at the Irish border, see Wilson 1993c). Because of the nature of participant observation, still the mainstay of anthropological research, it is all but impossible for ethnographers to avoid understanding the local informal economy. As such, ethnographers can do much to fill in the gaps in the social science of public policy in Europe, precisely because of their perspective from the "ground up."

Other problems in the social fabric of Ireland are also drawing the attention of ethnographers, many of whom wish to apply their research findings in order to alleviate the conditions of the poor and dispossessed, whose ranks are perceived by many Irish people to be on the rise. Ethnographic methods, in particular participant observation, allow anthropologists to describe the experiences of traveling people (Helleiner 1993) and homeless men (O'Sullivan 1993) in ways that enable readers to experience, if only vicariously, the everyday pressures to survive, in a society that prides itself on its culture, civilization, and charity. And while Irish social environments suffer from a variety of human forces, so too does the physical environment, on an island that is increasingly becoming one of the tourist havens for the people of the European Union precisely because of its traditional ways and unspoiled environment. Urban planners, government leaders, industrial developers, and environmental lobbies are engaged in what seems to some to be a never-ending debate over the future of the Irish landscape, a battle of wills in which some anthropologists have been active campaigners (Milton 1993, 1994; Peace 1993). These anthropologists, like many of their colleagues, are adding to a scholarly movement that is also a movement of concerned citizens who want to use their research in ways that matter to the quality of the lives of the people among whom they live and work.

New social actors are changing the configurations of policymaking in Ireland and Northern Ireland, where top-down decision making is being challenged by a wide range of interest groups, lobbies, concerned community councils, and new issue-oriented political parties. Traditional forms of politics are being transformed in Ireland precisely because many local communities and groups of citizens are aware of alternative avenues in the construction of the social policies that directly affect them. There are many reasons for this relatively recent awareness of the issues and roles of public policy in the daily lives of Ireland's citizens, and in the research agendas of Ireland's anthropologists, but one of the most important agents for change in this regard has been the European Union.

THE EUROPEAN UNION

Relative to other research and publishing, and despite the importance of the European Union, there has been very little research done by anthropologists throughout Europe on the institutions and policies of the European Union, partly due to the ethnographer's emphasis on local communities and the methodological difficulties of conducting field research from a locality up and out to the centers of political and economic decision making that are external to the community being studied. It may surprise some, however, that the anthropological investigation of various aspects of the European Union, in the ways its policies are experienced at local levels, and in the ways it is defining and transforming a wide range of social identities, is becoming a strong theme in anthropological research in Ireland. This interest is resulting in a growing literature on both "Europe" in Ireland and on an anthropology of the European Union in general (see, for example, Dilley 1989; Sheehan 1991; Shutes 1991, 1993; Wilson 1993a, 1993b, 1993c). This emphasis has much to do with contesting notions of "being" or "becoming" European in Ireland. "Europe" in the guise of the European Union is very important to many Irish people, and thus is important in anthropology because of the discipline's goal of chronicling and understanding the social and cultural formations to everyday life. It is far from an exaggeration to say that the European Union has become an integral factor in everybody's daily life in Ireland, North and South, and it is perceived as such by Irish people. This is due to a number of factors that, although not peculiar to Ireland in the European Union, have given Ireland a unique configuration of "Europeanness."

There are many elements in the "European" identities that Irish people have either adopted or rejected. Many Irish people in an economy that has long been dominated by farming and the food industries have benefited from the Common Agricultural Policy. There is a rich history of many ties to what is perceived to be the best of European culture. Among them are the connections fostered by emigration in the modern era; political republicanism shared with continental partners; the traditions of Christianity; colonialism and postcolonialism; and a shared Celtic past. Many Irish look to the European Union as a possible arena within which to solve the problems of nationalism and sectarianism in Northern Ireland. Many others deny a European identity precisely because the European Union may help to change the constitutional character of both the Republic of Ireland and Northern Ireland. Whatever the cause, Irish people are aware of the moves originating at local, national, and European levels, to have them one day acknowledging their European identity. Some welcome this, others oppose it. But the debate over European identity is growing in Ireland, and may be raging in the very near future when and if the peace dividend in Northern Ireland demands a larger role with the European Union, or when the subsidies to the Irish Republic are curtailed, or whenever the issues of sovereignty are raised in the British parliament. This chapter has suggested that anthropological research in Ireland has developed a number of identity crises over the years (see also Wilson 1994a). One thing is certain, however. The anthropology of the European Union in Ireland is already established, and will be both witness and analyst of the future impact of Europe in Ireland.

CONCLUSION

Although anthropological research in Ireland has increasingly turned to the study of public policy formation, its most important contribution to comparative European ethnology may be in the analysis of policy impact and reception at local levels. Ethnographic research provides long-term chronicles of social and political change, from perspectives that seek to privilege local reactions to ideas and actions that originate in distant capital cities. In the Irish context, the dictates of policy have had a wide range of effects on youth culture, the informal and illegal economies, and new social and political movements like feminism and environmentalism, among many others. A full understanding of the ways in which policies are articulated and internalized in local community life is necessary to any social science of law and politics in Ireland and in wider Europe. Because of their use of qualitative and quantitative methods, over relatively long periods of time, in localities, in order to contextualize the objective outcomes of policy within personalized, interested, and symbolically charged local cultures and communities, anthropologists may be in the best position among all social scientists to provide the information necessary for the understanding of wider European social formations, not least of which is the European Union, in the everyday lives of Europeans.

NOTE

1. "The Troubles" is the Irish term for the civil and terrorist war that has been waged in Northern Ireland since 1969, and that, at the time of writing this chapter, is in a state of cease-fire.

CHAPTER 9

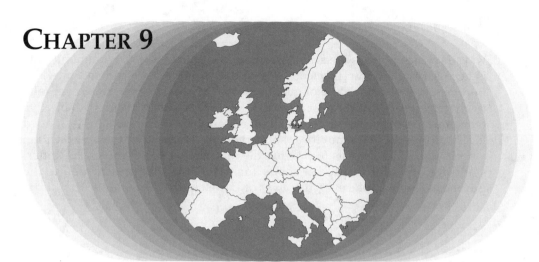

A FORTY-YEAR RETROSPECTIVE OF THE ANTHROPOLOGY OF FORMER YUGOSLAVIA

Linda A. Bennett
University of Memphis

Anthropological research conducted in former Yugoslavia has undergone substantial change over the past forty years.[1] Trends in the nature of this work are organized in this chapter into three periods: the late 1950s through the 1970s, the 1980s, and the 1990s. These designations are based upon: (1) the relationship between anthropologists from the United States and former Yugoslavia in carrying out anthropological studies; (2) the relative emphasis upon applied issues; (3) specific topics of research; and (4) responses by anthropologists to the traumatic developments and terrible events since 1991 due to the war. The primary focus of the chapter is on work in sociocultural anthropology, while also encompassing some of the recent research in biological or biocultural anthropology. Although I deal mainly with studies conducted by American anthropologists either predominantly on their own or in concert with colleagues in former Yugoslavia, I present some of the work of anthropologists in former Yugoslavia, especially those studies that have been published in English.[2] In addition, I include several recent studies conducted by other Europeans that are published in English.

PERIOD 1: 1950S–1970S

While the beginning point of the chapter is forty years ago, my own vantage point goes back twenty-six years. In 1970, at the onset of my doctoral studies, I decided to become a "Yugoslavist" anthropologist. I made this decision mainly on the basis of observations made during two weeks spent in Slovenia and Croatia in 1970 and upon reading about post-World War II Yugoslav society and its "mosaic" of cultures (e.g., Domenach and Pontault 1963). As I immersed myself in publications from anthropological fieldwork conducted since the Second World War, I envisioned a research project that seemed within the tradition of ongoing research. I planned a study of socialization patterns and decision making among young people growing up in a small island town (Vela Luka on Korčula, Croatia) under the impact of macro-level economic and educational changes in the wider society.

This was a prime time to begin fieldwork in former Yugoslavia; several anthropologists had just completed or were in the midst of conducting dissertation research representing communities in all six republics. As I began my initial review of studies published in English, three earlier publications were particularly useful for getting oriented to the field. First, Joel Halpern and Barbara Kerewsky-Halpern, who began conducting fieldwork in 1953, had published books and articles on Orašac in the Šumadija region of Serbia. The first edition of *A Serbian Village* was published in 1957 (Halpern) and described day-to-day life, the life cycle, and the annual ritual life of the village, as well as villagers' relationship to the outside world. It addressed changes in Orašac from the nineteenth century through 1955; a subsequent edition was published in 1966 and traced further changes since 1955. Halpern and Kerewsky-Halpern published a book in 1972 on their work in Orašac entitled *A Serbian Village in Historical Perspective* (revised edition 1986).

Second, Vera Stein Erlich's *Family in Transition: A Study of 300 Yugoslav Villages* was based upon interviews collected before the Second World War. It was published in English in 1966 and was particularly informative since it offered cross-cultural comparisons between family structures characteristic of villages in several regions of former Yugoslavia: Macedonia, Sandžak, Bosnia and Herzegovina, Serbia, Montenegro, Vojvodina, Croatia, Slavonia, and Dalmatia. It remains a very relevant data source.

Third, Eugene A. Hammel's study *Alternative Social Structures and Ritual Relations in the Balkans*, published in 1968, analyzed social structure and ritual relations in Serbia, eastern Montenegro, and southwestern Macedonia. A major focus of this work was on the structure, function, and continuity of godparenthood (*kumstvo*) in these parts of the Balkans. It, too, took a comparative perspective across different regions and generations.

Each of these anthropologists placed their observations and conclusions within a clear historical context, acknowledging the abundant sociocultural changes that had taken place in former Yugoslavia due to overwhelming political and economic transformations in the nineteenth and twentieth centuries.

During the early post-World War II period, considerable ethnological research was being conducted in the various Yugoslav republics. These include, for example, the work of Milovan Gavazzi in Zagreb; Milenko Filipović in Bosnia-Herzegovina; Borivoje Drobnjaković in Serbia; Boris Orel in Slovenia; Jovan Vukmanović in Montenegro; and Branislav Rušić in Macedonia (Halpern 1970).

By the late 1960s several American anthropologists had conducted dissertation research in former Yugoslavia. Three were Hammel's students at the University of California, Berkeley, two of whom did their research in Serbia and paid particular attention to the role of urbanization and industrialization within two different communities. Bette Stubing Denich conducted her fieldwork in Titovo Užice, Serbia, completing her dissertation in 1969, on *Social Mobility and Industrialization in a Yugoslav Town*. Second, Andrei Simic finished his dissertation in 1970 and published a book in 1973 based on his fieldwork conducted in Belgrade, entitled *The Peasant Urbanites: A Study of Rural-Urban Mobility in Serbia*. William G. Lockwood, a third student of Hammel's, carried out his fieldwork in western Bosnia, focusing on the peasant marketplace. He completed his dissertation in 1970 and in 1975 published a book entitled *European Moslems: Economy and Ethnicity in Western Bosnia*. Lockwood has published several articles growing out of his research in western Bosnia, with a particular focus on issues of kinship among Bosnian Muslims (e.g., 1972a and 1974).

During the 1960s and early 1970s four other American anthropologists also conducted dissertation research in other parts of the country. Irene Winner did her fieldwork in a Slovenian village, finishing her dissertation at the University of North Carolina, Chapel Hill, in 1967. *A Slovenian Village: Zerovnica* was published in 1971.

Second, Christopher Boehm, a graduate student at Harvard University who carried out fieldwork in Montenegro, completed his dissertation in 1972, entitled *Montenegrin Ethical Values: An Experiment in Anthropological Method*. Since then, Boehm has published two books based on his Montenegrin studies: *Montenegrin Social Organization and Values* (1983) and *Blood Revenge: The Enactment and Management of Conflict in Montenegro and Other Tribal Societies* (1984).

Third, David Rheubottom, a graduate student at the University of Rochester, conducted fieldwork in the Republic of Macedonia and completed his dissertation in 1970, entitled *A Structural Analysis of Conflict and Cleavage in Macedonian Domestic Groups*. And fourth, Brian C. Bennett did his fieldwork in the community of Sutivan on the island of Brač in Croatia, completing his dissertation at the University of Southern Illinois in 1972, and his book entitled *Sutivan: A Dalmatian Village in Social and Economic Transition* was published in 1974. His later research led to writings on socio-economic changes in former Yugoslavia, particularly in Dalmatia (e.g., B. Bennett 1976, 1979).

During the late 1970s, Frank A. Dubinskas, a graduate student at Stanford University, conducted fieldwork in yet another part of former Yugoslavia, Slavonia in eastern Croatia. His dissertation entitled *Performing Slavonian Folklore: The Politics of Reminiscence and Recreating the Past* was completed in 1983. With a strong focus on folklore and especially musical performance, Dubinskas also stressed historical influences on contemporary village and town life in Slavonia. He later published an analysis of the role of drinking in the singing of songs in Slavonia (1992).

Before I left for the field in 1973, I was able to meet with Lockwood, Boehm, Denich, and Rheubottom. Shortly after I arrived in Zagreb, I had a chance to meet with anthropologists Milovan Gavazzi, Dunja Rihtman-Auguštin, Olga Supek, Sanja Aleksandra Lazarević, linguist Rudolf Filipović, and sociologist Miro Mihovilović, among others, and I was privileged to visit Vera Erlich in her home in Zagreb. Thus, I was fortunate to have contact with quite a number of the anthropologists who had already influenced my way of viewing anthropology in former Yugoslavia through their writings.

Two major themes seem to characterize this period of anthropological research. The first and quite obvious one is the impact of political-economic-social change in the post-World War II period under the new communist system on the lives of people living in a wide variety of communities (from the urban capital city of Belgrade to villages throughout the various republics). The role of the "peasant worker," for example, garnered particular attention during this time (e.g., Lockwood 1973).

In addition, anthropologists such as Hammel, Rheubottom, and Boehm stressed continuity and change in kinship and social structure. As part of this focus, considerable interest was placed on the continuity and change in the *zadruga* household-family structure throughout the quite distinct Yugoslav lands, and on historical evidence for its differential form, function, and vitality. For example, Erlich, Hammel, and Rheubottom published chapters regarding the zadruga in Brynes's volume on *Communal Families in the Balkans* (Erlich 1976; Hammel 1972 and 1976; and Rheubottom 1976).

The topic of the *zadruga* was, of course, addressed by anthropologists in former Yugoslavia as well. For example, building upon the work and tradition of Milovan Gavazzi's work on the structure and function of zadrugas during the nineteenth and twentieth centuries (Gavazzi 1960), in the 1960s several anthropologists began research on eight regions of former Yugoslavia (including, for example, the town of Hvar on the island of Hvar in Croatia, the district of Jastrebarsko in western Croatia, the District of Valpovo in northeastern Slavonia, and the District of Subotica in Vojvodina), with the results of their work published in 1992 (Barbarić et al.). Over the past forty years anthropologists have continued to address the topic of the *zadruga* but have also addressed new issues. For example, during a later period Petrović reported a study of individual property rights of women in *zadruge* from several regions in former Yugoslavia (1991).

This initial post-World War II period of anthropological fieldwork by American anthropologists in former Yugoslavia could be described as (1) being conducted primarily by individual anthropologists having cooperative but not strongly collaborative ties to anthropologists in former Yugoslavia in the sense of conducting joint research; (2) not explicitly applied in its orientation; and (3) focused on the general topics of culture change since the Second World War, variation in social organization and social structure over time and space, and contemporary folklore in light of its historical past.

Period 2: 1980s

COLLABORATIVE WORK

It would be misleading to suggest that a totally new way of doing anthropology in former Yugoslavia emerged during the 1980s, but there is solid evidence to suggest that substantial changes did occur. Generally speaking, there was more explicit collaborative research, as was also the case in other European societies (L. Bennett 1991). Additionally, greater emphasis was placed upon applied studies, and—in addition to a continuing interest in culture change, folklore, and social structure—many new topics of research emerged.

These developments were, in part, influenced by new regulations in the former Yugoslav republics that were passed in the early 1970s requiring foreign anthropologists (and other scientists) to have a sponsoring institution in Yugoslavia. As a result, it was virtually impossible to do fieldwork without sponsorship and formal authorization. Foreign anthropologists who came into the country at an earlier time would more than likely have visited, at the very least, ethnologists and other colleagues in the republic where they were planning to do their fieldwork in order to obtain pertinent background information on the region, to establish social and collegial ties, and possibly to get entrée into the community of study. However, the resulting relationship was not typically formalized into collaborative projects. By 1973 a formal relationship had to be established in order for the foreign anthropologist to have the authority to collect field data. I believe this was one of many factors leading to an increase in intentional collaborations between anthropologists in that country and in the United States.

Another critical factor was the development and expansion of different fields of anthropology within former Yugoslavia. A number of professionals such as Dunja Rihtman-Auguštin, former director of the (now) Institute for Ethnology and Folklore Research, and Pavao Rudan, director of the (now) Institute for Anthropological Research, both in Zagreb, were very open to collaborative ties. Anthropologists in Zagreb, Belgrade, Ljubljana, and Sarajevo—as well as other urban centers—were clearly interested in working with anthropologists outside the country as well as within the country.

A clear sign of the movement toward more formal collaboration is a cross-over in graduate study that began to take place between anthropologists in former Yugoslavia and the United States during the 1980s. At least two anthropology students from Zagreb studied in the United States: Olga Supek, with William Lockwood and Sherry Ortner at the University of Michigan, and Jasna Čapo, with Eugene Hammel at the University of California, Berkeley (1990). Supek's dissertation entitled *A Hundred Years of Bread and Wine: Culture, History, and Economy of a Croatian Village* was completed in 1982 and led to further publications such as her article on the contrasts between peasant and capitalist worldviews during the 1930s (1989). Čapo's dissertation was completed in 1990, entitled *Economic and Demographic History of Peasant Households on a Croatian Estate*. More recently, Supek and Čapo have published a joint article drawing upon demographic and family data to elucidate the impact of emigration in parts of rural Croatia (1994).

Margaret Lethbridge-Çejku—from the United States—did her master's and doctoral studies in biological anthropology in Zagreb with Pavao Rudan as her mentor. She wrote her dissertation through the Institute for Anthropological Research, University of Zagreb, on *Osteoarthritis of the Hands in a Rural Population: Anthropological Research on the Island of Brač, Croatia* (1995). At least three other American anthropologists conducted their doctoral dissertation studies in Croatia during the 1980s. Mary Kay Gilliland, a graduate student at the University of California, San Diego, carried out research in 1982–1983 on women, family, culture change, and persistence in an Eastern Croatian town and village on the Bosnian border, in affiliation with the Department of Sociology, Philosophy Faculty, University of Zagreb. Her dissertation, entitled *The Maintenance of Family Values in a Yugoslav Town*, was completed in 1986 and led to several publications (e.g., Olsen 1989 and 1990). In the late 1980s, Maria Olujic, a student of Hammel's at the University of California, Berkeley, did her fieldwork in the region of Imotski, the Dalmatian hinterland of Croatia, on migration before and after World War II. Her dissertation is titled *People on the Move: Migration History of a Peasant Croatian Community* (1991). During this decade, she also wrote about the gender asymmetry in former Yugoslavia in spite of state reforms following the Second World War that were ostensibly to provide legal equality for women (1990).

Paul Gordiejew, a doctoral student at the University of Pittsburgh, began his fieldwork on Jewish ethnic identity and ritual in Belgrade and Sarajevo as well as other parts of former Yugoslavia. He completed his dissertation entitled *The Effects of History, Imposition, and Disjuncture on the Phases of Yugoslav Jewish Ethnicity* in 1993.

With the reported appearance of the Virgin Mary in the peasant village of Medjugorje in southeastern Herzegovina in 1981, considerable attention has been brought to this part of former Yugoslavia. Millions of pilgrims have traveled to Medjugorje from throughout the world. Mart Bax, an anthropologist from the Netherlands, began fieldwork in Medjugorje in 1983 on politics and religion as evidenced through the Medjugorje phenomenon (1987, 1993). Since he continued his work there into the 1990s after the outbreak of war, the issue of violence became intertwined with politics and religion in his analysis and writing. In this work, published as a book entitled *Medjugorje: Religion, Politics, and Violence in Rural Bosnia* (1995), Bax argues that in the context of the war, the apparitions "not only had to do with intra-church discord, but also with long-standing disputes and conflicts among segments of the local population" (1995, xviii).

INTERNATIONAL CONTACTS

Several developments expanded the international ties of anthropologists in former Yugoslavia during this period. Planning for and holding the 1988 International Congress of Anthropological and Ethnological Sciences in Zagreb stimulated considerable contact between anthropologists in the former Yugoslavia and those from many other countries. Close to one hundred countries were represented by the participants at the Congress.

Second, the annual course on "Anthropology and Health" was held in Dubrovnik at the InterUniversity Centre (IUC) for Postgraduate Studies since 1984 until the IUC was brutally shelled in 1991 and experienced extensive destruction. It has been rebuilt and is again being used for IUC programs. During the 1980s particularly, the IUC was considered to be a "neutral" meeting ground for people from East and West, and colleagues from around the entire country of former Yugoslavia regularly attended meetings there. I met many anthropologists and other professionals from throughout the country during the 1980s at the IUC. The Anthropology and Health Course of the IUC continues to be a major forum for anthropologists from a variety of countries for collaboration with anthropologists from Yugoslavia. In 1992, after one year when it could not be held because of the war, the course was held in Motovun on the Istrian Peninsula. It is now held annually on the island of Hvar.

An annual School of Biological Anthropology has been held in Zagreb each year for over two decades, providing another forum for international contacts.

COLLABORATIVE PROJECTS

Since 1983, the Bilateral Project of the Smithsonian Institution and the Institute for Medical Research and Occupational Health, Department of Anthropology (now the Institute for Anthropological Research) in Zagreb, with Pavao Rudan as the Principal Investigator, has been a major impetus for collaborative research in biocultural anthropology in Croatia (e.g., L. Bennett et al. 1983; and Rudan et al. 1987b). As a result of over a decade of joint study of biological and cultural microdifferentiation among rural populations on the middle Dalmatian islands and hinterland, a great number of collaborative articles and books have been published: for example, Rudan et al. (e.g., 1987a and 1987b, 1988) on isolation by distance in Middle Dalmatia; Smolej et al. (1987) on physiological variation and population structure on the island of Korčula; Sujoldžić et al. (1989) on migration within the island of Korčula and on linguistic variation in Middle Dalmatia historically and currently (1991), and isonomy and population structure on Korčula (1993); L. Bennett et al. (1989) on demographic structure and linguistic variation on the island of Korčula and the Pelješac Peninsula; and Zegura et al. on the population structure of the Pelješac Peninsula (1990) and on genetics, linguistics, and ethnohistory of the island of Brač (1991).

In addition to the project with anthropologists in the United States, the Zagreb group has worked jointly with anthropologist Andre Chaventre in

Paris in biocultural fieldwork on northern Dalmatian islands such as Olib and Silba (e.g., Sujoldžić et al. 1990) and on the island of Krk (e.g, Sujoldžić et al. 1992).

These two bilateral projects and others based at the Institute for Anthropological Research in Zagreb have led to a large number of publications continuing into the current decade: Mary Kay Gilliland (Olsen), Sanja Špoljar-Vržina, and psychiatrist Vlasta Rudan have worked jointly on a number of projects having to do with gender, family, migration, (e.g., Olsen et al. 1991; Olsen and V. Rudan 1992; V. Rudan and Olsen [1992]). Špoljar-Vržina has published migration data for Hvar (1992) and Korčula (1993), as part of the continuing analyses of population structure by the Institute in Middle Dalmatia.

APPLIED RESEARCH

Studies conducted by some anthropologists in former Yugoslavia during the 1980s also focused on clearly applied issues, especially in health areas. For example, in 1989 Deborah Padgett carried out a study of depressive morbidity among diabetic patients in Zagreb (1993). Over the decade I conducted alcoholism treatment research in Zagreb, Belgrade, and Ljubljana (L. Bennett 1985) and historical research on the temperance movement in former Yugoslavia (L. Bennett 1992). Robert Hayden conducted research on the use of workers' courts in former Yugoslavia (1985 and 1986) and on the impact of traffic safety legislation and the reception of the mandatory seatbelt laws in Yugoslavia (1989).

This trend of increasing applied studies has advanced considerably into the 1990s in response to the tragic outcomes of the war, especially with respect to work with refugees and displaced persons.

NEW TYPES OF PUBLICATIONS

During the late 1980s, work toward the publication of the volume on Europe (Central, Western, and Southeastern Europe) of the *Encyclopedia of World Cultures* was undertaken and published in 1992 (L. Bennett). Several contributions dealt with cultures or regions of former Yugoslav cultures: Slovenians (Portis-Winner); Croats (Čapo, Gelo, Macan, and Supek); Bosnian Muslims (Gratton); Serbs (Wagner); Dalmatians (Olujic); Slav Macedonians (Garber); Montenegrins (Wagner); and Vlachs (Sujoldžić). Details about demography, language, history, settlements, economy, kinship, marriage, family, sociopolitical organization, and religion and expressive culture are covered in these contributions.

Several anthropologists in former Yugoslavia have written about developments in the discipline of anthropology there. For example, in a volume of

Etnološki Pregled (*Ethnological Review*) published in Belgrade in 1988, five contributions from anthropologists reviewed developments in ethnology since 1945 in Serbia (Pavković, Bandić, and Kovačević); Croatia (Supek); Slovenia (Slavec); Bosnia and Herzegovina (Beljkašić-Hadžidedić); and Macedonia (Konstantinov). In a 1991 issue of *Studia Ethnologica* published in Zagreb, Čapo contributed an article on Croatian ethnology and its approach to culture. In addition to a continuing interest in research that draws upon considerable historical data to reconstruct cultural patterns of the nineteenth and earlier twentieth centuries, much of the domestic research focused on developments immediately at hand. A good example is Prica's analysis of the discovery and excavation of the Manduševac fountain in Ban Josip Jelačić Square in the middle of Zagreb (previously Republic Square) in 1986 and the subsequent outpouring of paper money into the fountain as an expression of "ritual manipulation of money" (1991, 219). These cited articles in *Etnološki Pregled* and *Studia Ethnologica* are published in English and reflect a much more extensive and valuable resource on the status of ethnology throughout most of former Yugoslavia prior to the war.

Anthropologists from the various republics of former Yugoslavia carried out substantial ethnological and folkloric fieldwork during this decade, some of which was published in English. For example, Mirjana Prošić-Dvornić from the Department of Ethnology at the University of Belgrade wrote an article in *Ethnological Review* in 1989 on how changes in clothing styles in Belgrade during the nineteenth century reflected wider sociocultural systemic changes. Zdeslav Dukat from the Institute for Ethnology and Folklore Research in Zagreb contributed an article to the Institute's publication *Narodna Umjetnost* on "Croatian Epic Folk Songs from Herzegovina and Dalmatia," as collected by Zlatko Tomačić in the 1960s (1993). Most of the articles in these two journals as well as *Studia Ethnologica* (published in Zagreb by the Ethnology Department of the University of Zagreb) and the *Etnološka tribina* (also published in Zagreb, by the Croatian Ethnological Society) include English-language summaries when the articles are written in a language other than English. Thus, a rich source of material that has been published within the former Yugoslavia is available.

PERIOD 3: 1990s

The ongoing war has dominated anthropological fieldwork and writing over the past five years. Many of the anthropologists who conducted what might be considered more traditional anthropological research during earlier periods have shifted the focus of their research and writings to the war situation (e.g., B. Bennett 1995; Hayden 1993; Olujic 1995d; to mention only three of many examples).

COLLECTIVE ACTION

Anthropologists in the United States have attempted to take certain collective actions with regard to the war. For example, in September 1991, a petition for peace was sent to major political leaders in the United States stipulating: "We strongly appeal to world leaders and citizens everywhere to make every possible effort to bring an end to the hostilities in Yugoslavia. Out of deep concern for the peoples in the Yugoslav territories, we urge that all channels be used to stop escalation of the violence" (Petition for Peace). Over fifty anthropologists who had worked in former Yugoslavia on research and other activities signed the petition.

In the summer of 1993, the officers of the Society for the Anthropology of Europe (SAE) appointed an ad hoc Committee on the Crisis in Former Yugoslavia to make recommendations to the SAE. The committee met at the 1993 American Anthropological Association meetings, and a final report was published in the *SAE Bulletin* in 1994 with eight recommendations for SAE action. The first of eight recommendations, for example, states: "Anthropological research on issues related to the current conflict in former Yugoslavia is crucial and should be encouraged."

These are only two examples of the various types of actions anthropologists in the United States have taken collectively regarding the war; most responses to the war have been done on an individual basis through letters and telephone calls, support for people there, staying in contact with friends and colleagues, participating in conferences held there, and collaborating in war-related research. To say that the past four to five years have been an extremely disturbing time for anthropologists who had worked in former Yugoslavia is a vast understatement; virtually everyone has reported feeling powerless to take any really constructive action.

WAR-RELATED RESEARCH AND REPORTS

Not surprisingly, much of the anthropological research being conducted now in former Yugoslavia deals with war-related issues. Most of this research is being carried out in a collaborative manner. For example, Gilliland et al.'s work (1993) focuses on Croatian and Bosnian refugee experience. Her research is being carried out in collaboration with the Centre for the Study of Refugee and Displaced Families, which is directed by Sanja Špoljar-Vržina in Zagreb. In 1993–1995 Maria Olujic carried out a project on the meaning and experience of sexual coercion and war rapes in Croatia and Bosnia-Herzegovina under a grant from the Guggenheim Foundation (Collvard and Wallman 1993; Olujic 1995a, 1995b, and 1995c). Archaeologists have dealt with the effects of the war as well. A recent report by Cal Calabrese (1994) briefly described his experience on a mission to Vukovar to investigate mass graves. In this brief report he describes the wartime conditions they encountered as they attempted to complete their two-month mission and the importance of their work: "We see first hand the destructive power struggles in the guise of ethnic and religious hatreds. At the same time, we have the chance to resolve the disappearance of many families' loved ones and assist a war crimes investigation. This is truly applied archeology" (p. 9).

Although relatively limited war-related research has been conducted by American anthropologists in former Yugoslavia thus far, a plethora of articles has been published recently in which the authors attempt to unravel some of the roots of the war and its horrendous inhumanity. For example, Robert Hayden (1992) describes the creation of what he terms constitutional nationalism in the former Yugoslav republics (1992) as a critical factor in the hostilities which ensued. Eugene Hammel draws upon migration history in the Balkans to propose some explanations for the development of the war in former Yugoslavia (1993b).

SPECIAL PUBLICATIONS ON THE WAR AND THE QUESTION OF IDENTITY

In a Special Issue of *The Anthropology of East Europe Review* on "The Yugoslav Conflict" edited by David A. Kideckel and Joel M. Halpern and introduced by Halpern (1993), several anthropologists and other authors from various countries offered their perspectives on the war situation. Certain articles in this issue offer perspectives on the overall situation in former Yugoslavia by way of attempting some explanations for the eruption of war (e.g., Denich; Hayden; Hammel; and Simić), with respect to such factors as the political-historical roots of conflict going back at least to the tenth and eleventh centuries; the particular atrocities that occurred during the Second World War; the expression of ethnic antagonisms and insensitivities since the Second World War; and eruptions of particularly potent nationalisms in former Yugoslavia. Specific topics addressed include the question of the extent of ethnic intermarriage over the prior three decades (Botev); this article led to a somewhat heated discussion of the interpretation of available figures regarding ethnic intermarriage in former Yugoslavia between Gagnon (1994a and 1994b) and Simić (1994).

Most of the articles in this special issue present personal experiences and insights regarding the war. Several articles deal with issues from specific republics of former Yugoslavia or regions: B. Bennett on his experience in a Croatian island village in the summer of 1991; Olsen on her experience in Slavonia in the 1981–1991 decade; Bringa on her perspectives on Bosnia-Herzegovina based on her fieldwork experience there in the late 1980s and early 1990s; Minnich on his vantage point from Slovenia and especially the Slovene perspective on its secession and independence; Reineck's depiction of Albanians in Kosovo and their own changing sense of national identity; Schwartz on his fifteen-year experience in the Prepsa Lake region of Macedonia, especially with regard to the 1991 independence of the

Macedonian Republic; Despalatović's reflections on Croatia from 1960–1992 and Povrzanović's direct experience in the ethnography of war in Croatia in 1991–1992; and Prošić-Dvornić's report on and analysis of The Student Protest in Belgrade in 1992. Prošić-Dvornić observes the following:

> The students offered their own cultural, social, and moral principles to fill the abyss left after total destruction of the previous order.... Their actions were directed toward pinpointing problems and frustrations. This strategy was the exact opposite of the official society's attitudes, speech, and behavior. The students wished to make their message loud and clear and to articulate differences with the government. Their attitude toward work and duty was, "Problems were there to be solved, work was there to be done, the only important thing is to have it well organized and to find the right person at the right time for the job." This ethos was a world apart from the ideas held by many of their elders. (p. 112)

In addition to this and other special publications on the war in former Yugoslavia, several anthropologists have published articles with analyses of the situation itself (e.g., Bakić-Hayden and Hayden 1992; Denich 1994; Hammel 1993a, 1993b, 1994; and Hayden 1992 and 1993). For example, in 1994 Eugene Hammel wrote a commentary for the *AAA Newsletter* (April 1994) entitled "Meeting the Minotaur," in which he asks provocative questions regarding our right as anthropologists to impose Euro-American concepts such as "human rights" and "individualism" in situations such as the war in the Balkans and the need to recognize our own cultural imperialism in doing so. There was a strong response to Hammel's commentary (see the October 1994 newsletter p. 2) as well as to certain articles published in the special issue of *The Anthropology of East Europe Review* on the Yugoslav crisis.

Considerable writing and publication of books and articles by anthropologists regarding the war have been published in Zagreb. Two major illustrations of this work include a book edited by Feldman, Prica, and Senjković on *Fear, Death, and Resistance: An Ethnography of War: Croatia 1991–92* published by the Institute of Ethnology and Folklore Research (1993), which was published in English. According to the Editorial Board, the authors represented in this book have "recorded and systematized the chaos around them and inside them, but they have also recognized order in chaos" (1993, 1). As such, they did not try to "explain the war," but instead attempt to develop a methodology for gathering information and analyzing it from people who experienced the war. Renata Jambrešić contributes a chapter on ethnonyms from recorded narratives collected from displaced people from Banija (in the Krajina region) (1993), and Maja Povrzanović writes about fear within the context of everyday life of people in wartime in Croatia (1993).

In 1995 a special issue of *Collegicum Antropologicum* was published on the overall topic of "Socio-Cultural Analyses of the Political and Economic Democratization Processes in East/Central Europe, " edited and introduced by

B. C. Bennett. Feldman (1995), Jambrešić (1995b), Povrzanović (1995), Prica (1995), and Senjković (1995b) have articles in this volume as well. Gender roles and the war are addressed in various ways in publications during this period. For example, Ceribašić draws upon popular musical expression in Croatia and Serbia in the early years of the war to elucidate gender roles (1995).

Several other anthropologists from former Yugoslavia have dealt with various aspects of the war. The 1992 volume of *Studia Ethnologica* published by the Sveučilište u Zagrebu Filozofski Fakultet Etnološki Zavod in Zagreb is devoted to the traditional culture of *Hrvatska Baranja*, a region bordering Croatia and Hungary to the north of the city of Osijek. During the war, tremendous destruction took place in this region which had been ethnically heterogeneous, with Croats, Hungarians, Germans, and Serbs living there. Most of the Croats and Hungarians were expelled in 1991. Topics such as traditional costumes (Maglica), the history and geography of the region (Klemenčić), and ethnological records (Lechner) are addressed in the dozen chapters, each of which includes a summary in English. A number of studies regarding the refugees from former Yugoslavia—whether Moslems, Croats, or Serbs—within and without the previous national borders have been carried out. This has been a focus of a session organized by Éva V. Huseby-Darvas at the 1993 American Anthropological Association and the focus of a Special Issue of *The Anthropology of East Europe Review* (1995) that she edited on "Refugee Women of the Balkans." Papers were published regarding refugees from former Yugoslavia on the narratives of Bosnian and Croatian refugees on the island of Hvar as a reflection of the impact of the war on ethnic and gender identities (Gilliland et al. 1995a and 1995b); narratives of female refugees in Hungary (Huseby-Darvas 1995); and the phenomenal trauma experienced by refugees and displaced persons because of rape, torture, and war (Olujic 1995c and Markowitz 1995).

DEVELOPMENTS IN ANTHROPOLOGY IN 1995–1996

The war in former Yugoslavia has further stimulated a long-standing interest in nationalism and questions of identity, especially ethnic identity, addressed by anthropologists and others. As an example, in 1994 the Societé Internationale d'Ethnologie et de Folklore (SIEF) at its fifth Congress in Vienna focused on "The Ethnic Paradigm and the Turn of the Centuries." Following the Congress, the journal *Ethnologia Europaea* published a special issue on "Ethnic and National Identities." Dunja Rihtman-Auguštin and Reana Senjković of the Institute of Ethnology and Folklore Research in Zagreb contributed papers. Rihtman-Auguštin contrasts the perspectives of Serbian and Croatian anthropologists living in earlier periods of the twentieth century— such as Jovan Cvijić, Dinko Tomašić, Jozo Tomaševich, and Vera St. Erlich with respect to research on national character. In her introduction, she observes that the authors of the articles in the Special Issue on "War among the Yugoslavs" in *The Anthropology of East Europe Review* (1993) appear to "have been confused and shared the same or even greater difficulties as we, the natives have, when discerning between facts and political propaganda of the parts in conflict" (1995, 61). In her article, she examines the particular promotion of heroism as a dominant value, and points out that such promotion of heroism in the war in the early 1990s in Croatia has not served to protect people from post-traumatic stress disturbances. Reana Senjković addresses the recent development of national identity in Croatia, focusing on the 1990–1992 period. In particular, she analyzes the iconography of the war and the strong influence of the mass media in the construction of national identity (1995a).

Anthropological research in Bosnia-Herzegovina by anthropologists from outside former Yugoslavia has been quite limited except for the work of Lockwood in western Bosnia in the 1960s; Gordiejew on Jewish life and identity in Sarajevo in the 1980s; and the fieldwork of Bax in Medjugorje in the 1980s. Beginning in the late 1980s, however, Norwegian anthropologist Tone Bringa began her dissertation research in central Bosnia in a Muslim-Croatian village, entering the village in 1988. Her research was focused on the Moslem population. In 1993 when she revisited the village, she found that none of the Muslims remained and all Muslim homes had been destroyed. Thus, over a period of six years, she witnessed phenomenal changes and devastation. Her study entitled *Being Muslim the Bosnian Way: Identity and Community in a Central Bosnian Village* was published in 1995. It provides a very thorough discussion, substantiated by ethnographic and historical data, of the issue of ethnonational identity of Muslims in Bosnia.

Developments regarding the formation and work of the international criminal tribunal have been written about by Paul Magnarella (1995 and 1996). The special circumstances of Macedonia are dealt with by Tony Velovski (1995), especially with regard to its identity as a state as well as individual identity. After five months of living in Macedonia, he observes the striking contrasts between generations and between the fixtures of the socialist past and contemporary consumer culture.

Two international conferences devoted to the topic of the war, violence, and recovery were held in Zagreb in 1995. The Institute of Ethnology and Folklore Research organized the first conference (March-April) on "War, Exile, Everyday Life." Scholars from Germany, the United States, United Kingdom, the Netherlands, Norway, Austria, Slovenia, Greece, France, and Croatia presented papers. Ger Duijzings from the Netherlands delivered a paper on the virtual total outmigration of Croatian refugees from villages in western Slavonia in 1992. Renata Jambrešić (1995a) presented a semantic analysis of narratives from the war. Sanja Martić-Biočina discussed the difficulties and misunderstandings between refugees from Bosnia-Herzegovina and health professionals in the Netherlands who were attempting to provide services to the refugees. Maja Povrzanović and Ines Prica (1995) drew upon data from forty-five life histories of eleven-to-fourteen-year-old refugee children in Zagreb. These life histories typically include depictions of prewar life, the war, and the postwar period. Sanja Špoljar-Vržina addressed questions about the difficulties of determining the most appropriate therapeutic treatment for refugees and displaced persons, as seen through the experience of those on the Island of Hvar. Natalija Vrečer of the Department of Ethnology and Cultural Anthropology in Ljubljana, Slovenia, also described the experience of refugee children from Bosnia-Herzegovina in Celje, Slovenia, during the 1992–1994 period of the war, especially difficulties meeting the children's developmental needs (1995).

Later in 1995 (October) another international conference was held in Zagreb (October), this one on the topic of *(En)gendering Violence, Terror, Domination, Recovery*, organized by Maria Olujic. Presenters from the United States, Croatia, Australia, Greece, and Norway presented papers. They focused on the issue of patriarchy in Croatia (Čapo Žmegač 1995); the effects of gender on war testimonies (Jambrešić 1995a); refugee children's life histories (Povrzanović 1995b); and rape in Croatia and Bosnia (Olujic 1995b). The series of papers is to be published in a volume on *Gendered Violence*, edited by Olujic (n.d.).

SIGNS OF THE FUTURE

Even in the midst of the trauma of war in former Yugoslavia, anthropological research and writing continues. In addition to the journals cited above, which are published in Zagreb, *Glasnik Etnografskog Muzeja* and *Glasnik Etnografskog Instituta* continue to be published in Belgrade. Reportedly most, if not all, of the ethnologists who were in Sarajevo before the war have remained there; anthropological journals as of 1996 were reportedly still not being published in Bosnia-Herzegovina. In Slovenia, anthropological researchers are very active, especially the archaeologists, according to verbal accounts. It is probably clear from the cited materials in this chapter that considerable anthropological research is being carried out in Croatia.

I anticipate that throughout the remaining 1990s anthropological research in former Yugoslavia will evidence (1) continuing, if not increasing, collaboration with foreign colleagues; (2) a strong focus on practical issues and problems such as refugee resettlement and readjustment, physical and emotional health, Post-Traumatic Stress Disorder among children and adults, gender roles, ethnicity, the impact of outmigration and population movements, and economic recovery, to note only a few areas of concern; and (3) a continuing emphasis on work within a particular political context (e.g., Croatia, Slovenia, Serbia, etc.) rather than across political boundaries. These circumstances provide an opportunity as well as a responsibility for anthropologists from abroad to cooperate in scholarly activities of colleagues in former Yugoslavia to the extent that it is possible to do so.

Acknowledgements

Many colleagues helped me gather material for this chapter, and I greatly appreciate their willing assistance and suggestions. Maria Olujic and Olga Supek read an earlier version of the chapter and offered very helpful comments and provided certain material that I did not have easily available to me regarding recent anthropological work in former Yugoslavia. Mary Kay Gilliland, Robert Hayden, Margaret Lethbridge-Çejku, and Mirjana Prošić-Dvornić, in particular, helped by sending reprints and/or answering my questions. I am, of course, responsible for any oversights or mistakes made in the chapter, and I apologize for them in advance. This chapter is dedicated to the memory of Frank A. Dubinskas.

Notes

1. Although "anthropology" in former Yugoslavia typically denotes biological anthropology, and "ethnology" denotes sociocultural anthropology, in this chapter the term "anthropology" encompasses both.

2. I have attempted to take into account anthropological studies—especially those of anthropologists from the United States—carried out in all regions of former Yugoslavia. In my summary of work over the past decade and especially since the start of the war in 1991, however, my review is clearly more thorough with regard to fieldwork in Croatia. This mainly reflects my access to published material as well as the degree to which studies are being conducted in each region.

CHAPTER 10

UTTER OTHERNESS:
WESTERN ANTHROPOLOGY AND EAST
EUROPEAN POLITICAL ECONOMY

David A. Kideckel
Central Connecticut State University

In the development of the anthropology of Europe I see fascinating contrasts between the practices of western (mainly American) anthropology in East European societies, compared to both the work of East European ethnographers in Eastern Europe and western anthropologists in Western Europe. As discussed below, American and Western European anthropologists in East Europe were continuously influenced by East Europe's marginal and highly charged political economic circumstances, defined below as "utter otherness." To address the value laden quality of the East that resulted from its socialist economy and adversarial Cold War political identity, western anthropologists throughout the Cold War sought to describe the region in terms that ameliorated these differences to western audiences. They focused intensively on people's daily lives and thus humanized the socialist system. This approach, however, has changed considerably in the current period.

Emerging from socialism allegedly on a path to democracy and the market, East Europe nonetheless remains conceptually distinct from the West, though now more through the focus of its economies than as an adversary of its politics. The greater role of the West in East European change defines a new regional anthropology, focused on problem solving and policy but increasingly distanced from the region's peoples. The "utter otherness" of the East is thus reconfigured. No longer is the region considered a zone of socialist machinations and superstitious peasants. However, neither is it a place granted the same self-identification and self-determination assumed for western states and individuals.

UTTER OTHERNESS DEFINED AND OPERATIONALIZED

Debates about the position of Europe within anthropological discourse have long focused on questions of its "otherness" (Cole 1977; Herzfeld 1987b). This theme was especially well-developed in the American Anthropological Association session on the History of Europeanist Anthropology for which this chapter was originally written. In that session most papers were characterized by the central place of this issue. However, two that avoided the question were concerned with Eastern Europe: Linda Bennett's on the history of Yugoslav anthropology and mine on changing anthropological practice in East Europe. Thinking of the session while revising this chapter, I questioned the apparent lack of concern for otherness in the anthropology of the East. Its absence implied an assumption about the nature of East European life. Similarly the "East Europe as problem" focus of the two essays also seemed to speak to the relationship of East and West in both Europeanist anthropology and world geopolitics. The answer to the absence of the otherness discourse was, after a time, apparent. Analyses of Eastern Europe are not in the main concerned with its otherness since that, I think, is assumed from the start. The region is, in fact, the *sine qua non* of otherness and was defined as such since the two halves of the continent diverged in the long sixteenth century during the formation of the so-called modern world system. As East Europe is considered the *locus classicus* of cultural and political economic difference, its interpreters are then freed (or forced, as the case may be) to explore more problematic issues in the region's anthropology. In Linda Bennett's case, this concerned changes in anthropological interest in the Yugoslav regions related to changing interethnic relations and, in my case, shifting motivations of anthropological practitioners correlated with changing East European political economy. In both, however, "otherness" remained the unstated subtext.

Thus, the history of western anthropological thought and practice in and about the East must be understood as motivated by a different problematic than Europeanist anthropology in general. The anthropological problematic in Western Europe is one of self-knowledge. It asks "what can anthropology in Europe and European communities really tell us about ourselves?" This focus is perhaps best exemplified by Cole's notion of Europe as "part-way home" and even Herzfeld's "looking glass of marginal Europe."

The anthropology of the East, on the other hand, was an anthropology of relation. As the region was physically (both geographically and "racially") proximate but somewhat distant in cultural and political economic terms, westerners—fearing to be seen too much akin to these others—originally looked at the East and asked "how is it different from us?" Thus, the need to define the East as other produced a distancing anthropology that, as with Africa, New Guinea, and Native America, first was geared toward explaining unfamiliar customs and habits. It is no accident, then, that the anthropology of East Europe traces its origins to accounts of travelers like Edith Durham (1987), strangers in strange lands, while that of the West is traced to history and political economy. In other words, though anthropologists in Europe sought out and often labored to define the "other,"[1] such activities were superfluous in Eastern Europe. For the West's own sake, the East had to be considered an utter other, more different precisely because of its proximity.

East European otherness dates to West European capitalist expansion when its peasant-based and often highly differentiated class system was produced by trade with the developing West (cf. Wallerstein 1974) and conquest by foreign and extractive empires (cf. Chirot 1976; McNeill 1964; Stahl 1979). This otherness, always a tar baby for the West as Sarajevo (1914 and 1995) readily attests, was amplified after World War II. As the lands between Germany and the Soviet Union became dominated by ostensibly socialist political economies, and the world and continent were caught in the grip of the Cold War, the interpretation of East European culture was further distanced from the prevailing discourse of Europeanist anthropology and thrown back on its own explanatory concepts and research problems. This is especially seen in the late 1950s and 1960s, the earliest period after the onset of the Cold War when western anthropologists were first allowed access to the East European field.

Considering anthropology in Eastern Europe at this time, it is instructive to contrast it with practices in both West Europeanist anthropology and those of native East European practitioners. At first blush, throughout the 1950s and 1960s, all these genres appear similar; each was dominated by the so-called community studies approach. However, on closer examination the rationale for such studies, the kinds of information on which they focused, the kinds of purposes to which they were put, and even the relationship of anthropologist and community differed greatly within them. So great were the differences that Hungarian ethnographer Tamás Hofer saw them as polar contrasts.

In his now-classic 1968 *Current Anthropology* article, Hofer compared American and native Europeans at work in European villages. According to Hofer, both approaches were community-based, but differed greatly in their approaches to community. Europeans made short frequent field trips to collect detailed, descriptive, ethnographic data of mainly folkloric and family customs in a few select communities. They developed close relationships with the communities they studied, as did Hofer and his colleague Edit Fél in the village of Átány, Hungary (Fél and Hofer 1969). In contrast, following Anthony Wallace (1966), Hofer likened American practices to slash-and-burn farming. The anthropologist/farmer prepared the village field site/garden plot via fieldwork, but cultivated it less for ethnography than for theoretical generalization, and then abandoned it for another theoretical interest/village community elsewhere.

Rethinking this discussion, however, it is clear that Western/American anthropological work in East European communities neither agreed with East European ethnographic approaches nor with western slash-and-burn theoreticians. In fact, as the "utter otherness" of Eastern Europe now had ominous political implications, it forced Western/American anthropologists to reflect on the distancing of the East. Responding to and challenging the imperatives of the Cold War, they combined the theoretical interests of the typical American approach with the in-depth focus on (and I dare say equal personal commitment to) the communities under study by East and Central European ethnographers.

As a brief example, consider the American research effort at the time in Yugoslavia, then thought a relatively liberal and "maverick" marxist state. Mirroring the East European ethnographic tradition, a selection of books based on Yugoslav research show them especially notable for their strong ethnographic component (Halpern 1967 [1956]; Halpern and Kerewsky Halpern 1972), for their concern with traditional social relations (Hammel 1968), and for their community focus (Lockwood 1975; Simic 1973). Despite these concerns, however, each work still sought to tie events and relationships within particular communities to a field of both national and international political and economic relations, to larger ethnic and national traditions, and to issues of large-scale social change. The latter were seen to be motivated by general modernization processes as well as by socialist state policy and practice. Subsequently, these activities and publications about Yugoslavia extended to elsewhere in the region. As other countries, notably Hungary and Romania, opened their borders to western anthropologists, the wedding of community study and theoretical inquiry was continually reproduced.

I explore this research strategy in more detail and suggest it as predicated partially on the nature of the socialist state, but also as a response to Cold War rhetoric and the possibilities of East-West conflict. Certainly the practices of western anthropologists in Eastern Europe borrowed theoretical principles and research strategies from the dominant western paradigm.[2] However, it differed sufficiently to assume an underlying divergent rationale.

ANTHROPOLOGY IN THE SOCIALIST EAST: CONFRONTING THE COLD WAR[3]

The forty-odd years of socialist dominance in East Europe provided a unique anthropological challenge. The mutual demonization of the East European states by the West and of the West by the socialist bloc was the dominant context in which the anthropology of East Europe was carried out. Though western anthropologists were largely animated by theoretical contributions, the Cold War gave them an additional charge: to enable greater degrees of mutual understanding and thus limit the spread and possible destructiveness of Cold War hostility. To this end western anthropologists in East European communities often saw themselves as cultural mediators translating each of these two adverse political economic systems to each other in terms accessible to both sides.

Taking the Hofer critique to heart, western, especially American, anthropology as practiced in East Europe implicitly challenged both the Hoferian image of the detached, theoretical anthropologist, and theoretically narrow

European ethnography. In this way, then, Cold War stereotypes of East European society regularly produced in the western press and academy were also debunked. In combining the two approaches, western work in East Europe first provided color to socialist life by attention to ethnography. Additionally, through theory emphasizing the linkages of communities within the state and international system, it also offered a nuanced analysis of socialism and a powerful critique of unidimensional views of it. A range of anthropological field practices, research orientations, and personal approaches thus all helped bridge the political, economic, and cultural gap between East and West. They partially dispelled what Steve Sampson and I (Kideckel and Sampson 1984; Sampson and Kideckel 1989) spoke of as western "politico-centrism" and the "verdict mentality," which rushed to judge the entire socialist system by the slightest flaws and glitches.

Western anthropological research in Cold War Eastern Europe was especially oriented to deflating many of the myths about socialist life. Models of East Europe deriving from western political science and economics faculties were particularly challenged. These models defined East Europe as characterized by totalitarian political economy, brutal atheism, domination of Soviet-style institutions, homogeneity of life from one East European state to another, and the loss of community identities under collectivist policies. In contrast, though anthropologists recognized the realities of the centralized state, they saw them as capable of manipulation by local community practice (Kideckel 1982), variably applied depending on region and group (Hann 1980), challenged by practices as apparently politically neutral as folklore (Kligman 1981, 1988; Silverman 1983), and neutralized and transformed by the extensive web of personal ties and networks that characterized the socialist bureaucracy and ubiquitous second economy (Sampson 1987; Wedel 1985).

Prevailing anthropological research in Cold War Eastern Europe still echoed dominant disciplinary concerns and included analyses of the social structure of domestic groups, peasant economics, oral tradition, religion and ritual, and labor migration (see Halpern and Kideckel 1983). But all of these, and even work emphasizing world system or political economic perspectives (Beck and Cole, eds. 1981; Verdery 1983), had a distinctly local cast, since it concerned the intersection of these large-scale forces with events and circumstances at the local level. Given this orientation, Rudolf Bahro's concept of "actually existing socialism" (1978) was informally modified by anthropologists away from its original meaning of societies that diverge from their ideological underpinnings due to hierarchy in the division of labor. The transformed concept spoke to the diversity of influences, especially those locally derived, on the organization and practices of the socialist state.

To an extent, the Cold War also demanded personal commitments on the part of anthropologists. Thus, unlike the Hoferian slash-and-burner, western anthropologists in the East European field typically developed long-term relationships with particular communities and regions during their research. Examples from this period are found in every East European country with an active anthropological research tradition. These include Gail Kligman in Ieud in the Romanian Marāmureş (1981); Chris Hann in the Hungarian *tanya* settlement Tazlár (1980); Zdenek Salzmann and Vladimir Scheuffler in Komárov, Bohemia (1974); not to mention Joel Halpern and Barbara Kerewsky Halpern in the Serbian Šumadija village of Orašac, Yugoslavia, the archetypical anti-Hoferian case (1972).[4]

Certainly these long-term anthropologist-community relationships also represented anthropologists' recognition of and adaptation to the East European political vicissitudes. Integration within local community networks and affective relationships with their responsible cadres could often short-circuit tedious administrative procedures for securing housing, receiving permission to consult archives and other documents, and otherwise carry out fieldwork. In the Romanian case such relationships were necessary to even speak with informants in their homes unaccompanied by political authorities.[5] But whatever the specific motivations, the emphasis on personal experiences within these communities expressed at professional meetings and in publications, gave socialism a human face and a lived dimension.

Aside from challenging Cold War mythologies by integrating community studies and theories of socialist social organization, the collaboration and easy relationship that western scholars and their East European counterparts established also furthered the dialogue between capitalist West and socialist East. In fact, though Hofer suggests that slash-and-burners mainly ignored and denigrated European scholarship (1968, 314–315), an intense collaboration between western scholars and East European intellectuals was one of the hallmarks of the anthropological effort in the Cold War East. Again, this was facilitated by the formal organizational ties and permissions researchers needed to work in East Europe. Despite its rationale, however, this collaboration had a number of salutary results.

Though it often placed East European scholars and their home institutions as supervisors over westerners, it also gave each access to the other's networks, conceptual apparatus, and histories. More than this, however, there was a political dimension to the collaboration of western anthropologists and East European scholars that offered a practical challenge to the Cold War. Collaboration between western anthropologists and East European scholars provided both with a range of benefits unavailable in their own societies. Westerners were not only exotic but their presence gave East Europeans access to professional resources (e.g., books, journals) and, more important, a bit of political wiggle room. In particular, westerners were used as sounding boards for ideas generally not acceptable within prevailing socialist dogma. Western anthropologists, on the other hand, received recognition and prominence in the highest social, political and academic circles of these nations, something sorely wanting in our societies. In fact, as the personal ties to communities and countries that anthropologists developed were so extensive, they even led, on occasion, to accusations of fellow traveling; of defending some increasingly indefensible behavior and sordid political practice.

Finally East-West collaboration resulted in a growing mutual respect manifested in a mirroring of research styles and strategies on the parts of both easterners and westerners. This is well illustrated by the experience of the University of Massachusetts' "Romanian Research Group," active from 1973 through 1978. Adopting a number of pages from Romanian research styles and social science history,[6] the members of this group were similarly organized as a research team, arrayed themselves across an ecological sample of communities within the same region to consider the range of possible state-region-community interactions, and gave regular reports to host Romanian scholars and institutions. Subsequent to returning to the United States, the group hosted three Romanian scholars at the Amherst campus, who were initiated into the research styles and theoretical debates prevalent in American anthropology of the time.

THE TRANSFORMATION OF EAST EUROPE[7]

As is now the stuff of legend, socialist East Europe fell apart in 1989. The weight of state neglect and class contradictions, local challenges of one sort or another, Polish pope and unions, the expansion of international communication networks, the opening of borders, and moribund dictators all combined to bring down the increasingly flimsy structure that was the socialist East. What was left was inchoate and ill-defined, but like any vacuum or frontier was ripe for the filling (cf. Kideckel 1993a). Thus, what is now glossed as "the transition" spawned a diversity of attempts to remold the East into a social system more attuned and accessible to the rest of the world but, in particular, to its erstwhile competitors in the developed West.

This is not the place to evaluate the essence of the transition, either in general or as manifested in particular national conditions. To again cite Bahro (1978), what we are confronted with is not so much the formation of new societies based on new principles, as "actually existing uncertainty" (see also Kideckel 1995a; Sampson 1995, on the questionable nature of the transition concept). Nonetheless, the confused nature of the transition and the large efforts of western governments and multilateral organizations like the World Bank and International Monetary Fund to more fully open the East to the global system has produced a social and scientific environment of the East European states that allows for a remarkably changed role for western social science, anthropology included.

To a great extent, even as the region began to be opened to more comprehensive international relations, its "otherness" was reinforced in Western eyes by the romantic picture of the transition first painted in the media. The sudden end to the Cold War, an essential part of the world scene for those coming of age in the post-World War II period, produced an extraordinary sense of the possible and of the excitement of the historical moment. This was intensified by televised images of the Berlin Wall being breached and torn down, holes in Romanian flags, and Albanians dripping off rooftops to catch a glimpse of then Secretary of State James Baker. Taken together, such images made the cities of the region inviting to legions of expatriates even as it made the study of East Europe more attractive to previously distant western intellectuals.

Thus, the romanticization of the transition and the possibilities of the East European future also implicitly offered a large role for intellectuals. As with socialist central planning before it, the transition required new policy, technical change, and a reworking of government, education, and social procedures to name a few. In response to these images and its promises, then, large numbers of individuals who previously avoided East Europe began to see it as a fertile, exciting, and relatively empty niche for scientific practice. Western anthropologists with little previous interest in the region suddenly began to pontificate on events in the East (cf. Harris 1992). Furthermore, granting agencies like the United States National Science Foundation, not previously known for their presence in socialist Europe, began to devote a significant share of their social science funding for 1993 and beyond for research related to democratization and privatization, with much of this money specifically ear-marked for anthropologists (Plattner et al. 1993).[8]

Now, defining a place as "other" is tantamount to its objectification. Thus, it is not surprising that the reality of the East still diverges greatly from western social scientific perceptions about it. Instead of societies eagerly awaiting western advice and scientific communities anxious to benefit from western wisdom, western social scientists entering East Europe find an intensely politicized environment where successful practice demands circumspection and a knowledge of networks more than it does laptops and note-taking skills. The scientific communities within transitional Europe are rapidly changing and forcing equally rapid changes in the relationship between themselves and their western counterparts, and in western practice as well.

Perhaps the most significant change in regional science affecting western practices in the region is its rapid privatization and decreased state support. Thus, the economic decline of the transition, and the shift to private funding all limit resources for scientific practice. Simultaneously, the greater political openness of the state makes access to western resources for East Europeans more plausible and thus also heightens competition for them. Eastern scientific institutes are still dominated by many of the same persons who held sway at the end of socialism. However, their lives are now taken up by the need to find contracts and resources to support their struggling existence and maintain their diminished staffs. In response to this competitive, resource-poor environment, then, there is a marked increase in East European requests to westerners for the various perquisites of the international intelligentsia—trips abroad, computers, electronic communication devices, space in respected journals, and the like.

This heightened competitive environment in the East tends to produce a dichotomous western response. On one hand, the possibility of cooperation

and collaboration in social science institution building motivates some westerners to mentor such institutions or even to move to the East for long
stretches of collaborative activity. On the other hand, other westerners blanch
at the steady drumbeat of instrumental requests and, instead, withdraw from
collaborative relations. More significantly, there is even a heightened sense of
competition between easterners and westerners over scientific access and
resources in the East. As discussed below, this is particularly spurred by an
increased number of western social scientists serving as well-paid consultants
to western government, multilateral, and nongovernmental agencies offering
aid to the region, positions largely excluding East Europeans (see Kideckel
1995b; Wedel 1994).

Along with changes in the relationships between eastern and western
social scientists, a new kind of exposure to actual social conditions and
processes in transitional East Europe also shapes changing western anthropological practices and orientations. In the socialist past, the dominant activity of
many East European social scientists and their institutions was contract work
for the government and planning bureaucracy. However, these same kinds of
inquiries were either not of interest or were simply off-limits to western scholars who worked in the region. In contrast, today the political economic transformation has brought into the open a host of real-life problems characterizing
East European life at the same time it encourages greater western recognition
of and involvement in them. In particular the renewed links with western governmental and financial institutions gives these institutions a large financial
and political stake in the resolution of such problems. Consequently they often
turn to members of the western scientific community for assistance in their resolution.

The list of serious issues with great actual or potential impact on East
European realities and hence, of great interest to western institutions and their
social science adjutants boggles the mind. A few of the more tendentious ones
include environmental degradation and rehabilitation, privatization of production resources and housing stock, reinvigorating the role of nongovernmental
organizations in regional life, managing the infusion of foreign assistance in
the region, and restructuring political organization and administration. Also of
particular but unfortunate significance is the critical problem of intensifying
ethnic antagonism and conflict, which itself implicates issues of international
and internal migration, the definition of the state, and evolving world geopolitics to name a few. Finally, it should be noted that each of these are general
East European problems on which each regional state has its own take.
Further, each also has its own unique issues like Romanian orphans, Albania's
lack of critical resources, Poland's tendentious labor history, and the recent
separation of the Czech Republic and Slovakia to name a few.

Though these problems are impressive for their diversity, they share two
qualities that impact on the changing practice of western anthropology in the
region. First is their essential difference from issues obtaining in Western
Europe, and second their near-exclusively practical nature. Thus, the East's

newly accessible problems and the premium its governments and their western patrons place on solving them offer social scientists and other intellectuals the perfect environment for the application of theory to actual reality. In contrast, in the west of Europe large-scale theoretical issues and problems of definition still tend to occupy the work of anthropology. Consequently, more than a few western experts are ready to step into the fray for the excitement and rewards tied to the analysis and resolution of problems of the transition. As they do, however, they are again encouraged to see the East as a zone of difficulty and of problems to be resolved. Thus, despite monumental changes in the East, the transition furthers the objectification of East by West and reproduces its utter otherness, even as it is reincorporated into the western political and economic sphere of influence.

ANTHROPOLOGICAL PRACTICE IN THE NEW EASTERN EUROPE

The reemergence of the market and international economic (some would argue dependency) linkages and the prevailing problematic of East European social systems is reflected in the development of analogous practices among western social scientists. Leaving behind Cold War cultural mediation, cross-cultural understanding, and intense involvement with East European scholarly and local communities, western anthropologists have gravitated toward a policy-oriented, can-do social science that, among other things, offers itself to eastern governments for help in institution building and to western agencies for consulting. In this reorientation two general trends are apparent. First, there is a changing focus of research from local to national research sites and problems, and less a preoccupation with describing and explaining the life circumstances of real people than a concern to outline the transformation of East European socio-political systems as a whole.[9] Second, there is a shift from research concerned with social and ideological questions to those oriented to practical economic and political ones. In both, however, the subtextual theme remains Eastern Europe as a thing apart, an utter other.

A brief analysis of recent grant proposals, applications for doctoral dissertation funding, and other projects submitted to major East Europeanist anthropology funding agencies illustrate these trends.[10] These data derive from my review of titles of U.S. National Science Foundation funded research projects available on the Internet, IREX-funded projects listed in a data base currently being developed,[11] funded projects listed in the Annual Report of the Wenner-Gren Foundation (Wenner-Gren Foundation 1994), and from other research proposals that have crossed my desk during various phases of their review process. My data are especially complete for anthropological projects funded by IREX in 1990–1991. During this period IREX funded thirty-nine separate grants to individuals identified as anthropologists of which twenty-three went to ostensibly cultural anthropological projects. Sixteen of these (70 percent) were projects of a decidedly practical and/or applied nature dealing with ethnicity and cultural preservation (N=6), labor in transitional capitalist economies (N=5), health and environmental issues (N=3), and demographic change (N=2).

Similarly, many of the East Europeanist anthropology projects reviewed by the NSF or Wenner-Gren, funded or not, were also decidedly policy-oriented. For 1992–1993, Wenner-Gren funded five small grant projects for Eastern Europe, only one of which was of marginal practical utility. Two of the remaining four focused on economic transformations related to capitalist privatization, one on changing Albanian identity in the potential hot-spot of Kosovo, and one on the politics of reproduction in Romania. Furthermore, a preponderance of proposals received by Wenner-Gren, in keeping with American fashion, dealt with issues of East European identity but almost exclusively from a political standpoint. Even the NSF has begun to fund cultural anthropological research in Eastern Europe and recently signed on to support three projects, one on the role of foreign aid in the contemporary region to which I am a collaborator with principal investigator Janine Wedel, another two dissertation projects on environmentalism in Slovakia and the cultural beliefs and identities of government economists in Slovenia.

Along with applied or practically-oriented research, anthropologists are increasingly active as consultants to both East European governments and nongovernmental organizations (NGOs) and to American and West European governmental and multilateral agencies. In these areas anthropologists whom I know or of whom I have heard are increasingly active in analyses of agricultural privatization and land use, the development of NGOs for purposes of democratization, the delivery of health care services, the expansion and systemization of university library collections, the analysis of media efficacy, the development of political parties and democratic government, and the formulation and evaluation of legislation and policy in the above domains. Beginning essentially from a zero-point before 1989, anthropologists in Eastern Europe have since worked for USAID, the World Bank, the European Union's PHARE program, Oxfam, the Red Cross, United Nations Development Program, and the UN High Commissioner on Refugees, to name only those agencies most visible in the transition. To an extent, this changed research and practice orientation results from the first-time availability of such opportunities. During socialism, as discussed, such opportunities were forestalled by the stand-offish relationship of the Eastern states with western financial and governmental institutions. However, as the end of state socialism precipitated a transfer of western financial resources and assistance eastward, donor governments and agencies have reached out for advice to those with experience in the region. The financial and political power and cultural capital of such actors not only makes for the greater availability of resources for consulting but also provides an imprimatur of respectability for it as well.[12]

Most important, this changed career orientation also precipitates a transformation in the way East Europe is conceptualized in the western mindset and treated by western researchers. Rather than a place to be understood in and on its own terms (see Fabian 1983), a zone begging for a deepened inter-cultural subjectivity, the reintegrating East is a place that western society demands be mastered and tamed. The interpretive requirements of historical understanding in East Europe have been replaced willy-nilly by facile discussions of the "end of history" (Fukuyama 1989) and technocratic attempts to be midwife to a democratic market system through structural adjustment, legal reform, and double-entry bookkeeping.

Still, despite these pressures, western anthropology's course in East Europe is not set. It remains to be seen what, if anything, changing anthropological practice in a changing East Europe means for each of the parties in this *pas de deux*. Despite our new tendency to de-emphasize community-oriented research and cultural mediation, the transformation offers extraordinary opportunities for the development of anthropological practice and knowledge and even greater opportunities for extending cross-cultural understanding and intercultural subjectivity. Policy-related research and other activities do not necessarily limit this possibility. In fact, the kind of understanding derived from anthropological knowledge of state-local interrelationships is not only critical for the formation of efficacious policy and institutions in the new East Europe but can be simultaneously used to better understand local life and the pressures that confront citizens in the transition. What is required, however, is a willingness to stand up for our first principles and commitments to the demands of the agencies and institutions who seek our knowledge and skills to move their own agenda (cf. Wedel and Kideckel 1994).

Of what, however, does such a defense consist? Our first challenge is to confront the policy agenda that defines the essences of contemporary East Europe in practical as opposed to critical terms. Anthropological work in the region can and must comprise both so that our policy work is informed by critical purposes and our critical commitments—to social equity, interethnic communication and cooperation, and participatory politics, to name a few—can shape the formulation of policy-oriented research. Anthropologists can also contribute to centering policy debates on actual realities. To do so, we must offer information that takes into account the diversity of regions, communities, and subcultural groups. In this way we can help move policy research away from implicit assumptions of social homogeneity and its use of aggregate data to support them. Furthermore, by a focus on diverse real life circumstances, we can maintain the personal relationships with East European communities that marked our approach in the Cold War years. Even more, however, we can continue to show that the ultimate problematic of the East European transformation is not some mystical and reified market or set of political principles. Rather, the goal and focus of the transition must be on the diverse peoples who, through their own actions and sacrifice, opened their lives to that transformation and to us. By recognizing their struggle we can especially help dispel the utter otherness in which our colleagues, friends, and informants had and have been conceptually imprisoned by a West intent on their pacification.

NOTES

1. David Kertzer's analysis of the anthropology of Italy in this volume is instructive. As he shows, the self-conscious attempt to find the other in Europe is particularly reflected in the "southern" focus of Italianist anthropology.

2. Hofer (1968, 313) even makes a strong case that, for Americans, theoretical generalization was a necessary condition for career advancement.

3. For a more general discussion of the role of anthropology in and at the end of the Cold War, see Kideckel 1989.

4. The career of the Halperns in Orašac was even recognized by the Yugoslavs themselves, who produced and broadcast a video in 1988 about their work and personal relationships there.

5. The Romanian Official Secrets Act, passed in 1974, forbade foreigners to reside in private Romanian homes and required that all Romanians who had contact with foreign citizens report the nature of that contact in writing to police within twenty-four hours.

6. Much of our work clearly mirrored the activities of the so-called "Gusti school" of Romanian sociology, active in that country in the years between the two world wars. This was frequently and positively noted by Romanian scholars throughout our stay.

7. With the end of the Cold War and the attempted transition to democracy and the market, social scientific discourse has revivified the terminological distinction between Eastern and Central Europe. The former now includes Romania, Bulgaria, Albania, and, excluding the Baltic states, the European states of the former Soviet Union, i.e., Belarus, Moldova, and Ukraine. Central Europe is comprised of the Baltic states (Estonia, Latvia, and Lithuania), Poland, the Czech and Slovak Republics, Hungary, Slovenia, and Croatia. Rump Yugoslavia, Bosnia, and F.Y.R. Macedonia have their own special status. However, in this chapter as well as in other works (Kideckel, ed. 1995) I continue to use the term Eastern Europe to define the territories of the formerly state socialist nations for a number of reasons. For one, the problematic of the transition continues to unite these states. For another, the distinction tends to demonize or "Orientalize" (see Said 1979) the so-called East Europeans while placing the Central European states firmly in the group of civilized Western nations. These distinctions, then, are not merely terminological but have large consequences for the conceptualization and treatment of these groups of states in diplomacy, foreign assistance, and other international practices. There will come a time when we can wipe out the distinctions entirely and speak only of Europe, but we have yet to reach that moment.

8. Stuart Plattner, head of the NSF's Anthropology section, attended various gatherings of Europeanists at the 1993 AAA annual meeting. At these

venues he regularly appealed to anthropologists interested in East European privatization and democratization to apply for an increasing amount of NSF funds devoted specifically to these purposes.

9. I try to offer somewhat of a corrective to this in a recently published volume (Kideckel, ed. 1995).

10. In this discussion I focus nearly exclusively on funded research. Titles of nonfunded applications are not readily available.

11. I wish to thank Eric Fowkes of the Information Systems office at the International Research and Exchanges Board for making the 1990–1991 data base available. Data for 1992 to the present are currently being coded and are unavailable. Furthermore, though funded grants are listed in the Board's quarterly newsletter, "IREX News in Brief," these are not broken down by grantee discipline and are thus unreliable for this chapter.

12. Though there are greater opportunities for those previously involved in research in Eastern Europe to serve the policy needs of Western governments and financial institutions, consultancies in East Europe are still mainly offered to those lacking experience in the region. Factors for this appear to be (1) the narrower scope of the former East European research effort; (2) the unfamiliarity of East Europeanist researchers with the ways of western agencies; and (perhaps) (3) the lingering suspicion of those previously involved in East European research by the western policy community (see Kideckel 1995b; Wedel 1994 for supplementary discussions on this issue).

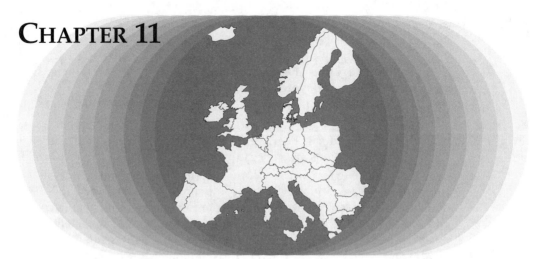

CHAPTER 11

AN ANTHROPOLOGY OF THE EUROPEAN UNION, FROM ABOVE AND BELOW

Thomas M. Wilson
The Queen's University of Belfast

In 1975 Jeremy Boissevain, in an essay introducing a volume written by members of the European-Mediterranean Study Group of the University of Amsterdam, spelled out the central problem addressed by the book's contributors. In so doing, he also identified key theoretical and methodological problems in the anthropology of Europe at the time, and problems that I suggest in this chapter are still of concern to anthropologists in Europe, and anthropologists of Europe. As Boissevain said,

> Political, religious and economic relationships [in Europe's villages] clearly do not exist in isolation at a local level. They are influenced by relationships and processes that lie beyond the community at regional, national and even supra-national levels. (1975, 9)

He went on to identify terms like "group, village, community, culture, society," which were used by anthropologists to indicate "socially significant entities," and he reviewed concepts, such as "brokerage, encapsulation, penetration, folk-urban, great tradition and little tradition, absorption and acculturation," which were used by anthropologists to make sense of the relations between these entities (see Boissevain 1975, 9). He was critical of the ways these concepts continued to be used almost exclusively in the study of small-scale, fairly isolated communities. As Boissevain charged,

> To polarize part and whole, micro and macro, community and nation in the

study of complex European societies by reifying them as separate categories does violence to the nature of the dynamic relationships between them, and the meaning they have to the people involved. Yet here lies the rub. Anthropologists have done little to systematize their thinking on the nature of these relationships to avoid this static polarization and reification. (Boissevain 1975, 9)

Boissevain was not alone in making these claims. In the 1970s and 1980s a number of other influential anthropologists made similar moves to reset the anthropological agenda in Europe, and in so doing to fuel a variety of theoretical debates in anthropological theory and method of significance beyond Europe. People like Eric Wolf, John Cole, Jane and Peter Schneider, Susan Tax Freeman, Anton Blok, John Davis, and Ralph Grillo[1] (among many others—this list is not exhaustive) have made important contributions to the anthropology of Europe that have at least one theme in common—that of taking anthropology beyond the locality in order to understand communities' relationships with people and institutions of the region, nation, and state. As Cole and Wolf said in *The Hidden Frontier* (1974),

[W]e are convinced of the utility of an approach that sees the *relation* between village and nation as problematic, and hence as a source of potential insights. That relation is for us not simple and mechanical; rather, we understand it as complex and dialectical. It is dialectical because village and total society exist in opposition and often in contradiction. It is dialectical because these two units in opposition interpenetrate each other and act upon one another in social and cultural interchanges. It is dialectical, finally, in that this interaction generates an ongoing transformation over time, which subjects the narrower unit to ever more comprehensive processes of integration, or synthesis. As anthropologists, we want to focus on the transformations worked upon small populations; but we also want to know something of the way in which what happens at the village level supports or stands in contrast to the character and direction of movement in the larger system. (Cole and Wolf 1974, 3–4)

Evocative calls to arms such as this have influenced many anthropologists of Europe and elsewhere, as well they should. But there continues to be much more that can and should be done in the anthropology of culture and power, in investigating the dialectical relations between localities and higher and wider levels of sociocultural, political, and economic integration. There is perhaps no better place to focus such studies, or to revitalize them, than in the Europe of today, the so-called "New Europe." I return to Boissevain, whose short essay in 1975 can still serve as both a summation and a reordering of the anthropological agenda in Europe. Boissevain contended that anthropological interest in Europe would grow because "Europe's complexity is precisely what makes it such a fascinating and important area of research" (1975, 11). He singled out many reasons why anthropologists should and would focus on Europe, including the relevance of European societies for the study of imperialism, capitalism, urbanization, industrialization, class conflict, state formation, national integration, bureaucratization, and commercialization. There is little to dispute in this contention. But he also identified many processes and institutions that may prove daunting to anthropologists. "The high degree of centralization, the interrelation between various levels of integration, the impact of multiple long-term processes, the sweep of change that can be documented across centuries still overwhelm many anthropologists" (Boissevain 1975, 11). As a result, these anthropologists, in Boissevain's words, "have sought refuge in villages.... They have tribalized Europe" (1975, 11).

It is not my intention in this chapter to engage in debate on the current state of the anthropology of Europe, or to provide a historical analysis of the merits of community studies (although I am aware that this chapter is related to both). My goal is to outline the many ways in which an anthropology of the European Union, which includes the past anthropology of the European Economic Community and the European Community (now officially and terminologically superseded in most contexts by the European Union, or EU), reflects the attempts by a variety of anthropologists to study issues of culture and power at supranational, national, and local levels, the integration and disintegration of relations between these levels, and the sweep of long-term and wide-ranging sources of cultural change.

Anthropologists and other ethnographers who study the EU have attempted to achieve the goal set by Cole and Wolf, to understand the transformations wrought on localities by people and institutions in wider society, and to understand the ways in which local communities can affect, and in some cases effect, that change. This is a difficult task, overwhelming in many ways. Some anthropologists who have undertaken it have chosen to concentrate their energies at the centers of power in the EU, among the Eurocracy and EU elites, including but not limited to regional and national government leaders and representatives, political party leaders, bureaucrats, lobbyists, and interest groups. I call this the top-down approach, looking from above at the EU as a political and social system. Other anthropologists have focused their attention on localities and institutions at lower levels of integration, and, in particular, on the impact of the EU on everyday life and the efforts of people to influence EU and national policymakers. This is the bottom-up approach, or the EU from below.

AN ANTHROPOLOGY OF THE EU

Why should anthropologists study the EU? This may at first glance be a self-serving question. But it would be an exaggeration to suggest that the sociocultural anthropology of Europe has kept pace with the startling developments in the EU over the last decade, or, for that matter, since the original EEC was formed in 1957. An analysis of the history and structure of the EU as a political, economic, social, and cultural entity is beyond the scope of this chapter. Suffice it to say that the EU is a social system of more than 360 million people, incorporating fifteen countries,[2] which as an intergovernmental body makes or influences policies that affect every aspect of life within its boundaries. Because of membership in the EU, all political action, economic decision making, social movements, and production of culture (low and high, popular and elite), once principally situated within the nation and the state and thus, once the problematic domains for anthropologists seeking to escape the constraints of the community method, are now firmly within the expansive arena of the largest interstate and international political system in the world. If the annual statistics of EU budgets, salaries, legislation, litigation, and dissemination of Euro-image and Euro-information were not enough to convince any social scientist of the need to study all European social formations within the EU context, then consider that the foods Europeans eat, the roads they travel, the beaches and forests they walk, the schools they attend, and the television they watch are but a sample of the conditions of daily life that bear the stamp of EU policy and administration. And the EU is growing. By the turn of the century, it is possible that there will be twenty member states, with a queue of Central and Eastern European countries in the wings. In short, and regardless of the past debates in places like the United Kingdom over whether the EU should widen itself or deepen its commitment to the creation of a new supranational body within its present structure and with its current membership (for a review of these two positions, see Bull 1993), the EU has become and will increasingly become a powerful actor in any new world order. In fact, the EU will define that new world order, and transform everyday life in Europe, from the Atlantic to the Urals and beyond.

As I have argued elsewhere (Wilson 1993a), I suggest that, with a few and recent exceptions, the EC has not been prominent in the ethnography or in macrosociological analyses of Europe conducted by anthropologists since the Community's inception. Over the last few years, however, there are indications that this situation is changing. Although categorizing the anthropological studies of the EU by pigeon-holing them into the two divisions of the "EU from above" (or perhaps it is more appropriate to call it the "EU from the center"), and the "EU from below" (in terms of the local community and beyond, or the "EU from the margins"), may be doing them a slight injustice, I think it a useful exercise in order to show some of the imbalance in our anthropological approach to the EU, a result of our methodological difficulties in ethnographic studies of culture, power, nations, and states.

THE EU FROM ABOVE

Perhaps the most promising, and in some senses the easiest, area of study of the EU is among the government leaders, bureaucrats, and lobbyists at the centers of EU power and decision making, in Brussels, Strasbourg, and

Luxembourg. I suggest that this may be a relatively easy way to study the EU precisely because these three places have been transformed by the presence of the EU; they have become "European" cities and the capitals of the new EU Europe. If there is any one place to study the dialectical relations between local communities and the higher levels of power, then it is in one of these cities where all the nations of Europe come and interact with not only the constituent units of the EC Commission, Council, and Parliament, but also the agents of the relevant regions and states that house them. Ethnographic analyses of these places are all but nonexistent, perhaps marking them as the ultimate examples of, to use Estellie Smith's phrase, the "incidental urban entities" of the EC (Smith 1993). Many anthropologists over the years have turned their critical eye to bureaucrats in a number of settings (the best recent example is Herzfeld 1992), and they have mapped out a number of successful strategies for conducting ethnographic studies among bureaucratic and government elites.

Restrictive access to the halls of power in the EU is the key obstacle, but at least six ethnographers have achieved success in this vein. Marc Abélès, Irène Bellier, and Maryon McDonald have been conducting research among the members of the European Commission in Brussels and elsewhere, and among the Members of the European Parliament (MEP), in Strasbourg, Brussels, and in the MEPs' home countries. Douglas Holmes recently completed a long-term research project in both the Parliament and the Commission. Little of this research on the Commission has been published to date, although Abélès has been productive in terms of his analysis of the European Parliament, including its everyday formal and informal politics, and the work and social schedules of the MEPs (Abélès 1992, 1993; see also Bellier 1995). McDonald's research continues at the Commission, and she has lately been involved in a mammoth enterprise to bring the anthropology of Europe, in terms of its breadth and depth, to the Commission's attention, and in particular to the attention of the think tank set up by the EU Commission president, Jacques Delors, to advise him on the scope of European life and integration (a suggestion of some of her research interests can be found in McDonald 1993). Others have worked on policy and policymakers in Brussels and Strasbourg. Cris Shore and Annabel Black have been investigating cultural policies (Shore 1993), European identity, and the cultural construction of Europe as seen from Brussels (Shore and Black 1992). Shore is at present designing a long-term project to study a number of the Commission's directorates, or policy departments.

Although appearing on the surface to be exciting and glamorous, this sort of research among people with power in the EU capitals is not as easy as it might at first seem. I surmise that he, and all the anthropologists who study EU elites, have had some difficulty in doing research among Eurocrats precisely because these civil servants and functionaries are educated, very busy, and perhaps at times more eager to interview the anthropologist about methods and audience than they are to answer questions. Their replies to interview questions also have a touch of the "official line" (Shore, personal communication), an occupational hazard to be considered by those who seek to conduct "fieldwork" among literate and powerful international elites.

The reluctance on the part of anthropologists to brave research among Eurocrats, or among the communities of people in Brussels and Strasbourg of which the Eurocrats are members, should not be surprising. There are clear problems of access to people and data; research in these central metropolises of Europe is extremely expensive; respondents are busy, elusive, and dispersed (at least after working hours); and anthropological research in particular is a largely unknown quantity to the people of the EU hierarchies, with the result that there is even less time and money available at their end for our ethnographic interests.

THE EU FROM BELOW

The importance and relevance of studies of power brokers in the EU capitals are apparent. Most anthropological studies of the EU have not been conducted among European elites, however, and although there is a growing literature in the ethnography of Europe within a variety of EU contexts, most of these studies focus primarily on local communities. Because historically there has been a preference in anthropological research in Europe toward the analysis of small communities, isolated locations, and people with little wealth and power, most of the anthropological approaches to the EU have centered on the impact of EU policies on a range of local social and political formations. Since local communities seldom have a clearly defined notion of the "Europe" of the EU, and often even less idea of how their communities are part of the total society that the EU represents, their role in the EU often appears to be reactive rather than proactive. Policies are experienced at local levels, but the means to affect the policy-making process at the level of the EU are either not at these communities' disposal or are perceived by them to be absent. As a result, the anthropology of the EU lacks a strong applied anthropological or policy-oriented character. There are exceptions, however, precisely because the EU since its inception has reconfigured a wide range of traditional ties between localities and nations and states.

Christian Giordano (1987) has analyzed the wine war between Italian and French peasants and agricultural cooperatives, in one of the earliest efforts to construct an ethnographic component to the understanding of the EC. Edward LiPuma and Sarah Keene Meltzoff (1989, 1994) have examined the ways in which Galician and other Iberian fishermen and their communities have adapted to EU fisheries policy, and they are among the few anthropologists who have attempted to chronicle ways in which local associations have carried the fight for their European rights to national capitals and to Brussels itself. Because the most important area of EU policy competence and power has been in agricultural policy, specifically in the Common Agricultural Policy, it is not surprising that most studies of rural Europe that focus on the EU are of the policy roller-coaster that farmers have been on since the 1970s. EU agricultural policy has transformed a host of past relationships between national governments and their countries' farmers, resulting in the loss of patronage and clientage, weakening farmer support for their traditional political parties, and providing the basis for new national and international farmers lobbies, as well as the financial means and political influence to create new forms of political action. I have studied the ways in which the Irish Farmers Association has helped to redefine local politics in Ireland (Wilson 1989a), which has had a number of knock-on effects on local notions of class and culture (Wilson 1988). André Jurjus (1993) has demonstrated how Dutch and Spanish farmers have developed diverging regional structures to deal with their volatile national and international markets. Mark Shutes (1991, 1993) has predicted that the EU will threaten the entire way of life of small farmers in Ireland and elsewhere in Europe, precisely because the EU as a market-driven economic system will cease to subsidize peasant and post-peasant farmers in its effort to maximize profit and productivity. To achieve this, the EU must also remove the financial support it has previously supplied to national governments, largely through its Structural and Cohesion Funds, which member states have used to subsidize their farmers in order to protect them from the vagaries of the free EU market, thereby guaranteeing farmers' support for political parties and governments. This inherent contradiction between the political goals of member nations and states, on the one hand, and the goals of the Eurocracy and other European elites to achieve economic and political union at a European, perhaps continental, level, on the other hand, is another area of great potential interest to anthropologists, especially in terms of conflicts over policy and the values and meanings of identity and political culture.

The EU has had an important effect on a wide range of social and cultural identities in Europe, forcing many groups of people to reconstruct their notions of nation, state, and sovereignty, and to renegotiate the many symbolic markers to the boundaries between groups that the EU, as a postmodern political structure, has transformed. Thus, Estellie Smith (1993) has investigated the changing role of cities in Europe; Parman (1993) has explored a variety of new community symbolic boundaries in Scotland, which are a direct result of EU membership; Alexandra Jaffe (1993a) has examined Corsicans' attempts to renegotiate their land as both region and nation in France and the EU; and Janeen Arnold Costa (1993) has looked at the impact of globalization and EU policies on images of self and possessions in Greece. Much of the anthropology of the EU, in fact, is the study of transnationals and transnationalism, in which the powerless of Europe and immigrants from elsewhere must negotiate themselves *as* "Europeans," as must influential elites such as bankers, as McDonogh (1993) and Gullick (1993) have respectively shown us. And the more that the EU is perceived by Europeans and anthropologists as a source of the attack on the traditional nation-state, then the more will nationalism figure prominently in our daily lives and privileged discourse (for a review of ways in which nationalism, the EU, and French scholarship are intertwined, see Varenne 1993b; for a view on Irish resistance to European integration, see Sheehan 1991). Perhaps there is no better arena in which to study the processes of nationalism and transnationalism than at the international borders between the states of Europe, where the EU's integration policies have resulted ostensibly in a "Europe without Frontiers," but where reduced barriers to commerce have not affected cultural and political constructions of the frontiers between nations and states (Wilson 1993b; Donnan and Wilson 1994).

"WHOSE HOME DO WE GO TO?"

In a piece that I wrote introducing a book of essays in the anthropology of the EU, I endorsed John Cole's 1977 suggestion that anthropologists' reluctance to conduct field research in the predictable and comfortable cultures of a "home" had for too long stultified the development of an anthropology of Europe. In his view the anglophone anthropologists of the time had come only "part-way home" because they not only avoided many European field sites but they also eschewed theories and methods that would allow them to understand the political economy of Europe beyond the local community (Cole 1977; Wilson 1993a; see also Ulin 1991). Almost twenty years later many anthropologists of Europe have still not found their way home. This may not be for the want of trying. As Irish publicans have been known to complain at a bar's closing time, in an effort to shame patrons out the door, "Have you no homes to go to?" One of the intentions of this chapter is to point out that Europe, at least in the guise of the EU, has become so volatile that anthropologists are as confused as are (other) Europeans about the location and the number of homes they have. None of the traditional symbols and institutions of hearth and home have gone untouched by a multitude of competing "Euro-isms." If the EU cannot desist from altering the elements of culture that define "home" to many Europeans (elements ranging from the bullfight in Spain, to the "pinta" milk in Britain, to the red sausage in Ireland), then many of the symbolic cornerstones to European society may be in jeopardy. It is no wonder that the anthropology of the EU has had difficulty finding its way along a path that is far from clear.

Nonetheless, an anthropology of the EU has many paths open before it. Some of the most productive and relevant may be in the application of ethnographic methods and anthropological theories to the totality of the EU as a set of cultural relations. I began this chapter by reviewing some of the writings by scholars who have been pointing out for some time that the anthropology of Europe must be an anthropology of nation and state. As Verdery indicated a few years ago, the nation is an element of the cultural relations between state and subject (1992, 8; see also Wilson 1993a, 18). We must also remember that the EU is a social system in which regions and states act as elements in the relations between subjects and the supranation. These elements are understood by Europeans to be about culture and power. As a consequence of this fact, which is so clearly appreciated by very many of the EU's people, I suggest that the anthropology of the EU is an anthropology of power in Europe. As Ghani correctly stipulated in his review of Eric Wolf's "anthropological quest": "Culture is never external to power, for all modes of power are cultural relationships in space and time" (1995, 42). The ways in which culture and power are meaningful in Europeans' lives, and the ways they are able to withstand or effect cultural change in the midst of EU building, should be the concern of anthropologists now and in the future.

One thing should be clear to all anthropologists of Europe, however. Although we may still be failing to articulate aspects of the total society, in local communities and beyond, in ways elicited by the scholars with whom I began this chapter, we must be clear that the supranation or superstate of the EU is not a nation and it is not a state. Although we may use the same tools and methods to study the EU as we would when studying nations and states beyond our communities, we must not confuse method and subject. As Walker Connor has been warning social scientists for years, in regard to "nation," "state" and "ethnic group," we must be clear about our definitions (Connor 1978). So too must we be aware that the EU is a new type of sociopolitical configuration, which is as new, surprising, and daunting to the peoples of Europe as it is to us. It is the process of constructing itself that may be the most exciting aspect of the cultural relations of the EU to Europeans. Perhaps our attempts to understand this process, which goes beyond the mechanisms and issues of nation and state building, will be the most exciting aspect of the EU to anthropologists. One thing is certain. Many national elites and state governments and bureaucracies are losing power in and to the EU. The current home for this power, and the fate of the peoples who will be the winners and losers in the creation of a European Union, are elements of the political culture of all of the localities, nations, and states of the EU. The future anthropology of Europe may very well stand or fall on our ability to understand and to adapt to this fact.

NOTES

1. Many publications are testament to the repeated calls by these authors to redirect the anthropological agenda in Europe. Some important examples are Blok 1974; Cole and Wolf 1974; Davis 1977; Freeman 1973; Grillo 1980; Schneider and Schneider 1976; Wolf 1982.

2. In 1995 Austria, Finland, and Sweden joined the EU member states Germany, France, Italy, The Netherlands, Belgium, Luxembourg, The United Kingdom, Denmark, Ireland, Greece, Spain, and Portugal.

CHAPTER 12

THE PLACE OF EUROPE IN GEORGE P. MURDOCK'S ANTHROPOLOGICAL THEORY

Mark T. Shutes
Youngstown State University

> There is a story, perhaps apocryphal, of the three tribal chiefs who were asked what their people did with their fathers when they died. One chief replied, "We eat them." Another said, "We burn them." And the third said, "We bury them." Each chief was unbelievably shocked by the repulsive, barbarous, and sacrilegious practices of the other two. Anthropology as a comparative science of man seeks, along with sociology and psychology, systematically to study and to understand the many different kinds of behavior found in the thousands of human societies known to history and ethnography, for only with such a cross-cultural approach will it be possible to create a science of human behavior. (Murdock 1957a, 249)

As I was passing Murdock's office, he asked me to come in for a moment. With another of what seemed to be an endless supply of Lucky Strikes dangling from his lips, he managed a sly smile and handed me the typed document that he was reading. "Tell me what you think of this," he said, "just read the introduction." By now, he had removed the cigarette and was offering me a huge grin. I noticed that the article was a submission for the journal *Ethnology*, and that its topic was the social organization of some Eastern European group. As I turned to the beginning, the very first word of the first line was "Therefore," followed by a comma and a long ending paragraph that continued beyond the first page. In spite of myself, I began to laugh out loud, and found that Murdock was laughing, just as heartily, right along with me! It seems the poor author had jumbled up his pages in a rush to submit the document, and had placed his concluding remarks at the very beginning. "I've said that anthropologists often jump to conclusions too quickly," he said through tears of laughter, "but this is the worst example yet!" Then he suddenly became serious and said: "This (the article) is about Europe and so I thought you'd be interested in reading it, but it isn't the kind of work we've been talking about. It pays no attention to the individual as decision-maker, and it doesn't place the system of social organization into any framework of economic reality. As anthropologists, we have got to learn to do these things" (Author's personal journal, Autumn 1972).

INTRODUCTION

The name George P. Murdock has become almost synonymous with cross-cultural studies, and with the painstaking reading, coding, and sampling of ethnographic materials in order to arrive at statistically valid generalizations about various aspects of human behavior, most notably, in his own case, kinship and social organization. Some would reject such work as epitomizing an "old-fashioned" approach and view attempts to seek regularities in the universe of coded ethnographic material as (perhaps) valiant, but (certainly) futile (cf. Guyer 1996, 112–113; Linnekin 1996, 115–116). Fewer still would associate Murdock with European anthropology and a strong concern for the role of individual decision-making in molding and shaping human behavior.

As one of Murdock's last students, I find such assessments of his work to be inadequate and inaccurate, and in this discussion of his contribution to the anthropological theory of Europe I hope to be able to demonstrate that: (1) Murdock viewed Europe as the key area for future anthropological research and that he urged students such as myself toward a path of European ethnography and ethnology; (2) his research strategy was, from the very beginning, systematic and open-ended, incorporating as it did the widest possible range of social science theory and method, and that this kind of approach, while certainly rare in our discipline, will never be out of fashion; (3) it was the systematic and open-ended character of his research that lead him to ultimately reject as "myths" the majority of the key anthropological concepts of his time and to offer an alternative strategy for future social science; and (4) the European stage acted as a catalyst for his new formulations both because it was underrepresented ethnographically and because he viewed the underrepresentation as being symptomatic of faulty theoretical concepts.

MURDOCK AND EUROPEAN ETHNOGRAPHY/ETHNOLOGY

As a graduate student of Murdock's interested in continuing my research in rural Ireland, I was somewhat surprised by the fieldwork advice that he offered me. There was no discussion of the accuracy of my ethnographic cod-

ing, or the problems of world sampling, or the adequacy of the statistical procedures in my research, or any of the other cross-cultural processes that I had
expected. Rather, Murdock encouraged me to examine my rural ethnographic
data from a strategic, decision-making perspective, and never to lose sight of
the fact that individuals were at the heart of any notion of change that I might
develop. They made decisions as individuals. They renegotiated older patterns
of acceptable behavior with each other. They actively participated in changing
their lives. It was my task as an anthropologist to document these processes
and to identify the factors that contributed to their decisions. In addition, I was
to be wary of any explanation for change that talked about such processes at
the "mythical level" of culture, such as the (then) strongly held notion that
"peasant" farmers' decisions about production were governed exclusively by a
set of universally shared traditional cultural values rather than by differing
local ecologies and/or changing market considerations.

Later I came to realize that the procedures he recommended demanded
greater rigor at all levels of the analysis. Since the suggested research strategy
hinged upon the documentation of individual farmers' decisions, ethnographic
variability had to be recorded at the individual farm household level, including family histories and complete ecological, technological, social, economic,
political, and religious data for every household member, since any and all of
these variables might have affected a farmer's decision-making process, and
different farmers may have been affected by different variables.

The focus of the analysis itself shifted from an identification of the characteristics shared by members of a farming community to an identification of
the ways in which individual members of the community farmed, and the
extent to which they agreed and disagreed about the nature of their enterprises
and their relationships to each other and to the greater world around them.
Where they agreed upon priorities, they shared behavioral expectations and
strategies, and where they disagreed, they negotiated new strategies with each
other and changed. But there was never a point of stasis in the analysis, never
a period of unchanging cultural tradition upon which to drape one's ethnographic cloak. It was all becoming. The extent to which anthropologists could
document and understand the process depended upon the rigors of their data
collection and their willingness to suspend their biases about culture and collective behavior and examine individuals in the process of creative interaction
in a world where knowledge is not perfect and change is a constant.

Murdock had become convinced that the same general principles applied
whether the focus was on rural Ireland or highland New Guinea: greater
ethnographic rigor and a shift in focus from the group to the individual. But he
was particularly interested in applying these new anthropological procedures
to the European continent and he was acutely aware of the lack of adequate
anthropological studies within Europe. In the mid-1950s, the Human Relations
Area Files (HRAF) had subcontracted numerous monographs on cultures
within the Soviet Bloc and in other areas in Europe (cf. HRAF Monographs
#1–12, 15, 18–20, 22, 25, 34, 35, 41), and later published an extensive ethno-

graphic bibliography for both Europe (Theodoratus 1969) and the Circum-Mediterranean (Sweet and O'Leary 1969). Murdock also expressed this concern in the introduction to the Ethnographic Atlas (1967, 2):

> The case is still different for Europe … an area for which ethnographic responsibility rests primarily with sociologists and historians rather than anthropologists. The author … has included only a small and unrepresentative fraction of the many adequately described societies—and these only because of his conviction that the exclusion of the Western peoples and their cultures from the ethnographic universe is totally unwarranted.

Murdock was greatly influenced by the early work of Fredrik Barth and his colleagues on the entrepreneurs of Northern Norway (1967a) and Barth's essay on social change (1967b). These were some of the first works that Murdock insisted I read because he believed that they represented a major contribution to the modern ethnographic literature for Europe and because they emphasized the role of individual decision-making in shaping behavior. Indeed, he refers to Barth's approach as "perhaps the most promising recent development in anthropological science" (1971, 23).

Murdock's European interests also had a strong influence on other graduate students at the University of Pittsburgh. In the decade of the 1970s, many students began their professional anthropological careers with a European fieldwork experience, and the majority of them pursued themes of economic and political decision-making (cf. Armstrong 1976; Frolander-Ulf 1978; Glascock 1973; Greenwood 1970; Halpern 1978; Hearn 1978; Kane 1977; Young 1975).

MURDOCK'S SYSTEMATIC APPROACH

To discuss the continuing relevance of Murdock's approach to both general anthropological and European anthropological theory, it is important first to address the common (but erroneous) assumptions regarding his work.

(1) Murdock was not a rigid positivist by any reasonable definition of that term. His views of the relationship between his own research and pure science demonstrates this fact quite pointedly. *Webster's Third New International Dictionary* defines positivism as "the theory or doctrine that society is susceptible of analysis in purely objective mechanistic terms and that social values or normative standards are mere epiphenomena." In 1950, Murdock stated that cross-cultural research of the sort that was being carried out by his Institute of Human Relations "offers no promise of substantial advance in either pure sci-

ence or interdisciplinary integration," and that any claims to the contrary were "illusory" (1950, 573–574). Further, he suggested that

> [p]erhaps, then, the sciences and humanities are not so distinct ... if there is such a genuine overlap and interpenetration, it may possibly seem less humiliating to recognize the essentially closer affiliation of area research with the humanities than with the sciences. (576–577)

These are hardly the thoughts of a rigid positivist. Indeed, this quote is even more relevant when one considers that it came only a year after the publication of *Social Structure*, Murdock's most famous international work, and the one to which most critics usually refer as being evidence of his strong positivist/materialist approach (cf. McGee and Warms 1996, 262). Rather, the above words indicate someone coming to the distinct recognition that such strict approaches to anthropological research cannot be fully realized (note the use of the words "less humiliating").

(2) Murdock was not a cultural determinist of any sort. He did not believe that culture was a monolith of values that unconsciously shaped and determined all individuals under its influence in exactly similar ways. According to Murdock (1941, 141–142),

> Society ... with the environment, poses problems for the individual, teaches him time-tested cultural solutions, and enforces his observance of them. The solutions themselves, or culture, reside only in the habit systems of individuals, constituting such of their habits as the members of a society or group share with one another. Of itself, therefore, culture can exert no influence upon an individual; expressions like "the coercion of custom" and "cultural compulsives" are meaningless and misleading. Culture is merely the lesson to be learned; the teacher and disciplinarian is society or its agents—parents, associates, wielders of authority, etc. ... Interpersonal relationships constitute the cement of society. Whenever two persons come into face-to-face association they adjust their behavior to one another, in part by bringing into play cultural norms with which they are already familiar, and in part by developing new reactions through the learning process.

From the above it is readily apparent that Murdock viewed culture not as a rigidly deterministic set of inviolate rules, but rather as only a part of the on-going "negotiations," if you will, between individuals, that could also involve non-normative and other creative aspects. The most important locus of behavior, for Murdock, was always the individual, and not the group. Consider the following:

> Anthropologists are fond of considering culture as a closed system, self-per-
> petuating and self-propagating. Nothing could be further from the fact.
> Like all habits, those of the cultural order persist only if they are reinforced
> or rewarded. Unless they achieve for individuals in the mass a favorable
> balance of satisfactions, they decline and suffer extinction.... Nor is culture
> change autonomous, springing from preexisting culture. On the contrary,
> its source is to be sought in actual behavior. When this fails to achieve satis-
> factions, the collective habits which find expression therein undergo modifi-
> cation. Individual after individual resorts to random behavior, out of which
> innovations spring, or adoption of the alternative cultural solutions offered
> by other societies. (1941, 144–145)

Nor did he subscribe to the notion that knowledge and analysis of culture
represented the pinnacle of social science research, or that culture was irre-
ducible to other domains, such as society or the individual, but rather saw
these three factors as "so intimately intertwined that there is probably no social
science datum which is not at the same time individual, social, and cultural,
and which cannot be approached from any of the three angles" (1941, 140). He
was more of an open-ended interactionist or behavioral science theorist, con-
versant with, and willing to entertain, theoretical notions drawn from anthropology, sociology, psychology, psychiatry, and other disciplines, so long as
they added to our knowledge of how individual human beings reacted to one
another within variable social settings.

(3) Murdock did not believe that cross-cultural research represented the
single most important method for examining the complexities of human
behavior, nor that coded references to human behavior of the sort found in the
Human Relations Area Files (HRAF) could adequately represent the totality of
these complexities. Comparing pure science research methods with cross-cultural ones, he stated,

> Basically a scientific principle or "law" is merely a statement of an invari-
> able relationship between phenomena whereby one characteristic changes
> in a precisely defined manner as another or others are altered in an equally
> definite manner. It is a peculiarity of pure science that once such a relation-
> ship has been established, experimentally or otherwise, the scientist no
> longer has the slightest interest in the phenomena themselves, whether they
> be objects or events. The abstracted relationship is his only concern.... Area
> research has no such interest in the discovery and validation of abstract
> principles, and certainly no such indifference to its data after they have
> been analyzed. On the contrary, it seeks to order its data into meaningful
> configurations, and afterwards to preserve them intact in their significant
> relationships with one another. (1950, 572)

For Murdock, maintaining the ethnographic context of coded data was
essential to the enterprise of cross-cultural research, and he does not confuse,

nor conflate, method with theory in this regard. Burton et al. have recently confirmed this assessment when they state that "neither Murdock nor other cross-cultural coders claimed that there was as much information in the codes as in the original ethnographies, yet cross-cultural researchers are often treated as if they had done so" (1996, 119).

Since the inception of the original Cross-Cultural Survey in 1937, Murdock always had two very clear objectives for the project:

> In addition to its practical objective of facilitating diverse forms of social science research, the Cross-Cultural Survey has a special theoretical objective. It is organized so as to make possible the formulation and verification, on a large scale and by quantitative methods, of scientific generalizations of a universally human or cross-cultural character. (1940, 364)

As can be seen from the above, Murdock, true to his behavioral science orientation, wanted to provide a quick and inexpensive way for all behavioral scientists to gain access to cross-cultural data in order to examine any number of theoretical propositions about human behavior. But also, and this point is crucial to future claims made in this chapter, he was designing a data base to test the scientific validity of anthropological theories of culture and its relationship to human behavior. From the same article as the above, he continued,

> [I]t seems premature to conclude that anthropology cannot be made a science until, using all known safeguards, we have made at least one serious and systematic attempt to formulate scientific generalizations about man and culture which will withstand a quantitative test. Anthropology has many objectives. That envisaged by the Cross-Cultural Survey is not intended to supplant the others, nor does it lay claim to greater importance. It is simply regarded as legitimate, promising, and opposed by no insuperable theoretical obstacles.... The plan rests at bottom on the conviction that all human cultures, despite their diversity, have fundamentally a great deal in common, and that these common aspects are susceptible to scientific analysis. (1940)

Clearly, Murdock did not design his research strategy to answer the question of how the already scientifically valid theories and methods of anthropology can explain the cross-cultural regularities found in human behavior, but rather with the question of whether or not anthropological theories about such regularities, couched in what he viewed as their most rigorous methodological form, could be shown to be scientific at all. Can anthropology, in other words, be "made a science?" Murdock's personal belief at the outset of the project was that the answer would be "yes," but he was willing to let the rigors of the scientific method ultimately decide the issue (1940, 369–370). That anthropological theories of culture were at the heart of this "grand design" is also clear, since all of the seven fundamental assumptions he sets out to examine concern this concept (1940, 364–368).

Throughout his long career, and despite many other interests in more specific anthropological topics, Murdock and the staff of the HRAF remained true to these initial objectives. He encouraged ethnographic studies in geographic areas where the files were deficient, continuously reviewed new ethnographic material so as to include only the most rigorous and complete descriptions, and offered many refinements and samples of the total files that would meet the objections of "Galton's problem" of comparing data drawn from differing time periods and overlapping geographic and cultural space. He insisted that all ethnographic material be able to be coded in as similar a manner as possible, not because he believed that the codes were more important than the context, but because his test of the validity of anthropological theories as scientific demanded that the data from all societies be framed in the same way. As we have seen, he never lost sight of the very real possibility that a scientific anthropology would have to be rejected, and hence his insistence upon the primary importance of the ethnographic context and his view that, because of this contextual concern, cross-cultural research would never be the same as pure science research.

I contend that the nature and substance of Murdock's contribution to anthropological theory has been so badly misunderstood precisely because he carried out long-term systematic research on the theory of culture and the extent to which it could be understood via the rigors of the scientific method, and that he did so within a discipline where such research is rare. Considering that, during the sixty-year span of Murdock's career, anthropology had rigorously defended/attacked every conceivable position from nineteenth-century evolutionism to late-twentieth-century postmodernism, with many major theorists making two or more radical changes in approach during their own careers, it is not surprising that our discipline finds it difficult to classify and comprehend a single systematic approach, let alone one that was designed to test the scientific status of our major concepts.

ANTHROPOLOGICAL THEORY AS MYTH

By the beginning of the 1970s, Murdock, after 'a lifetime of professional trial-and-error' (1971, 23), became convinced that the concepts of culture and social system had no scientific validity. In his words,

> It now seems to me distressingly obvious that culture, social system, and all comparable supra-individual concepts, such as collective representations, group mind, and social organism, are illusory conceptual abstractions

inferred from observations of the very real phenomena of individuals interacting with one another and with their natural environments. The circumstances of their interaction often lead to similarities in the behavior of different individuals which we tend to reify under the name of culture, and they
cause individuals to relate themselves to others in repetitive ways, which
we tend to reify as structures or systems. But culture and social structure
are actually mere epiphenomena—derivative products of the social interaction of pluralities of individuals. More precisely, they resemble the illusory
constructs so prevalent in the early days of the natural sciences, such as
those of phlogiston and the luminiferous ether in physics, and systems of
theory based upon them have no greater validity or utility ... they cannot
legitimately be used to explain human behavior. Culture and social aggre-
gates are explainable as derivates of behavior, but not *vice versa*. All systems
of theory which are based on the alleged or inferred characteristics of aggre-
gates are consequently inherently fallacious. They are, in short, mythology,
not science, and are to be rejected in their entirety—not revised or modified.
(emphasis Murdock) (1971, 19)

Having rejected the key concepts, Murdock also rejected the behavioral
theories based upon them, saying that

> ... what passes as theory in anthropology includes remarkably few proposi-
> tions which meet the basic requirements of science, that is to say, which
> explicitly state relationships between phenomena, specify precisely how
> these change as relevant variables are altered, and support such statements
> with adequate validating evidence. It consists in the main of what George
> Homans (1967, 10–19) calls 'nonoperating definitions' and 'orienting state-
> ments.' Prominent among the former are the concepts of culture and social
> system. (1971, 20)

Murdock found it 'inconceivable' that there could be such profound lack
of agreement over basic theoretical issues in any 'established fields of science,'
and that what anthropology was producing was 'not scientific theory in any
real sense but something much closer to the unverifiable dogmas of differing
religious sects' (1971, 19). In sum, he rejected it all, including 'the bulk of my
own work' (1971, 20). But he was not willing to reduce the entire anthropological endeavor to the realm of the humanities. In a presagement of the current
positivist-interpretivist debate, he says the following about the symbolic
approaches that were only then emerging in anthropology:

> I suspect that my skepticism stems primarily from an awareness of how
> vastly easier it is to speculate than it is to validate.... I am by no means con-
> vinced that what is postulated is actually a scientific myth. At least some of

the proponents insist that the symbolic connections they note are strictly metaphorical rather than causal, which would remove their theories from the realm of science to that of the humanities. If this is the case, their alleged discoveries are as scientifically irrelevant as are the latest fashions in literary criticism. (1971, 23)

He suggested a number of related ways in which anthropology could revitalize its claim to being a 'genuine and full-fledged science of man' (1971, 22), which can be summarized as follows: (1) that we retain our tradition of accurate descriptive ethnography, but that we (2) harness those descriptions to a more dynamic behavioral theory that emphasizes individuals as active and creative decision makers that regularly negotiate with each other in order to acquire that which met their needs. The new locus of study for Murdock was, therefore, the individual, rather than some mythological notion of group, which necessitates, for him, a closer alignment of anthropology with behavioral psychology and decision-making theory (1971, 22–ff.).

DISCUSSION

It is clear to me from the above, and from numerous private conversations with him, that Murdock was convinced that Europe was the ideal setting to test some of the aspects of his new approach to anthropology, both because it was an underrepresented area ethnographically, and because the underrepresentation itself was indicative of our faulty theoretical notions. In other words, we had devised a set of fatally flawed concepts to explain the behavior of the rest of the world that we could not easily apply to our own kind of society, hence the paucity of ethnographic material for the European continent. And so, in his view, why not begin again with a set of all-inclusive concepts such as those suggested above, and why not begin in those societies where we had already implicitly credited such concepts? To start in Europe with a new foundation for our discipline seemed, therefore, a doubly-sound course of action to him. We have also seen that Murdock's own ideas were stimulated and reinforced by the work of the Norwegian social anthropologists, particularly Fredrik Barth. I also suspect that such views were hatching for a long period of time, as is witnessed by his strong push for European ethnographic materials as far back as the 1950s.

Europe acted as a catalyst in the refinement of Murdock's views about human behavior, and in his remaining professional years he encouraged me and others to examine Europe as an ethnographic and ethnological workshop. I have found Murdock's theoretical guidance of my early work in Europe to be invaluable. The idea of emphasizing individuals as strategic thinkers and active participants in the shaping of their lives has been a central theme in my own work on Irish and Greek farmers (Shutes 1987, 1989, 1991, 1992, 1993, 1994, 1996), and has intensified my awareness of the need for more comprehensive ethnographic description when moving from a group model to an individual one, as Murdock suggested. But beyond this level, I believe that Murdock's larger contribution to the anthropological theory in Europe lies in the fact that he offers us both a model for how to carry out systematic inquiry into human behavior, and solutions for how to create a new and myth-free version of our discipline based upon the individual as an active decision-maker. Murdock's work represents the rarest of all anthropological accomplishments: systematic, open-ended inquiry into the validity of our most basic concepts and assumptions about human behavior. It is perhaps a measure of our unfamiliarity with such approaches that his work could erroneously be classified as "old-fashioned" positivism, or cultural determinism, or materialism, or any of the other titles we have given to our numerous theoretical bathwaters.

We have seen how Europe influenced Murdock's work, but how have his views influenced our work in Europe? Murdock spent his life systematically evaluating our most fundamental concepts by the most rigorous methods known to him, and he found them to be totally lacking in validity. He rejected our notions of collective behavior as "myths" and found them to be bereft of any true explanatory power, particularly with respect to the process of change. He challenged us to realign anthropology in order to reclaim the importance of the individual as strategist and decision-maker and thereby salvage anthropology's claims to being a social science, and he reemphasized the importance of more intensive descriptive ethnography in this realignment. Besides his students mentioned earlier, many anthropologists working in Europe have now begun to arrive at similar conclusions. Wilson (1993a, 20), for example, states that ethnographic treatments that emphasize decision-making and the ways in which Europeans are contesting and negotiating the new domains produced by the EU should be a major focus for anthropological study. Sutton has also noted that ethnography in Greece "has increasingly moved toward examination of ways in which individuals interpret and contest dominant value structures and normative patterns, inserting considerations of gender, ethnicity, and regional marginality," which she views as a positive step away from earlier community studies models dominated by functionalist approaches (1996, 9). In Ireland, a number of anthropologists have documented the importance of decision-making models in understanding the lives of Irish farmers (cf. Curtin 1986; Shutes 1991, 1993; Wilson 1988, 1989a, 1990a). Jurjus (1993) also views such models as crucial to understanding the changes in farmers' production strategies in Holland and Spain.

Clearly, not all of the modern ethnographic literature from Europe is emphasizing individual decision-making models in the manner that Murdock described (Ulin 1991). Europe has become the proving ground for a number of diverse approaches ranging from materialist to interpretive (Wilson 1993a, 19). But the majority of these approaches also reject the old theoretical concepts and examine the individual actor in new and dynamic ways (cf. Cohen 1987;

Harding 1984; Herzfeld 1985, 1987b; Holmes 1989; Kertzer 1980; McDonogh 1986; Parman 1990; Rogers 1991a; Schneider and Schneider 1976; Wilson and Smith 1993; and Wolf 1982), which was certainly part of Murdock's intent, if not his precise methodology, for an all-inclusive anthropology. Consider a statement he made almost fifty years ago:

> Perhaps they (sciences and humanities) differ primarily only in degree, with the former laying greater emphasis upon the establishment of universally valid abstract principles, and the latter upon the understanding of phenomena in the contexts in which they naturally occur. (1950, 576)

Given the dynamic status of the anthropology of Europe today, I think it is safe to assume that such developments would bring a different kind of smile to Murdock's face than the one that I remember from that day in his office in 1972, for the ethnographic and ethnological literature on Europe is serving to transform the discipline of anthropology in very much the way that he imagined it would.

CHAPTER 13

THE MEANING OF "EUROPE" IN THE AMERICAN ANTHROPOLOGIST (PART I)

Susan Parman
California State University, Fullerton

I n the following chapter, the journal *American Anthropologist* is treated as a foreign country within which I have attempted to do fieldwork on when, where, how, and why the topic of "Europe" has occurred in anthropological discourse.

It is reasonable to ask, as Timothy H. H. Thoresen did in his review of three selections of papers from the *American Anthropologist* (1979, 194), who reads old journal articles? And who reads the *American Anthropologist*—to which I would add, why read anthropological articles about Europe? The first question is about the significance of history, the second is about whether the *American Anthropologist* represents a reasonable sample of the discipline, and the third is about the place of Europe in the anthropological imagination.

I concur with Thoresen that the *American Anthropologist* may not provide a complete map of the territory of disciplinary anthropology, but understanding its major themes and trends, especially from an historical perspective, provides an effective vehicle for a broader understanding of the discipline. Reading old journal articles is in itself interesting (like ethnographers immersing themselves in the experience of the field, historians risk discovering things they did not expect to find), but in addition it has become apparent that one of the most important developments within twentieth-century anthropology has been the emergence of a critical examination by anthropologists of their own history. As they become more aware of the historical trends and disciplinary biases that shape their research, they learn as much about themselves as they do about the Other that is the presumed focus of their research, and that the Other is itself a product of western constructions and resolutions (see, for example, Pandian 1985). A critical history of anthropology must address and make explicit the meaning of the West, and especially Europe as the quintessential West.

METHOD: THE INDUCTIVE EUROPE

To observe the meaning of "Europe" in patterns of discourse is quite different from beginning with the definition of "Europe" as a culture area or a continent. Many courses on Europe begin with the latter. For example, using the definition of a culture area as "any large area, usually contiguous, that is inhabited by people of a particular culture, a land upon which the visible imprint of that culture has been placed" (Jordan 1973, 7), the cultural geographer Terry Jordan defined twelve traits that distinguish the European culture area: being of "Caucasian race," speaking an Indo-European language, having a religious tradition of Christianity, high level of literacy, low mortality rate, low population increase, per capita annual income of $1,000 or more, over 60 percent of the population living in cities, 35 percent or more of the work force involved in industry, a certain density of railroad network, no violent or illegal overthrow of government since 1950, and at least 100 kilograms of fertilizer applied to each hectare of arable land per year (Jordan 1973, 10). To this list are often added the traits of democracy (versus tyranny), creative innovation (versus passive conservatism), and science (versus custom).

Anthropologists may claim to be less culturally biased in their definitions of European culture area(s) (emphasizing, for example, ecological adaptations, settlement patterns, division of labor, kinship and social structure, as in Arensberg 1963; Gilmore 1982; Halpern and Kideckel 1983; Kenny 1963; and Pitkin 1963), but the point is that a trait list has severe limitations. If taken at face value, it is subject to nit-picking (where, in Jordan's trait list, would Basques, Hungarians, Turks, immigrants, poor rural populations, and the former Yugoslavia fit?), and it glosses over the point that all definitions involve symbolic contrasts in specific contexts.

The definition of Europe as a "continent" demonstrates this point. Europe is often defined as a continent; but as a mere one-fifth of the vast Eurasian landmass, Europe hardly qualifies as "a sizable landmass that stands more or less separate from other landmasses." The definition of Europe as a separate continent must be understood not as a geographical fact but as a cultural reality, a conceptual contrast constructed through comparison and relationship. Geographic and cartographic conventions (e.g., medieval T-O maps showing the world subdivided into three continents—Asia, Europe, and Africa—occupied by the three sons of Noah) reflect these relational contingencies. An example of a relational definition of what it means to be European is provided by Segal (1991), who argued that from the late seventeenth century on, in the context of New World plantations that relied on the unfree labor of "Africans," peoples who had previously thought of themselves as being of diverse class and national origin were rendered into a singular race identified as "European."

In my inductive reading of the *American Anthropologist*,[1] I attempted to understand the relational context in which "Europe" was used. It became clear that "Europe" is a complex and multivocal symbol in the history of American anthropology. Sometimes serving as the unexamined comparative framework (civilized, progressive, rational, etc.) in contrast to which the anthropological imagination constructs its exotic Other, the Europe of anthropological imaginings may also be rendered peripheral, marginal, exotic, orientalized (as represented, depending on the comparative context, by such groups as Celts, Slavs, gypsies, Latins, communists, peasants, Eastern Europeans, Catholics, and people variously defined as magical, fragmented, irrational, concrete, communal, stagnant, ahistorical, and even humanistic). Fixing Europe in the lens of critical analysis has the potential to illuminate the processes by which Us and Other are constructed—the Us referring not only to cultural identity (European qua western, American qua European) but to disciplinary identity as well (for example, anthropology distinguishing itself from sociology).

The following sections explore three patterns in the way "Europe" is used, or what Europe "means" in the American anthropological imagination (as represented in the pages of the *American Anthropologist*). These three patterns do not exhaust the discourse on Europe in this journal, but are prominent enough to serve as initial examples:

1. Through a series of contrasts (such as East versus West, nomadic versus sedentary, peasant versus urban, communist versus capitalist, Latin/Germanic versus Slavic, pre-Indo-European versus Indo-European), American anthropologists used discourse on Europe to explore and define the boundaries of the Occident (the West, conceived of as the essentialist match to Edward Said's Orient).

2. American anthropologists used discourse on Europe to explore and define their own physical identity as Americans sharing a European/"White" biological heritage.

3. In addition, discourse on Europe played an important role in helping American anthropologists explore and define the disciplinary boundaries of anthropology.

The citations are hardly comprehensive (the chapter would sink, like a ship overweighted with bibliographic lumber) and are often chosen not only because they are representative of the pattern but because of the odd spin they place on the pattern. The primary focus of this chapter (Part I) is on the period leading up to the 1970s. A second paper (Part II), describing developments that have occurred within American anthropology since the 1970s when the "anthropology of Europe" acquired institutional support, will be published at a later date.

OCCIDENTALIZING EUROPE

"Occidentalism" is an inversion of Edward Said's "Orientalism" (1978). Several anthropologists (e.g., Nader 1989; Carrier 1994) have coined the term occidentalism to make the point that the process of orientalizing a subject (that is, creating an essentialized image of the Orient that is absolutely different from the West) requires occidentalizing its counterpart (that is, creating an essentialized image of the West that is absolutely different from the Orient). Orientalisms define the boundary of the West, as occidentalisms define the boundary of the orient.[2] Without an orientation, we are nowhere; without a fall there can be no rising.[3]

"Occidentalizing Europe" would seem to be redundant. If Europe is the quintessential West, how can it be occidentalized? Isn't Europe, by definition, the Occident?

"Occidentalizing Europe" refers to the process by which Europe (or parts of Europe) are essentialized through the use of contrastive sets. In occidental discourse, "Europe" has the potential to be used as a symbolic vehicle that conveys the meaning of essential difference between Us and Other. Describing latitude, longitude, capitals, rivers, and mountain ranges within the geographical region labeled Europe is not an example of occidentalization, whereas a statement such as "Europe is defined as a Christian (versus Muslim/pagan/etc.) country" is an example of occidentalization.

"Occidentalizing Europe" also refers to the process by which regions, peoples, and eras within the geographical region of Europe serve as vehicles to convey essential difference. (It would be as reasonable to use the phrase "orientalizing Europe," because in the process of describing some groups—for example, urban dwellers—as embodying the essence of Occident/West/Us, other groups serving as a contrastive set—in this case, rural dwellers—are represented as embodiments of Orient/non-West/Other.)

In the *American Anthropologist*, certain groups, times, or regions of Europe were occidentalized as indigenous or autochthonous, historical, and progressive, in contrast with others that were orientalized as foreign, timeless, timelocked, or undeveloped. Sometimes the groups, times, or regions changed their signification, resulting in the geographical West becoming orientalized and the geographical East becoming occidentalized. For example, when the "civilized Ancient East" was considered the source of the foundations of Western Civilization, it was more occidental than the "barbaric" Celts or Teutonic hordes ravaging western Europe. Depending on the context in which the occidental/oriental contrast was constructed, the position of the orientalized Other might be occupied by Celts, Lapps, Basques, gypsies, peasants, nomadic pastoralists, ancient Greeks, Romans, Etruscans, or pre-Indo-Europeans. When Protestantism defined the West (as individualistic and a promoter of economic dynamism), Catholicism became the Other (as communal and tradition-bound); when Christianity was used to define the West, Islam became the Other; when Islam was interpreted as a Great Tradition—literate, enshrining the knowledge of the Greeks, urban—it was occidentalized (that is, incorporated into the essentialized image of the Occident/Europe/Us), and the barbaric hordes of western Europe pounding at the door of learning became the orientalized Other.

The following chart delineates some of the structural contrasts of occidental and oriental characteristics found in discourse on Europe in the *American Anthropologist*.

OCCIDENT/US	ORIENT/OTHER
TEMPORAL CONTEXT	
of the historical present	of a previous historical period
Indo-European	pre-Indo-European
Greco-Roman	pre-Greco-Roman
GEOGRAPHIC CONTEXT	
Western Europe	Eastern Europe
Eastern Europe (as place of Indo-European development)	Western Europe (not yet Indo-Europeanized)
northwestern Europe	southern/eastern Europe
democratic Europe	communist Europe
Greco-Roman/Islamic/Byzantine/Eastern (civilized)	Celtic/Germanic/Scandinavian/Western (barbarian)
German	Celtic
Teutonic	Latin
Teutonic/Latin	Slavic
rustic nationalist roots (Celtic, Germanic, etc.)	externally introduced influences ("East")
Indo-European	non-Indo-European

Occident/Us	Orient/Other
CULTURAL CONTEXT	
has history	has no history
literate/historical depth	oral/ethnographic present
creative	noncreative/stagnant
questions, challenges, thinks	mimics, accepts authority, submits
scientific	humanistic
modernized/modernizing	traditional
politically stable	politically labile
democratic	orientally despotic
Indo-European tripartite ideology	non-Indo-European (other ideologies)
Indo-European languages	non-Indo-European languages
agricultural/sedentary	pastoralist/nomadic
urban	rural
associative	communal
united	fragmented
individualistic	submerged in group
rational	irrational/prerational/magical
abstract	concrete
Christian	non-Christian/pagan
Protestant	Catholic
secular learning	ecclesiastical learning

Temporal boundaries between Occident and Orient refer to boundaries that define European autochthony (that is, when Europe became distinctively European), or to boundaries that divide contemporary peoples who participate actively in and belong to the present from contemporary peoples who, through their conservatism and tradition-bound behavior, are chained eternally to the past (the Moderns versus the Living Fossils). *Geographic* boundaries may be linked with temporal boundaries (that is, not only when but where did Europeans first become distinctively European; which parts of Europe are "modern" and which more closely resemble the past). *Cultural* boundaries refer to those linguistic, cognitive, technological, political, religious, and affiliative characteristics used, from one context to another, to distinguish Occident from Orient. Characteristics may be listed under more than one heading depending on the temporal, geographical, or cultural context in which they are used (for example, "Indo-European" may be used to refer to a linguistic group emerging at a certain period of time, a population in a particular geographic region, or a set of mythical/religious cultural traits).

Geographic areas and cultural characteristics or groups defined as marginal are especially significant in defining the criteria by which occidental and oriental boundaries are established, because arguments tend to be more explicit—when and why are geographic areas such as Eastern Europe, Russia, Greece (and the Mediterranean in general), Israel (and the Middle East), Turkey, and India defined as occidental or oriental? Are Celts, Scandinavians, Basques, Etruscans, nomads, and peasants occidental or oriental, and why?

EUROPEAN AUTOCHTHONY: INDIGENOUS IDENTITIES

Archaeologists and linguists in particular played an important role in attempting to identify the temporal, geographic, and cultural roots of the Occident, or when, where, and how Europe became distinctively European.

When East Was West   When civilization was the primary essence of the Occident to late-nineteenth- and early-twentieth-century writers, the essential West was constituted in the geographic East or the Mediterranean South, not in northwestern Europe. Babylonia, Egypt, Sumeria, and the Middle East in general (as variously defined "cradles of civilization" or home of the "peoples of the Bible") represented occidentalizing influences. In contrast, pre-Hellenic Greeks, Scandinavians, and Celts were uncivilized barbarians. But various authors during the twentieth century, especially V. Gordon Childe, began to question whether "oriental" influences were significant in producing an occidental culture, and began to look for autochthonous roots in the geographic west.

The Celts, Scandinavians, and the rural Volk or peasants in general were sometimes orientalized as rural, tradition-bound, pagan peoples in contrast with urban/civilized, dynamic, Christian peoples; but sometimes they also were used—often in the context of nationalist, grass-roots movements—to represent the authentic, autochthonous Europe. The Irish tended to carry the greatest burden of Celtic orienticity, followed by the French and to a lesser extent the Scots and Welsh.

Indo-Europeans   Linguists and archaeologists writing about "Indo-Europeans" were, in effect, presenting evidence about the issue of European autochthony: Where and when did the people speaking a single Indo-European tongue (from which other languages diverged) emerge? What distinctive cultural characteristics did they have? Of the many articles and reviews, two stand out as interesting examples. In 1949, Andrews wrote a curious article called "The Bean and Indo-European Totemism," in which he argued that because the Greeks and Romans had many beliefs relating to the bean but none about totemism, totemism did not exist among Indo-Europeans (and thus served as a cultural boundary between Occident and Orient).

Dumezil, in *Archaic Roman Religion* (reviewed by Barrett 1973), analyzed the myths of archaic Rome in search of Indo-European elements—seeking, on the one hand, to identify the occidental cultural complex that could be linked with particular peoples in the past; and, on the other, to affirm the essential hierarchical superiority of Indo-Europeans (for example, he attacked "primitivists" who said early Romans could be equated with modern-day primitives). Early Romans, he said, were religiously and politically sophisticated, and shared with Vedic Indians, Iranians, Celts, and the ancient Scandinavians a tripartite ideology (a hierarchy of three political domains—ruler-priests, warriors, and herder-cultivators—matched by three domains in the supernatural realm— sovereignty, physical power, and fertility) that was a distinctive feature of the mythological and religious structure of all Indo-European people.

    Candidates for Autochthony   Arguments about the best candidates for European autochthony (who is most distinctively European) emphasized different criteria. For example, de Laet, in his book *The Low Countries* (Hatt 1958), argued that "all cultural developments characteristic of north-western Europe" were felt there; that it was a natural crossroad between north and south, east and west, "a sort of synthesis of Europe, just as it is now." Frequently occurring candidates for Essence of Occident were the Scandinavians/Nordics, Germans (sometimes described as Teutons), and occasionally the Celts, Basques, and Etruscans.

    The Scandinavians, like the Celts, had a long history of being identified with European autochthony, and were as likely to be orientalized as occidentalized depending on what boundaries were being scrutinized. After being popular as temporally marginal, orientalized primitives (along with the Celts) in the nineteenth and early twentieth centuries, they were revived in the 1960s in articles that emphasized their contribution to European foundations.

    The position of the Germans along occidental/oriental boundaries shifted considerably. Whereas they appear in the late nineteenth and early twentieth centuries as barbarians being contrasted with the Greeks and Romans, from about 1930 on they became occidentalized as the representatives of Indo-European culture, sometimes battling with the Celts for this title (see Voegelin 1935 for the Germans; Childe 1937 for the Celts), or with the Romans (see Van Nostrand 1956 for the Teutons; Foltiny 1959 for the Romans).

    Other regions and groups used as candidates for European autochthony were the Basques; and in 1959 the Etruscans joined the contenders for occidentity (see Angel 1959, 334).

    The Case of Greece   As Herzfeld has made clear in a variety of writings (especially 1987b), Greece has provided a significant arena in which the occidental/oriental contrast has been explored, in particular in relation to questions about the origins of Western civilization. Greece is geographically and culturally ambiguous, straddling "European and Islamic Worlds" (Shimkin

1955), or presented as a Christian country that nevertheless harbors pagan rituals. One of the most remarkable illustrations of the marginality of Greece in the pages of the *American Anthropologist* is an article by J. Lawrence Angel called "Social Biology of Greek Culture Growth" (1946).

Angel was a student of Hooton who became known for his paleopathological studies of skeletal populations. The Greeks, although "our chief cultural ancestors" (1946, 493), were conceived of as biological hybrids, and much of his paper is an attempt to come to terms with the implications of "mixing" for culture growth. His article is a fascinating view of Greece as boundary between Occident and Orient, like the edge of a raw volcano spewing the raw energy that gets shaped into the form of civilization—a place of Nordic aristocracy (1946, 494, 515–516) and "orientalizing" influence (1946, 497), a place where an expanding prehistoric population met challenges through "diffusion of Near Eastern traits," a classic Hellenic civilization produced by "heterogeneous mongrels both ethnically and biologically," a population that changed from a Mediterranean to an Alpine norm (1946, 525), and through all the diverse interaction generated the cultural energy that produced Western civilization.

THE OCCIDENTAL PEOPLES OF HISTORICAL/PROGRESSIVE TIME VERSUS THE ORIENTAL TIMELESS/TIMELOCKED/UNDEVELOPED OTHER

As Fabian clearly demonstrates in his book *Time and the Other* (1983), an important aspect of anthropological rhetoric is to imprison the anthropological subject in a time warp. Temporal orientalizing occurs when a contrast is constructed between peoples outside of time or caught in time (having no history, unable to change because of conservatism and tradition-bound behavior, linked to a past that has never changed) and peoples inside of or controlling time (changing, evolving, progressing, able to separate modern from archaic periods in their own history and to confine other peoples in those archaic periods). Sometimes history is conceived of as a progression from childish stages of development (characterized, for example, by oral communication, concrete thinking, and communalism) toward an adult level (characterized, for example, by literacy, abstract reasoning, and individualism); and the peoples linked with the earlier stages—whether contemporary "living fossils" or historical peoples used as models of undeveloped primitiveness—are orientalized as the timeless or timelocked Other. An important attribute of being timeless, timelocked, and/or undeveloped is that such peoples are assumed to have an unambiguous identity

The Case of Greeks, Scandinavians, and Celts   Early Greeks, Scandinavians, and Celts, conceived of as uncivilized barbarians, were orientalized in articles that equated them with contemporary nonwestern peoples; and contemporary Celts and Greek peasants—peasants in general—are still frequently interpreted as living fossils.

Jennifer Brown's article, "Plato's Republic as an Early Study of Media Bias and a Charter for Prosaic Education" (1972), described a Greece at the margins of historic/modern/European time: an orientalized, nonliterate Greece in which knowledge was based on orally conveyed, vividly described myths that did not encourage the young "to analyze, to consider alternatives, to ask abstract or generic questions like 'What is justice?'..." (Brown 1972, 673). In contrast, the literate (occidentalized) Greece was represented by Plato, who used "the newly powerful medium of prose writing or discursive symbolism ... to substitute rational, explicit control and direction for the conglomerate of traditional belief that was being passed on without criticism or analysis" (Brown 1972, 673). Orientalized Greece used a "negative feedback system" that promoted equilibrium and stability. Occidentalized Greece used a "positive feedback system" that transcended tradition, challenged conventions, and contributed to "a new period of intellectual searching, uncertainty, and confusion—known to historians as the Hellenistic period." (Brown 1972, 674) Orientalized Greece was homogeneous; occidentalized Greece was heterogeneous and syncretic. Brown's article is one of the more interesting examples of articles and reviews in the *American Anthropologist* that distinguished early from later Greek thought, and linked the former with nonwestern primitives and modern peasantry, the latter with Western civilization. Other articles compared contemporary nonwestern peoples not only with early Greek but with early Irish and Scandinavian peoples and periods as well, as when Beckwith (1922, 311) compared contemporary Polynesian riddles with "the Scandinavian Edda and Greek tales of Oedipus and the riddle of the Sphinx." A frequent theme was to link European prehistoric art with contemporary nonwestern art, distinguishing, for example, causal-and-history-minded psychological orientations from nonhistorical orientations (Chapman 1968), prerational representation from historic and civilized (Fritz 1974).

Although Childe praised "Irish proletarians of unidentified physical type" (1937, 22) for their prehistoric industry in pushing Britain into the Bronze Age without the help of the eastern Mediterranean, writers such as Hallan L. Movius argued that the Irish remained imprisoned in the Mesolithic and the unprogressive past long after the rest of Europe had progressed:

> [B]ecause of Ireland's insular position there was a marked lag in the introduction of new ideas.... Dr. Movius is clearly able to demonstrate the survival, even into early Christian times, of a culture essentially to be regarded as stemming from the old food-gathering traditions of the Mesolithic.... The story of Ireland "in insular isolation on the outermost periphery of western Europe" is essentially one of lagging response to new influences and of strange survivals out of the millennial past ... the influences of Ireland's peculiar geographical situation ... cast long shadows down her later history. (Eiseley 1945, 152–153)

In other examples, the Irish represent the Celts as an orientalized culture in the midst of the Occident, as in Levin's (1972) review of a book on Indo-Europeans, and in particular a chapter called "Celtic Suretyship, a Fossilized Indo-European Institution?" in which he found evidence of three stages of prehistoric Irish law in the Gaelic spoken in contemporary Ireland.

Eastern and Western Europe   The demarcation between Eastern and Western Europe was used in the pages of the *American Anthropologist* to discuss the process of modernization, the difference between peasant and urban society, the incursion of Slavic/Greek/Turkish/pagan influences and their effect on European culture, and the difference between communism and democracy. In contrast with archaeological studies such as those by Gimbutas that stressed Eastern Europe as the cauldron of Indo-European autochthony, writings about cultural differences portrayed Eastern Europe as nonhistorical, traditional-peasant-communal. Western Europe was historical, stable, modernized, innovative, and Christian in contrast with the ahistorical, unstable, primitive, conservative, pagan, and ambiguously bounded Eastern Europe. In 1923, for example, Arnold Van Gennep established an opposition between two "principles," a social process involving history that resulted in the stable nations of Western Europe, and a nonhistorical social process involving totemism that resulted in nonstable social groups; groups such as the Poles were portrayed as transitional between these European and oriental processes, and were in the process of working themselves up the developmental ladder toward stable nationhood (Faye 1923). This contrast became more prominent during the study of European peasant communities in the 1950s and 1960s, as in Earl Count's review of Benet's book about *Peasant Poland* (1952b), in which he said that Benet's ethnography "presents us with that culture from which we detached ourselves ere the Occidental machinery had been fairly built. That culture, no less than the exotics, stands to be ground under by the Occidental machine.... Ethnological treatment of the European peasant is no less a rescue job than the others are" (Count 1952b, 543).

Between 1930 and 1945, the Soviet Union began to loom large on the intellectual horizon of American anthropologists, and to the formulation of Occidental/Oriental contrast was added capitalism versus communism, Western democracy versus Tsarist/Communist [Oriental] despotism. During the 1950s, George Peter Murdock, in reviewing Karl Wittfogel's book *Oriental Despotism: A Comparative Study of Tribal Power* (1957b, 545–547) commented that this book will "provide for the first time a solid theoretical framework on which the 'free world' might base a positive assault on the foundations of Communism and Fascism to replace the unorganized rearguard defense which it has presented for some decades to the ideational attacks of its enemies. The political and social systems of Soviet Russia, Communist China, and recent Nazi Germany fall clearly into the pattern of bureaucratic Asiatic despotism." This contrast shaped conceptions of Europe even after the fall of the Berlin wall in 1989.

One of the earliest references to the European Community in the *American*

Anthropologist occurred in a review (Douglass 1970b, 643) of a book about European peasantry in which East and West were defined in terms of their approach to the "peasant problem" as they (in the form of eastern and western blocs in Europe) debated "a common agricultural policy for the European Economic Community."

ORIENTALIZING EUROPE

Although the title of this section was called "Occidentalizing Europe," it would have been just as reasonable to call it "Orientalizing Europe." In the examples provided above, anthropologists were conducting a discourse on the temporal, geographic, and cultural boundaries of the West by defining, in multiple and changing ways, the characteristics of the orientalized/non-West.

Why do new and changing definitions sweep through the anthropological imagination, taking up the burden of contrast, continuing the occidental/oriental dialogue? Why, for example, during the period 1930–1970, did the distinction between nomadic and sedentary populations become such a frequently used device to explore the margins of European civilization? Besides numerous items on nomadism as a category in itself, the settled peasant cooperatives of Russia were contrasted with Central Asian and Turkic nomads, the Scythians were linked with the early Celts as incomparable horsemen, the linguistically distinctive Hungarians (Finno-Ugric as opposed to Indo-European) were identified as pastoralists, the nomadic Sarakatsani represented the Greeks, the camel-breeding Bedouin were romanticized as warrior nomads at the fringes of civilization, and the reindeer-herding Lapps become a popular ethnographic topic.

At the very least, it would be reasonable to say that the boundaries between Occident and Orient varied in relation to historical contingencies, policies of modernization, and nationalism; in other words, the poetics of representing Europe reflected shifting relationships of power. For example, the Soviet Union represented Asiatic despotism when contrasted with Western democracy. Scottish crofters were portrayed as survivals from the Iron Age when discussed in the context of modernization, but in the context of nationalism, rural societies were portrayed as the cradle, core, and essence of European identity. But in addition to these relational factors, certain themes (time and nomadism, among others) seemed to emerge and take hold, to run their course as romantic or reflective themes in the anthropological imagination.

OCCIDENTALIZING AMERICANS: RACE, IMMIGRATION, AND EUGENICS

From 1888 through the 1930s the largest category of items dealing with Europe in the *American Anthropologist* related to racial classifications, especially of groups attempting to emigrate to the United States. Of particular interest were anomalous categories along the occidental/oriental divide, for example, Armenians, Turks, Greeks, and Jews, whose origins ("Asiatic" or "Aryan") were in dispute. One of the purposes of such studies was to help the United States formulate policies of immigration that would weed out "undesirables." Eugenics was considered to be a form of "applied anthropology" (Hooton 1926, 552). Charlotte Day Gower's study of a Sicilian village community, usually touted as the first European community study, was done to provide background information on "the problem of the Sicilian immigrant to the U.S." (Anonymous 1929, 823).

At the turn of the century, the cephalic index and pigmentation were used to classify Jews, Armenians, Turks, and Greeks as being "of Asiatic origin" (e.g., Fishberg 1902 and 1903); characteristics such as blondness and blue eyes derived from "Aryan mixture." Boas himself contributed an article called "The Cephalic Index," filled with erudite mathematics that he said should be used "to investigate racial characters" (1899, 461), but by 1911 he was being criticized for his new position that head shape was subject to the influence of the environment. Other anthropologists continued to use head shape, the cephalic index, and speculations about characteristics of brain, intelligence, and race throughout the twentieth century (cf. Newman 1962), but the most racist writings in the *American Anthropologist* were concentrated in the period of high immigration in the 1920s and 1930s, and, with a few interesting exceptions, declined in number after World War II.

A few examples illustrate the tone of this discourse. In 1924, Spier reviewed S. J. Holmes's book, *Studies in Evolution and Eugenics*, in which Holmes argued that "panmixia" interfered with natural selection, and that immigration from southern and eastern Europe of "racially low" populations would degrade civilization. In his review of the new journal, *Annals of Eugenics: A Journal for the Scientific Study of Racial Problems*, Hooton noted that half of the first issue concerned Russian and Polish Jewish children who, as immigrants to Britain, were found to be "inferior physically and mentally" to the "Gentile population" (1926, 552–553).

Books on immigration were commonly reviewed. What is usually described as the earliest European community study, by Charlotte Day Gower, was rooted in immigrant studies. Funded by the SSRC, her project was called "An Ethnological and Sociological Study of a Typical Sicilian Village Community as a Contribution to the Background of the Problem of the Sicilian Immigrant to the U.S." (Anonymous 1929, 823). The complete title of Thomas and Znaniecki's book on Polish peasants (reviewed by Kroeber in 1930) was, we should remember, *The Polish Peasant in Europe and America*.

Anthropologists read and commented on books about the racial characteristics of different nations and of Europe in general (for example, see Hooton's 1929 review of Gunther's book, *The Racial Elements of European History*), and proposed studies that would help to distinguish the role of biology from the role of culture, separate animal-like from human traits, and debate whether civilization was more likely to arise from racial purity or mixture. Robert Lowie reviewed a book called *The Racial Basis of Civilization: A Critique of the Nordic Doctrine* (1928, 317–319), pointing out that the author believed in eugenics and the "inferiority of the Negroids, but not of the Alpines and Mediterraneans." He took issue with the author's criticism of anthropologists who say that all races are equal; Lowie argued that they do *not* say that all races are equal; rather, they question the proofs about the differences.

Lowie's acceptance of the possibility of racial inequality soon became a minor voice in a rising chorus of procultural-determinism and anti-Nazi sentiment that became clearly visible in the 1930s and culminated in the post-World-War-II 1940s. The concept of "Nordic purity" and validity of the concept of race itself were widely questioned. In a review of an introductory text in physical anthropology in 1931, Kroeber (1931) noted that anthropometrical measurements were used to define Mediterranean, Alpine, Nordic, Mongoloid, Negroid, and Australoid races, but he questioned the meaning of "race" in the light of results that located Alpines in Peru and said that Polynesians were Mediterranean. Some books attacked heredity in favor of environment influences (e.g., Garth's review of Otto Klineberg's book, *Negro Intelligence and Selective Migration* [1936, 130–131]) whereas others supported the idea that heredity played a major role in intelligence (among the white race, however, differences in intelligence were "natio-mental rather than racial" [Gower 1938, 322]).

Writers began to examine the history of racist concepts, and to evaluate the "mythology of race," especially in the light of Nazi applications of the concept of race. Jacques Barzun's book, *The French Race*, was not about biology but about the history of the Nordic race idea in France (Schapiro 1933, 536), and his book, *Race: A Study in Modern Superstition*, was listed under New Publications (1938, 172). Montagu (1942, 374) concluded that the concept of race was "a fatuous kind of abstraction," and in 1944 (pp. 254–255) reviewed two books by sociologists concerned with how the "White" American maintained the mythology of race. Hofstadter's book, *Social Darwinism in American Thought, 1860–1915* (Bennett 1945, 451), described the eugenics movement as a powerful American racist philosophy and the reviewer noted that Roosevelt himself was full of "Germanic tribal superiority" slogans. Opler (1944, 448–459) said that after World War I, the United States and Britain refused to support a proposed racial equality clause in the Covenant of the League of Nations. "The 1924 Immigration Bill, often called the 'Nordic Bill,' was the supreme triumph of the organicists. It provided for total Oriental exclusion and discriminated against the peoples of southern and eastern Europe." (1944, 448) Opler established a link between the writings of physical anthropologists and the racist writings of the Nazis and others. He said that after World War II anthropologists should reject the organicist interpretation, and achieve, through an emphasis on behavior, "that triumph ... which may yet make us finally and completely human" (p. 459). Honigsheim (1945) said that the collapse of Hitler should reaffirm the principles of the French Enlightenment. A booklet for high school students by Hortense Powdermaker, called *Probing our Prejudices* (Montagu 1945, 451), said we must eliminate phrases such as "purity of racial heritage" and define clearly such concepts as race, heredity, and environment.

Given such sentiments, one might expect that after World War II the issue of race would disappear as a scientific category and as a significant tool by which boundaries of identity were established. However, the concept of race continued to be dealt with in the *American Anthropologist* in three major contexts:

1. The Middle East posed a problem of identity for American Jews after the founding of the state of Israel. The boundaries between "European Jews" and "Oriental Jews," and between Israelis (as occidentalized) and Arabs (as orientalized) were explored by means of biological and cultural contrasts.

2. Britain, which was inundated with "Commonwealth" peoples, posed a problem of identity for Americans, who by and large have given Britain (and the image of Britain as a homogeneous society of white, Anglo-Saxon Protestants) a central role in their myths of provenience. Immigration of Commonwealth peoples resulted in two types of people, white and colored, the specific referents of which varied from one context to another (e.g., the classification of "Negroes," "Chinese," and "Moslems" as "colored" [Landes 1959, 173]).

3. In the United States, the "racial" subdivisions of Europe such as Alpine, Mediterranean, and Nordic were no longer significant (although American anthropologists were still interested enough in the topic to review books on racial classifications written by Europeans, including one that subdivided European racial categories into Polynesian, Mediterranean, Atlanto-Mediterranean, Alpine, Basque, Dinaric, Armenian, and "Oriental"—the latter including "Eastern Baltic, Nordic, Dalic, Lapp, and Celtic types" [Holloway 1972, 146–147]). In the United States, different patterns of immigration pitted Europeans in general against non-European immigrants (as in California, where the Chinese had to contend with prejudice from a united front of Euro-Americans, and where "Mexicans" sought to define their complex heritage); but the debate on race continued, primarily in the context of black/white relationships.

The discussion of race in the United States, especially as it pertained to black/white categories, fell into three categories:

1. Writings that validated the concept of race. (See, for example, Buettner-Janusch, who argued that "anyone who reads [Stanley] Garn's book [on *Human Races*] and continues to maintain that racial difference, or race, is

a myth, must indeed be blinded by divine vision. The trend to diminish or minimize the fact of racial differences has been most unfortunate in anthropology" [1962, 902].)

2. Writings that discussed the social causes of distinctiveness and discrimination.

3. Writings that attacked the concept of race itself and examined the epistemological foundations of racist and biased thinking in the social sciences. (See, for example, Montagu, who argued "that all those who continue to use the term 'race' with reference to man, whether they be laymen or scientists, are 'for sacred rites unfit'" [1962, 919]; or Haller's article on race and the concept of progress in nineteenth-century American ethnology [1971] in which he argued that nineteenth-century ethnologists used the concept of evolution as a teleological projection of Anglo-Saxon race achievement). The nature-nurture debate was revived in the context of sociobiology (for example, in discussions of Robert Ardrey, Napoleon Chagnon, and Derek Freeman's attack on Margaret Mead.)

EUROPE AND THE DISCIPLINARY BOUNDARIES OF ANTHROPOLOGY

I suggested at the beginning of this chapter that American anthropologists used Europe not only to explore and define the boundaries of their own identity as Americans participating in a European/Western heritage, but to explore and define the disciplinary boundaries of anthropology. I use this section to draw attention to a few trends in anthropology that have only tangential relevance to the study of Europe: the territorial mutterings over the boundary between anthropology and sociology (and between anthropology and Folklore studies in the context of Europe), and the change from particularistic, psychohistorical studies of nonwestern peoples, especially American Indians, to universalistic, generalizing studies that embraced the whole of humanity.

Many of the writings in the *American Anthropologist*, especially before 1945, drew clear-cut boundaries between the responsibilities of anthropologists and sociologists. Anthropologists were defined as people who studied small-scale, relatively nonchanging, nonwestern peoples, especially the American Indian, as part of a philosophy of cultural salvage, an attempt to collect the remnants of memory cultures. The study of complex, dynamic, innovative western peoples was thought of as belonging to the province of sociologists. In an article about teaching anthropology, Wallis (1924, 284) stated explicitly that anthropology "deals with non-European peoples and non-European fields of knowledge" (whereas by 1952 Earl Count, in his review of the fiftieth anniversary meeting of the American Anthropological Association, wondered why American Indian studies were always considered anthropological but some linguistic and archaeological studies—such as Indo-European, Finno-Ugrian, Semitic-Hamitic, and Seino-Tibetan—were not [Count 1952a, 124]).

The liminality of Europe in the anthropological canon is indicated by the difficulty with which editors of the *American Anthropologist* classified items pertaining to Europe. For example, until 1930 any books relating to Europe in the book review section were placed under the heading "Miscellaneous," and after 1930, when a category called "Europe" appeared (with one entry), European titles were placed under a variety of headings, including "Eurasia," "General," "Miscellaneous," or the combined category "Europe and Asia" (or "Asia and Europe," or "Europe and Asia Minor"), unlike categories such as "North America" and "Africa" that remained relatively stable. "Europe" began to appear more regularly as a category in the 1940s, appearing in 1943, then regularly in the years 1946–1948; "Ireland" had its own separate category in 1945. In 1949 the method of categorizing subject matter in book reviews and new publications changed from geographical area to the more familiar categories of General and Theoretical, Ethnography and Ethnology, Archaeology, and Other, and in 1965 a new section, Film Review, was added, as well as a new subdivision in Book Review called "Culture Change, Applied Anthropology, and Economic Development."

Studies done in Europe were usually classified by reviewers as examples of "folklore." American anthropologists reviewed European journals such as *Folk-liv, Acta Ethnologica et Folkloristica Europaea* that was first started in 1936 (reviewed in 1949, 498), or reviewed books that reflected the folklore bias of European ethnology. During the 1950s various letters were exchanged between European and American anthropologists over whether Redfield's approach to the study of peasant or folk culture was new or just a version of the long-term interest of Central European ethnologists in *Volkskunde.*

In 1962, while reviewing a German book on folk culture as influenced by the technical world, Lange entered into a fascinating discourse on the study of peasants in New and Old World contexts. He began by quoting Redfield who in *Peasant Society and Culture* (1956) had noted that "Until recently the peasantry of the Old World were the business, not of anthropology, but of other disciplines"—namely, Folklore (1962, 1073). Folklorists studied European peasant communities; anthropologists studied non-European primitives. The community study model embraced by anthropologists was not initially considered appropriate to European peasant communities because of this disciplinary distinction, or as Lange commented, "The student of peasant life characteristically did not make holistic community studies" (p. 1073). The folklorist was concerned with "timeless" folk identity and traditional practices (or as Mandelbaum said, the "fossil customs of rustic people" [1963, 140], studied out of an idyllic search for one's past in the history of the common people, a study born of the Romantic movement rather than a scientific, worldwide, collaborative effort to understand and classify human custom) and had to be careful to distinguish between "legitimate folk culture" and "flagrant misrepresentations staged by European communities for their tourist appeal" (p. 1075) or culture that had undergone too much change. When such groups innovated and became too professional, they lost "the spontaneity and authenticity of the folk characteristics" (p. 1074). There are two interesting aspects of this review: One is the implicit contrast between folk and urban cultures (and the assumption that change represented loss and inauthenticity); the other is the association of European peasant studies with folklore studies rather than anthropology.

In contrast with folklore journals, however, were new journals, surveys, and publication series concerned with establishing a global perspective on anthropology that included Europe. The Columbia University Project in Contemporary Cultures produced several publications on eastern Europe, including Zborowski and Herzog's *Life Is with People: The Jewish Little Town of Eastern Europe* (1952) and David Rodnick's anticommunist-tinged book, *The Strangled Democracy: Czechoslovakia 1948–1969* (reviewed by Lockwood in 1972, who noted that most information came from 1949 and reflected "the Patterns of Culture approach that was popular at that time" [1972, 850]). HRAF (Human Relations Area Files) produced its bibliographic summaries and reviews, and at the end of the 1950s Murdock produced his world ethnographic sample and the *Outline of World Cultures* (in 1957 and 1958, respectively). HRAF and New Mexico's Museum of International Folk Art sponsored the project called the *Visual Files Coding Index* that attempted to organize visual materials in a manner comparable to textual materials in the HRAF (Force 1962). HRAF sponsored numerous publications related to Europe, one of the most notable being Theodoratus's bibliography on Europe (1969).

In 1959 Gordon Hewes commented that American anthropologists had done fieldwork in a wider diversity of regions, with more approaches and techniques, than their counterparts in non-English-speaking countries but that the time had come for a worldwide synthesis of cultural data in many languages (especially German, French, Italian, and Russian)—a need being met by HRAF, international symposia, the projected international journal *Current Anthropology*, and the global research of people like Sorokin and Toynbee in sociology and history, and the work of Kroeber, Redfield, and Steward in anthropology. An interest in how other European countries were doing anthropology resulted in three articles appearing in 1959 on the anthropology of Sweden, Germany, and Austria, respectively. The *Biennial Review of Anthropology*, with its summaries and reviews of the various branches and current topics of anthropology, appeared at the beginning of the 1960s, as did the Spindler Case Studies in Cultural Anthropology (its first European case study was Ernestine Friedl's *Vasilika: A Village in Modern Greece*, published in 1962).

Between about 1930 and 1945, the boundary between anthropology and sociology was no longer defined by the study of nonwestern as opposed to western societies, but by the techniques used to study society. Applied anthropology no longer meant eugenics (the race concept used in social policy) but the use of social and psychological concepts to solve problems in the modern world, both at home and abroad. The journal *Applied Anthropology* included articles about Europe by sociologists, and anthropologists such as W. Lloyd Warner made significant contributions (such as definitions of class and caste) to sociology. Chapple, Arensberg, and Coon wrote textbooks advocating the study of "human relations" rather than "cultures."

The disciplinary boundaries of anthropology and sociology were some-times sharply debated over the issue of community studies. For example, although Erna Gunther said that the Lynds' *Middletown* was sociology rather than anthropology, she suggested that the authors were doing the same thing that anthropologists do when studying a nonwestern, small-scale, "primitive" society. That is, instead of dealing with single issues or problems, as sociol-ogists usually do, they showed "the interrelation of the various activities indulged in by this community" (1930, 319). To W. Lloyd Warner, anthropol-ogy provided detailed information about individuals and was comparative (cf. Meggars 1946); but when it dealt with "our own behavior" (see next para-graph), he tended to call it comparative sociology.

Meggars, in her view of "Recent Trends in American Ethnology" (1946), noted the recent turn from primitive peoples to "studies of modern communi-ties." The leader in this area, she said, was W. Lloyd Warner who, between 1930–1934, was involved in the research that culminated in *Yankee City*, and whom she quotes as saying that "It seems likely that once we place the study of civilization in the framework of an inductive, systematic, comparative soci-ology, we can increase our knowledge of our own social behavior" (Meggars 1946, 191). By "our own" behavior, Warner had in mind an implicit West that included representative samples from the United States (the east coast, west coast, south, and midwest) and Ireland. The development of "an inductive, systematic, comparative sociology" was not accomplished by this research, Meggars said (p. 194), in part because the research was so disparate. *Yankee City* was preoccupied with the mathematics of class; the work by Powdermaker, Davis, and the Gardners in Mississippi during 1933–1935 (later by Dollard) concentrated on the psychological effects of caste and class. The only work that corresponded to "standard" anthropology was the work done in Ireland beginning in 1931 by Warner, Arensberg, and Kimball (Meggars 1946, 193), which was followed by the publication of *The Irish Countryman* in 1937 and *Family and Community in Ireland* in 1940.

Some anthropologists sought to reconcile the study of modern society with the models provided by anthropology. For example, in 1946 Junek, who had an applied background working on modern hospitals, said that anthropol-ogists should look at the "total pattern" of "their own western civilization" (Junek 1946, 397). He identified sixteen complexes of "Euro-American" or "Western" or "civilized" peoples (Junek 1946, 398) using Kroeber's 1923 study of cultural accretions among American Indians that included the modern fac-tory system, mass education, dependence on steam, scientific food packing, etcetera. By describing these "scientific-technical complexes" that are the "mainstays of the total pattern" (p. 399), he limned the boundaries of "civiliza-tion."

During the period 1930–1945, not only were sociologists frequently quoted but developments in anthropology—particularly the influence of British structure-functionalism at the University of Chicago via Radcliffe-Brown and Fred Eggan, and the development of the folk-urban continuum under Redfield and Park—provided a theoretical context in which community studies and functionalist analysis in complex societies could be accepted as anthropological. Although Conrad Arensberg's *The Irish Countryman* was listed under New Publications in 1937 but not reviewed, by 1941 Cora Du Bois was calling Arensberg and Kimball's *Family and Community in Ireland* a classic of functional analysis. In 1944, the sociologist William Foote Whyte published an article in the *American Anthropologist* called "Sicilian Peasant Society." Whyte used Charlotte Gower's unpublished manuscript from the Department of Anthropology at the University of Chicago, as well as turn-of-the-century Italian publications, and commented that "Until recently anthropologists have been concentrating their attention upon primitive societies and have done little research into the peasant communities of civilized societies" (1944, 65). Bennett suggested that von Martin's *Sociology of the Renaissance* could be compared with Redfield's folk-urban continuum with its polar type of Middle Ages (folk) compared to the early Renaissance (urban) (1946a, 274).

Besides the trends toward interdisciplinary commingling of anthropology and sociology, World War II exerted a significant influence on the goals and methods of anthropologists, as reflected in an article written by John Gillin in 1949. Gillin suggested that if anthropologists were to make a significant contribution to world peace, they must shift their focus from "primitives" to "moderns," and should change from "deductive" methods (as used, for example, in the psychological theories of Benedict and Gorer) to "inductive" methods based on fieldwork. Although, in comparison with "primitive cultures," "modern cultures" were more heterogeneous, showed more borrowing and innovation ("particularly true of Western civilization" [Gillin 1949, 396]), and posed problems for traditional anthropological study because of their large scale, these problems could be overcome by using large research teams and by focusing on community studies (best represented, he said, by the work of Warner and the Lynds). (Gillin's interest in a global approach to the problems of the modern world is reflected in his choice of books to review, such as his review of Grinker's *Toward a Unified Theory of Human Behavior* [1957]. Eric Wolf showed a similar range of interests—e.g. Wolf 1957b.)

As president of the American Anthropology Association (AAA), Gillin continued these ideas in his presidential address, "More Complex Cultures for Anthropologists" (1967), in which he said that anthropology was being brought into the modern world and was becoming of greater interest to more people, including businesses and government. Although some anthropologists, such as Ruth Benedict, Margaret Mead, W. Lloyd Warner, and Charles Wagley, had studied whole nations and parts of the modern world, and trends had been studied by Toynbee and Sorokin, anthropologists needed to develop techniques to study both the details and the whole of complex societies just as traditional ethnologists studied details and the whole of "simple tribes." Although he gave examples of how to approach "the whole" of complex societies, none of his examples included Europe.

The movement toward global consciousness, the symbolic construction of identity, and the development of a universalistic theory reflected Americans' awareness that they were participants rather than powerful dictators in a global drama. These sentiments were reflected in the writings of an "Orientalist" writer—K. Kodanda Rao from India (Aginsky 1949, 493–494)—who, in a book published in 1949 called *East vs. West, a Denial of Contrast*, says that the concepts of culture pattern and diffusion were used "for political purposes and to aid in re-enforcing the shibboleth of racial inferiority and superiority" (1949, 493). "Civilization is a common heritage; each individual is heir to all knowledge ... the only right course is to secure universal accessibility to universal culture...." (1949, 494) Such thoughts were echoed over twenty years later by Tambiah who, in reviewing Louis Dumont's *Homo Hierarchicus: An Essay on the Caste System*, challenged the notion of "a dialectical confrontation between the *homo hierarchicus* of traditional society and the *homo aequalis* of modern society, between the mind of Western man and that of the Hindu Asian" (1972, 834) and asked to what extent the features dichotomized by Dumont are in fact part of universal man (also see Tyler 1972).

COMMUNITY STUDIES

The period between 1946 and 1970 saw an explosion of community studies. As Harold Orlans said in 1959 (p. 175), "If our teachers' generation was the era of ethnographies, surely ours is the era of community studies. The average ethnography was not intended to be more than a modest brick in the rising edifice of anthropology. The study of modern ... communities has fewer rules and greater ambitions." Community studies were not uniform in type, intention, or theoretical orientation. The concept of community was applied to rural peasant societies, mining towns, and even psychiatric hospitals (Wilkie 1959). The community was conceived of as a microcosm of large complex cultures (cf. Friedl 1966a), or as a stage in cultural development (cf. Tumin 1954; Steward 1956; and Petrullo 1957).

European community studies include the reissue of Arensberg's *Irish Countryman* (1951 [1937], 274), and articles and books about Belgium (Miner 1955), England (Orlans 1957; Richards 1970), France (Friedl 1958; Bernot 1966; Freeman 1968c), Greece (Friedl 1959, 1964, 1966b; Andromedas 1963; Gearing 1963; Pitt-Rivers 1965), Lapland (Paine 1960; Eidheim 1966; Pelto 1966a, 1967), Wales (Frankenberg 1961; Kimball 1967), Spain (Wolf 1963; Freeman 1968b), Ireland (Messenger 1964a), Malta (Boissevain 1964; Kenny 1966; Benedict 1970), Norway (Nash 1964), Denmark (Pitkin 1965), Turkey (Kasdan 1965), Italy (Silverman 1966), Russia (Krader 1968), Germany (Willems 1970), Hungary (Hammel 1970), and the Basques in Spain (Freeman 1970b).

A number of these articles signal an important theoretical shift in European community studies. Peasants were no longer isolated but involved in a web of social relationships, and they were no longer passive recipients of Great Traditions but active entrepreneurs and decision-makers actively constructing their cultural identity. Studies were explicit about stating the criteria by which culture-bearing units were identified, and by whom (for example, Moerman's article on ethnic identification among the Lue [1965] suggested that terms such as cultures, tribes, societies, and peoples should be critically examined to "discover the criteria used for ethnic labeling at different taxonomic levels" [p. 1225]). Silverman (1966) attempted to apply the "new ethnography" or "ethnoscience" to discover the code in the minds of the people by which positions in a system of social stratification were assigned. Basic classification systems were criticized, and histories of anthropology created a sense of critical perspective. Boissevain used network theory and the transactional analysis of Fredrik Barth to analyze the choices by individuals that generated "social forms and patterns of behavior" (Benedict 1970, 403). The emphasis on decision making appeared to be a transitional phase between Culture and Personality's concern with the individual, and symbolic anthropology's emphasis on the use of public symbols. The focus was not on culture content but on culture process.

A collection of papers by Arensberg and Kimball published between 1942 and 1963 on the topic of community (Friedl 1966a) included the two papers in which Arensberg explicitly formulated the concept of community (one written in 1954 and one in 1961). Arensberg thought of communities as being composed of interrelated social processes by which individuals perpetuated themselves and their culture in time and space. A community was like a machine that produced individuals who carried a specific culture. "An American community is that minimum set of interrelated roles and activities that will produce Americans, a Greek community, Greeks, and so on" (p. 1022). Different cultures had different community types, and anthropologists set out to discover what these community forms were, regardless of complexity or scale (thus European and American communities were just as valuable to developing a taxonomy of communities as were communities located anywhere else).

Community studies based in the United States seemed to pursue Gillin's prescription for their use as vehicles to tackle the world's problems; they were conceived of as small-scale samples of complex societies and were linked with applied anthropology and sociological studies. They combined a commitment to science (as an empirical, inductive approach based on case studies and the search for general laws or regularities) with the desire of a wealthy country tired of war to embrace a global, holistic perspective on the world—as reflected, for example, in the complete title of Robert Redfield's book, *The Little Community: Viewpoints for the Study of a Human Whole*, as reviewed by Julian H. Steward (1956)—identified by Leslie White (1969) as the person who, after laxative companies, was most concerned with human regularity.

American anthropology lurched across the stage of Europe, borrowing eclectically, influenced by applied concerns, committed to scientific principles and humanistic attachments to the personal narrative, influenced by British structure-functionalism and British preference for social structure versus culture (thus tending toward social structural units of analysis such as stratification systems) and yet wed to the concept of culture (with its implications of cultural types such as rural folk/urban modern, and ultimately of symbolic inventions of identities and communities), and seeking a platform to synthesize global cross-cultural laws.

Community studies based in Europe took many directions, in some cases following the traditional anthropological pattern of a lone fieldworker studying a cultural isolate—the "orientalized" Europe of peasants, nomads, and linguistic holdouts. Arensberg's *Irish Countryman* was reissued in 1950, and it is ironic that this work is often cited as exemplary of this tradition, as Arensberg more appropriately belongs in Gillin's camp, as illustrated, for example, by his article on "American communities" published in 1955, and by his more generic treatment of the concept of community published in 1961.

The relationship between community studies and peasants was complex. An argument about whether peasant communities belonged to the province of folklorists rather than anthropologists was hammered out among Americans and Europeans. When anthropologists studied peasant communities (such as Arensberg 1937), they were initially not interested in their peasantness but in their characteristics as a unit of analysis. Later, when the concept of "peasant" was developed (especially through the work of George Foster, whose article "Peasant Society and the Image of Limited Good" [1965] contributed greatly in advancing the notion of a "peasant type" beyond the folk/urban continuum of Redfield, and through the work of Mintz and Wolf who were more interested in their economic characteristics), Europe was of interest not as a place in itself but as the historical source of New World customs (Foster in Spain) or as a site to do comparative tests of the influence of history and economics (e.g., Cole 1973; and Cole and Wolf 1974 in the Alpine communities).

The first attempt to classify European community studies (in the context of a clearly defined geographic, linguistic, culture area) was the article by Robert and Gallatin Anderson called "The Indirect Social Structure of European Village Communities" (1962). Their concern with the structure of class in small rural communities continued the work of Pitt-Rivers, Warner, Moss, and Cappannari; their focus on indirect structure and voluntary associations echoes Plotnicov's "flexible-structure" groups (1962), with the same implicit message that in developing a category to describe "Europe," they needed a conceptual device that connoted modernism, urbanism, and westernization. "A special form of sodality, the form generally meant when the term 'voluntary association' is used, is part of Western urban rather than peasant culture. Deriving historically from Roman cities and persisting and developing in urban areas, it is a well defined institution...." (p. 1022) It is particularly interesting that, despite their focus on an urban-based concept, they choose to locate their comparative study in rural communities, despite the existence of research in urban areas (such as the Firth/Bott material from England). This was, after all, the era of community studies. Although the article has few implications for theory beyond the limited focus of their particular interests, it is useful for its insights into European ethnography at the time: the existence of a course on Europe at Mills (1960), a faculty discussion group at Berkeley, an SSRC (Social Science Research Council) Research Training Fellowship in Denmark in 1956–1957, an NSF (National Science Foundation) postdoctoral fellowship in France in 1957–1959; and a bibliographic overview of existing work in Europe.

In 1971, Robert Anderson wrote "Voluntary Associations in History" (1971b) which, while not specifically about Europe, continued ideas developed in his 1971 book, *Traditional Europe* (and provoked a reaction from Clifton Amsbury regarding whether voluntary associations were a feature of medieval civilizations and other preindustrial state-ruled societies—e.g., Amsbury 1972). Both were attempts to integrate anthropology and history, which brought to the fore the incongruencies of the two disciplines. Historians developed their craft in the context of great religions, the views of kings and the power elite, the sweep of dynasties, the archival records of the literate winning side. Anthropologists, on the other hand, spoke for the common man, the anonymous informant, "those great orphans of history, the peasantry and the proletariat" (Anderson 1971b, 213). In European history, voluntary associations belonged to the province of the merchant guilds, not peasants whose lives were organized primarily in terms of territory and kinship. As the traditional framework of village life broke down, as the industrial revolution transformed the context of work, and as peasants moved to the city, voluntary associations performed the same function that they did in Africa (e.g., as described by Kenneth Little in his 1965 book, *West African Urbanization: A Study of Voluntary Associations in Social Change*). The Andersons had described the use of voluntary associations among Ukrainian immigrants to France (1962), a study that Anderson referred to in his 1971b article (and also to Michael Kenny's study of Spanish expatriates in Mexico in 1962). While Anderson continued to use an implicit functionalist assumption that individuals caught in the disorder of social change would find voluntary associations contributing to social stability as adaptive mechanisms for traditional institutions (Anderson 1971b, 209), other writers were branching out in quest of different, nontraditional models to explain social organization in Europe: nongroup networks, flexible-group concepts, factions, and conflict.

Anderson's use of the term "voluntary association," and Amsbury's critique, promoted discussion in the pages of the *American Anthropologist* of what terms were legitimate for anthropologists to use when they studied Europe or societies other than the small-scale and the "primitive." (See, for example, Brown 1973.)

It is ironic that as American anthropology struggled to develop a universal system of analysis and to move away from its preoccupation with "primitives" (as illustrated by the numerous articles and reviews about ecological models, unified theories of behavior, general systems theory, the development of world ethnographies and culture-historical syntheses), its most promising candidate for critical self-reflection, Europe, remained largely orientalized— Europeanist anthropologists paying lip service to the notion of "complex society" but conceptualizing the scope of their study largely in terms of small-scale functionalist systems. European peasants, however, were somewhat different from peasants as conceived of in other parts of the world. Rather than being eternally timelocked in an undifferentiated stage of primitive development, the subjects of European community studies were frequently given a history of their own (for example, Turney-High linked the Walloon-speaking peasants of his Belgian community with the Celtic Belgae conquered by Caesar and the Knights Templar of the thirteenth century [Miner 1955]), and European peasants tended to be interpreted as entrepreneurs and decision makers actively constructing their cultural identity, departing from stereotypes about passive peasants. European peasants (that is, truly "western" rather than nonwestern or peripherally western [Willems 1970, 528]) were represented as choosing to retain their peasant way of life in close proximity to the cities, as active integrators (rather than the rural extreme) of an urban/rural binary opposition (Willems 1970), as manipulators of economic opportunities (Douglass 1970a).

In 1970 William Douglass reviewed S. H. Franklin's book, *The European Peasantry: The Final Phase* (1970b). He said that in trying to characterize "contemporary rural areas of Germany, France, Italy, Yugoslavia, and Poland" (p. 641), Franklin was "aware of the inadequacies" of the typical anthropological model of peasantry provided by Redfield (peasants as representing the folk/rural extreme in a folk-urban continuum, peasants as the "little tradition" in a national structure, peasants as basically passive). In other words, European peasants required a different theoretical model. Departing from Redfield and Co., Franklin borrowed the term of French rural sociologists, the *chef d'entreprise* who was the prime actor in the peasant family, "the manipulator of economic opportunities within an essentially monetized economy" (p. 642).

Gamesmanship, as in the work of Goffman in Scotland beginning in the 1950s, was a model widely applied in Europeanist studies, especially in writings about nomads (especially Lapps) and "active" peasants (see Lemert 1972). The concern with "social interaction" took many forms. It sometimes connoted microlevel analysis, local and specific, with an emphasis on individuals making choices (gamesmanship, strategy, front stage and back stage). But with the influence of the sociologist Alfred Schutz (and others, including Harold Garfinkel and Harvey Sacks), it became a vehicle for analyzing language and behavior in everyday interaction, and for bridging the gap between folk and analytic models (see, for example, Blount 1974).

In the 1970s anthropologists began to use Europe as a context for exploring issues in urban anthropology (e.g., Hammel in Yugoslavia in 1970). In 1970, Richard Fox, reviewing E. A. Gutkind's book, *Urban Development in Southern Europe: Italy and Greece* (published as part of a series titled International History of City Development), said that "Each month brings forth still another community study of ethnic enclaves and shantytowns in one or another great urban center. But city form as social statement and urban pattern as cultural catalog have not yet engendered great interest among anthropologists…. Perhaps this failure to see urban space as cultural representation reflects an ahistorical bias in much urban anthropology, as well as an often insufficient cross-cultural perspective" (p. 1520). Gutkind, an architect and city planner, studied urban space as it was defined and developed in Italy and Greece to "present a worldwide survey of the origin and growth of urban civilization" (p. 1520).

Urban anthropology got its primary start in studies of African cities, and in the pioneering work of Raymond Firth on kinship studies in London. Since anthropology was supposed to be concerned with small-scale units, how were anthropologists to study cities? The African material followed tribal peoples into the city and studied their adaptation; Europeanists tended to follow peasants into the cities for the same reason (to discuss demoralization or adaptation). But new methodologies began to emerge: network analysis, nongroups, gamesmanship, strategies, decision making, and active evaluation of choices. As Weingrod noted in reviewing Mangin's edited collection, *Peasants in Cities: Readings in the Anthropology of Urbanization* (1972a), "In striking contrast to many of the early 20th century analyses of European peasant migrations (the classic example is Thomas and Znaniecki's *The Polish Peasant in Europe and America*) which stressed social and cultural disorganization, these studies by anthropologists emphasize the variety of strategies utilized by peasant migrants as they learn to cope with their new environment" (pp. 89–90). "What is involved … is a somewhat different view of social change and the character of culture. The view of culture that guides these essays is of a set of norms and customs that are flexible, changing to meet new conditions, ever-adaptive and finely calculated" (p. 90). Mangin expressed skepticism over Oscar Lewis's culture of poverty writings, and the view of peasants as being locked into traditional attitudes and values.

Community studies seemed to provide a method by which anthropologists could preserve the holistic, case-study approach but still study "modern" societies. But as they did so, they began to ask new questions and develop new approaches, and they no longer took for granted certain assumptions about the organization, structure, and continuity of culture.

TOWARD AN ANTHROPOLOGY OF EUROPE

An "anthropology of Europe" is different from "Europe in anthropology." Europe in the sense of the cultural and biological referent of the "West" or "Us" has been both explicitly and implicitly present in anthropological discourse since the founding of anthropology; indeed, it is inherent to the calculus of the anthropological imagination. But in addition to this role, Europe began to emerge in the pages of the *American Anthropologist* as the focus of ethnographic investigation—not just as an extension of American concern about immigrants from southern and eastern Europe (or as background material to peasant studies in Latin America) but as part of the decolonization of the traditional arena of anthropological investigation, and in the context of anthropology's mandate to develop universal categories and comparative models. The nature of these investigations still reflected the earlier modes of thought, but anthropology was going through an expansive, reflective, and experimental stage, and Europe was put to use as part of this process.

It is in this context that the emergence of an anthropology of Europe must be understood. The chapters in this collection of readings provide insight into the critical period of the 1970s and 1980s when an anthropology of Europe began to enter the anthropological imagination with the solidity, theoretical relevance, and stability of an Africa, India, or New Guinea—contested, perhaps, but with organizational validity in field programs, ethnographies, and structural recognition.

And thus this chapter (and the book) comes to an end at the threshold between back stage and front stage. A future project will describe the organizational structure and theoretical developments within American anthropology that have made the anthropology of Europe an explicit and problematic player on the field of the anthropological imagination. The stage has been set.

NOTES

1. I began reading the *American Anthropologist* from the first volume with the intent, originally, of writing a footnote in a paper that referred to the founding of the Society for the Anthropology of Europe. I did not expect to find many references to Europe until the 1950s (when community studies began to be a popular item of study), and after the founding of the SAE I expected to find a qualitatively different set of papers. What I found instead were numerous references to Europe and the West, and out of curiosity I started over again and tried to let the material speak for itself. What was the context in which "Europe" was used? What did "Europe" mean to American anthropologists at different periods of the development of the discipline? I found that the most interesting comments were not in articles but in commentary, in book reviews and letters to the editor where sociologists attacked anthropologists for writing about Europe (it was not appropriate subject matter for them), or where physical anthropologists debated the Europeanness of various immigrants to the United States. Archaeologists looked for Europe in various patterns of material remains; cultural anthropologists charted centers and peripheries and focused on different topics that reflected changing fads (e.g., patterns of creativity, nomads) or theoretical perspectives (e.g., urban anthropology, politics of identity).

    To say that I read the *American Anthropologist* from 1888 to the present is both correct and incorrect. I read, page by page, from the beginning, but I read to assess relevance, and then read in detail the material I judged to be relevant. I took notes on contextual material (e.g., Volume 25, published in 1923, contained George T. Flom's article, "Figures of Ships and the Four-Spoked Wheel in Ancient Irish Sculpture," as well as Robert Lowie's review of Sapir's *Language*, Gifford's review of Malinowski's *Argonauts of the Western Pacific*, Kroeber's review of Ogburn's *Social Change*, and Lowie's review of Thurnwald's *Psychologie des primitiven Menschen*). The most interesting item in Volume 25 was Faye's review of Van Gennep's *Traité Comparatif des Nationalites* that linked Europe with history, distinguished stable Western Europe from unstable Eastern Europe, and established an opposition between two "principles," the European and the Oriental.

Although it might be interesting to count the number of items pertaining to different themes that appeared during different periods, I did not collect the data in a manner that would lend itself to this type of analysis. I read for themes and took notes on the most interesting examples (very often the argumentative items that took up a theme after it had matured and that added to it in some distinctive way). For example, between 1888 and 1970 I took notes on 1,120 items—123 between 1888 and 1929, 437 between 1930 and 1949, and 560 between 1950 and 1970 (after which I began to take notes directly onto a computer and the number of items escalated dramatically).

In effect, I treated the pages of the *American Anthropologist* as informants' statements about a cultural domain to be analyzed emically for its distinctive elements and principles of order.

2. "This can be said ... of all identity or all identification: There is no self-relation, no relation to oneself, no identification with oneself, without culture, but a culture of oneself as a culture of the other, a culture of the double genitive and of the difference to oneself. The grammar of the double genitive also signals that a culture never has a single origin" (Derrida 1992, 10).

3. When we orient ourselves, we establish a direction. We look to the east, to the rising of the sun (L. *orient* - [stem of *oriens*] the east, sunrise, noun use of present participle of *oriri*, to rise). The setting or fall of the sun gives us occidental, or the west; but it also gives us cadaver (fallen, perished), and cadenza (the elaborate flourish introduced near the end of an aria).

BIBLIOGRAPHY

Abélès, Marc
  1989   Jours Tranquilles en 89: Ethnologie Politique d'un Département Français. Paris: Odile Jacob. 1991 translation, Quiet Days in Burgundy: A Study of Local Politics. Tr. Annella McDermott. Cambridge University Press.
  1992   La Vie Quotidienne au Parlement Européen. Paris: Hachette.
  1993   Political Anthropology of a Transnational Institution: The European Parliament. French Politics and Society 11(1):1–19.
  1995   Villageois et Bureaucrates: Nouvelles Approches de L'anthropologie Nord-Américaine. Revue Française de Science Politique 45:486–491.

Aginsky, Burt W.
  1949   *Review of* East vs. West, A Denial of Contrast, by K. Kodanda Rao. American Anthropologist 51:493–494.

Allen, Peter Sutton
  1972   *Review of* three films: The Anastenaria, The Kalogeros, and The Aegean Sponge Divers. American Anthropologist 74:1581–1585.
  1973   Social and Economic Change in a Depopulated Community in Southern Greece. Ph.D. Dissertation, Anthropology Department, Brown University.
  1976   Aspida: A Depopulated Maniat Community. *In* Regional Variation

in Modern Greece and Cyprus: Toward a Perspective on the Ethnography of Greece. M. Dimen and E. Friedl, eds. Annals of the New York Academy of Sciences, Vol. 268:168–198.

1992   Greek Anthropology Comes of Age. Modern Greek Studies Yearbook 8:446–459.

1993   *Review of* Iceman, Archaeology 46(3):66–67

1994   The Anthropology of Greece. Anthropology Newsletter 35(4 April):24–25.

Allen, Peter S., and Carole Lazio
1982   Archaeology on Film: A Comprehensive Guide to Audio-Visual Materials. Boston: Archaeological Institute of America.

Allen, Peter S., et al.
1978   Five Views of Kypseli (a film review). Reviews in Anthropology 5(1):129–142.

Althabe, Gérard, Daniel Fabre, and Gérard Lenclud, eds.
1992   Vers une Ethnologie du Présent. Paris: Maison des Sciences de l'Homme.

Amsbury, Clifton
1972   Reply to Robert T. Anderson. American Anthropologist 74:770.

Anderson, Robert T.
1965   Studies in Peasant Life. *In* Biennial Review of Anthropology 1965. B. J. Siegel, ed. Pp. 176–210. Stanford, California: Stanford University Press.

1971a   Traditional Europe: A Study in Anthropology and History. Belmont, CA: Wadsworth Publishing Co.

1971b   Voluntary Associations in History. American Anthropologist 73:209–222.

Anderson, Robert T., and Barbara Gallatin Anderson
1962   Voluntary Associations among Ukrainians in France. Anthropological Quarterly 35(4):158–168.

Anderson, Robert T., and Gallatin Anderson
1962   The Indirect Social Structure of European Village Communities. American Anthropologist 64:1016–1027.

1965   Bus Stop to Paris: The Transformation of a French Village. New York: Doubleday.

Anderson-Levitt, Kathryn
1987   Cultural Knowledge for Teaching First Grade: An Example from France. *In* Interpretive Ethnography of Education at Home and Abroad. G. Spindler and L. Spindler, eds. Pp. 171–194. Hillsdale, NJ: Lawrence Erlbaum.

Andrews, Alfred
1949   The Bean and Indo-European Totemism. American Anthropologist 51:274–292.

Andromedas, John
  1963   *Review of* Rainbow in the Rock: The People of Rural Greece, by Irwin
          T. Sanders. American Anthropologist 65:434–435.

Angel, J. Lawrence
  1946   Social Biology of Greek Culture Growth. American Anthropologist
          48:493–533.
  1959   *Review of* The Etruscans, by Raymond Bloch. American
          Anthropologist 61:334.

Anonymous
  1929   Announcements of SSRC Fellowships. American Anthropologist
          31:823.

Apolito, Paolo, ed.
  1993   Sguardi e Modelli: Saggi Italiani di Antropologia. Milan: Angeli.

Appadurai, Arjun
  1986   Theory in Anthropology: Center and Periphery. Comparative
          Studies in Society and History 28:356–361.

Aranda, Francisco
  1976   Luis Buñuel: A Critical Biography. New York: Da Capo.

Arensberg, Conrad
  1937   The Irish Countryman: An Anthropological Study. (Reissued in 1950.
          Reprinted in 1958 by Peter Smith.) Cambridge, MA: Macmillan.
  1955   American Communities. American Anthropologist 57:1143–1162.
  1961   The Community as Object and as Sample. American Anthropologist
          63:241–264.
  1963   The Old World Peoples: The Place of European Cultures in World
          Ethnography. Anthropological Quarterly 36:75–99.

Arensberg, Conrad and Solon T. Kimball
  1968   [1940] Family and Community in Ireland. Rev. ed. Cambridge:
          Harvard University Press.

Armstrong, K. V.
  1976   The Participation of Scottish Women in Village Politics. Ph.D.
          Dissertation, University of Pittsburgh.

Badone, Ellen
  1989   The Appointed Hour: Death, Worldview and Social Change in
          Brittany. Berkeley: University of California Press.

Badone, Ellen, ed.
  1990   Religious Orthodoxy and Popular Faith in European Society.
          Princeton: Princeton University Press.

Bahro, Rudolf
  1978   The Alternative in Eastern Europe. London: NLB.

Bakić-Hayden, Milica and Robert M. Hayden
  1992   Orientalist Variations on the Theme 'Balkans': Symbolic Geography
          in Recent Yugoslav Cultural Politics. Slavic Review 51(1):1–15.

Banfield, Edward
    1971   The Moral Basis of a Backward Society. Riverside, NJ: The Free
            Press.

Barbarić, Anamarija, Andrija Stojanović, Stjepan Janjić, Tihomira Stepinac,
        Durđica Palošija, Žarko Spaniček, and Milana Cernelić
    1992   Seljačke Obiteljske Zadruge 2 (Peasant Joint Families-Zadrugas 2).
            Zagreb: Otvoreno Sveučilište.

Barbichon, Guy
    1991   Le Huron Chez Narcisse: Un Regard Renouvelé de L'anthropologie
            Américaine sur la France. Ethnologie Française 21:56–66.

Barnouw, Erik
    1983   Documentary: A History of the Non-Fiction Film. Oxford: Oxford
            University Press.

Barrett, Richard
    1973   Review of Archaic Roman Religion: With an Appendix on the
            Religion of the Etruscans, by Georges Dumezil. American
            Anthropologist 75:1028–1030.

Barth, Fredrik
    1967a   The Role of the Entrepreneur in Social Change in Northern Norway.
            Bergen, Norway: Universitetsforlaget.
    1967b   On the Study of Social Change. American Anthropologist
            69:661–669.
    1972   Analytical Dimensions in the Comparison of Social Organizations.
            American Anthropologist 74:207–220.

Bastos, Cristina
    1988   The Northeastern Algarve and the Southern Iberia Family Pattern.
            Journal of Family History 13:111–122.

Bax, Mart
    1973   Harpstrings and Confessions. Amsterdam: University of
            Amsterdam.
    1975   The Political Machine and Its Importance in the Irish Republic.
            Political Anthropology 1:6–20.
    1987   Religious Regimes and State Formation: Towards a Research
            Perspective. Anthropological Quarterly 60(1):1–12.
    1993   Power and the Definition of the Sacred: Popular Religious Regime
            Formation in Former Yugoslavia. Etnološka Tribina 16:119–132.
    1995   Medjugorje: Religion, Politics, and Violence in Rural Bosnia.
            Amsterdam: VU University Press.

Beck, Sam, and John W. Cole, eds.
    1981   Ethnicity and Nationalism in Southeastern Europe. Papers on
            European and Mediterranean Societies, No. 14. Amsterdam:
            University of Amsterdam Anthropology-Sociology Center.

Beckwith, Martha W.
    1922   Hawaiian Riddling. American Anthropologist 24:311–331.

Beidelman, T. O.
    1970   *Review of* The Divine Twins: An Indo-European Myth in Germanic
            Tradition. American Anthropologist 72:1148–1149.

Beljkašić-Hadžidedić, Ljiljana
    1988   Ethnological Work in Bosnia and Herzegovina from 1945 to the
            Present. Etnološki Pregled (Ethnological Review) 23–24:65–73.

Bell, Desmond
    1990   Acts of Union: Youth Culture and Sectarianism in Northern Ireland.
            London: Macmillan Publishers.

Bellier, Irène
    1993   L'ENA Comme si Vous y étiez. Paris: Seuil.
    1995   Moralité, langue et pouvoirs dans les institutions européenes. Social
            Anthropology 3:235–250.

Belmonte, Thomas
    1979   The Broken Fountain. New York: Columbia University Press.

Benedict, Burton
    1962   Stratification in Plural Societies. American Anthropologist
            64:1235–1246.
    1970   *Review of* Hal-Farrug: A Village in Malta, by Jeremy Boissevain.
            American Anthropologist 72:403–404.

Bennett, Brian C.
    1974   Sutivan: A Dalmatian Village in Social and Economic Transition. San
            Francisco, CA: R and E Research Associates.
    1976   Rural Community Planning Alternatives: The Yugoslav Model—
            Local Participation in Social Change. Planning Frontiers in Rural
            America: A Report to the Senate Subcommittee on Agriculture and
            Forestry, Washington, D.C.
    1979   Peasants, Businessmen, and Directions for Socio-Economic Change
            in Rural Coastal Dalmatia, Yugoslavia. Balkanistica V. Columbus,
            Ohio: Slavica Publishers.
    1993   Ideological Accommodation and Reconciliation in a Croatian
            Community. The Anthropology of East Europe Review 11(1–2):21–26.
    1995   An Outline of Socio-Cultural Analyses and Discourse on War,
            Ethnicity, and Change in Croatia and Eastern/Central Europe:
            Introduction to the Themes and Articles. Collegium
            Antropologicum 19(1):1–6.

Bennett, John W.
    1945   *Review of* Social Darwinism in American Thought, 1860–1915, by
            Richard Hofstadter. American Anthropologist 47:451.
    1946a   *Review of* Philosophy in a New Key: A Study in the Symbolism of
            Reason, Rite, and Art, by Suzanne K. Langer. American
            Anthropologist 48:463–464.
    1946b   *Review of* Sociology of the Renaissance, by Alfred von Martin.
            American Anthropologist 48:271–274.

Bennett, Linda A.
    1985   Treating Alcoholism in a Yugoslav Fashion. East European
              Quarterly XVIII(4):495–519.
    1991   From Solo Research to Collaborative European Studies. The
              Anthropology of East Europe Review 10(1):25–28.
    1992   The Temperance Movement in Yugoslavia: The Role of the Medical
              Professional, 1900–1940. Contemporary Drug Problems: 75–107.

Bennett, Linda A., Volume Editor
    1992   Encyclopedia of World Cultures Volume IV: Europe (Central,
              Western, and Southeastern Europe). David Levinson, series editor.
              Boston: G. K. Hall and Co.

Bennett, Linda A., J. L. Angel, D. F. Roberts, and P. Rudan
    1983   Joint Study of Biological and Cultural Variation in Dalmatian
              Village   Populations,   Project   Description.   Collegium
              Anthropologicum 7:195–199.

Bennett, Linda A., A. Sujoldžić, and P. Rudan
    1989   Contrasts in Demographic Structure and Linguistic Variation on the
              Island of Korčula and the Pelješac Peninsula, Yugoslavia. Ethnologia
              Europeae 19:141–168.

Bent, J. Theodore
    1885   Aegean Islands: The Cyclades, or Life among the Insular Greeks.
              London: Longsmans Green.

Beriss, David
    1993   High Folklore: Challenges to the French Cultural World Order.
              Social Analysis 33:105–129.

Berkowitz, Susan
    1984   Familism, Kinship and Sex Roles in Southern Italy: Contradictory
              Ideals and Real Contradictions. Anthropological Quarterly
              57(2):83–92.

Bernal, Martin
    1987   Black Athena: The Afroasiatic Roots of Classical Civilization. New
              Brunswick, NJ: Rutgers University Press.

Bernot, Lucien
    1966   *Review of* Bus Stop for Paris: The Transformation of a French Village,
              by Robert T. Anderson and Barbara Gallatin Anderson. American
              Anthropologist 68:786–788.

Bialor, Perry A.
    1976   The Northwest Corner of the Peloponnesus: Mavrikion and Its
              Region. *In* Regional Variation in Modern Greece and Cyprus:
              Toward a Perspective on the Ethnography of Greece. M. Dimen and
              E. Friedl, eds. New York Academy of Sciences 268:22–235.

Blacking, John, Kieran Byrne, and Kate Ingram
    1989   Looking for Work in Larne: A Social Anthropological Study. *In* Social

> Anthropology and Public Policy in Northern Ireland. Hastings
> Donnan and Graham McFarlane, eds. Pp. 67–89. Aldershot: Avebury.

Blim, Michael L.
> 1990   Made in Italy: Small-Scale Industrialization and Its Consequences.
>   New York: Praeger.

Blok, Anton
> 1974   The Mafia of a Sicilian Village, 1860–1960. Oxford: Basil Blackwell.

Blount, Ben
> 1974   *Review of* Studies in Social Interaction, edited by David Sudnow.
>   American Anthropologist 76:111–112.

Blum, R. and E.
> 1970   The Dangerous Hour: The Lore and Culture of Crisis and Mystery in
>   Rural Greece. London: Chatto and Windus.

Boas, Franz
> 1899   The Cephalic Index. American Anthropologist 1:448–461.

Boehm, Christopher
> 1972   Montenegrin Ethical Values: An Experiment in Anthropological
>   Method. Ph.D. Dissertation, Anthropology Department, Harvard
>   University.
> 1983   Montenegrin Social Organization and Values: Political Ethnography
>   of a Refuge Area Tribal Adaptation. New York: AMS Press.
> 1984   Blood Revenge: The Enactment and Management of Conflict in
>   Montenegro and Other Tribal Societies. Philadelphia: University of
>   Pennsylvania Press.

Boissevain, Jeremy
> 1964   Factions, Parties, and Politics in a Maltese Village. American
>   Anthropologist 66:1275–1287.
> 1975   Introduction: Towards a Social Anthropology of Europe. *In* Beyond
>   the Community: Social Process in Europe. Jeremy Boissevain and
>   John Friedl, eds. The Hague: Department of Educational Science of
>   the Netherlands.
> 1979   Towards a Social Anthropology of the Mediterranean. Current
>   Anthropology 20:81–93.

Boissevain, Jeremy, and John Friedl
> 1975   Beyond the Community: Social Process in Europe. The Hague:
>   Department of Educational Science of the Netherlands.

Botev, Nikolai
> 1993   Seeing Past the Barricades: Ethnic Intermarriage in Yugoslavia
>   During the Last Three Decades. The Anthropology of East Europe
>   Review 11(1–2):27–34.

Boyarin, Jonathan
> 1991   Polish Jews in Paris: The Ethnography of Memory. Bloomington:
>   Indiana University Press.

Brandes, Stanley
    1975   Migration, Kinship and Community: Tradition and Transition in a Spanish Village. New York: Academic Press.
    1980   Metaphors of Masculinity. Philadelphia: University of Pennsylvania Press.

Bremer, Fredericka
    1863   Greece and the Greeks: The Narrative of a Winter Residence in Greece and Its Islands. Mary Hewitt, tr. London. 2 vols.

Brettell, Caroline B.
    1977   Ethnicity and Entrepreneurs. Portuguese Immigrants in a Canadian City. *In* Ethnic Encounters: Identities and Contexts. George L. Hicks and Philip E. Leis, eds. Pp. 169–180. North Scituate, Mass: Duxbury Press.
    1979   Emigrar para Voltar: A Portuguese Ideology of Return Migration. Papers in Anthropology 20:1–20.
    1981   Is the Ethnic Community Inevitable? A Comparison of the Settlement Patterns of Portuguese Immigrants in Toronto and Paris. Journal of Ethnic Studies 9:1–18.
    1982   We Have Already Cried Many Tears: The Stories of Three Portuguese Migrant Women. Cambridge, Mass: Schenkman Publishing Company.
    1983   Emigração, a Igreja e a Festa Religiosa do Norte de Portugal: Estudo de um Caso. Estudos Contemporaneos 5:175–204.
    1984   Emigration and Underdevelopment: The Causes and Consequences of Portuguese Emigration to France in Historical and Cross-Cultural Perspective. *In* Portugal in Development: Emigration, Industrialization and the EEC. Thomas Bruneau et. al., eds. Pp. 65–82. Ottawa: University of Ottawa Press.
    1986   Men Who Migrate, Women Who Wait: Population and History in a Portuguese Parish. Princeton: Princeton University Press.
    1989   Emigration and Household Structure in a Portuguese Parish. 1850–1902. Journal of Family History 13:33–58.
    1990a   The Priest and His People: The Contractual Basis for Religious Practice in Rural Portugal. *In* Religious Orthodoxy & Popular Faith in European Society. Ellen Badone, ed. Pp. 55–75. Princeton: Princeton University Press.
    1990b   Leaving, Remaining, and Returning: Some Thoughts on the Multifaceted Portuguese Migratory System. *In* Portuguese Migration in Global Perspective. David Higgs, ed. Pp. 61–80. Toronto: The Multicultural History Society of Ontario.
    1991   Kinship and Contract: Property Transmission and Family Relations in Northwestern Portugal. Comparative Studies in Society and History 33:443–465.
    1992   *Review of* Pre-Bureaucratic Europeans, by Jan Brøgger. American Ethnologist. 19:851–852.

1993a   The Emigrant, the Nation, and the State in Nineteenth and Twentieth Century Portugal. Portuguese Studies Review 2:51–64.

1993b   Archives and Informants: Reflections on Juxtaposing the Methods of Anthropology and History. Historical Methods 25:28–36.

1994   Women Are Migrants Too: A Portuguese Perspective. *In* Urban Life. 3rd ed. George Gmelch and Walter Zenner, eds. Prospect Heights, IL: Waveland Press.

Brettell, Caroline B., and Patricia A. deBerjeois
1992   Anthropology and the Study of Immigrant Women. *In* Seeking Common Ground: Multidisciplinary Studies of Immigrant Women in the United States. Donna Gabaccia, ed. Pp. 41–63. Westport, CT: Greenwood Press.

Brettell, Caroline B., and Rui Feijó
1991   Foundlings in 19th Century Northwestern Portugal: Public Welfare and Family Strategies. *In* Enfance Abandonée et Société en Europe, XIV–XX Siecle. Pp. 273–300. Rome: École Francaise de Rome: Actes de Colloque Internationale.

Breuner, Nancy F.
1992   Cult of the Virgin Mary in Southern Italy and Spain. Ethos 20:66–95.

Bringa, Tone R.
1993   Nationality Categories, National Identification and Identity Formation in 'Multinational' Bosnia. The Anthropology of East Europe Review 11(1–2):69–76.

1995   Being Muslim the Bosnian Way: Identity and Community in a Central Bosnian Village. Princeton: Princeton University Press.

Brody, Hugh
1973   Innishkillane. London: Allan Lane.

Brøgger, Jan
1990   Pre-Bureaucratic Europeans. A Study of a Portuguese Fishing Community. Oslo: Norwegian University Press.

Brown, D. E.
1973   Voluntary Association: A Further Comment. American Anthropologist 75:309–310.

Brown, Jennifer
1972   Plato's Republic as an Early Study of Media Bias and a Charter for Prosaic Education. American Anthropologist 74:672–675.

Brown, Peter J.
1981   Cultural Adaptations to Endemic Malaria in Sardinia. Medical Anthropology 5:311–339.

Brown, Peter J., and Elizabeth D. Whitaker
1994   Health Implications of Modern Agricultural Transformations: Malaria and Pellagra in Italy. Human Organization 53:346–351.

Buckley, Anthony D.
    1982   A Gentle People: A Study of a Peaceful Community in Northern
            Ireland. Cultra: Ulster Folk and Transport Museum.

Buechler, Hans C., and Judith-Maria Buechler
    1981   Carmen: The Autobiography of a Spanish Galician Woman.
            Cambridge: Shenkman Publishing Company.
    1987   Migrants in Europe: The Role of Family, Labor, and Politics. New
            York: Greenwood Press.

Buettner-Janusch, John
    1962   *Review of* Human Races, by Stanley M. Garn. American
            Anthropologist 64:902–903.

Bufwack, Mary S.
    1982   Village without Violence: An Examination of a Northern Irish
            Community. Cambridge, MA: Schenkman.

Bull, Martin
    1993   Widening Versus Deepening the European Community: The
            Political Dynamics of 1992 in Historical Perspective. *In* Cultural
            Change and the New Europe. Thomas M. Wilson and M. Estellie
            Smith, eds. Boulder: Westview Press.

Burguière, André
    1978   The New Annales. Review 1:195–205.

Burton, M. L., C. C. Moore, J. W. M. Whiting, and A. K. Romney
    1996   Regions Based on Social Structure. Current Anthropology
            37(1):87–111.

Calabrese, Cal
    1994   Report from the Balkans: Investigating Mass Graves for the UN.
            Federal Archeology 7(2):9.

Callier, Colette
    1966   Soajo: Une Communauté Feminine Rurale de l'Alto Minho. Bulletin
            des Etudes Portugaises 27:237–278.

Callier-Boisvert, Colette
    1968   Remarques sur le Système de Parenté et sur la Famille au Portugal.
            l'Homme 8:88–103.
    1990   Femme et Mère Celibataires dans le Nord-Ouest du Portugal,
            1860–1986. Ethnologie Francaise 2:189–202.

Campbell, John K.
    1964   Honour, Family and Patronage: A Study of Institutions and Moral
            Values in a Greek Mountain Community. Oxford: Clarendon Press.

Čapo Jasna
    1990   Economic and Demographic History of Peasant Households on a
            Croatian Estate. Ph.D. Dissertation, Anthropology Department,
            University of California, Berkeley.

1991   Croatian Ethnology, the Science of Peoples or the Science of Culture? Studia Ethnologica 3:17–25.

Čapo Žmegač, Jasna
1995   Patriarchy or Seniority in Croatia: Regional and Historical Perspective. Paper presented at an international conference on (En)gendering Violence: Terror, Domination, Recovery. October, Zagreb, Croatia.

Čapo, Jasna, Jakov Gelo, Trpimir Macan, and Olga Supek
1992   Croats, *In* The Encyclopedia of World Cultures Volume IV: Europe. Linda A. Bennett, vol. ed., David Levinson, series ed. Pp. 72–75. Boston: G. K. Hall and Co.

Cappanari, Stephen
1973   *Review of* Torregreca: Life, Death, Miracles, by Ann Cornelisen; *and* Milocca: A Sicilian Village, by Charlotte Gower Chapman. American Anthropologist 75:427–428.

Caraveli, Anna
1980   Bridge Between Worlds: The Women's Ritual Lament as Communicative Event. Journal of American Folklore 93:129–157.
1986   The Bitter Wounding: The Lament as Social Protest in Rural Greece. *In* Gender and Power in Rural Greece. J. Dubisch, ed. Pp. 169–194. Princeton: Princeton University Press.

Carrier, James, ed.
1995   Occidentalism: Images of the West. Oxford: Clarendon Press.

Caws, Peter
1970   What Is Structuralism? *In* Claude Levi-Strauss: The Anthropologist as Hero. E. Hayes and T. Hayes, eds. Pp. 197–215. Cambridge: M.I.T. Press.

Cecil, Rosanne
1989   Care and Community in a Northern Irish Town. *In* Social Anthropology and Public Policy in Northern Ireland. Hastings Donnan and Graham McFarlane, eds. Pp. 107–121. Aldershot: Avebury.
1993   The Marching Season in Northern Ireland: An Expression of Politico-Religious Identity. *In* Inside European Identities: Ethnography in Western Europe. Sharon Macdonald, ed. Pp. 146–166. Providence: Berg.

Ceribašić, N.
1995   Gender Roles During the War: Representations in Croatian and Serbian Popular Music 1991–1992. Collegium Antropologicum 19(1):91–101.

Chapman, Anne
1968   *Review of* The Art of Two Worlds: Studies in Pre-Columbian and European Cultures, by Alfred B. Schuster. American Anthropologist 70:402–403.

Chapman, Charlotte Gower
  1971   [1935] Milocca: A Sicilian Village. Cambridge: Schenkman.

Charbonnier, Georges
  1969   Conversations with Claude Levi-Strauss. London: Jonathan Cape.

Childe, V. Gordon
  1937   The Antiquity of the British Bronze Age. American Anthropologist
            39:1–22.

Chirot, Daniel
  1976   Social Change in a Peripheral Society: The Creation of a Balkan
            Colony. New York: Academic Press.

Chiva, Isac
  1987   Entre Livre et Musée: Emergence d'une Ethnologie de la France. *In*
            Ethnologies en Miroir. Chiva and Jeggle, eds. Pp. 9–33. Paris:
            Maison des Sciences de l'Homme.

Claverie, Elisabeth, and Pierre Lamaison
  1982   L'impossible Mariage: Violence et Parenté en Gévaudan 17e, 18e,
            19e Siècles. Paris: Hachette.

Clark, Mari
  1983   Variations on Themes of Male and Female: Reflections on Gender
            Bias in Fieldwork in Rural Greece. Women's Studies 102:117–133.

Clifford, James
  1988   The Predicament of Culture. Cambridge: Harvard University
            Press.

Cohen, A. P.
  1987   Whalsay. Manchester: Manchester University Press.

Cohen, Eugene
  1970   *Review of* The Study of an Italian Village, by A. L. Maraspini.
            American Anthropologist 72:405–407.

Cohn, Werner
  1972   *Review of* Gypsies: Wanderers of the World, by Bart McDowell.
            American Anthropologist 74:25.

Cole, John W.
  1973   Social Process in the Italian Alps. American Anthropologist
            75:765–786.
  1977   Anthropology Comes Part-Way Home: Community Studies in
            Europe. Annual Review of Anthropology 6:349–378.

Cole, John W., and Eric R. Wolf
  1974   The Hidden Frontier: Ecology and Ethnicity in an Alpine Valley.
            New York: Academic.

Cole, Sally
  1991   Women of the Praia: Work and Lives in a Portuguese Coastal
            Community. Princeton: Princeton University Press.

Colvard, Karen, and Joel Wallman
    1993   1993 Report of the Harry Frank Guggenheim Foundation. New
            York: Guggenheim Foundation.
Connor, Walker
    1978   A Nation Is a Nation, Is a State, Is an Ethnic Group, Is a.... Ethnic
            and Racial Studies 1(4):379–388.
Costa, Janeen Arnold
    1988   The History of Migration and Political Economy in Rural Greece: A
            Case Study. Journal of Modern Greek Studies 6(2):159–186.
    1993   The Periphery of Pleasure or Pain: Consumer Culture in the EC
            Mediterranean of 1992. *In* Cultural Change and the New Europe.
            Thomas M. Wilson and M. Estellie Smith, eds. Pp. 81–98. Boulder:
            Westview Press.
Counihan, Carole
    1984   Bread as World: Food Habits and Social Relations in Modernizing
            Sardinia. Anthropological Quarterly 57(2):47–59.
    1988   Female Identity, Food, and Power in Contemporary Florence.
            Anthropological Quarterly 61(2):51–62.
    1993   The Periphery of Pleasure or Pain: Consumer Culture in the EC
            Mediterranean of 1992. *In* Cultural Change and the New Europe.
            Thomas M. Wilson and M. Estellie Smith, eds. Boulder: Westview Press.
Count, Earl
    1952a   *Review of* The 50th Anniversary Meeting of the AAA. American
            Anthropological Association 54:123–125.
    1952b   *Review of* Song, Dance, and Customs of Peasant Poland, by Sula
            Benet. American Anthropologist 54:542–543.
Cowan, Jane
    1990   Dance and the Body Politic in Northern Greece. Princeton: Princeton
            University Press.
    1991   Going Out for Coffee? Contesting the Grounds of Gendered
            Pleasures in Everyday Sociability. *In* Contested Identities: Gender
            and Kinship in Modern Greece. E. Papataxiarchis and P. Loizos, eds.
            Princeton: Princeton University Press. Pp. 180–202.
Cresswell, Robert
    1969   Une communante rurale de 'Irlande. Paris: Institute de
            Ethnographie.
Cronin, Constance
    1970   The Sting of Change: Sicilians in Sicily and Australia. Chicago:
            University of Chicago Press.
Crozier, Maurna
    1989   'Powerful Wakes': Perfect Hospitality. *In* Ireland From Below. Chris
            Curtin and Thomas M. Wilson, eds. Pp. 70–91. Galway: Galway
            University Press.

Cucchiari, Salvatore
1988   Adapted for Heaven: Conversion and Culture in Western Sicily. American Ethnologist 15:417–441.

Currier, Richard
1976   Social Interaction and Social Structure in a Greek Island Village. *In* Regional Variation in Modern Greece and Cyprus: Toward a Perspective on the Ethnography of Greece. M. Dimen and E. Friedl, eds. New York Academy of Sciences 268:308–313.

Curtin, Chris
1986   The Peasant Family Farm and Commoditization in the West of Ireland. *In* The Commoditization Debate: Strategy and Social Network. N. Long, J. D. van der Ploeg, C. Curtin, and L. Box. Papers of the Department of Sociology No. 17, pp. 58–76. Agricultural University, Wageningen, The Netherlands.

Curtin, Chris, and Colm Ryan
1989   Clubs, Pubs, and Private Houses in a Clare Town. *In* Ireland From Below. Chris Curtin and Thomas M. Wilson, eds. Pp. 128–143. Galway: Galway University Press.

Curtin, Chris, and Tony Varley
1989   Brown Trout, 'Gentry' and Dutchmen: Tourism and Development in South Mayo. *In* Ireland from Below. Chris Curtin and Thomas M. Wilson, eds. Pp. 207–223. Galway: Galway University Press.

Curtin, Chris, Hastings Donnan, and Thomas M. Wilson, eds.
1993a   Irish Urban Cultures. Belfast: Institute of Irish Studies Press.
1993b   Anthropology and Irish Urban Settings. *In* Irish Urban Cultures. Chris Curtin, Hastings Donnan, and Thomas M. Wilson, eds. Pp. 1–21. Belfast: Institute of Irish Studies Press.

Curtin, Chris, and Thomas M. Wilson, eds.
1989a   Introduction. *In* Ireland from Below. Chris Curtin and Thomas M. Wilson, eds. Pp. vi–xvi. Galway: Galway University Press.
1989b   Ireland from Below: Social Change and Local Communities. Galway: Galway University Press.

Cutileiro, Jose
1971   A Portuguese Rural Society. Oxford: Clarendon Press.

Danforth, Loring, and Alexander Tsiarias
1982   The Death Rituals of Rural Greece. Princeton: Princeton University Press.

Davis, John
1973   Land and Family in Pisticci. London: Athlone.
1977   People of the Mediterranean: An Essay in Comparative Social Anthropology. London: Routledge and Kegan Paul.

de Boulay, J.
1974   Portrait of a Greek Mountain Village. Oxford: Clarendon Press.

Denich, Bette
    1969   Social Mobility and Industrialization in a Yugoslav Town (Titovo Uzice, Serbia). Ph.D. Dissertation, Anthropology Department, University of California, Berkeley.
    1993   Unmaking Multi-Ethnicity in Yugoslavia: Metamorphosis Observed. The Anthropology of East Europe Review 11(1–2):43–53.
    1994   Dismembering Yugoslavia: Nationalist Ideologies and the Symbolic Revival of Genocide. American Ethnologist 21(2):367–390.

Denoon, Donald
    1983   Settler Capitalism. The Dynamics of Dependent Development in the Southern Hemisphere. Oxford: Clarendon Press.

Derrida, Jacques
    1992   The Other Heading: Reflections on Today's Europe. Bloomington: Indiana University Press.

Despalatović, Eleanor
    1993   Reflections on Croatia, 1960–1992. The Anthropology of East Europe Review 11(1–2):100–107.

Diamandouros, Nikiforos
    1993   The Dialectics of Ambivalence: Images of the Greek "Self" and the European "Other" in Contemporary Greek Culture. Plenary Address, 1993 Modern Greek Studies Symposium. Berkeley, CA.

Dias, A. Jorge
    1953   Rio de Onor: Comunitarismo Agro-pastoril. Porto.
    1961   Portuguese Contribution to Cultural Anthropology. Johannesburg: Witwatersrand University Press.
    1981   Vilarinho da Furna, Uma Aldeia Comunitaria. Lisbon: Imprensa Nacional. 1st ed., Porto, 1948.

Dilley, Roy
    1989   Boat Owners, Patrons and State Policy in the Northern Ireland Fishing Industry. In Social Anthropology and Public Policy in Northern Ireland. Hastings Donnan and Graham McFarlane, eds. Pp. 122–147. Aldershot: Avebury.

Dimen, Murial
    1976   Regional Studies and their Potential Value for the Ethnography of Modern Greece and Cyprus. In Regional Variation in Modern Greece and Cyprus: Toward a Perspective on the Ethnography of Greece. M. Dimen and E. Friedl, eds. New York Academy of Sciences 268:3–9.

Dimen, Muriel, and Ernestine Friedl, eds.
    1976   Regional Variation in Modern Greece and Cyprus: Toward a Perspective on the Ethnography of Greece. Annals of the New York Academy of Sciences, Vol. 268.

Domenach, Jean-Marie, and Alain Pontault
    1963   Yugoslavia. New York: Viking Press.

Donnan, Hastings
   1994   'New' Minorities: South Asians in the North. *In* The Unheard Voice:
            Social Anthropology in Ireland. Pol O Muiri, ed. Pp. 11–14. Belfast:
            Fortnight Educational Trust.

Donnan, Hastings, and Graham McFarlane
   1986   Social Anthropology and the Sectarian Divide in Northern Ireland.
            In The Sectarian Divide in Northern Ireland Today. Richard Jenkins,
            Hastings Donnan, and Graham McFarlane, eds. Pp. 23–37. Royal
            Anthropological Institute of Great Britain and Ireland. Occasional
            Paper, no. 41.
   1989   Introduction: Social Anthropology and Public Policy in Northern
            Ireland. *In* Social Anthropology and Public Policy in Northern
            Ireland. Hastings Donnan and Graham McFarlane, eds. Pp. 1–25.
            Aldershot: Avebury.

Donnan, Hastings, and Graham McFarlane, eds.
   1989   Social Anthropology and Public Policy in Northern Ireland.
            Aldershot: Avebury Press.

Donnan, Hastings, and Thomas M. Wilson
   1994   An Anthropology of Frontiers. *In* Border Approaches:
            Anthropological Perspectives on Frontiers. H. Donnan and T. M.
            Wilson, eds. Lanham, MD: University Press of America.

Douglas, Mary
   1966   Purity and Danger: An Analysis of Concepts of Pollution and Taboo.
            New York: F. A. Praeger.

Douglass, William A.
   1967   Opportunity, Choice-Making, and Rural Depopulation in Two
            Spanish Basque Villages. Unpublished Ph.D. Dissertation,
            University of Chicago.
   1969   Death in Murélaga: Funerary Ritual in a Spanish Basque Village.
            Seattle: University of Washington Press.
   1970a   Peasant Emigrants: Reactors or Actors. *In* Migration and
            Anthropology. Robert F. Spencer, ed. Seattle: Proceedings of the
            1970 Annual Spring Meeting of the American Ethnological Society.
   1970b   *Review of* The European Peasantry: The Final Phase, by S. H.
            Franklin. American Anthropologist 72:641–643.
   1975   Echalar and Murélaga: Opportunity and Rural Depopulation in Two
            Spanish Basque Villages. New York: St. Martin's Press.
   1984   Emigration in a South Italian Town: An Anthropological History.
            New Brunswick: Rutgers University Press.
   1991   The Joint Family Household in Eighteenth-Century Southern Italian
            Society. *In* The Family in Italy from Antiquity to the Present. David
            I. Kertzer and Richard P. Saller, eds. Pp. 286–303. New Haven: Yale
            University Press.

1996   Azúcar Amargo. Vida y Fortuna de los Cortadoros de Caña Italianos y Vascos en la Australia Tropical. Lejona: Servicio Editorial, Universidad del Pais Vasco.

Douglass, William A., and Jon Bilbao
1975   Amerikanuak: Basques in the New World. Reno: University of Nevada Press.

Downs, Mary, Peter S. Allen, Mark J. Meister, and Carole Lazio
1994   Archaeology on Film. Dubuque, IA: Kendall/Hunt.

Dubisch, Jill
1972   The Open Community: Migration from a Greek Island Village. Ph.D. Dissertation, University of Chicago.

1974a   The Domestic Power of Women in a Greek Island Village. Studies in European Society 1(1):23–33.

1974b   Honor and Shame in a Complex Society. Paper presented at the annual meeting of the American Anthropological Association, Mexico City.

1977   The City as Resource: Migration from a Greek Island Village. Urban Anthropology 6(1):65–83.

1983   Greek Women: Sacred or Profane? Journal of Modern Greek Studies 1(1):185–202.

1986   Introduction and Preface. *In* Gender and Power in Rural Greece. Pp. 3–41. Princeton: Princeton University Press.

1989   Death and Social Change in Greece. Anthropological Quarterly 62(4):189–200.

1995   In a Different Place: Pilgrimage, Gender and Politics at a Greek Island Shrine. Princeton: Princeton University Press.

Dubisch, Jill, ed.
1986   Gender and Power in Rural Greece. Princeton: Princeton University Press.

Du Bois, Cora
1941   *Review of* Family and Community in Ireland, by Conrad M. Arensberg and Solon T. Kimball. American Anthropologist 43:460–461.

Dubinskas, Frank A.
1983   Performing Slavic Folklore: The Politics of Reminiscence and Recreating the Past, Ph.D. Dissertation, Anthropology Department, Stanford University.

1992   Managing Merriment. Contemporary Drug Problems 19(1):109–132.

Duijzings, Ger
1995   The Exodus of Letnica. Croatian Refugees from Kosovo in Western Slavonia. Paper presented at an international conference on War, Exile, Everyday Life. March–April, Zagreb, Croatia.

Dukat, Zdeslav
    1993   The Song of Kontreš Harambaša as Recorded in Tomičić's Collection
            of Croatian Epic Folk Songs From Herzegovina and Dalmatia.
            Narodna Umjetnost 30:357–370.

Dumas, Christos G.
    1983   Thera, Pompeii of the Ancient Aegean: Excavations at Akrotiri,
            1967–79. New York: Thames and Hudson.

Dunn, Stephen P.
    1962   *Review of* Education and Professional Employment in the USSR, by
            Nicholas de Witt. American Anthropologist 64:903–904.
    1971   *Review of* The Russian Colonization of Kazakhstan, 1896–1916, by
            George J. Demko. American Anthropologist 73:871.
    1973   *Review of* (!)Qué Gitano!: Gypsies of Southern Spain, by Bertha B.
            Quintana and Lois Gray Floyd. American Anthropologist 75:1816.

Durham, Edith
    1987   [1909] High Albania. Boston: Beacon Press.

Ehrmann, Jacques, ed.
    1970   Structuralism. New York: Doubleday.

Eidheim, Harald
    1966   Lappish Guest Relationships under Conditions of Cultural Change.
            American Anthropologist 68:426–437.

Eipper, Chris
    1986   The Ruling Trinity: A Community Study of Church, State and
            Business in Ireland. Aldershot: Gower.

Eiseley, Loren
    1945   *Review of* The Irish Stone Age, by Hallam Movius Jr. American
            Anthropologist 47:152–153.

Erlich, Vera St.
    1966   Family in Transition: A Study of 300 Yugoslav Villages. Princeton:
            Princeton University Press.
    1976   The Last Big Zadrugas: Albanian Extended Families of the Kosovo
            Region. *In* Communal Families in the Balkans: The Zadruga. Robert F.
            Byrnes, ed. Pp. 244–251. Notre Dame: University of Notre Dame Press.

Evans, Sir Arthur J.
    1921   The Palace of Minos: A Comparative Account of the Successive
            Stages of the Early Cretan Civilization as Illustrated by the
            Discoveries at Knossos. London: Macmillan.

Fabian, Johannes
    1983   Time and the Other: How Anthropology Makes Its Object. New
            York: Columbia University Press.

Farber, Bernard
    1968   Comparative Kinship Systems: A Method of Analysis. New York:
            Wiley.

Faubion, James D.
  1993   Modern Greek Lessons: A Primer in Historical Construction.
          Princeton: Princeton University Press.

Faye, P. L.
  1923   *Review of* Traité Comparatif des Nationalites, by A. Van Gennep.
          American Anthropologist 25:412–416.

Fél, Edit, and Tamás Hofer
  1969   Proper Peasants: Traditional Life in a Hungarian Village. Viking
          Fund Publications in Anthropology, No. 46. New York: Wenner-
          Gren Foundation for Anthropological Research.

Feldman, Allen
  1991   Formations of Violence. Chicago: University of Chicago Press.

Feldman, Lada Čale
  1995   The Image of the Leader: Being a President, Displaying a Cultural
          Performance. Collegium Antropologicum 19(1):41–52.

Feldman, Lada Čale, Ines Prica, and Reana Senjković, eds.
  1993   Fear, Death, and Resistance: An Ethnography of War: Croatia
          1991–1992. Zagreb: Institute of Ethnology and Folklore Research.

Fernandez, James
  1983   Consciousness and Class in Southern Spain (review essay).
          American Ethnologist 10(1):165–173.
  1986   Persuasions and Performances: The Play of Tropes in Culture.
          Bloomington: Indiana University Press.

Fishberg, Maurice
  1902   Physical Anthropology of the Jews. I.—The Cephalic Index.
          American Anthropologist 4:684–705.
  1903   Physical Anthropology of the Jews. II.—Pigmentation. American
          Anthropologist 5:89–106.

Foltiny, Stephen
  1959   *Review of* The Tongues of Italy, by Ernst Pulgram. American
          Anthropologist 61:339–341.

Force, Roland W.
  1962   *Review of* Visual Files Coding Index, by Robert Bruce Inverarity.
          American Anthropologist 64:212–213.

Forman, Shepard, and Joyce Riegelhaupt
  1979   The Political-Economy of Patron-Clientship: Brazil and Portugal
          Compared. *In* Brazil: Anthropological Perspectives. Essays in Honor
          of Charles Wagley. Maxine L. Margolis and William E. Carter, eds.
          Pp. 379–400. New York: Columbia University Press.

Foster, George
  1965   Peasant Society and the Image of Limited Good. American
          Anthropologist 67:293–315.

Foster, George M., and Robert V. Kemper, eds.
    1974   Anthropologists in Cities. Boston: Little, Brown

Fouque, Ferdinand
    1869   Une Pompeii Antehistorique. Revue des Doux Mondes 39.
    1879   Santorin et Ses Eruptions. Paris: Maison et Cie.

Fox, Richard G.
    1970   *Review of* Urban Development in Southern Europe: Italy and Greece, by E. A. Gutkind. American Anthropologist 72:1519–1521.

Frankenberg, Ronald
    1961   *Review of* Welsh Rural Communities, by David Jenkins et al., eds. American Anthropologist 63:1370.

Franklin, S. H.
    1969   The European Peasantry: The Final Phase. London: Methuen.

Freeman, Susan Tax
    1968a   Corporate Village Organization in the Sierra Ministra: An Iberian Structural Type. Man 3:477–484.
    1968b   Religious Aspects of the Social Organization of a Castillian Village. American Anthropologist 70:34–49.
    1968c   *Review of* Chanzeaux: A Village in Anjoy, edited by Laurence Wylie. American Anthropologist 70:126–127.
    1970a   Neighbors. Chicago: University of Chicago Press.
    1970b   *Review of* Death in Murélaga: Funerary Ritual in a Spanish Basque Village, by William A. Douglass. American Anthropologist 72:1112–1113.
    1972a   *Review of* Irrigation and Society in Medieval Valencia, by Thomas Glick. American Anthropologist 74:163–164.
    1972b   *Review of* Social Change in a Spanish Village, by Joseph Aceves. American Anthropologist 74:882–883.
    1973   Introduction: Studies in Rural European Social Organization. American Anthropologist 75:743–750.

Friedl, Ernestine
    1958   *Review of* Village in the Vaucluse, by Laurence Wylie. American Anthropologist 60:962–963.
    1959   The Role of Kinship in the Transmission of National Culture to Rural Villages in Mainland Greece. American Anthropologist 61:30–38.
    1962   Vasilika: A Village in Modern Greece. New York: Holt, Rinehart and Winston.
    1963   Studies in Peasant Life. *In* Biennial Review of Anthropology 1963. B. J. Siegel, ed. Pp. 276–306. Stanford, CA: Stanford University Press.
    1964   Lagging Emulation in Post-Peasant Society. American Anthropologist 66:569–586.
    1966a   *Review of* Culture and Community, by Conrad M. Arensberg and Solon T. Kimball. American Anthropologist 68:1022–1024.
    1966b   *Review of* Social Change in a Greek Country Town: The Impact of

Factory Work on the Position of Women, by Ioanna Lambiri. American Anthropologist 68:1532–1533.

1967   The Position of Women: Appearance and Reality. Anthropological Quarterly 4(3):97–108.

1995   The Life of an Academic: A Personal Record of a Teacher, Administrator, and Anthropologist. Annual Review of Anthropology 24:1–19.

Fritz, Margaret C.

1974   *Review of* Prehistoric European Art, by Walter Torbugge. American Anthropologist 76:399–401.

Frolander-Ulf, M. C.

1978   Women: The Cattle Keepers of Eastern Finland. An Analysis of the Economic and Political Roles of Women in Kuusisaari Village in the Twentieth Century. Ph.D. Dissertation, University of Pittsburgh.

Fukuyama, Francis

1989   The End of History. The National Interest. Summer 1989.

Gaboriau, Patrick

1993   Clochard: l'Univers D'un Groupe de sans-Abri Parisians. Paris: Julliard.

Gaetz, Stephen

1992   Planning Community-Based Youth Services in Cork, Ireland: The Relevance of the Concepts "Youth" and "Community." Urban Anthropology 21(1):91–113.

1993   Who Comes First? Teenage Girls, Youth Culture and the Provision of Youth Services in Cork. *In* Irish Urban Cultures. Chris Curtin, Hastings Donnan, and Thomas M. Wilson, eds. Pp. 143–159. Belfast: Institute of Irish Studies Press.

Gagnon Jr., V. P.

1994a   Letters: Reaction to the Special Issue of AEER War among the Yugoslavs. The Anthropology of East Europe Review 12(1):50–51.

1994b   Reply to Simić. The Anthropology of East Europe Review 12(2):35.

Galani-Moutafi, Vasiliki

1993   From Agriculture to Tourism: Property, Labor, Gender, and Kinship in a Greek Island Village (Part One). Journal of Modern Greek Studies 11(2):241–270.

1994   From Agriculture to Tourism: Property, Labor, Gender, and Kinship in a Greek Island Village (Part Two). Journal of Modern Greek Studies 12(1):113–132.

Galanopoulos, A. G.

1958   Zur Bestimmung des Alters des Santorin-kaldera. Annales Geologiques des Pays Helleniques 9.

Galt, Anthony

1980   Structure and Process in Social Stratification on the Island of Pantelleria, Italy. Ethnology 19:405–425.

1985   Does the Mediterraneanist Dilemma Have Straw Horns? American Ethnologist 12:369–371.

1991   Far from the Church Bell. Cambridge: Cambridge University Press.

Garber, Vesna

1992   Slav Macedonians. Encyclopedia of World Cultures Volume IV: Europe, Linda A. Bennett, vol. ed., David Levinson, series ed. Pp. 238–242. Boston: G. K. Hall and Co.

Garth, Thomas R.

1936   *Review of* Negro Intelligence and Selective Migration, by Otto Klineberg. American Anthropologist 38:130–131.

Gavazzi, Milovan, ed.

1960   Seljaćke Obiteljske Zadruge (Peasant Joint Families—Zadrugas). Ethnological Institute of the Faculty of Philosophy, University of Zagreb.

Gearing, Fred

1963   *Review of* Vasilika: A Village in Modern Greece, by Ernestine Friedl. American Anthropologist 65:1170–1172.

Geertz, Clifford

1961   Studies in Peasant Life. *In* Biennial Review of Anthropology. B. J. Siegel, ed. Pp. 1–41. Stanford, CA: Stanford University Press.

Gefou-Madianou, Dimitra

1993   Mirroring Ourselves through Western Texts: The Limits of an Indigenous Anthropology. *In* The Politics of Ethnographic Reading and Writing: Confrontations of Indigenous and Western Views. H. Driessen, ed. Pp. 160–179. Saarvrucken and Fort Lauderdale: Verlag Breitenbach Publishers.

Gewertz, Deborah, and Frederick Errington

1991   We Think, Therefore They Are? Occidentalizing the World. Anthropological Quarterly 64(2):80–91.

Ghani, Ashraf

1995   Writing a History of Power: An Examination of Eric R. Wolf's Anthropological Quest. *In* Articulating Hidden Histories: Exploring the Influence of Eric R. Wolf. Jane Schneider and Rayna Rapp, eds. Berkeley: University of California Press.

Gibbon, Peter

1973   Arensberg and Kimball Revisited. Economy and Society 2:479–498.

Gibbon, P., and C. Curtin

1976   The Stem Family in Ireland. Comparative Studies in Society and History 20(3):429–453.

1983a   Irish Farm Families: Facts and Fantasies. Comparative Studies in Society and History 25(2):375–380.

1983b   Some Observations on The Stem Family in Ireland Reconsidered. Comparative Studies in Society and History 25(2):393–395.

Gibbon, P., and M. D. Higgins
    1974   Patronage, Tradition and Modernization: The Case of the Irish 'Gombeenman.' Economic and Social Review 6:27–44.
    1977   The Irish 'Gombeenman': Re-incarnation or Rehabilitation. Economic and Social Review 8:313–320.

Gilliland, Mary Kay
    1986   The Maintenance of Family Values in a Yugoslav Town. Ph.D. Dissertation, Anthropology Department, University of California, San Diego.

Gilliland, Mary Kay, Sanja Špoljar-Vržina, and Vlasta Rudan
    1995a   Reclaiming Lives: Variable Effects of War on Gender and Ethnic Identities in the Narratives of Bosnian and Croatian Refugees. The Anthropology of East Europe Review 13(1):30–39.
    1995b   Interviews with Displaced Persons and Refugees on the Island of Hvar: Themes and Introductory Findings. Collegium Antropologicum 19(1):103–111.

Gilliland Olsen, Mary Kay
    1993   Bridge on the Sava: Ethnicity in Eastern Croatia, 1981–1991. The Anthropology of East Europe Review 11(1–2):54–62.

Gillin, John
    1949   Methodological Problems in the Anthropological Study of Modern Cultures. American Anthropologist 51:392–399.
    1957   *Review of* Toward a Unified Theory of Human Behavior, edited by Roy R. Grinker. American Anthropologist 59:1092–1093.
    1967   More Complex Cultures for Anthropologists. American Anthropologist 69:301–302.

Gilmore, David
    1982   Anthropology of the Mediterranean Area. Annual Review of Anthropology 11:175–205.
    1987   Introduction: The Shame of Dishonour. *In* Honor and Shame and the Unity of the Mediterranean. David Gilmore, ed. Pp. 2–21. Washington, DC: American Anthropological Association.

Giordano, Christian
    1987   The 'Wine War' between France and Italy: Ethno-Anthropological Aspects of the European Community. Sociologia Ruralis 27:56–66.

Giovannini, Maureen
    1981   Woman: A Dominant Symbol within the Cultural System of a Sicilian Town. Man 16:408–426.

Glascock, A. P.
    1973   Decision-Making among Migrants to Dublin, Ireland. Ph.D. Dissertation, University of Pittsburgh.

Gmelch, George
    1977   The Irish Tinkers. Menlo Park, CA: Cummings.
    1986a   Return Migration. Annual Review of Anthropology 9:135–159.

1986b   Return Migration to Rural Ireland. *In* Return Migration and Regional Economic Problems. R. L. King, ed. London: Croom Helm.

Gmelch, George, and Sharon Bohn Gmelch
1985   The Cross-Channel Migration of Irish Travelers. The Economic and Social Review 4:287–296.

Gmelch, Sharon Bohn
1986   Nan: The Life of an Irish Traveling Woman. New York: W. W. Norton.
1989   From Poverty Subculture to Political Lobby: The Traveler Rights Movement in Ireland. *In* Ireland from Below. Chris Curtin and Thomas M. Wilson, eds. Pp. 201–319. Galway: Galway University Press.

Goldey, Patricia
1981   Emigração e Estrutura Familiar. Estudos Contemporâneos 2(3):111–128.

Gordiejew, Paul
1993   The Effects of History, Imposition, and Disjuncture on the Phases of Yugoslav Jewish Ethnicity. Ph.D. Dissertation, Anthropology Department, University of Pittsburgh.

Gower, Charlotte
1938   *Review of* Primitive Intelligence and Environment, by S. D. Porteus. American Anthropologist 40:321–322.

Goy, Joseph
1986   Rurale (histoire). *In* Dictionnaire des Sciences Historiques. André Burguière, ed. Pp. 609–615. Paris: PUF.

Gratton, Nancy E.
1992   Bosnian Muslims. Encyclopedia of World Cultures Volume IV: Europe, Linda A. Bennett, vol. ed., David Levinson, series ed. P. 36. Boston: G. K. Hall and Co.

Greenwood, D. J.
1970   Agriculture, Industrialization, and Tourism: The Economics of Modern Basque Farming. Ph.D. Dissertation, University of Pittsburgh.

Gregory, David
1978   La Odisea Andaluza: Una Emigración Intereuropea. Madrid: Tecnos.

Grillo, R. D.
1980   Introduction. *In* "Nation" and "State" in Europe: Anthropological Perspectives. R. D. Grillo, ed. London: Academic Press.

Groger, B. Lisa
1979   Of Men and Machines: Co-operation among French Family Farmers. Ethnology 20:1163–1176.

Gullick, Charles J. M. R.
1993   Cultural Values and European Financial Institutions. *In* Cultural

Change and the New Europe. Thomas M. Wilson and M. Estellie Smith, eds. Pp. 203–221. Boulder: Westview Press.

Gunther, Erna
1930   *Review of* Middletown, by Robert Lynd and Helen Lynd. American Anthropologist 32:319–320.

Guyer, J. I.
1996   Comments on Burton, et al. Current Anthropology 37(1):112–113.

Haddon, A. C., and C. R. Browne
1891–93 Ethnography of the Aran Islands, Co. Galway. Proceedings of the Royal Irish Academy 18:768–830.

Hall, Peter A.
1995   The State of European Studies. European Studies Newsletter 24(5/6):6–16.

Haller Jr., John S.
1971   *Race* and the Concept of Progress in Nineteenth Century American Ethnology. American Anthropologist 73:710–724.

Halpern, J.
1978   Working in the Factory: Resistance to Industrialization in Rural Ireland. Ph.D. Dissertation, University of Pittsburgh.

Halpern, Joel M.
1967   [1956] A Serbian Village: Social and Cultural Change in a Yugoslav Community. New York: Harper and Row.
1970   Ethnology in Yugoslavia since World War II: A Review of Research and Publications. East European Quarterly IV (3):328–342.
1993   Introduction. Special Issue: The Yugoslav Conflict, The Anthropology of East Europe Review 11(1–2):5–13.

Halpern, Joel M., and Barbara Kerewsky-Halpern
1972   A Serbian Village in Historical Perspective. New York: Holt, Rinehart and Winston. Rev. ed. 1986, Prospect Heights, IL: Waveland Press.

Halpern, Joel M., and David A. Kideckel
1983   Anthropology in Eastern Europe. Annual Review of Anthropology 12:377–402

Hammel, Eugene A.
1967   The Jewish Mother in Serbia: Or, Les Structures Alimentaires de la Parente. *In* Essays in Balkan Ethnology. W. G. Lockwood, ed. 1:55–62. Berkeley, Kroeber Anthropological Society Papers, Special Publications.
1968   Alternative Social Structures and Ritual Relations in the Balkans. Englewood Cliffs, NJ: Prentice Hall.
1969   Structure and Sentiment in Serbian Cousinship. American Anthropologist 71:285–293.
1970   *Review of* Proper Peasants: Traditional Life in a Hungarian Village,

edited by Edit Fél and Tamás Hofer. American Anthropologist 72:1110–1111.

1972   The Zadruga as Process. *In* Household and Family in Past Time. Peter Laslett, ed. Pp. 335–374. Cambridge: Cambridge University Press.

1976   Some Medieval Evidence on the Serbian Zadruga: A Preliminary Analysis of the Chrsobulls of Decani. *In* Communal Families in the Balkans: The Zadruga. Robert F. Brynes, ed. Pp. 100–116. Notre Dame: University of Notre Dame Press.

1993a   The Yugoslav Labyrinth. The Anthropology of East Europe Review 11(1–2):35–42.

1993b   Demography and the Origins of the Yugoslav Civil War. Anthropology Today 9(1):4–9.

1994   Meeting the Minotaur. Anthropology Newsletter 35(4):48.

Hann, Chris
1980   Tazlár: A Village in Hungary. London: Cambridge University Press.

Hanson, Allan
1989   The Making of the Maori: Culture Invention and Its Logic. American Anthropologist 91:890–902.

Harding, S. F.
1984   Remaking Ibieca: Rural Life in Aragon under Franco. Chapel Hill: University of North Carolina Press.

Harris, Marvin
1992   Distinguished Lecture: Anthropology and the Theoretical and Paradigmatic Significance of the Collapse of Soviet and East European Communism. American Anthropologist 94(2):295–305.

Harris, Rosemary
1961   The Selection of Leaders in Ballybeg, Northern Ireland. The Sociological Review (NS) 9:137–149.

1972   Prejudice and Tolerance in Ulster. Manchester: Manchester University.

Hatt, Gudmund
1958   *Review of* The Low Countries, by S. J. de Laet. American Anthropologist 60:1241.

Hayden, Robert M.
1985   Who Wants Informal Courts? Paradoxical Evidence from a Yugoslav Attempt to Create Workers' Courts for Labor Cases. American Bar Foundation Research Journal. Spring 1985(2):293–326.

1986   Popular Use of Yugoslav Labor Courts and the Contradiction of Social Courts. Law and Society Review 20(2):229–251.

1989   Cultural Context and the Impact of Traffic Safety Legislation: The Reception of Mandatory Seatbelt Laws in Yugoslavia and Illinois. Law and Society Review 23(2):285–294.

1992   Constitutional Nationalism in the Formerly Yugoslav Republics. Slavic Review 51(4):654–673.

1993   The Triumph of Chauvinistic Nationalisms in Yugoslavia: Bleak Implications for Anthropology. The Anthropology of East Europe Review 11(1–2):63–68.

Hearn, T. R.
1978   The Sea Hunters: A Study of an Artisanal Fishery in Western Brittany. Ph.D. Dissertation, University of Pittsburgh.

Heider, Karl, and Carol Hermer
1995   Films for Anthropological Teaching. 8th ed. Washington: American Anthropological Association.

Helleiner, Jane
1993   Traveler Settlement in Galway City: Politics, Class and Culture. *In* Irish Urban Cultures. Chris Curtin, Hastings Donnan, and Thomas M. Wilson, eds. Pp. 181–201. Belfast: Institute of Irish Studies Press.

Herzfeld, Michael
1980   Honor and Shame: Some Problems in the Comparative Analysis of Moral Systems. Man 15:339–351.
1982   Ours Once More: Folklore, Ideology, and the Making of Modern Greece. Austin: University of Texas Press.
1985   The Poetics of Manhood: Contest and Identity in a Cretan Mountain Village. Princeton: Princeton University Press.
1987a   As in Your Own House: Hospitality, Ethnography and the Stereotype of Mediterranean Society. *In* Honor and Shame and the Unity of the Mediterranean. David D. Gilmore, ed. Pp. 75–89. Washington, D.C.: American Anthropological Association.
1987b   Anthropology through the Looking Glass: Critical Ethnography in the Margins of Europe. Cambridge: Harvard University Press.
1992   The Social Production of Indifference: Exploring the Symbolic Roots of Western Bureaucracy. Oxford: Berg.

Hewes, Gordon W.
1959   World Ethnographies and Culture-Historical Syntheses. American Anthropologist 61:615–630.

Hiller von Geartrigen, F.
1895   Thera: Untersuchenger, Vermessungen and Ausgrabungen in 1909 den Jahren 1895–1898. 4 vols. Berlin.

Hilowitz, Jane
1976   Economic Development and Social Change in Sicily. Cambridge: Schenkman.

Hirschon, Renee
1983   Women, the Aged, and Religious Activity: Oppositions and Complementarity in an Urban Locality. Journal of Modern Greek Studies 1(1):113–130.
1989   Heirs of the Greek Catastrophe: The Social Life of Asia Minor Refugees in Piraeus. Oxford: Clarendon Press.

Hirschon, Renee, ed.
  1984   Women and Property—Women as Property. New York: St. Martin's
           Press.

Hobsbawn, Eric, and Terence Ranger, eds.
  1983   The Invention of Tradition. Cambridge: Cambridge University Press.

Hofer, Tamás
  1968   Comparative Notes on the Professional Personality of Two
           Disciplines: Anthropologists and Native Ethnographers in Central
           European Villages. Current Anthropology 9(4):311–315.

Hoffman, Susanna M.
  1973   Kypseli—Women and Men Apart—A Divided Reality. Film,
           Distributed by Extension Media Center. Berkeley, CA: University of
           California.
  1976   The Ethnography of the Islands: Thera. *In* Regional Variation in
           Modern Greece and Cyprus: Toward a Perspective on the
           Ethnography of Greece. Muriel Dimen and Ernestine Friedl, eds.
           Annals of the New York Academy of Sciences 268:328–340. New
           York: New York Academy of Sciences.
  1976   Kypseli: A Marital Geography of a Greek Village. *In* Lifelong
           Learning, Vol. 45, no. 58. Berkeley: University Extension, University
           of California.
  1978   Comments on the Reviews of Kypseli: Women and Men Apart—A
           Divided Reality. Reviews in Anthropology 5(1):129–142.
  1980   The Classified Man. New York: Coward McCann.
  1981   The Nature of Culture, for Faces of Culture, Public Broadcasting
           System Film Series.
  1988a   Men Who Are Good for You and Men Who Are Bad. Berkeley, CA:
           Ten Speed Press.
  1988b   Good and Plenty: America's New Home Cooking. New York:
           Harper and Row.
  1988c   The Controversy about Kypseli. *In* Anthropological Filmmaking. J.
           Rollwagen, ed. New York: Harwood Academic Publishers.
  1990   The Well-Filled Tortilla. New York: Workman.
  1993a   The Return of the Thief: Greek Identity and the Resurgence of
           Xenophobia in the Face of the Influx of Albanian Immigrants. Paper
           read at MGSA Meetings, Oct. 1993.
  1993b   Transformation without Memory, Change without Nostalgia: An
           Example from a Greek Village. Paper read at AAA Meetings, Nov.
           1993.
  1994   Up from the Embers: A Disaster Survivor's Story. Clinical Quarterly,
           National Center for Post-Traumatic Stress Disorder. Palo Alto, CA.
           4(2):15–17.
  1995a   Ruing the Theft of History, Feeling the Rise of Nostalgia. Paper read
           at Modern Greek Studies Association Meetings, Oct. 1995.

1995b Culture Deep and Custom Old among the Coals: The Reappearance of a Traditional Cultural Grammar in the Aftermath of the Oakland Berkeley Firestorm. Paper read at AAA Meetings, Nov. 1995.

1996 The Well-Filled Microwave. New York: Workman.

1997 The Olive and the Caper: Anthropology and Adventures in Greek Food. New York: Workman.

Holloway, Ralph
1972 *Review of* Evolution des Vertebres: De Leur Origine a l'Homme, by Georges Vanderbroek. American Anthropologist 74:146–147.

Holmes, Douglas R.
1989 Cultural Disenchantments: Worker Peasantries in Northeast Italy. Princeton: Princeton University Press.

Homans, G.
1967 The Nature of Social Science. New York: Harcourt, Brace & World.

Honigsheim, Paul
1945 Voltaire as Anthropologist. American Anthropologist 47:104–118.

Hooton, E. A.
1926 *Review of* Annals of Eugenics: A Journal for the Scientific Study of Racial Problems. American Anthropologist 28:551–553.

1929 *Review of* The Racial Elements of European History, by Hans F. K. Gunther. American Anthropologist 31:165–166.

Horn, David G.
1991 Constructing the Sterile City: Pronatalism and Social Sciences in Interwar Italy. American Ethnologist 18:581–601.

1994 Social Bodies: Science, Reproduction, and Italian Modernity. Princeton: Princeton University Press.

Howe, Leo
1989a Unemployment, Doing the Double and Labor Markets in Belfast. *In* Ireland from Below. Chris Curtin and Thomas M. Wilson, eds. Pp. 144–164. Galway: Galway University Press.

1989b Social Anthropology and Public Policy: Aspects of Unemployment and Social Security in Northern Ireland. *In* Social Anthropology and Public Policy in Northern Ireland. Hastings Donnan and Graham McFarlane, eds. Pp. 26–46. Aldershot: Avebury.

1990 Being Unemployed in Northern Ireland. Cambridge: Cambridge University Press.

HRAF Monographs #1
1955 The Cheremis. New Haven: Human Relations Area Files, Inc.

HRAF Monographs #2
1955 Finland. New Haven: Human Relations Area Files, Inc.

HRAF Monographs #3
1955 The Lapps. New Haven: Human Relations Area Files, Inc.

HRAF Monographs #4
1955   The Estonians. New Haven: Human Relations Area Files, Inc.

HRAF Monographs #5
1955   The Hungarians. New Haven: Human Relations Area Files, Inc.

HRAF Monographs #6
1955   The Mordva. New Haven: Human Relations Area Files, Inc.

HRAF Monographs #7
1955   The Ostyak and The Vogul. New Haven: Human Relations Area
          Files, Inc.

HRAF Monographs #8a
1955   The Votyak. New Haven: Human Relations Area Files, Inc.

HRAF Monographs #8b
1955   The Zyryans. New Haven: Human Relations Area Files, Inc.

HRAF Monographs #9
1955   The Livonians. New Haven: Human Relations Area Files, Inc.

HRAF Monographs #10
1955   The Vespians. New Haven: Human Relations Area Files, Inc.

HRAF Monographs #11
1955   The Votes. New Haven: Human Relations Area Files, Inc.

HRAF Monographs #12
1955   The Karelians. New Haven: Human Relations Area Files, Inc.

HRAF Monographs #15
1955   Czechoslovakia. New Haven: Human Relations Area Files, Inc.

HRAF Monographs #18
1955   Lithuania. New Haven: Human Relations Area Files, Inc.

HRAF Monographs #19
1955   Belorussia. New Haven: Human Relations Area Files, Inc.

HRAF Monographs #20
1955   Ukraine. New Haven: Human Relations Area Files, Inc.

HRAF Monographs #22
1955   Poland. New Haven: Human Relations Area Files, Inc.

HRAF Monographs #25
1955   Social and Cultural Change in a Serbian Village. New Haven:
          Human Relations Area Files, Inc.

HRAF Monographs #34
1955   The Soviet Zone of Germany. New Haven: Human Relations Area
          Files, Inc.

HRAF Monographs #35
1955   The Caucasus. 2 vols. New Haven: Human Relations Area Files, Inc.

HRAF Monographs #41
1956   Latvia. 2 vols. New Haven: Human Relations Area Files, Inc.

Humphreys, Alexander
    1966   New Dubliners: Urbanization and the Irish Family. London:
            Routledge and Kegan Paul.

Huseby-Darvas, Éva V.
    1995   Voices of Plight, Voices of Paradox: Narratives of Women Refugees
            from the Balkans and the Hungarian Host Population. The
            Anthropology of East Europe Review 13(1):15–22.

Institute für Wissenschaftlichen Film
    1995   Ethnologie Europa Medienkatalog. Göttingen.

Jaffe, Alexandra
    1993a   Corsican Identity and a Europe of Peoples and Regions. In Cultural
            Change and the New Europe. Thomas M. Wilson and M. Estellie
            Smith, eds. Boulder: Westview Press.
    1993b   Obligation, Error, and Authenticity: Competing Cultural Principles
            in the Teaching of Corsican. Journal of Linguistic Anthropology
            3:99–114.

Jambrešić, Renata
    1993   Banija: An Analysis of Ethnonymic Polarization. In Fear, Death, and
            Resistance: An Ethnography of War: Croatia 1991–1992. Feldman et
            al. Pp. 73–118. Zagreb: Institute of Ethnology and Folklore Research.
    1995a   On Gender-Affected War Testimonies. Paper presented at an
            international conference on (En)gendering Violence: Terror,
            Domination, Recovery. October, Zagreb, Croatia.
    1995b   Testimonial Discourse between National Narrative and
            Ethnography as Socio-Cultural Analysis. Collegium
            Antropologicum 19(1):17–27.

Jenkins, Richard
    1983   Lads, Citizens, and Ordinary Kids. London: Routledge and Kegan
            Paul.
    1986   Northern Ireland: In What Sense 'Religions' in Conflict? In The
            Sectarian Divide in Northern Ireland Today. Richard Jenkins,
            Hastings Donnan, and Graham McFarlane, eds. Pp. 1–21. Royal
            Anthropological Institute of Great Britain and Ireland. Occasional
            Paper no. 41.

Jordan, Terry G.
    1973   The European Culture Area: A Systematic Geography. New York:
            Harper and Row.

Junek, Oscar Waldemar
    1946   What Is the Total Pattern of Our Western Civilization? Some
            Preliminary Observations. American Anthropologist 48:397–406.

Jurjus, André
    1993   Farming Styles and Intermediate Structures in the Wake of 1992. In
            Cultural Change and the New Europe: Perspectives on the

European Community. T. Wilson and E. Smith, eds. Pp. 99–122. Boulder: Westview Press.

Kane, Eileen
1977   The Last Place God Made: Traditional Economy and New Industry in Rural Ireland. New Haven: HRAF Press.
1979   The Changing Role of the Family in the Rural Irish Community. Journal of Comparative Family Studies 10:141–162.

Kane, Eileen, John Blacking, Hastings Donnan, and Graham McFarlane
1988   A Review of Anthropological Research, North and South. In The State of Social Science Research in Ireland. Liam O'Dowd, ed. Dublin: Royal Irish Academy.

Karakasidou, Anastasia
1993   Politicizing Culture: Negating Ethnic Identity in Greek Macedonia. Journal of Modern Greek Studies 11(1):1–28.

Karnoouh, Claude
1980   Le Pouvoir et la Parenté. In Paysans, Femmes et Citoyens: Luttes pour le Pouvoir dans un Village Lorrain. Lamarche, Rogers and Karnoouh. Pp. 141–206. Le Paradou: Actes Sud.

Kasdan, Leonard
1965   Review of Life in a Turkish Village, by Joe E. Pierce. American Anthropologist 67:559–560.

Keith-Ross, Jennie
1977   Old People, New Lives: Community Creation in a Retirement Community. Chicago: University of Chicago Press.

Kenna, Margaret
1976   Houses, Fields and Graves: Property and Ritual Obligation on a Greek Island. Ethnology 15:21–34.
1977   Greek Urban Immigrants and Their Rural Patron Saint. Ethnic Studies 1:14–23.
1993   Return Migrants and Tourism Development: An Example from the Cyclades. Journal of Modern Greek Studies 11(1):75–96.

Kenny, Michael
1962a   [1961] A Spanish Tapestry: Town and Country in Castile. Bloomington: Indiana University Press.
1962b   Twentieth Century Spain Expatriates in Mexico: An Urban Sub-Culture. Anthropological Quarterly 35(4):169–180.
1963   Europe: The Atlantic Fringe. Anthropological Quarterly 36:100–119.
1964   Review of Mediterranean Countrymen: Essays in the Social Anthropology of the Mediterranean, edited by Julian Pitt-Rivers. American Anthropologist 66:130–132.
1966   Review of Saints and Fireworks: Religion and Politics in Rural Malta, by Jeremy Boissevain. American Anthropologist 68:788–790.

Kenny, Michael, and David I. Kertzer, eds.
  1983   Urban Life in Mediterranean Europe: Anthropological Perspectives.
           Urbana: University of Illinois Press.

Kertzer, David I.
  1980   Comrades and Christians: Religion and Political Struggle in
           Communist Italy. Cambridge: Cambridge University Press. Rev. ed.
           published by Waveland Press, 1990.
  1983   Urban Research in Italy. *In* Urban Life in Mediterranean Europe.
           Michael Kenny and D. Kertzer, eds. Pp. 53–75. Urbana: University of
           Illinois Press.
  1984   Family Life in Central Italy, 1880–1910. New Brunswick, NJ: Rutgers
           University Press.
  1991   *Review of* Italian Communism, by Cris Shore. Man 26:565–566.
  1993   Sacrificed for Honor: Italian Infant Abandonment and the Politics of
           Reproductive Control. Boston: Beacon Press.

Kertzer, David I., and Dennis P. Hogan
  1989   Family, Political Economy, and Demographic Change: The
           Transformation of Life in Casalecchio, Italy, 1861–1921. Madison:
           University of Wisconsin Press.

Kertzer, Morris N.
  1947   With an H on My Dog Tag. New York: Behrman House.

Keur, John Y., and Dorothy L. Keur
  1955   The Deeply Rooted: A Study of a Drents Community in the
           Netherlands. Monographs of the American Ethnological Society 25.
           Netherlands: Royal VanGorcum Ltd.

Khera, Sigrid
  1972   An Austrian Peasant Village under Rural Industrialization.
           Behavioral Science Notes 7:31–32.
  1973   Social Stratification and Land Inheritance among Austrian Peasants.
           American Anthropologist 75:814–823.

Kideckel, David A.
  1982   The Socialist Transformation of Agriculture in a Romanian
           Commune, 1945–1962. American Ethnologist 9(2):320–340.
  1989   Anthropology in the Common European Home: Notes on the End of
           the Cold War (Maybe). Paper presented at Annual Meeting,
           American Anthropological Association, Washington, D.C.
  1993a   The Solitude of Collectivism: Romanian Villagers to the Revolution
           and Beyond. Ithaca: Cornell University Press.
  1993b   Us and Them Redux: Concepts of East and West in the East
           European Transition. Proceedings of the Conference on East
           European Cultures after Communism: Tradition, Modernity,
           Postmodernity. Radziejowice, Poland. Warsaw: Polish Academy of
           Sciences.

1995a   Introduction: Local Life in the East European Transition. *In* East
          European Communities: The Struggle for Balance in Turbulent
          Times. David A. Kideckel, ed. Pp 1–6. Boulder, CO: Westview Press.
1995b   A Tale of Two Clients: Comparing Western Agricultural
          Privatization Aid in Albania and Romania. Paper presented at
          Annual Meeting, American Association for the Advancement of
          Slavic Studies. Philadelphia, PA.

Kideckel, David A., ed.
1983   Political Rituals and Symbolism in Socialist Eastern Europe. Special
          Issue, Anthropological Quarterly 56(2).

Kideckel, David A., and Joel M. Halpern, eds.
1993   Special Issue: The Yugoslav Conflict. The Anthropology of East
          European Review 11(1–2).

Kideckel, David A., and Steven L. Sampson
1984   Fieldwork in Romania: Political, Practical, and Ethical Aspects. *In*
          Anthropological Research in Romania. J. W. Cole, ed. Pp. 85–102.
          Amherst: University of Massachusetts Anthropology Research
          Report No. 24.

Kimball, Solon T.
1967   *Review of* A North Wales Village: A Social Anthropological Study, by
          Isabel Emmett; *and* The Shearers and the Shorn: A Study of Life in a
          Devon Community, by E. W. Martin. American Anthropologist
          69:105–106.

Klemenčić, Mladen
1992   Baranja, Povjesno-Geografski Pregled (Baranja, Historico-
          Geographical Review). Hrvatska Baranja, Studia Ethnologica 4:15–20.

Kligman, Gail
1981   Căluş: Symbolic Transformation in Romanian Ritual. Chicago:
          University of Chicago Press.
1988   The Wedding of the Dead: Ritual, Poetics, and Popular Culture in
          Transylvania. Berkeley: University of California Press.

Komito, Lee
1984   Irish Clientelism: A Reappraisal. Economic and Social Review
          15(3):173–194.

Konstantinov, Miloš
1988   Ethnology of the Macedonians. Etnološki Pregled (Ethnological
          Review) 23–24:75–88.

Krader, Lawrence
1968   *Review of* The Peasants of Central Russia, by Stephen P. Dunn and
          Ethel Dunn. American Anthropologist 70:592–593.

Kroeber, A. L.
1931   *Review of* An Introduction to Physical Anthropology, by E. P. Stibbe.
          American Anthropologist 33:231.

Landes, Ruth
  1959   *Review of* Coloured Minorities in Britain, by Sydney Collins.
          American Anthropologist 61:173–174.

Lange, Charles H.
  1962   *Review of* Volkskultur in der technischen Welt, by Hermann
          Bausinger. American Anthropologist 64:1073–1075.

Larsen, S. S.
  1982a   The Two Sides of the House: Identity and Social Organization in
          Kilbroney, Northern Ireland. *In* Belonging: Identity and Social
          Organization in British Rural Cultures. A. P. Cohen, ed. Pp. 131–164.
          Manchester: Manchester University Press.
  1982b   The Glorious Twelfth: The Politics of Legitimation in Kilbroney. *In*
          Belonging: Identity and Social Organization in British Rural
          Cultures. A. P. Cohen, ed. Pp. 278–291. Manchester: Manchester
          University Press.

Laslett, Peter
  1965   The World We Have Lost. New York: Charles Scribner's Sons.

Lawrence, Denise
  1988   Menstrual Politics: Women and Pigs in Rural Portugal. *In* Blood
          Magic: The Anthropology of Menstruation. Thomas Buckley and
          Alma Gottlieb, eds. Pp. 117–136. Berkeley, CA: University of
          California Press.

Lazio, Carole
  1995   Eleven Film and Video Events Planned in Europe between Fall
          1995 and Fall 1996. Old World Archaeology Newsletter
          18(3):12–15.

Leach, Edmund
  1961   Rethinking Anthropology. London: Athlone Press.
  1967   Brain-Twister. The New York Review of Books 9(6):6–10.
  1969   Genesis as Myth and Other Essays. London: Jonathan Cape.

Lechner, Zdenka
  1992   Etnološki Zapisi iz Baranje (Ethnological Records from Baranja).
          Hrvatska Barnaja, Studia Ethnologica 4:209–217.

Lem, Winnie
  1991   Gender, Ideology, and Petty Commodity Production in Languedoc,
          France. *In* Marxist Approaches to Economic Anthropology. Alice
          Littlefield and Hill Gates, eds. Pp. 103–117. Lanham: University Press
          of America.

LeMaster, Barbara
  1993   When Women and Men Talk Differently: Language and Policy in
          the Dublin Deaf Community. *In* Irish Urban Cultures. Chris Curtin,
          Hastings Donnan, and Thomas M. Wilson, eds. Pp. 123–141. Belfast:
          Institute of Irish Studies Press.

Lemert, Edwin
    1972   *Review of* Strategic Interaction, by Erving Goffman. American
            Anthropologist 74:8–10

Lenclud, Gérard
    1987   Anthropologie et Histoire, Hier et Aujourd'hui en France. *In*
            Ethnologie en Miroir. Chiva and Jeggle, eds. Paris: Maison des
            Sciences de l'Homme.

Lethbridge, Çejku, Margaret
    1995   Osteoarthritis of the Hands in a Rural Population: Anthropological
            Research on the Island of Brač, Croatia. Ph.D. Dissertation,
            Anthropology Department, University of Zagreb.

Levi-Strauss, Claude
    1963   Structural Anthropology. Pp. 186–205. New York: Basic Books.
    1966a   The Savage Mind. Chicago: University of Chicago Press.
    1966b   Anthropology: Its Achievements and Future. Current Anthropology
            7(2):124–128.
    1969   The Raw and the Cooked. New York: Harper and Row.

Levin, Saul
    1972   *Review of* Indo-European and Indo-Europeans, by George Cardona,
            et al. American Anthropologist 74:927–929.

Lewis, Oscar
    1951   Life in a Mexican Village; Tepotzlan Restudied. Urbana: University
            of Illinois Press.

Le Wita, Beatrix
    1988   Ni Vue, ni Connue. Paris: Fondation de la Maison des Sciences de
            l'Homme. 1994 translation, French Bourgeois Culture. Tr. J. A.
            Underwood. Cambridge: Cambridge University Press. 1994.

Leyton, Elliott
    1966   Conscious Models and Dispute Regulation in an Ulster Village. Man
            (NS)1:534–542.
    1970   Sphere of Inheritance in Aughnaboy. American Anthropologist
            72:1378–1388.
    1974   Opposition and Integration in Ulster. Man (NS)9:185–198.
    1975   The One Blood: Kinship and Class in an Irish Village. St. John's
            Institute of Social and Economic Research: Memorial University of
            Newfoundland.

Limon, Jose E.
    1991   Representation, Ethnicity, and the Precursory Ethnography: Notes
            of a Native Anthropologist. *In* Recapturing Anthropology. Richard
            G. Fox, ed. Pp. 115–136. Santa Fe: School of American Research
            Press.

Linnekin, J.
    1996   Comments on Burton, et al. Current Anthropology 37(1):115–116.

LiPuma, Edward, and Sarah Keene Meltzoff
    1989   Toward a Theory of Culture and Class: An Iberian Example. American Ethnologist 16(2):313–334.
    1994   Economic Mediation and the Power of Associations: Toward a Concept of Encompassment. American Anthropologist 96:31–51.

Littleton, C. Scott
    1966   The New Comparative Mythology. Berkeley: University of California Press.

Llobera, Josep R.
    1986   Fieldwork in Southwestern Europe: Anthropological Panacea or Epistemological Straitjacket? Critique of Anthropology 6:25–33.

Lockwood, William G.
    1970   Selo and Carsija: The Peasant Market Place as Mechanism of Social Integration in Western Bosnia. Ph.D. Dissertation, Anthropology Department, University of California, Berkeley.
    1972a   Converts and Consanguinity: The Social Organization of Moslem Slavs in Western Bosnia. Ethnology 11:55–79.
    1972b   *Review of* The Strangled Democracy: Czechoslovakia 1948–1969, by David Rodnick. American Anthropologist 74:849–850.
    1973   The Peasant-Worker in Yugoslavia. Studies in European Society 1(1):91–110.
    1974   Bride Theft and Social Maneuverability in Western Bosnia. Center for Russian and East European Studies No. 104:253–269.
    1975   European Moslems: Economy and Ethnicity in Western Bosnia. New York: Academic Press.

Loizos, Peter, and E. Papataxiarchis, eds.
    1991   Contested Identities: Gender and Kinship in Modern Greece. Princeton: Princeton University Press.

Lowie, Robert
    1928   *Review of* The Racial Basis of Civilization: A Critique of the Nordic Doctrine, by Frank H. Hankins. American Anthropologist 30:317–319.

McCann, May
    1994   A Woman's Voice: A Feminist Looks at Irish Anthropology. *In* The Unheard Voice: Social Anthropology in Ireland. Pol O Muiri, ed. Pp. 18–22. Belfast: Fortnight Educational Trust.

McDonald, Maryon
    1993   The Construction of Difference: An Anthropological Approach to Stereotypes. *In* Inside European Identities. Sharon Macdonald, ed. Oxford: Berg.

McDonogh, Gary
    1986   Good Families of Barcelona: A Social History of Power in the Industrial Era. Princeton: Princeton University Press.

1993   The Face Behind the Door: European Integration, Immigration, and
         Identity. *In* Cultural Change and the New Europe. Thomas M. Wilson
         and M. Estellie Smith, eds. Pp. 143–165. Boulder: Westview Press.

McFarlane, Graham
1979   Mixed Marriages in Ballycuan, Northern Ireland. Journal of
         Comparative Family Studies 10:191–205.
1989   Dimensions of Protestantism: The Working of Protestant Identity in a
         Northern Irish Village. *In* Ireland from Below. Chris Curtin and
         Thomas M. Wilson, eds. Pp. 23–45. Galway: Galway University Press.
1994   A Soft Voice: The Anthropology of Religion in Ireland. *In* The
         Unheard Voice: Social Anthropology in Ireland. Pol O Muiri, ed. Pp.
         15–18. Belfast: Fortnight Educational Trust. January.

McGee, R. J. and R. L. Warms
1996   Anthropological Theory: An Introductory History. Mountain View,
         CA: Mayfield Publishing Company.

McLaughlin, Eithne
1989   In Search of the Female Breadwinner: Gender and Unemployment
         in Derry City. *In* Social Anthropology and Public Policy in Northern
         Ireland. Hastings Donnan and Graham McFarlane, eds. Pp. 476–486.
         Aldershot: Avebury.

McNeill, William
1964   Europe's Steppe Frontier: 1500–1800. Chicago: University of Chicago
         Press.

Maddox, Richard
1993   El Castillo: The Politics of Tradition in an Andalusian Town.
         Urbana: University of Illinois Press.

Maglica, Nadja
1992   Naroda Nošnja Baranjski Hrvata (National Costume of the Croats
         from Baranja). Hrvatska Baranja, Studia Ethnologica 4:117–139.

Magliocco, Sabina
1993   The Two Madonnas: The Politics of Festival in a Sardinian
         Community. New York: Peter Lang.

Magnarella, Paul
1973   *Review of* Aspects of Modern Turkish Society: Six Papers, edited by
         Peter Suzuki. American Anthropologist 75:463–465.
1995   The International Criminal Tribunal for the Former Yugoslavia: Its
         Background, Legal Character, and Potential. The Anthropology of
         East Europe Review 13(1):54–60.
1996   The Conflicts of the Former Yugoslavia in the Courts. The
         Anthropology of East Europe Review 14(1):44–50.

Magnarella, Paul, and Orhan Turkdogan
1973   Descent, Affinity, and Ritual Relations in Eastern Turkey. American
         Anthropologist 75:1626–1633.

Mallory, J. D.
  1989   In Search of the Indo-Europeans: Language, Archaeology, and Myth. London: Thames and Hudson.

Mandelbaum, David G.
  1963   *Review of* General Ethnological Concepts (International Dictionary of Regional European Ethnology and Folklore, Volume I), by Åke Hultkranz. American Anthropologist 65:140–141.

Mangin, William, ed.
  1970   Peasants in Cities: Readings in the Anthropology of Urbanization. Boston: Houghton Mifflin Company.

Marinatos, Spyridon
  1939   The Volcanic Destruction of Minoan Crete. Antiquity 13:425–439.
  1950   About the Rumor of Atlantis. Cretan Chronicle 4.

Mark, Vera
  1987   In Search of the Occitan Village: Regionalist Ideologies and the Ethnography of Southern France. Anthropological Quarterly 60:64–70.

Markowitz, Fran
  1995   Discussion: Rape, Torture, Warfare ... and Refuge. The Anthropology of East Europe Review 13(1):44–50.

Martić-Biočina, Sanja
  1995   Cross-Cultural Misunderstandings—Examples of Providing Health Services to Refugees from Bosnia-Herzegovina in the Netherlands. Paper presented at an international conference on War, Exile, Everyday Life, March–April, Zagreb, Croatia.

Mauss, M.
  1967   The Gift. London: Routledge and Kegan Paul.

Mayer, A.
  1966   Quasi-Groups in the Study of Complex Societies. *In* The Social Anthropology of Complex Societies. Michael Banton, ed. Pp. 97–122. A.S.A. Monograph 4. London: Tavistock.

Mead, Margaret
  1940   The Mountain Arapesh. Anthropological Papers 37(3). American Museum of Natural History.

Megas, G., ed.
  1970   Folktales of Greece. Chicago: University of Chicago Press.

Meggars, Betty
  1946   Recent Trends in American Ethnology. American Anthropologist 48:176–214.

Meggitt, M. J.
  1964   Male and Female Relationships in the Highlands of Australian New Guinea. *In* New Guinea: The Central Highlands. J. B. Watson, ed. American Anthropologist 66: 204–223.

Mellen, Joan, ed.
    1978   The World of Luis Buñuel: Essays in Criticism. Oxford: Oxford
           University Press.

Messenger, Betty
    1975   Picking up the Linen Threads. Austin: University of Texas.

Messenger, John
    1962   A Critical Reexamination of the Concept of Spirits: With Special
           Reference to Traditional Irish Folklore and Contemporary Irish Folk
           Culture. American Anthropologist 64:367–373.
    1964a   Anthropology at Play: The Research Implications of
           Balladmongering. American Anthropologist 66:407–416.
    1964b   Literacy vs. Scientific Interpretation of Cultural 'Reality' in the Aran
           Islands of Eire. Ethnohistory 11:41–55.
    1968   Types and Causes of Disputes in an Irish Folk Community. Eire-
           Ireland 3:27–37.
    1969   Inis Beag. New York: Holt, Rinehart and Winston.
    1983   An Anthropologist at Play: Balladmongering in Ireland and Its
           Consequences for Research. Lanham, MD: University Press of
           America.
    1991   Personal Communication.

Michaelson, Evelyn, and Walter Goldschmidt
    1972   Female Roles and Male Dominance Among Peasants. Southwestern
           Journal of Anthropology 27:330–352.

Miller, Roy A., and M. G. Miller
    1978   The Golden Chain: A Study of the Structure, Function, and Patterning
           of Comparatico in a South Italian Village. American Ethnologist
           5:116–136.

Milton, Kay
    1993   Belfast: Whose City? In Irish Urban Cultures. Chris Curtin, Hastings
           Donnan, and Thomas M. Wilson, eds. Pp. 23–37. Belfast: Institute of
           Irish Studies Press.
    1994   An Environmentalist's Science: An Examination of Social Science and
           Social Change. In The Unheard Voice: Social Anthropology in Ireland.
           Pol O Muiri, ed. Pp. 8–10. Belfast: Fortnight Educational Trust.

Miner, Horace
    1955   Review of Chateau-Gerard: The Life and Times of a Walloon Village,
           by Harry Holbert Turney-High. American Anthropologist 57:159–161.

Minnich, Robert Gary
    1993   Reflections on the Violent Death of a Multi-Ethnic State: A Slovene
           Perspective. The Anthropology of East Europe Review
           11(1–2):77–84.

Moch, Leslie Page
    1992   Moving Europeans. Migration in Western Europe Since 1650.
           Bloomington: Indiana University Press.

Moerman, Michael
    1965   Ethnic Identification in a Complex Civilization: Who are the Lue? American Anthropologist 67:1215–1225.

Mogg, Janet Schreiber
    1973   To Eat the Bread of Others: The Decision to Migrate in a Province of Southern Italy. Ph.D. Dissertation, Anthropology Department, University of California, Berkeley.

Montagu, Ashley
    1942   The Genetical Theory of Race, and Anthropological Method. American Anthropologist 44:369–375.
    1944   *Review of* Race Riot, by Alfred McClung Lee and Norman Daymond Humphrey; *and* Race and Rumors of Race, by Howard W. Odum. American Anthropologist 46:254–255.
    1945   *Review of* Probing Our Prejudices, by Hortense Powdermaker. American Anthropologist 47:451.
    1962   The Concept of Race. American Anthropologist 64:919–928.
    1972   Sociogenic Brain Damage. American Anthropologist 74:1045–1061.

Moreno-Navarro, Isidoro
    1986   Trabajo de Campo en el Sur de Europa y Colonizacion Cientifica: El Caso de Andalucia. Paper presented at the Thirteenth European Congress for Rural Sociology, Braga, Portugal.

Moss, Leonard, and S. Cappannari
    1976   Mal'occhio—the Evil Eye Hovers Above. *In* The Evil Eye. C. Maloney ed. New York: Columbia University Press.

Moustaka, Calliope
    1964   The Internal Migrant. Athens Social Sciences Centre.

Murdock, George Peter
    1940   The Cross-Cultural Survey. American Sociological Review 5(3):361–370.
    1941   Anthropology and Human Relations. Sociometry 4:140–149.
    1950   The Conceptual Basis of Area Research. World Politics 2:571–578.
    1957a   Anthropology as a Comparative Science. Behavioral Science 2:249–254.
    1957b   *Review of* Oriental Despotism: A Comparative Study of Tribal Power, by Karl A. Wittfogel. American Anthropologist 59:545–547.
    1967   Ethnographic Atlas. Pittsburgh: University of Pittsburgh Press.
    1971   Anthropology's Mythology: The Huxley Memorial Lecture. Proceedings of the Royal Anthropological Society of Great Britain and Ireland. Pp. 17–24.

Nader, Laura
    1989   Orientalism, Occidentalism and the Control of Women. Cultural Dynamics 2:323–355.

Nash, Manning
    1964   *Review of* The Role of the Entrepreneur in Social Change in Northern

Norway, edited by Fredrik Barth. American Anthropologist 66:1432–1433.

Naupliotou, K. G.
1937   Thera in Ancient Times. *In* Thera: Collected Writings. M. A. Danezis, ed. Pp. 61–80. Athens: Academy of Athens.

Newman, Marshall T.
1962   Evolutionary Changes in Body Size and Head Form in American Indians. American Anthropologist 64:237–257.

Ninkovitch, D., and B. C. Heezen
1965   Santorini Tephra. London, Colston Papers 25.

Nurge, Ethel
1971   A Peasant Is as a Peasant Does. American Anthropologist 73:1259–1260.

Ogle, Shaun
1989   Housing Estate Improvements: An Assessment of Strategies for Tenant Participation. *In* Social Anthropology and Public Policy in Northern Ireland. Hastings Donnan and Graham McFarlane, eds. Pp. 90–106. Aldershot: Avebury.

Olsen, Mary Kay Gilliland
1989   Authority and Conflict in Slavonian Households: The Effects of Social Environment on Intra-Household Processes. *In* The Household Economy: Reconsidering the Domestic Mode of Production. R. Wilk, ed. Pp. 149–170. Colorado: Westview Press.
1990   Redefining Gender in Yugoslavia: Masculine and Feminine Ideals in Ritual Context. East European Quarterly 23(4):431–444.

Olsen, Mary Kay Gilliland, S. M. Špoljar Vržina, V. Rudan, and A. M. Barbarić-Keršić
1991   Normal Families? Problems in Cultural Anthropological Research Methods. Collegium Antropologicum 15(2):299–308.
1993   Bridge on the Sava: Ethnicity in Eastern Croatia, 1981–1991. The Anthropology of East Europe Review 11(1–2):54–62.

Olsen, Mary Kay Gilliland, and Vlasta Rudan
1992   Childlessness and Gender in Croatia: Examples from the Island of Hvar. Collegium Antropologicum 16(1):115–124.

Olujić, Maria
1990   Economic and Demographic Change in Contemporary Yugoslavia: Persistence of Traditional Gender Ideology. East European Quarterly 23(4):477–485.
1991   People on the Move: Migration History of a Peasant Croatian Community. Ph.D. Dissertation, Anthropology Department, University of California, Berkeley.
1992   Dalmatians. Encyclopedia of World Cultures Volume IV, Linda A. Bennett, vol. ed., David Levinson, series ed. Pp. 85–88. Boston: G. K. Hall and Co.

1995a   Coming Home: The Croatian War Experience. *In* Fieldwork under Fire. Carolyn Nordstrom and Antonius Robben, eds. Berkeley: University of California Press.

1995b   Representation of Experience and Survival of Genocidal Rape in Croatia and Bosnia. Paper presented at an International Conference on (En)gendering Violence: Terror, Domination, Recovery. October. Zagreb, Croatia.

1995c   Women, Rape, and War: The Continued Trauma of Refugees and Displaced Persons in Croatia. The Anthropology of East Europe Review 13(1):40–43.

1995d   Women and War: Sexual Coercion and Torture in Former Yugoslavia. Cultural Survival Quarterly.

Olujic, Maria, ed.

(n.d.)   Gendered Violence. Berkeley: University of California Press. Under review.

O'Neill, Brian

1987   Social Inequality in a Portuguese Hamlet. Cambridge: Cambridge University Press.

Opler, Morris E.

1944   Cultural and Organic Conception in Contemporary World History. American Anthropologist 46:448–460.

Orlans, Harold

1957   *Review of* Gosforth: The Sociology of an English Village, by W. M. Williams. American Anthropologist 59:733–734.

1958   *Review of* Two Studies of Kinship in London, edited by Raymond Firth. American Anthropologist 60:961–962.

1959   *Review of* People of Coal Town, by Herman R. Lantz; *and* Small Town in Mass Society: Class, Power and Religion in a Rural Community, by Arthur J. Vidich and Joseph Bensman. American Anthropologist 61:175–176.

O'Sullivan, Eoin

1993   Identity and Survival in a Hostile Environment: Homeless Men in Galway. *In* Irish Urban Cultures. Chris Curtin, Hastings Donnan, and Thomas M. Wilson, eds. Pp. 161–180. Belfast: Institute of Irish Studies Press.

Ottenberg, Simon

1971   *Review of* Social Networks in Urban Situations: Analyses of Personal Relationships in Central African Towns, edited by J. Clyde Mitchell. American Anthropologist 73:946–948.

Oyler John E.

1962   *Review of* The Germanic People, Their Origin, Expansion, and Culture, by Francis Owen. American Anthropologist 64:427–428.

Padgett, Deborah K.

1993   Sociodemographic and Disease-Related Correlates of Depressive

Morbidity among Diabetic Patients in Zagreb, Croatia. Journal of Nervous and Mental Disease 181(2):123–129.

Paine, Robert
1960   Emergence of the Village as a Social Unit in a Coast Lappish Fjord. American Anthropologist 62:1004–1017.

Pandian, Jacob
1985   Anthropology and the Western Tradition: Toward an Authentic Anthropology. Prospect Heights, IL: Waveland Press, Inc.

Panourgia, Neni
1994   Objects at Birth, Subjects at Death (review essay). Journal of Modern Greek Studies 12(2):261–270.

Papataxiarchis, Evthymios
1991   Friends of the Heart: Male Commensal Solidarity, Gender, and Kinship in Aegean Greece. In Contested Identities. P. Loizos and E. Papataxiarchis, eds. Pp. 156–179. Princeton: Princeton University Press.

Pardo, Italo
1989   Life, Death, and Ambiguity in the Social Dynamics of Inner Naples. Man 24:103–123.

Parman, Susan
1990   Scottish Crofters: A Historical Ethnography of a Celtic Village. Fort Worth, TX: Holt, Rinehart and Winston.
1993   The Future of European Boundaries. In Cultural Change and the New Europe. Thomas M. Wilson and M. Estellie Smith, eds. Pp. 189–202. Boulder: Westview Press.

Pavković, Nikola, Dušan Bandić, Ivan Kovačević
1988   Aspirations and Directions of the Development of Ethnological in the Socialist Republic of Serbia (1945–1983). Etnološki Pregled (Ethnological Review) 23–24:5–16.

Peace, Adrian
1989   From Arcadia to Anomie: Critical Notes on the Constitution of Irish Society as an Anthropological Subject. Critique of Anthropology 9(1):89–111.
1993   Environmental Protest, Bureaucratic Closure: The Politics of Discourse in Rural Ireland. In Environmentalism: The View from Anthropology. Kay Milton, ed. Pp. 189–204. London: Routledge.

Pehrson, Robert N.
1954   The Lappish Herding Leader: A Structural Analysis. American Anthropologist 56:1076–1080.

Pellegrino, Charles
1993   Unearthing Atlantis, an Archaeological Odyssey. New York: Vintage.

Pelto, Pertti J.
    1966a   *Review of* Sirma: Residence and Work Organization in a Lappish-Speaking Community, by Siri Lavik Dikkanen. American Anthropologist 68:785–788.
    1966b   *Review of* Lapponica. American Anthropologist 68:1044–1045.
    1967   *Review of* Coast Lapp Society II: A Study of Economic Development and Social Values, by Robert Paine. American Anthropologist 69:522–523.
    1971   *Review of* Reciprocity Systems of the Rural Society in the Finnish-Karelian Culture Area with Special Reference to Social Intercourse of the Youth, by Matti Sarmela. American Anthropologist 73:398–399.

Peristiany, John G.
    1967   Contributions to Mediterranean Sociology: Mediterranean Rural Communities and Social Change. Paris: Mouton.
    1987   Social Inequality in a Portuguese Hamlet. Cambridge: Cambridge University Press.

Peristiany, J. G., ed.
    1965   Honour and Shame: The Values of Mediterranean Society. London: Weidenfeld and Nicolson.

Petrović, Tihana
    1991   Women's Individual Property in South Slavic Zadrugas. Studia Ethnologica 3:193–200.

Petrullo, Vincenzo
    1957   *Review of* Peasant Society and Culture: An Anthropological Approach to Civilization, by Robert Redfield. American Anthropologist 59:352–353.

Pieterse, Jan Nederveen
    1991   Fictions of Europe. Race and Class 32(3):3–10.

Pina-Cabral, João de
    1986   Sons of Adam, Daughters of Eve: The Peasant World View of the Alto Minho. Oxford: Clarendon Press.
    1989   The Mediterranean as a Category of Regional Comparison. A Critical View. Current Anthropology 30:399–406.
    1991   *Review of* Pre-Bureaucratic Europeans: A Study of a Portuguese Fishing Community, by Jan Brøgger. Man 26:174–175.

Pitkin, Donald S.
    1963   Mediterranean Europe. Anthropological Quarterly 36:120–129.
    1965   *Review of* The Vanishing Village: A Danish Maritime Community, by Robert T. Anderson and Barbara Gallatin Anderson. American Anthropologist 67:532–533.
    1985   The House that Giacomo Built: History of an Italian Family, 1898–1978. Cambridge: Cambridge University Press.

Pitt-Rivers, Julian
    1954   People of the Sierra. Chicago: Aldine.
    1961   The People of the Sierra. Chicago: University of Chicago Press.
    1965   *Review of* Honour, Family and Patronage: A Study of Institutions
            and Moral Values in a Greek Mountain Community, by J. K.
            Campbell. American Anthropologist 67:557–559.
    1966   Honour and Social Status. *In* Honour and Shame. The Values of
            Mediterranean Society. J. G. Peristiany, ed. Pp. 19–78. Chicago:
            University of Chicago Press.
    1971   [1954] The People of the Sierra. Rev. ed. Chicago: University of
            Chicago Press.
    1977   The Fate of Sechem, or the Politics of Sex: Essays in the
            Anthropology of the Mediterranean. Cambridge: Cambridge
            University Press.
    1992   Postscript: The Place of Grace in Anthropology. *In* Honour and
            Grace in Anthropology. J. G. Peristiany and Julian Pitt-Rivers, eds.
            Pp. 215–246. Cambridge: Cambridge University Press.
    1993   The Spanish Bull-Fight and Kindred Activities. Anthropology Today
            9(4):11–15.

Pitt-Rivers, Julian, ed.
    1963   Mediterranean Countrymen: Essays in the Social Anthropology of
            the Mediterranean. The Hague: Mouton and Company.

Plato
    n.d.   Timaeus and Critias. R. G. Bury, tr. Loeb Classical Library.
            Cambridge: Harvard University Press.

Plattner, Stuart, Gary Aronsen, and Benjamin Abellera
    1993   Recent Trends in Funding Anthropological Research at the National
            Science Foundation. Human Organization 52:110–114.

Plotnicov, Leonard
    1962   Fixed Membership Groups: The Locus of Culture Process. American
            Anthropologist 64:97–103.

Portis-Winner, Irene
    1992   Slovenes. The Encyclopedia of World Cultures Volume IV: Europe,
            Linda A. Bennett, vol. ed., David Levinson, series ed. Pp. 85–88.
            Boston: G. K. Hall and Co.

Povzranović, Maja
    1993a   Ethnography of a War: Croatia 1991–1992. The Anthropology of East
            Europe Review 11(1–2):117–125.
    1993b   Culture and Fear: Everyday Life in Wartime. *In* Fear, Death and
            Resistance: An Ethnography of War: Croatia 1991–1992. Zagreb:
            Institute of Ethnology and Folklore Research Matrix Croatica X-
            Press. Pp. 119–150.
    1995   War Experience and Ethnic Identities: Croatian Children in the
            Nineties. Collegium Antropologicum 19(1):29–39.

Povzranović, Maja, and Ines Prica
    1995   Between Myth and History: Displaced and Refugee Children's Life Histories. Paper presented at an international conference on War, Exile, Everyday Life, March–April, Zagreb, Croatia.

Prica, Ines
    1991   Dossier 'Manduševac': The Ritual Manipulation of Money in Contemporary Zagreb. Studia Ethnologica 3:219–224.
    1995   Between Destruction and Deconstruction, The Preconditions of the Croatian Ethnography of War. Collegium Antropologicum 19(1):7–16.

Prošić-Dvornić, Mirjana
    1989   Changes in Cultural Systems as Reflected in Styles of Clothing. Ethnological Review (Etnološki Pregled) 25:111–125.
    1993   Enough! Ethnic Protest '92: The Youth of Belgrade in Quest of 'Another Serbia.' The Anthropology of East Europe Review 11(1–2):108–116.

Quigley, Carroll
    1966   Tragedy and Hope: A History of the World in Our Time. New York: Macmillan.
    1973   Mexican National Character and Circum-Mediterranean Personality Structure. American Anthropologist 75:319–322.

Rapoport, Robert N.
    1958   *Review of* Family and Kinship in East London, by Michael Young and Peter Wilmott. American Anthropologist 60:770–772.

Redfield, James
    1966   *Review of* Enter Plato: Classical Greece and the Origins of Social Theory, by Alvin W. Gouldner. American Anthropologist 68:1317–1318.

Redfield, Robert
    1930   Tepotzlan, a Mexican Village: A Study of Folk Life. Chicago: University of Chicago Press.
    1956   Obituary: Robert Niel Pehrson (1926–1955). American Anthropologist 58:357–359.
    1960   The Little Community and Peasant Society and Culture. Chicago: University of Chicago Press.

Reed-Danahay, Deborah
    1996   Education and Identity in Rural France: The Politics of Schooling. Cambridge: Cambridge University Press.

Reed-Danahay, Deborah, and Susan Carol Rogers
    1987   Introduction. Anthropological Quarterly 60:51–55. Special issue on anthropological research in France.

Reineck, Janet
    1993   Seizing the Past, Forging the Present: Changing Visions of Self and

Nation among the Kosova Albanians. The Anthropology of East Europe Review 11(1–2):85–92.

Reissman, Leonard
  1971   *Review of* Woodruff: A Study of Community Decision Making, by Albert and Ruth Conner Schaffer. American Anthropologist 73:943.

Reiter, Rayna
  1975   Men and Women in the South of France. *In* Toward an Anthropology of Women. K. Reiter, ed. Pp. 252–282. New York: Monthly Review Press.

Rheubottom, David B.
  1970   *Review of* Alternative Social Structure and Ritual Relations in the Balkans, by Eugene A. Hammel. American Anthropologist 72:404–405.
  1971   A Structural Analysis of Conflict and Cleavage in Macedonian Domestic Groups. Ph.D. Dissertation, Anthropology Department, University of Rochester.
  1976   Time and Form: Contemporary Macedonian Households and the Zadruga Controversy. *In* Communal Families in the Balkans: The Zadruga. Robert F. Brynes, ed. Pp. 215–231. Notre Dame: University of Notre Dame Press.

Richards, Audrey
  1970   *Review of* Akenfield: Portrait of an English Village, by Ronald Blythe. American Anthropologist 72:1518–1519.

Riegelhaupt, Joyce
  1964   In the Shadow of the City. Unpublished Dissertation, Columbia University.
  1967   Saloio Women: An Analysis of Informal and Formal Political and Economic Roles of Portuguese Peasant Women. Anthropological Quarterly 40:109–126.
  1973   Festas and Padres: The Organization of Religious Action in a Portuguese Parish. American Anthropologist 75:835–852.
  1979   The Corporate State and Village Non-Politics. *In* Contemporary Portugal. Lawrence Graham and Harry Makler, eds. Pp. 167–190. Austin: University of Texas Press.
  1981   Camponeses e Estado Liberal: A Revolta de Maria da Fonte. Estudos Contemporâneos 2(3):129–139.
  1984   Popular Anti-Clericalism and Religiosity in Pre-1974 Portugal. *In* Religion, Power, and Protest in Local Communities. Eric R. Wolf, ed. Pp. 93–115. Amsterdam: Mouton Publishers.

Rihtman-Auguštin, Dunja
  1984   Struktura Tradicijskog Mišljenja (The Structure of Traditional Thought). Zagreb: Školska Knjiga.
  1990   The Metamorphosis of Festivals in a Socialist Country. Ethnologia Europaea XX(2):97–106.

1995 Victims and Heroes. Between Ethnic Values and the Construction of Identity. Ethnologia Europaea 25(1):61–68.

Rodd, R.
1892 The Customs and Lore of Modern Greece. Chicago: Argonaut, Inc. Publishers.

Rogers, Susan Carol
1991a Shaping Modern Times in Rural France: The Transformation and Reproduction of an Aveyronnais Community. Princeton: Princeton University Press.
1991b L'ethnologie Nord-Américaine de la France: Entreprise Ethnologique Près de chez Soi. Ethnologie Française 21:5–12.

Romanucci-Ross, Lola
1991 One Hundred Towers: An Italian Odyssey of Cultural Survival. New York: Bergin and Garvey.

Rosaldo, Michelle, and Louise Lamphere, eds.
1974 Woman, Culture, and Society. Palo Alto: Stanford University Press.

Roseberry, William
1989 Anthropologies and Histories: Essays in Culture, History, and Political Economy. New Brunswick, NJ: Rutgers University Press.

Rosenberg, Harriet
1988 A Negotiated World: Three Centuries of Change in a French Alpine Community. Toronto: University of Toronto Press.

Ruane, Joseph
1989 Success and Failure in a West of Ireland Factory. In Ireland from Below. Chris Curtin and Thomas M. Wilson, eds. Pp. 165–185. Galway: Galway University Press.

Rudan, Pavao, et al.
1987a Isolation by Distance in Middle Dalmatia-Yugoslavia. American Journal of Physical Anthropology 74:417–426.
1987b Anthropological Investigations of the Eastern Adriatic, Book One: Biological and Cultural Microdifferentiation of Rural Populations of Korčula and Pelješac (In Croatian). Croatian Anthropological Society, Zagreb.

Rudan, Pavao, Diana Šimić, and Linda A. Bennett
1988 Isolation by Distance on the Island of Korčula: Correlation Analysis of Distance Measures. American Journal of Physical Anthropology 77:97–103.

Rudan, Vlasta, and Mary Kay G. Olsen
1992 Psychodynamics and Culture: A Reconsideration of Contemporary 'Migrant' Families in the Eastern Adriatic, Croatia. Rivista di Antropologia (Roma) LXX:247–255.

Said, Edward
1978 Orientalism. Harmondsworth: Penguin.

St. Clair, William
   1977   The Philhellenes and the War of Independence. *In* Greece in Transition: Essays in the History of Modern Greece 1821–1974. J. Koumoulides, ed. Pp. 272–282. London: Zeno Publishers.

Salamone, Stephen D.
   1987   In the Shadow of the Holy Mountain: The Genesis of a Rural Greek Community and Its Refugee Heritage. Boulder: East European Monographs.

Salzmann, Z., and V. Scheuffler
   1974   Komarov: A Czech Farming Village. New York: Holt, Rinehart and Winston.

Sampson, Steven L.
   1987   The Informal Sector in Eastern Europe. TELOS, No. 66 (Winter): 44–66.
   1995   All Is Possible, Nothing Is Certain: The Transition in a Romanian Village. *In* East European Communities: The Struggle for Balance in Turbulent Times. David A. Kideckel, ed. Pp. 159–176. Boulder: Westview Press.

Sampson, Steven L., and David A. Kideckel
   1989   Anthropology Going into the Cold: Research in the Age of Mutually Assured Destruction. *In* The Anthropology of War and Peace: Perspectives on the Nuclear Age. P. Turner and D. Pitt, eds. Pp. 160–173. South Hadley, MA: Bergin and Garvey.

Sant Cassia, Paul
   1991   Authors in Search of a Character: Personhood, Agency, and Identity in the Mediterranean. Journal of Mediterranean Studies 11:1–17.

Sant Cassia, Paul, with Constantina Bada
   1992   The Making of the Modern Greek Family: Marriage and Exchange in Nineteenth Century Athens. Cambridge: Cambridge University Press.

Saunders, George R.
   1979   Social Change and Psycho-Cultural Continuity in Alpine Italian Family Life. Ethos 7:206–231.
   1995   The Crisis of Presence in Italian Pentecostal Conversion. American Ethnologist 22(2): 324–340.

Schapiro, J. Salwyn
   1933   *Review of* The French Race, by Jacques Barzun. American Anthropologist 35:536.

Scheper-Hughes, Nancy
   1979   Saints, Scholars, and Schizophrenics: Mental Illness in Rural Ireland. Berkeley: University of California.

Schiller, Nina Glick, Linda Basch, and Cristina Blanc-Szanton, eds.
   1992   Towards a Transnational Perspective on Migration; Race, Class,

Ethnicity, and Nationalism Reconsidered. New York: New York Academy of Sciences.

Schneider, David M.
  1965   Some Muddles in the Models: Or, How the System Really Works. *In* The Relevance of Models for Social Anthropology. A.S.A. Monographs. I. M. Banton, ed. Pp. 25–86. New York: F. A. Praeger.
  1961   Matrilineal Kinship. Berkeley: University of California Press.

Schneider, Jane
  1971   Of Vigilance and Virgins: Honor, Shame, and Access to Resources in Mediterranean Societies. Ethnology 10:1–24.

Schneider, Jane, and Peter Schneider
  1976   Culture and Political Economy in Western Sicily. New York: Academic.
  1996   Other People's Children: Fertility Decline and the Ideology of Class in Sicily. Tucson: University of Arizona Press.

Schneider, Jane, Peter Schneider, and Edward Hansen
  1972   Modernization and Development: The Role of Regional Elites and Noncorporate Groups in the European Mediterranean. Comparative Studies in Society and History 14:328–350.

Schwartz, Jonathan
  1993   Macedonia: A Country in Quotation Marks. The Anthropology of East Europe Review 11(1–2):93–99.

Segal, Daniel A.
  1991   "The European": Allegories of Racial Purity. Anthropology Today 7(5):7–9.

Segalen, Martine
  1985   Quinze Générations de Bas-Bretons. Paris: PUF. 1991 translation, Fifteen Generations of Bretons: Kinship and Society in Lower Brittany, 1720–1980. Cambridge: Cambridge University Press.
  1989   Introduction. *In* L'autre et le Semblable. Segalen, ed. Pp. 7–14. Paris: CNRS.
  1990   Nanterriens: Les Familles dans la Ville. Toulouse: Presses Universitaires de Mirail.

Senjković, Reana
  1995a   The Use, Interpretation, and Symbolization of the National: Croatia 1990/92. Ethnologia Europaea 25(1):69–80.
  1995b   Ideologies and Iconographies. Croatia in the Second Half of the 20th Century. Collegium Antropologicum 19(1):53–63.

Seremetakis, C. Nadia
  1990   The Ethics of Antiphony: The Social Construction of Pain, Gender, and Power in the Southern Peloponnesus. Ethos 18(4):481–511.
  1991   The Last Word: Women, Death, and Divination in Inner Mani. Chicago: University of Chicago Press.

Shanklin, Eugenia
  1980   The Irish Go-Between. Anthropological Quarterly 53:162–172.
  1982   Donegal's Changing Traditions: An Ethnographic Study. New York:
            Gordon and Breach.

Shanks, Amanda
  1994   Cultural Divergence and Durability: The Border, Symbolic
            Boundaries, and the Irish Gentry. *In* Border Approaches:
            Anthropological Perspectives on Frontiers. Hastings Donnan and
            Thomas M. Wilson, eds. Pp. 89–100. Lanham: University Press of
            America.

Sheehan, Elizabeth A.
  1991   Political and Cultural Resistance to European Community Europe:
            Ireland and the Single European Act. Socialism and Democracy
            13:101–118.
  1993   The Academic as Informant: Methodological and Theoretical Issues
            in the Ethnography of Intellectuals. Human Organization
            52(3):252–259.

Shimkin, D. B.
  1955   *Review of* The Origins of European Thought about the Body, the
            Mind, the Soul, the World, Time, and Fate, by Richard B. Onians.
            American Anthropologist 57:368–369.
  1957   *Review of* The Bilateral Network of Social Relations in Konkama
            Lapps, by Robert H. Pehrson. American Anthropologist 59:734–736.
  1959   *Review of* Coast Lapp Society I: A Study of Neighbourhood in
            Revsbotn Fjord, by Robert Paine. American Anthropologist
            61:311–312.

Shore, Cris
  1993   Inventing the 'People's Europe': Critical Approaches to European
            Community 'Cultural Policy.' Man 28:779–800.

Shore, Cris, and Annabel Black
  1992   The European Communities and the Construction of Europe.
            Anthropology Today 8(3):10–11.

Shutes, Mark T.
  1987   Production and Social Change in a Rural Irish Parish. Social Studies
            9(3/4):17–28.
  1989   Changing Agricultural Strategies in a Kerry Parish. *In* Ireland from
            Below: Social Change and Local Community. T. Wilson and C.
            Curtin, eds. Pp. 186–206. Galway: Galway University Press.
  1991   Kerry Farmers and the European Community: Capital Transitions in
            a Rural Irish Parish. Irish Journal of Sociology 1:1–17.
  1992   Regional Study in the Korinthia—The Korinthia Exploration Project
            1991. OWAN 15(2):20–26.
  1993   Rural Communities without Family Farms? The Future of Family
            Dairy Farming in the Post-1993 European Community. *In* Cultural

Change and the New Europe: Perspectives on the European Community. T. Wilson and E. Smith, eds. Pp. 123–142. Boulder: Westview Press.

1994   Production-Oriented Ethnography: The Role of the Cultural Anthropologist in Multidisciplinary Approaches to Social Change. *In* Beyond the Site: Regional Studies in the Aegean Area. P. N. Kardulias, ed. Pp. 337–351. Lanham: University Press of America.

1996   Tailored Research: On Getting the Right Fit between Macro-Level Theory and Micro-Level Data. Journal of World Systems Research 2(Part 2):1–23.

Siegel, Bernard J.
1952   *Review of* Life in a Welsh Countryside, by Alwyn D. Rees. American Anthropologist 54:260–261.

Sills, David L.
1968   Voluntary Associations, II, Sociological Aspects. International Encyclopedia of the Social Sciences 16:362–379.

Silverman, Carol
1983   The Politics of Folklore in Bulgaria. Anthropological Quarterly 56(2):55–61.

Silverman, Marilyn
1989   A Labouring Man's Daughter: Constructing Respectability in South Kilkenny. *In* Ireland from Below. Chris Curtin and Thomas M. Wilson, eds. Pp. 109–127. Galway: Galway University Press.

Silverman, Marilyn, and P. H. Gulliver, eds.
1992   Approaching the Past: Historical Anthropology through Irish Case Studies. New York: Columbia University Press.

Silverman, Sydel
1966   An Ethnographic Approach to Social Stratification: Prestige in a Central Italian Community. American Anthropologist 68:899–921.

1975   Three Bells of Civilization: The Life of an Italian Hill Town. New York: Columbia University Press.

Simić, Andrei
1970   Cultural Factors in Yugoslav Industrialization. Ph.D. Dissertation, Anthropology Department, University of California, Berkeley.

1973   The Peasant Urbanites: A Study of Rural-Urban Mobility in Serbia. New York: Seminar Press.

1993   The First and Last Yugoslav: Some Thoughts on the Dissolution of a State. The Anthropology of East Europe Review 11(1–2):14–20.

1994   The Civil War in Yugoslavia: Do Ostensibly High Rates of Intermarriage Obviate Ethnic Hatreds as a Cause? The Anthropology of East Europe Review 12(2):33–34.

Simon, Rita J., and Caroline B. Brettell, eds.
1986   International Migration: The Female Experience. Totowa, NJ: Rowman and Allenheld.

Sitney, P. Adam
     1985   The International Dictionary of Films and Filmmakers. New York:
               Macmillan.

Slavec, Ingrid
     1988   Slovenian Ethnology between the Past and the Present. Etnološki
               Pregled (Ethnological Review) 23–24:37–59.

Sluka, Jeffrey
     1989   Hearts and Minds, Water and Fish: Support for the IRA and INLA
               in a Northern Irish Ghetto. Greenwich: JAI Press.
     1992a   The Anthropology of Conflict. *In* The Paths to Domination,
               Resistance, and Terror. Carolyn Nordstrom and JoAnn Martin, eds.
               Pp. 18–36. Berkeley: University of California Press.
     1992b   The Politics of Painting: Political Murals in Northern Ireland. *In* The
               Paths to Domination, Resistance, and Terror. Carolyn Nordstrom
               and JoAnn Martin, eds. Pp. 190–216. Berkeley: University of
               California Press.

Smith, M. Estellie
     1993   The Incidental City: Urban Entities in the EC of the 1990s. *In*
               Cultural Change and the New Europe. Thomas M. Wilson and M.
               Estellie Smith, eds. Pp. 47–60. Boulder: Westview Press.

Smolej, N., J. L. Angel, L. A. Bennett, D. F. Roberts, and P. Rudan
     1987   Physiological Variation and Population Structure on the Island of
               Korčula, Yugoslavia. Human Biology 59(4):667–685.

Society for the Anthropology of Europe
     1994   Final Report: SAE Committee on the Crisis in Former Yugoslavia.
               Bulletin of the Society for the Anthropology of Europe 8(1):1, 8.

Southall, Aidan, ed.
     1973   Urban Anthropology: Cross-Cultural Studies in Urbanization. New
               York: Oxford University Press.

Spencer, Robert F.
     1958   Culture Process and Intellectual Current: Durkheim and Ataturk.
               American Anthropologist 60:640–657.

Spencer, Robert F., ed.
     1970   Migration and Anthropology. Seattle: University of Washington
               Press.

Spier, Leslie
     1924   *Review of* Studies in Evolution and Eugenics, by S. J. Holmes.
               American Anthropologist 26:264–267.

Špoljar-Vržina, Sanja Marina
     1992   Estimation of the Population Structure Through Temporal Migration
               Analysis: An Example from the Island of Hvar, Croatia. Rivista di
               Antropolopogia (Roma) LXX:53–62.
     1993   Estimation of the Population Structure Through Temporal Migration

Analysis—Example from the Island of Korčula (Croatia). Collegium Antropologicum 17(1):7–16.

1995   Refugees and Displaced Persons on the Island of Hvar—In Search of the Ideal Perception of Their Everyday Needs. Paper presented at an international conference on War, Exile, Everyday Life, March–April, Zagreb, Croatia.

Špoljar-Vržina, S. M., S. Martić-Biočina, and M. K. Gilliland
1995   Beyond the Basic Needs—The Refugee and Displaced Person Families on the Island of Hvar (Croatia). Collegium Antropologicum 19(1):113–119.

Stahl, Henri H.
1979   Traditional Romanian Village Communities: The Transition from the Communal to the Capitalist Mode of Production in the Danube Region. London: Cambridge University Press.

Steward, Julian
1956   *Review of* The Little Community: Viewpoints for the Study of a Human Whole, by Robert Redfield. American Anthropologist 58:564–565.
1960   *Review of* The Evolution of Culture, by Leslie A. White. American Anthropologist 62:144–148.

Stott, Margaret
1993   Return Migrants and Tourism Development: An Example from the Cyclades. Journal of Modern Greek Studies 11(1):75–95.

Sujoldžić, A.
1991   The Population Study of Middle Dalmatia: Linguistic History and Current Regional Differentiation of Croatian Dialects. Collegium Antropologicum 15(2):309–322.
1992   Vlachs. The Encyclopedia of World Cultures Volume IV: Europe, Linda A. Bennett, vol. ed., David Levinson, series ed. Pp. 273–275. Boston: G. K. Hall and Co.
1993   Isonomy and Population Structure of the Island of Korčula (Croatia). Collegium Antropologicum 17(1):17–24.

Sujoldžić, A., A. Chaventre, and P. Rudan
1990   Arercu Demographique de la Population de l'ile d'Olib, Rad HAZU 449. Razred za Prirodne Znanosti 24:123–136.

Sujoldžić, A., V. Jovanovic, J. L. Angel, L. A. Bennett, D. F. Roberts, and P. Rudan
1989   Migration within the Island of Korčula, Yugoslavia. Annals of Human Biology 16(6):483–493.

Sujoldžić, A., A. Marković, and A. Chaventre
1992   The Population Structure of the Island of Krk—Geomorphology, Ethnohistory, Demography, and Linguistics. Collegium Antropologicum 16(2):413–425.

Supek, Olga
1982   A Hundred Years of Bread and Wine: Culture, History, and

Economy of a Croatian Village. Ph.D. Dissertation, Anthropology Department, University of Michigan.

1988   Ethnology in Croatia. Etnološki Pregled (Ethnological Review) 39(5):17–35.

1989   Peasant versus Capitalist Worldview in Vinogorje of the 1930s. Ethnological Review (Etnološki Pregled) 25:61–80.

Supek, Olga and Jasna Čapo

1994   Effects of Emigration on a Rural Society: Demography, Family Structure, and Gender Relations in Croatia. *In* Roots of the Transplanted. Dirk Hoerder and Inge Blank, eds. Boulder: East European Monograph.

Sutton, Susan Buck

1978   Migrant Regional Associations: An Athenian Example and Its Implications. Ph.D. Dissertation, Anthropology Department, University of North Carolina at Chapel Hill.

1988   What Is a "Village" in a Nation of Migrants? Journal of Modern Greek Studies 6(2):187–216.

Sveučilište u Zagrebu Filozofski Fakultet Etnološki Zavod

1992   Hrvatska Baranja (Croatian Baranja). Studia Ethnologica 4.

Sweet, L. E., and T. J. O'Leary, eds.

1969   Circum-Mediterranean Peasantry: Introductory Bibliographies. New Haven: Human Relations Area Files Press.

Symmons, Konstantin

1959   *Review of* Poland: Its People, Its Society, Its Culture, by Clifford R. Barnett, et al. American Anthropologist 61:134.

Szuchewycz, Bodhan

1989   The Meanings of Silence in the Irish Catholic Charismatic Movement. *In* Ireland from Below. Chris Curtin and Thomas M. Wilson, eds. Pp. 46–69. Galway: Galway University Press.

1996   Introduction: Past and Present in Rural Greece. *In* Contingent Countryside: Settlement, Economy, and Land Use in the Southern Argolid since 1700. S. Sutton, ed. Pp. 1–22. Stanford: Stanford University Press.

Tambiah, S. J.

1972   *Review of* Homo Hierarchicus: An Essay on the Caste System, by Louis Dumont. American Anthropologist 74:832–835.

Taylor, Lawrence

1980a   Colonialism and Community Structure in Western Ireland. Ethnohistory 27:169–181.

1980b   The Merchant in Peripheral Ireland: A Case from Donegal. Anthropology 4:63–76.

1981   'Man the Fisher': Salmon Fishing and the Expression of Community in a Rural Irish Settlement. American Ethnologist 8:774–788.

1989a   Bas in Eirinn: Cultural Constructions of Death in Ireland. Anthropological Quarterly 62(4):175–187.

1989b   The Mission: An Anthropological View of an Irish Religious Occasion. *In* Ireland from Below. Chris Curtin and Thomas M. Wilson, eds. Pp. 1–22. Galway: Galway University Press.

Theodoratus, R. J.
1969   Europe: A Selected Ethnographic Bibliography. New Haven Human Relations Area Files Press.

Thomas, William Isaac, and Florian Znaniecki
1918–21 The Polish Peasant in Europe and America. Chicago: The University of Chicago Press.

Thoresen, Timothy H. H.
1979   *Review of* Selected Papers from the American Anthropologist, 1888–1920, edited by Frederica de Laguna; 1921–1945, edited by George W. Stocking Jr.; and 1946–1970, edited by Robert Murphy. American Anthropologist 81:194–196.

Torgovnick, Marianna
1990   Gone Primitive. Chicago: University of Chicago Press.

Triolo, Nancy
1993   From Domestic Space to Private Place. On the Changing Social Context of Abortion in Sicily (1920–1960). Paper presented to the Conference on Aspetti della Storia della Maternità. Palermo, December.

Tumin, Melvin
1954   *Review of* Societies around the World, edited by Irwin T. Sanders, et al. American Anthropologist 56:493–499.

Turney-High, Harry Holbert
1953   Château-Gèrard: The Life and Times of a Walloon Village. Columbia: University of South Carolina Press.

Tyler, Stephen A.
1972   *Review of* Essays on the Caste System: The European Understanding of India, by Celestin Bougle. American Anthropologist 74:1380–1382.

1973   *Review of* Religion, Politics, and History in India: Collected Papers in Indian Sociology, by Louis Dumont. American Anthropologist 75:381–385

Ulin, Robert C.
1991   The Current Tide in American Europeanist Anthropology. Anthropology Today 7(6):8–12.

Vacalopoulos, Apostolos E.
1970   Origins of the Greek Nation: The Byzantine Period, 1204–1461. New Brunswick, NJ: Rutgers University Press.

1976   The Greek Nation 1453–1669. The Cultural and Economic Background of Modern Greek Society. New Brunswick, NJ: Rutgers University Press.

Van Nostrand, J. J.
1956   *Review of* Rome beyond the Imperial Frontiers, by Sir Mortimer Wheeler. American Anthropologist 58:757–758.

Varenne, Hervé
1993a   Dublin 16: Accounts of Suburban Lives. *In* Irish Urban Cultures. Chris Curtin, Hastings Donnan, and Thomas M. Wilson, eds. Pp. 99–121. Belfast: Institute of Irish Studies Press.
1993b   The Question of European Nationalism. *In* Cultural Change and the New Europe. Thomas M. Wilson and M. Estellie Smith, eds. Boulder: Westview Press.

Velovski, Tony
1995   Notes from the Field-Republic of Macedonia, March, 1995. The Anthropology of East European Review 13(1):70–73.

Verdery, Katherine
1983   Transylvanian Villagers: Three Centuries of Political, Economic, and Ethnic Change. Berkeley: University of California Press.
1992   Comment: Hobsbawm in the East. Anthropology Today 8(1):8–10.

Viazzo, Pier Paolo
1989   Upland Communities. Cambridge: Cambridge University Press.

Vincent, Joan
1983   Marriage, Religion, and Class in South Fermanagh, 1846–1920. *In* Emergent Structures and the Family. Owen Lynch, ed. Delhi: Hindustan Publishing Corporation.
1989   Local Knowledge and Political Violence in County Fermanagh. *In* Ireland from Below: Social Change and Local Communities. Chris Curtin and Thomas M. Wilson, eds. Pp. 92–108. Galway: Galway University Press.
1991   Irish Border Violence and the Question of Sovereignty. *In* The Anthropology of War and Peace. M. D. Zamora, B. B. Erring, and A. L. LaRuffa, eds. St. Mary's College of Bayonbong, Nueva Vizcaya: Rex Book Store.
1992   A Political Orchestration of the Irish Famine: County Fermanagh, May 1847. *In* Approaching the Past. Marilyn Silverman and P. H. Gulliver, eds. Pp. 75–98. New York: Columbia University Press.
1993   Ethnicity and the State in Northern Ireland. *In* Ethnicity and the State. Judith D. Toland, ed. Pp. 123–146. New Brunswick, NJ: Transaction Publishers.

Voegelin, C. F.
1935   *Review of* The Earliest Relations between the Celts and the Germans, by C. S. Elston. American Anthropologist 37:152.

Vrećer, Natalija
 1995   The Lost Way of Life: The Experience of Refugee Children in Celje from 1992 to 1994. Paper presented at an international conference on War, Exile, Everyday Life, March–April, Zagreb, Croatia.

Wagner, Richard
 1992   Montenegrins. *In* The Encyclopedia of World Cultures Volume IV: Europe. Linda A. Bennett, vol. ed., David Levinson, series ed. Pp. 171–174. Boston: G. K. Hall and Co.
 1992   Serbs. *In* The Encyclopedia of World Cultures Volume IV: Europe. Linda A. Bennett, vol. ed., David Levinson, series ed. Pp. 229–232. Boston: G. K. Hall and Co.

Wagner, Roy
 1975   The Invention of Culture. Englewood Cliffs, NJ: Prentice-Hall, Inc.

Walcot, P.
 1970   Greek Peasants Ancient and Modern: A Comparison of Social and Moral Values. New York: Barnes and Noble.

Wallace, Anthony
 1966   *Review of* The Revolution in Anthropology, by I. C. Jarvie. American Anthropologist 68:1254–1255.

Wallerstein, Immanuel
 1974   The Modern World System: Capitalist Agriculture and the Origins of the European World Economy in the Sixteenth Century. New York: Academic Press.

Wallis, Wilson D.
 1924   The Teaching of Anthropology. American Anthropologist 26:283–289.

Ward, Martha C.
 1994   The Hidden Life of Tirol. Prospect Heights, IL: Waveland Press.

Wedel, Janine R.
 1985   The Private Poland: An Anthropologist's Look at Everyday Life. New York: Facts on File.
 1994   U.S. Aid to Central and Eastern Europe, 1990–1994: An Inside Look at Aid Relations and Models. Washington, D.C. U.S. Congress Joint Economic Committee.

Wedel, Janine R., and David A. Kideckel
 1994   Studying Up: Amending the First Principles of Anthropological Ethics. Anthropology Newsletter 35(7):37.

Weigland, Phil C.
 1965   *Review of* Europe's Steppe Frontier, 1500–1800, by William H. McNeill. American Anthropologist 67:1604–1605.

Weingrod, Alex
 1972a   *Review of* Peasants in Cities: Readings in the Anthropology of

Urbanization, edited by William Mangin. American Anthropologist 74:88–90.

1972b   *Review of* Banditismo in Sardegna: La Vendetta Barbaricina Come Ordinamento Giuridico, by Antonio Pigliaru. American Anthropologist 74:848–849.

Wenner-Gren Foundation for Anthropological Research
1994   Report for 1992 and 1993. New York: Wenner-Gren Foundation for Anthropological Research, Inc.

Whitaker, Elizabeth D.
1992   Bread and Work: Pellagra and Economic Transformation in Turn-of-the-Century Italy. Anthropological Quarterly 65(2):80–90.

White, Caroline
1980   Patrons and Partisans: A Study of Politics in Two Southern Italian Comuni. Cambridge: Cambridge University Press.

White, Leslie
1938   *Review of* Thraldom in Ancient Ireland, by Carl O. Williams. American Anthropologist 40:321.
1969   Personal Communication.

Whyte, William Foote
1944   Sicilian Peasant Society. American Anthropologist 46:65–74.

Wilkie, Ray
1959   *Review of* The Psychiatric Hospital as a Small Society, by William Caudill. American Anthropologist 61:714–716.

Willems, Emilio
1970   Peasantry and City: Cultural Persistence and Change in Historical Perspective, a European Case. American Anthropologist 72:528–544.

Wilson, Thomas M.
1984   From Clare to the Common Market: Perspectives in Irish Ethnography. Anthropological Quarterly 57(1):1–15.
1988   Culture and Class Among the 'Large' Farmers of Eastern Ireland. American Ethnologist 15:678–693.
1989a   Large Farms, Local Politics, and the International Arena: The Irish Tax Dispute of 1979. Human Organization 48(1):60–70.
1989b   Broker's Broker: The Chairman of the Meath County Council. *In* Ireland from Below. Chris Curtin and Thomas M. Wilson, eds. Pp. 260–282. Galway: Galway University Press.
1990a   Ethnography and Political Science: Agricultural Politics in Eire. Politics 10(1):9–16.
1990b   From Patronage to Brokerage in the Local Politics of Eastern Ireland. Ethnohistory 37(2):158–187.
1993a   An Anthropology of the European Community. *In* Cultural Change and the New Europe: Perspectives on the European Community. Thomas M. Wilson and M. Estellie Smith, eds. Pp. 1–23. Boulder: Westview Press.

1993b   Frontiers Go but Boundaries Remain: The Irish Border as a Cultural Divide. *In* Cultural Change and the New Europe: Perspectives on the European Community. Thomas M. Wilson and M. Estellie Smith, eds. Pp. 167–187. Boulder: Westview Press.

1993c   Consumer Culture and European Integration at the Northern Irish Border. *In* European Advances in Consumer Research, Volume 1. W. Fred van Raaij and Gary J. Bamossy, eds. Pp. 293–299. Provo, UT: Association for Consumer Research.

1994a   A Question of Identity: Problems of Social Anthropology in Ireland. *In* The Unheard Voice: Social Anthropology in Ireland. Pol O Muiri, ed. Pp. 4–7. Belfast: Fortnight Educational Trust.

1994b   Symbolic Dimensions to the Irish Border. *In* Border Approaches: Anthropological Perspectives on Frontiers. Hastings Donnan and Thomas M. Wilson, eds. Pp. 101–118. Lanham, MD: University Press of America.

Wilson, Thomas M., and M. Estellie Smith, eds.
1993   Cultural Change and the New Europe: Perspectives on the European Community. Boulder: Westview Press.

Winner, Irene P.
1967   Zerovnica: A Slovenian Village. Ph.D. Dissertation, Anthropology Department, University of North Carolina.

1971   A Slovenian Village: Zerovnica. Providence: Brown University Press.

1972   *Review of* East European Quarterly. American Anthropologist 74:1410–1411.

Winston, Brian
1995   Claiming the Real: The Grierson Documentary and Its Legitimations. London: The British Film Institute.

Wittfogel, Karl A.
1967   *Review of* The Evolution of Urban Society: Early Mesopotamia and Prehispanic Mexico, by Robert McC. Adams. American Anthropologist 69:90–92.

Wojno, Mark Gregory
1982   Countrymen Return: Colonial Migration and Rural Economy in Northern Portugal. Ph.D. Dissertation, Michigan State University.

Wolf, Eric
1955   Types of Latin American Peasantry: A Preliminary Discussion. American Anthropologist 57:452–471.

1957a   Closed Corporate Peasant Communities in Meso-America and Central Java. Southwestern Journal of Anthropology 13:1–18.

1957b   *Review of* Man's Role in Changing the Face of the Earth, by William L. Thomas. American Anthropologist 1959:1089–1091.

1963   *Review of* A Spanish Tapestry: Town and Country in Castile, by Michael Kenny. American Anthropologist 65:432–434.

1966   Peasants. Englewood Cliffs, NJ: Prentice Hall.

1982   Europe and the People without History. Berkeley: University of California Press.

Wylie, Laurence
1964   [1957] Village in the Vaucluse: Life in a French Village. New York: Harper and Row.

Yanagisako, Sylvia J.
1991   Capital and Gendered Interest in Italian Family Firms. *In* The Family in Italy from Antiquity to the Present. David I. Kertzer and Richard P. Saller, eds. Pp. 321–339. New Haven: Yale University Press.

Yoon, Soon Young Song
1975   Provençal Wine Cooperatives. *In* Beyond the Community: Social Process in Europe. J. Boissevain and J. Friedl, eds. The Hague: Department of Educational Science of the Netherlands.

Young, T.
1975   The Dingle Commercial Fishermen: An Analysis of the Economic Action of an Irish Fishing Fleet. Ph.D. Dissertation, University of Pittsburgh.

Zakythinos, D. A.
1976   The Making of Modern Greece: From Byzantium to Independence. Oxford: Basil Blackwell.

Zegura, S. L., B. Janićijević, D. Šimić, D. F. Roberts, L. A. Bennett, and P. Rudan
1990   Population Structure of the Pelješac Peninsula, Yugoslavia. Human Biology 62:173–194.

Zegura, S. L., B. Janićijević, A. Sujoldžić, D. F. Roberts, and P. Rudan
1991   Genetics, Ethnohistory and Linguistics of Brač, Yugoslavia. American Journal of Human Biology 3:155–168.

Zonabend, Françoise
1980   La Mémoire Longue. Paris: PUF. 1984 translation, The Enduring Memory: Time and History in a French Village. Manchester University Press.
1989   La Presqu'ile au Nucléaire. Paris: Odile Jacob. 1993 translation, The Nuclear Peninsula. Cambridge University Press.

*Film Reviews (Prepared by Peter S. Allen)**

Aegean Sponge Divers. American Anthropologist 74 (December, 1972):1584–1585 (P. Allen).

Anastenaria. American Anthropologist 74 (December, 1972):1581–1584 (P. Allen).

Bandits of Orgosolo. American Anthropologist 74 (December, 1972):1574–1575 (T. Flores Fratto).

Basques of Santazi. American Anthropologist 90 (December, 1988):1045–1046 (S. Ybarrola).

Biquefarre. American Anthropologist 89 (December, 1987):1013–1014 (D. Reed-Danahay).

Chronicle of a Summer. American Anthropologist 80 (December, 1978):1020–1022 (J-P. Dumont).

Dead Birds. American Anthropologist 67 (December, 1965):1358–1359 (J. B. Watson).

Farrebique. American Anthropologist 80 (March, 1978):200 (L. Wylie).

The House that Giacomo Built. American Anthropologist 86 (December, 1984):1063 (D. Kertzer).

The Hunters. American Anthropologist 82 (March, 1980):228–229 (B. Nichols).

The Ice Man. Archaeology 46 (May/June, 1993):66–67 (P. Allen).

Kalogeros. American Anthropologist 74 (December, 1972):1581–1584 (P. Allen).

Kypseli: Women and Men Apart—A Divided Reality. American Anthropologist 79 (March, 1977):194 (M. Dimen-Schein).

Lascaux: Cradle of Man's Art. American Anthropologist 77 (December, 1975):919–920 (L. Freeman).

The Lascaux Cave: A Look at Our Prehistoric Past. Archaeology 45 (July/August, 1992):69 (P. Allen).

Life Chances: Four Families in a Changing Cypriot Village. American Anthropologist 78 (December, 1976):955–956 (E. Friedl).

Man of Aran. American Anthropologist 79 (September, 1977):749–751 (S. Kimball).

Nanook of the North. American Anthropologist 80 (March, 1978):196–197 (I. Jarvie).

The Shepherds of Berneray. American Anthropologist 85 (March, 1983):225–226 (G. Epple).

Sophia's People—Eventful Lives. American Anthropologist 90 (September, 1988):782 (P. Allen); Visual Anthropology 4 (1991):81 (J. MacClancy).

Village of Spain. American Anthropologist 77 (September, 1975):710 (P. Allen).

Vlach Gypsies. American Anthropologist 92 (June, 1990):554–555 (W. Lockwood).

THE FILMS OF COLETTE PIAULT

Everyday Is Not a Feast Day. American Anthropologist 84 (September, 1982):754–756 (P. Allen).

The Thread of the Needle. American Anthropologist 86 (June, 1984):510–511 (P. Allen).

My Family and Me. American Anthropologist 90 (June, 1988):491–492 (J. Cowan).

Charcoal Makers. American Anthropologist 94 (June, 1992):523–524 (P. Sant Cassia).

Review of Four Films by Colette Piault (Everyday Is Not a Feast Day; My Family and Me; Let's Get Married; and The Thread of the Needle). Commission on Visual Anthropology Review: Fall, 1990:42–43 (S. B. Sutton).

Six Views of a Greek Village (Everyday Is Not a Feast Day; The Thread of the Needle; Let's Get Married; My Family and Me; Charcoal Makers; and A Hard Life). Visual Anthropology 6 (1993):109–114 (M. Herzfeld).

See also commentary, Greece on Film, by Gillian Bottomley in Visual Anthropology 7 (1994):69–70.

THE FILMS OF BARRIE MACHIN

Passing Shadows. American Anthropologist 88 (December, 1986):1045–1046 (L. Danforth).

Passing Shadows, Warriors and Maidens, Warriors and Maidens: A Discussion with Margaret Papandreou and Leading Greek Feminists. Commission on Visual Anthropology Review (Fall, 1990):43–44 (P. Allen).

THE FILMS OF JEROME MINTZ

Pepe's Family. American Anthropologist 82 (March, 1980):226–227 (D. J. and P. F-C. Greenwood).

The Shoemaker. American Anthropologist 82 (March, 1980):226–227 (D. J. and P. F-C. Greenwood).

Carnaval De Pueblo. American Anthropologist 90 (September, 1988):781–782 (J. Dubisch).

Romeria: Day of the Virgin. American Anthropologist 90 (September, 1988):781–782 (J. Dubisch).

Jerome Mintz Retrospective: 1968–1986. Review of The Shoemaker; Pepe's Family; Perico the Bowlmaker; The Shepherd's Family; Carnaval de Pueblo; and Romeria: Day of the Virgin. Visual Anthropology 4 (1991):69–73 (D. Gilmore).

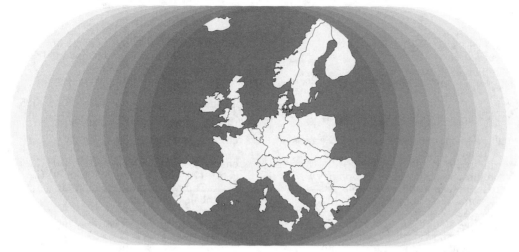

INDEX

A

Abélès, Marc, 29, 152
Across the Tracks: Vlach Gypsies in Hungary, 62
  (*see also* Film; Hungary)
Aegean Sponge Divers, 62 (*see also* Film; Greece)
Aginsky, Burt W., 189
Albania, 22, 63, 128, 142, 144, 146
The Albanians of Rrogam, 63 (*see also* Film)
Alcoholism, 125 (*see also* Drinking studies;
  Temperance movement)
Allen, Peter Sutton, 5, 6, 11, 44, 60–69, 91, 99
  (*see also* Film)
Alliata, Francesco, 66 (*see also* Film)
Alpine, 25, 26, 191
  as biological category, 177, 182, 183
Althabe, Gérard, 29
American Anthropological Association Film
  Festival, 63
American Anthropological Association, 3, 4, 8,
  9, 36, 40, 60, 67, 68, 71, 81, 127, 130, 135, 188
American Anthropologist:
  concept of race after World War II, 183
  Europe in, 3, 6, 11, 169–196 (*see also* Europe;
    Parman, Susan)
  method of analysis, 195–196
American anthropologists in Europe:
  criticism/views by native anthropologists,
    39, 78, 92 (*see also* Native anthropologists)

American anthropologists in Europe, *cont.*:
  ties with other disciplines and organiza-
    tions, 8–9 (*see also* European Association
    of Social Anthropologists)
American anthropologists: reacting to
  immigration, 180–184 (*see also* Eugenics;
  Race)
American anthropology:
  growing interest in West, 2, 28–29, 188
  history, 6, 10, 13, 15, 17, 157–168, 169–196
  interest in European anthropology, 29, 30,
    186
American Council of Learned Societies
  (ACLS), 19, 23
American Ethnological Society, 91
Amsbury, Clifton, 192
An Invisible Enemy, 63 (*see also* Film)
Anastenaria, 62 (*see also* Film; Greece)
Andalusia, 24, 65
Anderson, Barbara Gallatin, 25, 191
Anderson, Robert T., 13, 25, 83, 191, 192
Anderson-Levitt, Kathryn, 26
Andrews, Alfred, 175
Andromedas, John, 189
Angel, J. Lawrence, 176, 177
Anglophone Europeanist anthropology, 15,
  72, 73, 75, 77, 94, 100, 102, 103, 104,
  106
Annales history, 27–29